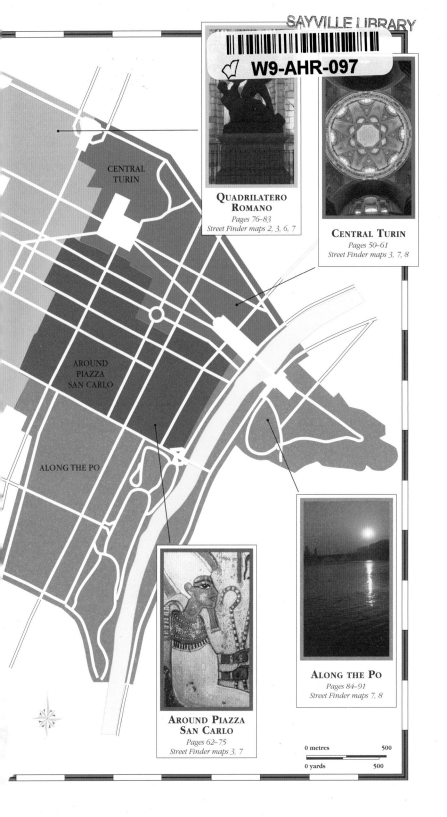

CENTRAL
TURIN

AROUND
PIAZZA
SAN CARLO

ALONG THE PO

**QUADRILATERO
ROMANO**
Pages 76–83
Street Finder maps 2, 3, 6, 7

CENTRAL TURIN
Pages 50–61
Street Finder maps 3, 7, 8

**AROUND PIAZZA
SAN CARLO**
Pages 62–75
Street Finder maps 3, 7

ALONG THE PO
Pages 84–91
Street Finder maps 7, 8

0 metres   500

0 yards   500

TURIN

EYEWITNESS TRAVEL GUIDES

TURIN

LONDON, NEW YORK,
MELBOURNE, MUNICH AND DELHI
www.dk.com

Produced by Fabio Ratti Editoria Srl, Milan, Italy

PUBLISHING CO-ORDINATOR Alberto Santangelo
EDITORIAL STAFF Fiorenzaa Bariatti, Prisca Destro

DESIGNERS
Andrea Barison, Oriana Bianchetti, Stefania Testa

ORIGINAL CONTRIBUTORS
Fabrizio Ardito, Anna Balbiano, Alberto Santangelo
Antonio Piccinardi, Michele Saviozzi

TRANSLATORS Susan Andrews, Louise Bostock

PICTURE RESEARCH Margherita Guerra

MAPS
Luca Signorelli, Bergamo – Studio Aguilar, Milan

ILLUSTRATIONS
Modi Artistici, Milan

Reproduced in Singapore by Colourscan
Printed and bound by Toppan in China

Dorling Kindersley Limited
PUBLISHER Douglas Amrine
PUBLISHING MANAGER Helen Townsend
EDITOR Fiona Wild
DTP Jason Little
RESTAURANTS Michael Palij MW
FACTCHECKER Leonie Loudon

First American Edition, 2005
05 06 07 08 10 9 8 7 6 5 4 3 2 1

Published in the United States by
DK Publishing, Inc.,
375 Hudson Street, New York, New York 10014

Copyright © Mondadori Electra SpA 2004.
Published under exclusive license by Dorling Kindersley Limited.
A Penguin Company.

ISBN 0-7566-1439-2
ISSN 1542-1554

THROUGHOUT THIS BOOK, FLOORS ARE REFERRED TO IN ACCORDANCE WITH
EUROPEAN USAGE, I.E., THE "FIRST FLOOR" IS THE FLOOR ABOVE GROUND LEVEL.

**The information in this
Eyewitness Travel Guide is checked regularly.**
Every effort has been made to ensure that this book is as up-to-date
as possible at the time of going to press. Some details, however,
such as telephone numbers, opening hours, prices, gallery hanging
arrangements and travel information are liable to change. The
publishers cannot accept responsibility for any consequences arising
from the use of this book, nor for any material on third party
websites, and cannot guarantee that any website address in this
book will be a suitable source of travel information. We value the
views and suggestions of our readers very highly. Please write to:
Publisher, DK Eyewitness Travel Guides,
Dorling Kindersley, 80 Strand, London WC2R 0RL, Great Britain.

CONTENTS

HOW TO USE THIS GUIDE 6

**Dancer in bronze,
Museo di Antichità, Turin**

INTRODUCING TURIN AND THE VALLEYS

PUTTING TURIN ON THE
MAP *10*

A PORTRAIT OF TURIN
AND THE VALLEYS *14*

TURIN AND THE VALLEYS
THROUGH THE YEAR *32*

THE HISTORY OF TURIN
36

**The Baroque dome (1680) of
the church of San Lorenzo**

◁ **The Gran Bosco of Salbertrand with the Rocciamelone in the background**

TURIN AREA BY AREA

CENTRAL TURIN 50

AROUND PIAZZA SAN CARLO 62

QUADRILATERO ROMANO 76

ALONG THE PO 84

FURTHER AFIELD 92

An atmospheric view of the Forte di Exilles in Val di Susa

River Po in Turin with the Mole Antonelliana in the background

THE VALLEYS AREA BY AREA

THE VALLEYS AT A GLANCE 108

VAL DI SUSA 110

THE CHISONE AND GERMANASCA VALLEYS 134

VAL PELLICE 154

TRAVELLERS' NEEDS

WHERE TO STAY 174

WHERE TO EAT 182

BARS AND CAFÉS 192

SHOPPING 196

ENTERTAINMENT 198

Chocolate cake made by a Turinese pastry chef

SURVIVAL GUIDE

PRACTICAL INFORMATION 204

One of the new underground trains in Turin

TRAVEL INFORMATION 208

TURIN STREET FINDER 216

GENERAL INDEX 228

ACKNOWLEDGMENTS 236

PHRASE BOOK 239

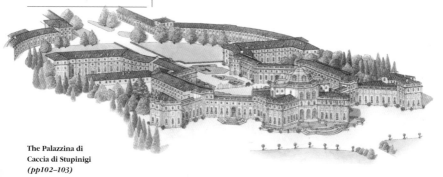

The Palazzina di Caccia di Stupinigi (pp102–103)

How to Use this Guide

This guide helps you to get the most from your visit to Turin and the nearby valleys by providing detailed information and expert advice. *Introducing Turin and the Valleys* maps the city and the valleys and summarizes their history and culture. Traditional festivals, exhibitions and events are listed in the section *Turin and the Valleys Through the Year*. *Turin Area by Area* and *The Valleys* Area by Area describe key sights using maps, photographs and detailed illustrations. Restaurant and hotel recommendations, along with historic cafés and lively night spots, are listed in *Travellers' Needs*, while the *Survival Guide* has tips on all kinds of practical matters, from making a telephone call to using local transport services, banks and post offices, as well as advice on what to do in an emergency.

TURIN AREA BY AREA

The city centre is divided into four areas, to which a further area beyond the city centre has been added, each identified by a colour code. The area colour codes are listed on the book's front flap. All the interesting sights in each area are listed under *Sights at a Glance*.

Sights at a Glance lists the chapter's most important sights by category: Churches, Museums, Art Galleries, Historic Buildings, Streets and Squares.

1 Introduction
This section describes the character and history of each area, along with an account of how the area has developed and what it has to offer the visitor today.

A locator map shows where you are in relation to the other areas in the city centre.

2 Street-by-Street Map
This gives a bird's-eye view of the area to visit. The numbering of the sights refers you to the more complete information which is given on the pages that follow the Street-by-Street map.

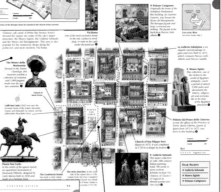

Suggested routes are marked in red and take in the area's most interesting streets.

3 Detailed information
All the main attractions are described individually. They are listed in order and follow the numbering on the area map. The practical information includes references to the Street Finder, opening hours and available facilities.

The coloured thumb tabs allow you to find each area easily.

1 Introduction
The landscape, history and character of each area is described, along with how the area has developed over the centuries and what it has to offer today.

THE VALLEYS

The valleys west of Turin are divided into three main areas, each with its own colour code. There is a general map on the inside cover showing these three areas. All the interesting places to visit are numbered and indicated on the map which can be found at the start of each chapter.

2 Pictorial Map
This shows the road network and gives an illustrated overview of the area. Interesting places to visit are numbered, and there are useful tips on getting around the area.

3 Detailed information
All the important places to visit are described in detail. They are listed in order and follow the numbering on the Pictorial Map. Information is given on how to reach the area by car or other means, along with details of important buildings and other sights.

4 Top Sights
Two or more pages are dedicated to monuments, parks and important sights. Historic buildings and parks are illustrated in detail. Museums and galleries are shown in bird's-eye view and the various sections are coloured to help you make the most of your visit.

Stars indicate the sights no visitor should miss.

INTRODUCING
TURIN AND THE VALLEYS

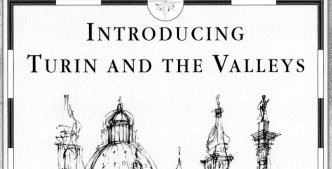

PUTTING TURIN ON THE MAP 10–13
A PORTRAIT OF TURIN AND THE VALLEYS 14–31
TURIN AND THE VALLEYS
THROUGH THE YEAR 32–35
THE HISTORY OF TURIN 36–47

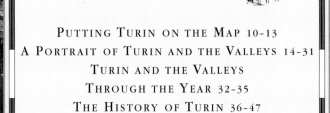

Putting Turin on the Map

Turin (Torino) is the administrative centre of the region of Piedmont and is the fourth largest city in Italy in terms of population (around 900,000). It is also one of the main cities in the industrial triangle that has made Italy's northwest an economically prosperous area. Proximity to France and the Alps has long had an effect on various aspects of the city's life and history, as well as its cultural development. The city is crossed by Italy's largest river, the Po, and three streams: the Dora, Stura and Sangone. The Turinese valleys, starting at Monviso, source of the river Po, are located between the Cozie and Graie Alps and include peaks over 3,000 m (9,845 ft) high, glaciers and ski resorts. Val di Susa is the largest and most densely populated, while Val Pellice, further to the south, is the home of the Waldensian religion. Between the two lies Val Chisone-Germanasca.

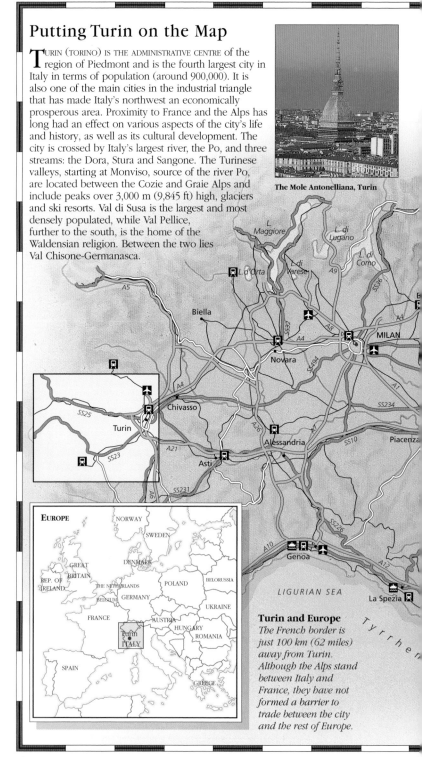

The Mole Antonelliana, Turin

Turin and Europe
The French border is just 100 km (62 miles) away from Turin. Although the Alps stand between Italy and France, they have not formed a barrier to trade between the city and the rest of Europe.

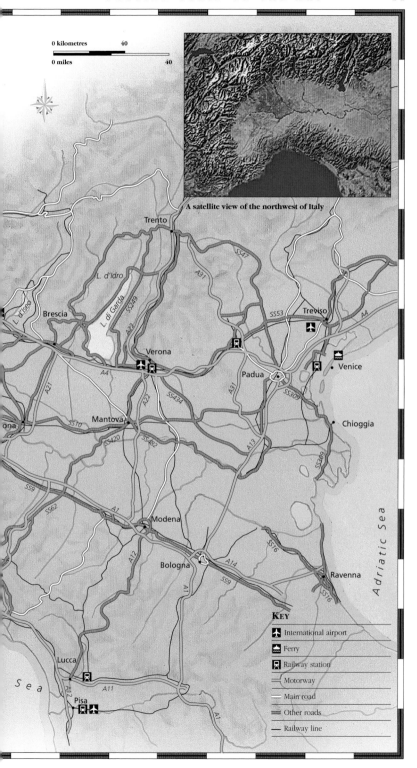

A satellite view of the northwest of Italy

Trento

L. d'Idro

L. di Garda

L. d'Iseo

Brescia

Verona

Treviso

Padua

Venice

Chioggia

Mantova

Modena

Bologna

Ravenna

Adriatic Sea

Lucca

Pisa

Sea

KEY

✈ International airport

⛴ Ferry

🚉 Railway station

━ Motorway

━ Main road

━ Other roads

━ Railway line

0 kilometres 40

0 miles 40

The Centre of Turin

THE CITY COVERS A LARGE AREA and is laid out in a grid pattern; maps reveal the neat regularity of the streets. At the heart of Turin is Piazza Castello, which is overlooked by Palazzo Madama and Palazzo Reale. Leading out of the square are Via Po, which runs to the east and the banks of the river, and Via Roma, which runs south to Piazza San Carlo, passing by Turin's main museums. Via Garibaldi, originally a Roman street, leads directly west into the city and boasts numerous churches and small squares of interest. At the edge of the historic centre are the two railway stations, Porta Nuova and Porta Susa. There are also many interesting attractions to visit in the areas beyond the city's centuries-old centre.

La Consolata
Much loved by the people of Turin, this church has a Romanesque bell tower and stands in a small square in the Quadrilatero Romano. In front is Al Bicerin, a café once patronized by the politician Cavour.

KEY

▢	Star sights
▤	Railway station
P	Parking
ℹ	Tourist information
✝	Church
✚	Hospital
▣	Police station
⊠	Post office

Piazza San Carlo
Palazzo Solaro del Borgo stands in the most elegant square in Turin, along with a monument to Emanuele Filiberto and numerous long-established restaurants and cafés.

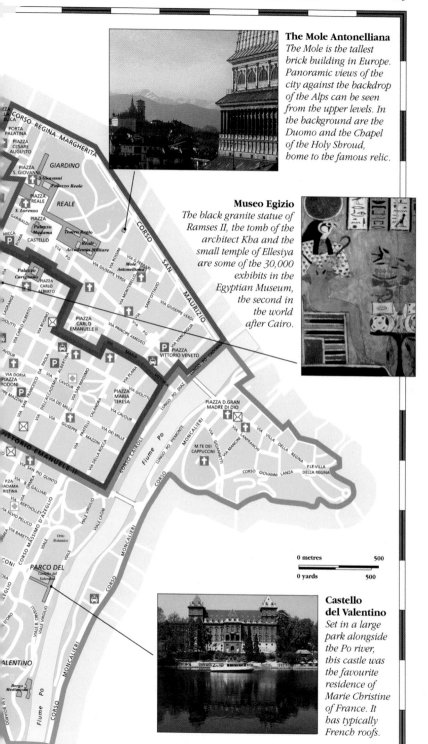

The Mole Antonelliana
The Mole is the tallest brick building in Europe. Panoramic views of the city against the backdrop of the Alps can be seen from the upper levels. In the background are the Duomo and the Chapel of the Holy Shroud, home to the famous relic.

Museo Egizio
The black granite statue of Ramses II, the tomb of the architect Kha and the small temple of Ellesiya are some of the 30,000 exhibits in the Egyptian Museum, the second in the world after Cairo.

0 metres 500
0 yards 500

Castello del Valentino
Set in a large park alongside the Po river, this castle was the favourite residence of Marie Christine of France. It has typically French roofs.

A PORTRAIT OF TURIN AND THE VALLEYS

A MUCH FOUGHT-OVER CITY, *a European power, the capital of the Savoy kingdom, and latterly an important industrial centre: centuries of change have influenced the city of Turin and its appearance. Lying at the foot of the Alps and bisected by the river Po, it is today a lively city with an eye on the future.*

A good way to understand the layout and nature of Turin is to study the view from the highest balcony of the Mole Antonelliana, the 19th-century building which is now home to the Museo del Cinema. A futuristic glass lift offers an unrivalled panorama as it rises to the top. From here, on clear, cold winter days, the austere, monumental blocks of Turin, the capital of Piedmont, are set against the spectacular snow-capped peaks of the Alps. Close by are the majestic mountains of Monviso, Rocciamelone and Monte Rosa, the closest of the range, which rises across Piedmont and neighbouring Val d'Aosta. These impressive peaks are

Art Nouveau glass

a reminder that the city was founded on mercantile trade across the Alps. Turin was for many centuries drawn to both Italy and its neighbour, cosmopolitan France. The mountain valleys that climb up towards Moncenisio and Monginevro to the west are just a short distance away from the city and its suburbs.

At the centre of the city are avenues created by the ruling House of Savoy, and beyond them are the industrial zones. Here are the old factories that produced the FIAT cars which filled Italian streets and became a symbol of post-war prosperity across the country. Today, the city is also renowned for other excellent products and its

Boats moored alongside the Castello del Valentino, with the peak of Monviso beyond

◁ **Turin's most notable landmark, the Mole Antonelliana, with the Alps in the background**

many tourist attractions, such as its Baroque and Art Nouveau architecture, its historic cafés and the famous *giandujotto* chocolates.

TURIN'S FINEST

Many of Italy's key institutions, such as the army, industry, cinema and the charitable institutions of Cottolengo and Don Bosco, originated in Turin, thanks to the good organizational skills and the belief in hard work which are characteristic values of the people of Turin. Many other important Italian institutions and companies also began life here: the publishing houses of Utet (1791) and Einaudi (1933), the Turin newspaper *La Stampa* (1895), Juventus football team (1897), SIP (an Italian telecoms company, 1924), RAI (the national broadcasting corporation) radio (1924) and its National Symphony Orchestra (1931), and the Lavazza (1894) and Ferrero (1946) companies. Turin is also the home of Istituto Elettrotecnico Nazionale, a prestigious research institute.

Juventus FC, founded in 1900

The FIAT assembly line in the 1960s

The city, innately conservative, has nonetheless fostered revolutionaries at times, and given voice to writers and intellectuals including Cesare Pavese, Antonio Gramsci, Giovanni Arpino, Piero Gobetti, Primo Levi and Alessandro Baricco.

Turin preserves little of its remote past and its appearance today is that of a French-influenced capital city which underwent much urban change between the 17th and 19th centuries. Piazza San Carlo, with its statue of a Savoy ruler (Emanuele Filiberto, duke of Savoy) in the centre, is Turin's favourite meeting place, while Piazza Castello represents the city's more official image. The streets in the centre are bordered by porticoes and it is here that the oldest and most famous cafés and *pasticcerie* can be found. Visitors can see Cavour's favourite table, the corner the Savoys chose to have a vermouth, Pavese's regular café. Among the cappuccinos and the famous sweets and chocolates – delectable *giandujotti* and *marrons glacés* – the daily ritual of meeting friends takes place.

Home-made chocolates

The Museo Egizio (Egyptian Museum) was founded thanks to collections donated by Vitaliano Donati and the Italian consul in Cairo, Bernardino Drovetti. The museum is of international importance, not only for the very

The interior of Caffè San Carlo in Turin

fine quality exhibits but also for the founding of the only school of Egyptology in Italy.

There are many other important institutions in Turin. After a pioneering climb to the top of Monviso, the Piedmontese mountaineer Quintino Sella founded the Club Alpino Italiano in 1863, the third in the world after the Alpine Club of London and the Association of Austrian Mountaineers.

Sestrière, with its tower hotels and ski facilities

"Doing things well" seems to be Turin's motto. This is true in the fields of religion and architecture too: the Baroque Cappella della Sacra Sindone, with the famous Holy Shroud, came to Turin from Chambéry when the Savoys decided to change the location of their capital, and is one of Italy's most famous pilgrimage spots.

Outside the city, religion and the Savoy dynasty combine in the Basilica di Superga; while the Savoy residences at Rivoli, Stupinigi, Agliè and Racconigi take you back in time to the golden age of Turin. The Parco del Valentino, set out in the mid-1800s on the banks of the Po, forms a green oasis, drawing the people of Turin to the riverside.

Traditional handicrafts

THE TURINESE VALLEYS

Devotion to the Alps – especially to the distinctive peak of Monviso, which is part of the city's backdrop – is heartfelt. The people of Turin ski on, climb and write about their mountains: and the city is also home to Italy's most important magazine on the subject. The first ski facilities appeared in Sestrière in around the 1930s. The fame of Piedmont's winter resorts, which developed from these early facilities, makes it a fitting setting for the 2006 Winter Olympics.

The valleys are also famous for the Waldensian religion. For eight centuries, the most important Protestant community in Italy has co-existed with its Catholic neighbours in the region between Val Pellice and Val Germanasca. Here, the Waldensians have created a piece of northern Europe in their "capital" Torre Pellice, and their culture and lifestyle fascinate visitors.

The traditional folk group, Aoute Doueire

Landscape, Flora and Fauna

THE MOUNTAINS SURROUNDING Turin are crowned with peaks which are visible from the city, particularly on clear, windy days. The valleys of Susa, Chisone and Pellice are each distinctive – each one's individual characteristics are brought about by its unique microclimate. Both mountains and valleys are home to wet or windy areas, dry or rainy slopes, sparse vegetation or broadleaved woodlands, forests of conifers, meadows and bare rocky slopes. The lakes of Avigliana enjoy a special climate, which has given rise to the presence of warm-climate plants such as wild prickly pears. In the upper Val di Susa, broadleaved trees alternate with conifers, creating a dark green area of woodland, home to deer and to wolves, and redolent with the scent of resin.

Certosa di Monte Benedetto, with Rocciamelone in the background

THE MOUNTAIN PEAKS

A number of major mountain peaks dominate the valleys. They include Rocciamelone, which overlooks the town of Susa; Chaberton, where visitors will find the ruins of a military installation, destroyed during World War II by cannon fire from the French town of Briançon; and the peaks of Rognosa and Platasse, which both exceed 3,000 m (9,845 ft), towering above the winter resort of Sestrière.

THE WOODLANDS

Large areas of woodland can still be found in these valleys. Greenery covers the north-facing slopes and it is still possible to see centuries-old chestnut forests in the lower Val di Susa. The chestnut has been the staple food for generations of the valley's inhabitants whose livelihoods were inextricably linked to the woods. Further up the valley you reach the dense, almost impenetrable wood of Salbertrand.

***Forests** of Scots and Arolla pines (Pinus sylvestris, P. cembra) are found halfway up. Mountain pines grow in Val Troncea.*

***Deer**, the most important of the ungulates (hoofed mammals), can weigh up to 210 kg (465 lb). The male has impressive antlers.*

***Dandelions** grow on the plains and in the mountains. From March to November you can see the yellow flowers which develop downy, white seed heads with maturity.*

***Larches** dominate at 1,000–2,000 m (2,380–6,560 ft) in the Val di Susa and the Val Chisone.*

WATER AND WATERFALLS

Water is plentiful in the valleys and there are numerous waterfalls: hydro-electric plants have, as a consequence, become a visible part of the landscape. Cascading waterfalls make spectacular sights in the winter when they freeze and turn into training grounds for adventurous ice climbers. These same falls often become dangerous and destructive in the spring due to the uneven terrain. You can travel down the torrents by canoe: along the Pellice from Chisone onwards, and along the river Po in the area of Villafranca Piemonte. You can also follow the swirling waters through the many gorges cut into the rock. The most popular routes are found near Novalesa (Rio Claretto and Marderello) or not far from Chianocco (Orrido di Foresto). In Val Pellice, rafting enthusiasts have set up trails in the gorges of Rouspart, near Villar Pellice.

A waterfall in Val Germanasca

THE LAKES

The numerous lakes in the area help to moderate the heat of the summer and the cold in winter. The two lakes of Avigliana are surrounded by woodland and are framed by a circle of hills of glacial origins, part of the ancient morainic amphitheatre. The protection given the area now that it is a natural park means that this territory retains an unspoilt fascination, which changes with the seasons and the time of day.

Fungi found in the foothills and valleys include porcini, puffballs, Caesar and honey fungus.

The chestnut grows naturally at 300–1,000 m (985–2,380 ft) and is typical of valleys in Piedmont. Individual specimens can reach 1,000 years of age and a height of 40 m (130 ft).

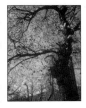

THE UPPER MEADOWS

Found between the tree-line and the higher mountains, these upper meadows are the last sight of green before the peaks. A dense, compact carpet of grass protects other plants from frost and the biting winds which blow from the north, even in the summer months. In spring, the meadows become a carpet of bright flowers, including linaria, gentianella and crocus – all well-adapted to the climate.

Good grazing land is found above the tree line. The pasture has been used for centuries by local farmers.

The vegetation changes with altitude. Over 600 different plant species are found in the Parco Naturale Orsiera-Rocciavré.

Parks and Reserves

IN THE 1960s the region of Piedmont set up an environmental protection programme. The project established numerous regional parks and reserves aimed not only at protecting the natural environment, but also at preserving the architecture and history of the valleys. All kinds of interesting trips can be made in this area: to the dense woodlands of Salbertrand, the Rocca di Cavour with its colourful rock paintings, the cross-country trails in Val Troncea in winter and the Chianocco nature reserve.

The common frog is protected at a special site at San Giorio di Susa, a haven for breeding frogs. The Lataste frog is also found in the Avigliana lakes.

The Riserva di Chianocco e Foresto in Val di Susa covers two deep, narrow ravines cut into the rock. Thanks to its particular microclimate, Chianocco supports a holm oak forest. Foresto can be reached by train.

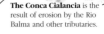

L. NERC

RIS. NAT. DI CHIANOCC E FORESTO

Susa

L. DI ROCCHEMOLLES

R. di Valfredda

PARCO NATURALE GRAN BOSCO SALBERTRAND

PARCO NATURALE ORSIERA ROCCIAVRE

Oulx

AREA LAGO BORELLO

Dora Riparia

T. Chisone

The marshes of Lago Borello are home to grey heron, mallard and other aquatic birds.

PARCO NATURALE VAL TRONCEA

T. Ripa

AREA CON CIALANCI

The Conca Cialancia is the result of erosion by the Rio Balma and other tributaries.

The Parco Naturale del Gran Bosco di Salbertrand covers the north-facing slope of the valley with its lush vegetation. Towards Bardonecchia, visitors are treated to wonderful views of this great green park. The large forest of conifers and alpine broad-leaved tree species is home to deer, roebuck and wolves, and has a fairy-tale fascination.

The Parco Naturale della Val Troncea was set up to preserve the entire Val Troncea, protecting both history and nature. The Chisone river divides the area in two, with steep rock faces on one side and gentler slopes and woods on the other. Old villages with 18th-century houses dot the landscape.

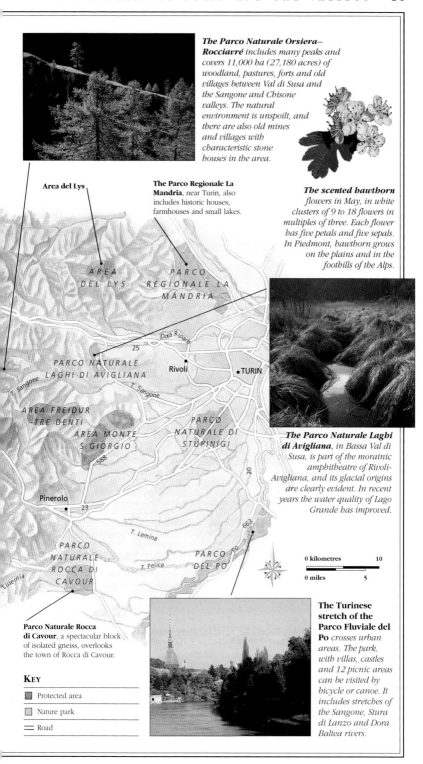

The Parco Naturale Orsiera–Rocciavré includes many peaks and covers 11,000 ha (27,180 acres) of woodland, pastures, forts and old villages between Val di Susa and the Sangone and Chisone valleys. The natural environment is unspoilt, and there are also old mines and villages with characteristic stone houses in the area.

Area del Lys

The Parco Regionale La Mandria, near Turin, also includes historic houses, farmhouses and small lakes.

The scented hawthorn flowers in May, in white clusters of 9 to 18 flowers in multiples of three. Each flower has five petals and five sepals. In Piedmont, hawthorn grows on the plains and in the foothills of the Alps.

AREA DEL LYS

PARCO REGIONALE LA MANDRIA

Dora Riparia

25

PARCO NATURALE LAGHI DI AVIGLIANA

Rivoli

•TURIN

T. Sangone

T. Sangone

AREA FREIDUR –TRE DENTI

AREA MONTE S. GIORGIO

588

PARCO NATURALE DI STUPINIGI

20

The Parco Naturale Laghi di Avigliana, in Bassa Val di Susa, is part of the morainic amphitheatre of Rivoli-Avigliana, and its glacial origins are clearly evident. In recent years the water quality of Lago Grande has improved.

Pinerolo

23

T. Lemina

PARCO NATURALE ROCCA DI CAVOUR

T. Pelice

Luserna

PARCO DEL PO

663

Po

0 kilometres   10

0 miles   5

The Turinese stretch of the Parco Fluviale del Po crosses urban areas. The park, with villas, castles and 12 picnic areas can be visited by bicycle or canoe. It includes stretches of the Sangone, Stura di Lanzo and Dora Baltea rivers.

Parco Naturale Rocca di Cavour, a spectacular block of isolated gneiss, overlooks the town of Rocca di Cavour.

KEY

	Protected area
	Nature park
══	Road

The Alps

TURIN AND THE PIEDMONTESE PLAIN are dominated by the majestic peaks of the western Alps. Although Monviso is the most impressive mountain visible from the city on clear, fine days, the entire view is spectacular. The Alpi Cozie, beginning at the Colle della Maddalena and ending at Moncenisio in Alta Val di Susa, reach a peak of 3,841 m (12,600 ft) at the top of Monviso. The mountain passes have been used since ancient times, including Monginevro (1,850 m/ 6,070 ft), not far from Clavière in Val di Susa, and Moncenisio (2,083 m/6,835 ft), just beyond the French border on the route linking Susa with the French Haute Savoie. In 1871, the 12-km (7-mile) excavations were completed for the oldest Alpine railway tunnel: the Frejus, still in use today.

Mont Blanc *(Monte Bianco) is the highest peak in Europe at 4,807 m (15,770 ft). It was first climbed in 1786 by Paccard and Balmat. Today, the summit can be reached by cable car. The Mont Blanc tunnel is 11.6 km (7 miles) long.*

Cervino
4,478 m/
14,695 ft

Chaberton *is one of the Alta Val di Susa peaks (3,131 m/ 10,275 ft) in French territory. Europe's highest fortress was located here during World War II.*

Monviso, *in the Alpi Cozie, is 3,841 m (12,600 ft) high. The river Po originates on the Coolidge glacier, facing northeast. The source is at Piano del Re, at 2,020 m (6,630 ft).*

Peak of Argentera
3,297 m/10,820 ft

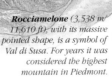

Rocciamelone *(3,538 m/ 11,610 ft), with its massive pointed shape, is a symbol of Val di Susa. For years it was considered the highest mountain in Piedmont.*

THE MAIN ALPINE PEAKS

Eight of the tallest peaks in Italy rise in the western and central Alps. Monte Bianco (Mont Blanc) is, at 4,807 m (15,770 ft), the highest mountain in Europe. The Alpi Cozie in Piedmont are home to Monviso, Punta Ramière (3,303 m/10,835 ft) at one end of Val Germanasca, Rocca d'Abin (3,378 m/ 11,085 ft) and Rocciamelone (3,538 m/ 11,610 ft), not far from Susa. In the Pre-Alps lie Orsiera (2,878 m/9,445 ft) and the mountains dividing the Chisone, Germanasca and Pellice valleys.

THE WESTERN ALPS

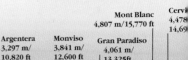

Mont Blanc
4,807 m/15,770 ft

Cervi
4,478
14,69

Argentera
3,297 m/
10,820 ft

Monviso
3,841 m/
12,600 ft

Gran Paradiso
4,061 m/
13,325ft

CAESAR AND MONGINEVRO

In *De Bello Gallico* (Gallic Wars), Julius Caesar describes crossing the Alps across the Monginevro pass, which he undertook in 58 BC. The pass was one of the easiest topographically, but it certainly presented dangers for the safety of travellers. During the march, Caesar and his five legions were attacked by the Gallic tribes of Graioceli, Ceutrones and Caturiges. Later, control of the Alpine passes was one of the incentives that drove the Romans to conquer the Piedmontese valleys or to establish an agreement with the local populations, as Augustus did with King Cozio and the 14 tribes who lived in the area around the Val di Susa. The event is commemorated by the Arco di Augusto (Arch of Augustus) in Susa.

Arch of Augustus, Susa

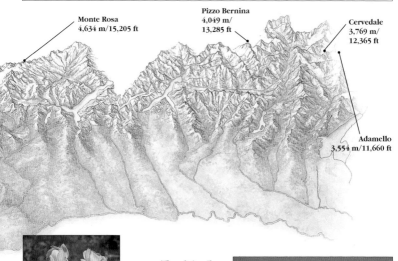

Monte Rosa
4,634 m/15,205 ft

Pizzo Bernina
4,049 m/
13,285 ft

Cervedale
3,769 m/
12,365 ft

Adamello
3,554 m/11,660 ft

The globe flower (Trollius europaeus) *can be seen from May to August above the tree line. It has a distinctive shape and bright golden yellow colour.*

The alpine ibex, *emblem of the Gran Paradiso reserve, can also be seen above 3,000 m (9,845 ft) in the Parco dell'Orsiera in the Alta Valle Po. At one time only the king was permitted to hunt them.*

THE WESTERN ALPS

Monte Rosa
4,634 m/
15,205 ft

Corno Bianco
3,320 m/
10,895 ft

Adula
3,402 m/
11,160 ft

Bernina
4,049 m/
13,285 ft

Adamello
3,554 m/
11,660 ft

Ortles
3,899 m/
12,795 ft

Palla Bianca
3,736 m/
12,260 ft

THE EASTERN ALPS

Gran Pilastro
3,509 m/
11,515 ft

Marmolada
3,342 m/10,965 ft

Picco dei
Tre Signori
3,499 m/
11,480 ft

The Turin Winter Olympics

Seventeen days of competitions, 15 sports (from classic events such as bobsleigh racing, to the newest sports, such as snowboarding), 84 titles and 246 medals. The Winter Olympics of Turin and its valleys will take place from 10–26 February 2006. Seven local communes are involved: Turin itself, Bardonecchia, Cesana, Pinerolo, Pragelato, Sauze d'Oulx and Sestrière. These areas are home to some of the most famous ski resorts in Italy and this prestigious event represents an opportunity to promote the area on an unprecedented scale.

torino 2006

***The official logo** of the 20th Winter Olympic Games is shown here. The 9th Paralympic Games take place 10–19 March.*

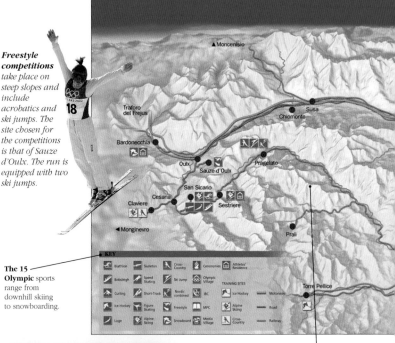

***Freestyle competitions** take place on steep slopes and include acrobatics and ski jumps. The site chosen for the competitions is that of Sauze d'Oulx. The run is equipped with two ski jumps.*

The 15 Olympic sports range from downhill skiing to snowboarding.

KEY

Biathlon   Skeleton   Cross-Country   Ceremonies   Athletes' Residence

Bobsleigh   Speed Skating   Ski Jump   Olympic Village   TRAINING SITES

Curling   Short-Track   Nordic combined   IBC   Ice Hockey   Motorway

Ice Hockey   Figure Skating   Freestyle   MPC   Alpine Skiing   Road

Luge   Alpine Skiing   Snowboard   Media Village   Cross-Country   Railway

Val Chisone and Germanasca
Pragelato is ideal for cross-country skiing. Its plains and forests offer long and spectacular routes for the cross-country events.

***Sestrière** is one of the resorts hosting the games. The area known as Via Lattea (Milky Way) is made up of Cesana, Clavière, San Sicario, Sauze d'Oulx and Monginevro. There are over 200 slopes, covering a total of 400 km (250 ft). The area is served by 91 ski lifts.*

***The ice hockey matches** (at the Palasport in Turin) are tests of physical strength and stamina. The players use hockey sticks to manoeuvre a puck to play a fast and furious game while striving to score a goal.*

Oval Lingotto was designed as the venue for the speed skating competitions and part of it will continue to be used for ice sports after the Olympic Games. The arena can hold 8,200 spectators and the entire building measures 210 x 127 m (690 x 415 ft).

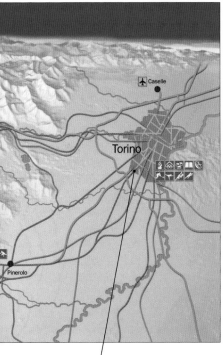

Turin is the organizing centre for the event, home to an Olympic village and press centres. Ceremonies and speed skating take place at Oval Lingotto, short track races and figure skating at the Palavela. Hockey matches are held at Torino Esposizioni and Palasport.

THE OLYMPICS IN THE VALLEYS

Pragelato will host the cross-country and ski jump events, while Pinerolo, on the plain, will be the venue for the curling competition. Clavière, Chiomonte and Prali will be training locations for the downhill and cross-country events, while at Torre Pellice an ice rink will be available to all the teams for training purposes.

Turin will be home to 2,500 athletes and 10,000 journalists, as well as members of the National Olympic Committee, trainers and national representatives.

Short track speed skating is a relatively new event at the Olympics. The individual and team races (at Turin's Palavela) are fast and exhilarating.

The Palavela in Turin is one of the buildings hosting the Olympic Games. The new design will incorporate and rejuvenate one of the city's emblematic buildings. Torino Esposizioni also undergoes radical alterations, and it will be converted into a venue for fairs and exhibitions after the games.

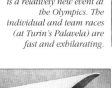

Turin's Architecture

THE REGULAR LAYOUT of Turin's streets and squares is the result of three phases of expansion carried out in the 17th and 18th centuries. At this time, Turin left much of its past behind and became the Baroque capital of a powerful kingdom. Among the architects at work during this period was Filippo Juvarra who designed, among other things, the façade of Palazzo Madama, a symbol of a city which has diverse architectural styles. Today, Turin continues to renew itself, with a clutch of futuristic buildings and a number of large urban projects under way.

Palazzo Madama mirrors the city's history through the various architectural styles revealed in the building.

ROMANESQUE AND GOTHIC

Little remains of medieval Turin. Traces of windows and towers are visible near Porta Palatina, Largo IV Marzo and in the streets and small squares around Via Garibaldi. Over time, some of the Romanesque churches, including Sant'Agostino and Consolata, have evolved in various styles. The church of San Domenico, altered over the years, is the only example of Gothic in Turin.

The Romanesque bell tower (40 m/130 ft) of the Santuario della Consolata is all that remains of what was originally the church of Sant'Andrea. It has double and triple openings in the upper part.

A Gothic window

RENAISSANCE

Renaissance architecture is characterized by the reappearance of Classical models in both civic and religious buildings from the 14th to the 16th century. Turin's first Renaissance monument was the Duomo, dedicated to San Giovanni.

Portals with bas reliefs

The Duomo (cathedral), completed in 1498, represents the only religious Renaissance building in Turin. The decoration on the façade was inspired by Classical Roman models while the interior has Gothic elements.

BAROQUE

The Baroque architecture of northwest Italy (17th–18th century) reached its height in Turin ruled by the House of Savoy, with works by architects of note such as Guarino Guarini and Filippo Juvarra. The most significant examples are the west façade of Palazzo Madama, the Stupinigi hunting lodge, the Basilica di Superga, Cappella della Sindone, Piazza San Carlo and San Lorenzo.

Rotonda   **Concave brick façade**

Ornate windows

Palazzo Carignano, designed in 1679–85 by Guarini, is one of the most original Baroque buildings in Piedmont. The curved façade, faced in bare brick, is highly innovative compared with the style of the period.

NEO-CLASSICAL AND THE 19TH CENTURY

In the second half of the 18th century, the Baroque style gave way to a return to the rational dictates of antiquity, giving rise to Neo-Classicism. Architecturally, the Neo-Classical style was characterized by an imposing quality, as seen in the buildings in squares such as Piazza Vittorio Veneto, Piazza Maria Teresa and Piazza Statuto.

The Mole Antonelliana was the highest building in the world at the time of its construction. Today, at 163.35 m (536 ft), it is the tallest brick building in Europe.

The Gran Madre stands on Piazza Vittorio Veneto, at the end of Vittorio Emanuele I bridge in an area of Turin with many Neo-Classical features. The temple, inspired by the Pantheon in Rome, was completed in 1831. Statues represent Faith and Religion.

Dome on a square base

THE NEW MILLENNIUM

Turin made its contribution to the architecture of the 20th century with the building of Lingotto (1916–22) by Giacomo Mattè Trucco, and the Palavela, built for the 1961 exhibition of Italy. The latter is being rebuilt for the Winter Olympics and is one of the major works being carried out in the city on an unprecedented scale: the Palazzo della Regione and the futuristic Biblioteca Civica are two more examples.

The Bolla conference hall by Renzo Piano at Lingotto

Sail structure rotated 60 degrees

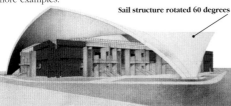

A helical ramp leads up to the testing track on the roof of the former FIAT factory at Lingotto.

The rebuilding of Palavela is the work of the architects Gae Aulenti and Arnaldo De Bernardi. The sail-like structure rests on only three bases. The internal circular base is 130 m (425 ft) across and the structure is 29 m (95 ft) high.

ART NOUVEAU

In the early 1900s, Turin was one of the capitals of Art Nouveau (known as Liberty style in Italy) and many examples of the floral and decorative style then in fashion in European cities can still be admired. Along the first stretch of Corso Francia, the major thoroughfare planned by Vittorio Amedeo II in 1711 to connect Castello di Rivoli to Palazzo Reale, are good examples. The interior of Caffè Mulassano, in Piazza Castello, has its original furnishings. In Corso Francia, there is Villino Raby (1901) at No. 8, while at No. 23 stands Palazzo della Vittoria (1925) which has a door-way decorated with two winged dragons. At No. 32 is Casa Macciotta (1904). Palazzo Fenoglio is in Via Principi d'Acaja, at No. 11.

Dragon, Palazzo della Vittoria

The façade of Palazzo Fenoglio-La Fleur (1902)

Architecture in the Valleys

W ITH TIME, people living in the mountains near
Turin adopted a style of architecture suited to the
climate, the location and their own requirements. The
social structure was that of a community and buildings
were constructed one against the other, so as to make
the most of the shelter provided by neighbouring
walls. Sloping roofs provided protection from the rain.
These old villages can usually be recognized by this
"enclosed" layout. Mountain houses are generally
characterized by the fact that the living quarters for
the family are often smaller than areas given over to
the storing of foodstuffs, farming equipment and
tools, and for farm animals.

*The murals of Usseaux, in Val
Chisone, are painted on the
walls of the houses and
represent scenes of traditional
village life, from the process of
making bread to community
entertainment, such as dances.*

*The houses are built of stone, with a large
single room on the ground floor for people and
animals, and a loft above for storing hay and
grain. Stables have a cross vault with a central
stone pillar. Where ceilings had wooden beams,
wooden pillars were not needed for support.*

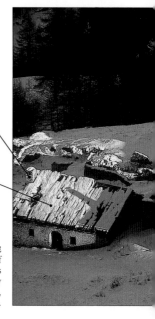

**Stone
chimney**

**Roof with
wooden
shingles**

A SMALL MOUNTAIN VILLAGE
Many communes in the Turinese valleys are made up of
various outlying wards, or hamlets, with typical houses
made of wood and stone. Some of the villages are very
old and are deliberately located near summer pastures,
in sunny spots sheltered from the wind.

*The old villages can be
recognized by their
"enclosed" layout, centred
around a parish church.
Typical stone houses have
wide overhanging roofs,
stone doorways and frescoes.
At one time villagers used a
public oven to bake bread
and there was often a mill
on the outskirts of the village.
Wash-houses, fountains
and sundials were other
common features of these
alpine villages.*

Windows *framed with floral frescoes became commonplace on many of the houses in the valleys from the early 1900s. Some also have Art Nouveau motifs. In Usseaux, the stone walls are frescoed.*

The mountain huts retain their original characteristics. Some still have wooden roofing, an alternative to flat stone tiling.

Stone walls

Fountains *are a common feature in the villages and some are very old. Examples are a square fountain with fleur-de-lys dated 1614 in Granges (Pragelato), hexagonal ones with the House of Savoy cross from 1748 in La Ruà and 17th-century fountains with geometric motifs in Traverses.*

Wood *is the chief material seen in alpine houses: it is used for details and for lintels above doors and windows. Furniture and work implements and tools are also often made of wood.*

BUILDING FOR TOURISM

In the 1930s, Sestrière became home to what is still one of the most striking buildings in western Piedmont. The tower hotel was designed by Vittorio Bonadè Bottino, and soon became an architectural symbol of a growing phenomenon: mass tourism. In the mountains, tourism took off after World War II, and in just a few decades the appearance of the towns and villages here changed. Fields were no longer plots of land used for agriculture, but potential building sites. Enormous apartment blocks, typical of the

The "tower" hotel in Sestrière

1950s, now rub shoulders with architectural gems, thanks to architects such as Carlo Mollino, a ski enthusiast who designed various buildings in these valleys. The recently-renovated sledge lift station at Lago Nero di Sauze d'Oulx is just one example.

Contemporary Art in Turin

TURIN IS A FORWARD-LOOKING CITY, and is known in Italy as the capital of contemporary art. Institutions such as the Galleria Civica d'Arte Moderna e Contemporanea (*see p83*), the Nuovo Centro per l'Arte Contemporanea at the Fondazione Sandretto (*see p94*) and Castello di Rivoli (*see p104*) have an international reputation. New exhibition spaces are being added all the time, and modern art can also be found on the streets and in the cafés along the river and in the city centre. From November to January the city hosts an open-air art and light show called Luci d'Artista.

Fountain-Igloo by Mario Merz, the first of 11 works in a major street-art project.

GALLERIA CIVICA D'ARTE MODERNA E CONTEMPORANEA (GAM)

Compenetrazioni Iridescenti, *Giacomo Balla (1917), is part of a series of abstract works revealing harmony of colour and pure geometric forms.*

Head of a Woman with Red Hair, *Modigliani (1915), is exhibited in the 20th-century section of GAM.*

The first floor of GAM houses permanent works from the 20th century, with examples of Divisionism, Pop Art, Arte Povera (poor art) and more recent experimental works. The illuminated sign outside the gallery, by Nannucci, claims, "All art has been contemporary".

FONDAZIONE SANDRETTO RE REBAUDENGO – NUOVO CENTRO PER L'ARTE CONTEMPORANEA

Opened in 2002, this new gallery covers an area of 3,500 sq m (37,675 sq ft) and is used for exhibitions, video installations and projects dedicated to new trends in modern art. The building, designed by the architect Claudio Silvestrin, occupies a former industrial site.

A video-installation by the Californian artist Doug Aitken was an exhibit in one of the gallery's first temporary exhibitions.

CASTELLO DI RIVOLI – MUSEO D'ARTE CONTEMPORANEA

Coloured panels and tower,
Sol LeWitt (1992), *occupies
one of the rooms in the
permanent collection (works
from the 1950s onwards).*

Created from sections of a
renovated Savoy castle, the
Castello di Rivoli museum
has housed contemporary art
since 1984. Temporary
exhibitions are held in the
17th-century Manica Lunga,
which is 147 m (480 ft) long.

ART IN THE OPEN AIR

Turin's streets and buildings also act as exhibition spaces.
The **Luci d'Artista** and **ManifesTO** events are held every
year between November and January. These exhibitions
combine light installations and enormous posters (*manifesti*)
by internationally renowned artists. They aim to bring art
onto the streets and to the people, and everyday places are
transformed according to the artists' inspiration and style.
Installing the lights for Luci d'Artista takes 30,000 hours, 100
km (62 miles) of wiring, 700,000 bulbs and the work of 100
technicians and craftsmen. Artists involved have included
Mario Merz, Rebecca Horn, Daniel Buren, Francesco Casorati,
Mario Airò and Jan Vercruysse. **ManifesTO** turns the streets
into works of art with enormous posters on the sides of the
buildings. Another event, **Artissima**, began in 1994 and is an

Fluctuating Waves **by Nancy
Dwyer in Parete ad Arte**

exhibition and market specializing in contemporary art. Today it is known as a showcase
for young artists and modern galleries. The works are mainly paintings, videos,
photographs and installations. Many works of art later become part of the city. This

A light installation by Luci d'Artista, Via Pietro Micca

happened with the **Museo d'Arte
Urbana Campidoglio** (Corso Tassoni,
Corso Lecce, Via Nicola Fabrizi and Via
Levanna), with *Piercing* by Corrado
Levi and the Gruppo Cliostradt in Via
Palazzo di Città, an untitled bronze
work by Giò Pomodoro in the gardens
of Piazza Adriano and the **Parete ad
Arte** by Nancy Dwyer in Piazza
Viglongo. "Public Art in Turin: 11
unexpected events on the Crossrail
System" will, when completed,
comprise a string of 11 street-art
installations positioned along the 3 km
(2 miles) of avenues cleared during the
construction of Turin's new railway.

TURIN AND THE VALLEYS THROUGH THE YEAR

IN SPRING splendid views of the Alpine range can be enjoyed from the terrace of the Mole Antonelliana, Monte dei Cappuccini, Superga and Lingotto. The parks along the Po provide welcome shade from the sultry summer heat, and the people of Turin seek out the open-air cafés of Murazzi and Valentino. Summer is celebrated with fireworks on the Po (Feast of San Giovanni) and with musical events. With autumn, the city returns to its normal routine with film festivals, the theatre season and concerts. Winter makes Turin the capital of the Alps, with tourists en route to the popular skiing resorts nearby. Every season is good for hiking and sport: the green parks and woods in the summer, the white-capped mountains in winter.

Vermouth, a popular aperitif

CioccolaTò, a celebration of chocolate in Turin

SPRING

SPRINGTIME brings with it fine sunny days when the breeze clears the air, the city takes on new colours and there is a wonderful view of the snow-capped peaks of the Alps. It is best to carry an umbrella, however; towards the end of the season the fine weather can quickly change to often violent thunderstorms.

MARCH

CioccolaTò, Turin *(Feb, Mar)*. Festival of chocolate with exhibitions, shows, tours, concerts. A pass allows you to taste delicacies in the city's cafés and *pasticcerie*.
Musica 90, Turin *(spring, autumn)*. Concerts of varied music from diverse geographical regions.

Eurojazz Festival, Ivrea and villages around Turin. After Carnival, the town becomes the European capital of jazz.

APRIL

Settimana della Carne, Pinerolo. Show of Piedmontese cattle, guided visits to farms, meat tasting.
Cantavalli *(Apr, May)*. Ethnic and folk music concerts in the Chisone-Germanasca valleys.
Valsusa Filmfest, Val Susa *(Apr, May)*. Films about regional history and the local environment.
Da Sodoma a Hollywood, Turin. International gay film festival.
Turin Marathon. Along the streets of the city centre, up the hill, along the Po to the Parco del Valentino.
Danza delle Spade, San Giorio di Susa *(Sun closest to 23 Apr)*. Commemoration of an uprising against feudal lords. Dances, processions and swordsmen.

MAY

Fiera Internazionale del Libro, Lingotto. A different country guests annually at the book fair.
Tastar de Corda, *(May–Jun)*. Exhibitions of harpsichords, lutes, harps and guitars. Concerts in Rivoli, Avigliana, Giaveno and Turin.
Parchi Storici Fioriti. Houses and private parks at Pinerolo, Pralormo and Racconigi are open to visitors.

Cattle consortium logo

The International Book Fair, held in May at Lingotto Fiere

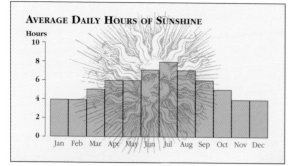

AVERAGE DAILY HOURS OF SUNSHINE

Hours

Jan Feb Mar Apr May Jun Jul Aug Sep Oct Nov Dec

Sunshine Hours
Turin's sunshine average is similar to other Mediterranean countries. However, in autumn and winter the sun is often obscured by haze. The towns in the valleys, surrounded by alpine peaks, are naturally shaded in the mornings and evenings.

Poppies in the Parco del Po

SUMMER

JUNE IS A PLEASANT TIME to visit Turin because of the mild weather and full calendar of cultural and sporting events. In July the sultry summer weather can get rather oppressive during the hottest part of the day. Shows and concerts move into the open air, the parks and the stadium. In August, when offices and factories close, the city empties and the streets are quiet and peaceful. Relief from the summer heat is easily found at a variety of alpine resorts, just a few kilometres away from Turin.

JUNE

Torino Punti Verdi, Turin *(until Sep)*. For visitors and locals alike, hundreds of entertaining events are held daily.
San Giovanni, Turin (*24 June*). The patron saint's day is celebrated with regattas and a firework display on the banks of the river Po.

Immagini dell'Interno, Pinerolo. International festival of puppet theatre with fine performances.
Experimenta, Turin *(until Nov)*. An interactive exhibition with a different scientific theme every year.
Festival delle Colline Torinesi *(until Jul)*. Young theatrical groups perform in Turin and nearby castles.

JULY

Traffic Torino Free Festival A festival of rock and new musical trends with international artists.
Festivalmontagna *(Jul, Aug)*. Theatre, music, nature and story-telling in Val Pellice.
Le Fenestrelle *(Jul–Sep)*. Shows performed inside the Fenestrelle fort with music, dance, images and words.
Sentinelle delle Alpi *(summer)*. A programme of musical and theatrical events,

Forte di Fenestrelle

shows and cinema in the forts of Exilles and Fenestrelle.
Vincoli Sonori, Pinerolo. This festival of klezmer and Gypsy music creates a very distinctive atmosphere in this mountain town.

AUGUST

Mostra Mercato dell'Artigianato, Pinerolo *(end Aug, beginning Sep)*. The streets in the city centre are filled with artisans showing their handicrafts.
Teatro Festival Sauze d'Oulx. A theatrical event in the town known as "the balcony of the Alps".
Bal do Sabre, Fenestrelle *(25 Aug)*. This festival features traditional sword-dancing and local costumes.

The Stadio delle Alpi, a venue for concerts as well as football matches

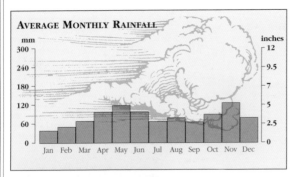

AVERAGE MONTHLY RAINFALL

Rainfall
The average monthly rainfall in the Turin area changes during the year. The rainiest season is autumn, when it may rain for days, while in late spring and summer the amount of rainfall can increase due to the often violent rainstorms and heavy downpours.

The Agnelli Auditorium in Turin

AUTUMN

SEPTEMBER in Turin gives you a real sense that the city is coming back to life. The inhabitants of Turin usually begin to return to the city at the end of August, and the city gets back to its normal routine in September. This is when many film festivals, artistic events, the theatre season and concert programmes begin. The weather in this season is changeable, and rainy spells often alternate with clear, bright, sunny days.

SEPTEMBER

Due Laghi Jazz Festival *(beginning Sep)*, Avigliana. The medieval Piazza Conte Rosso is the venue for jazz performances by national and international artists.
Identità e Differenza, Turin. Multicultural music, theatre and meetings organized by the city council.
Concorso Ippico Internazionale *(mid-Sep)*, Pinerolo. The town hosts this international equestrian event on the CSIA circuit, and riders from all over the world participate.
Torino Settembre Musica, Turin. Over 50 musical events, with all types of music and international guests. Venues include the Agnelli Auditorium and the Borgo Medioevale.

OCTOBER

Salone Internazionale del Gusto, Turin. Every two years, Lingotto Fiere hosts this international wine and gastronomic event with stands, workshops and seminars.
Teatro Stabile di Torino *(until May)*. The Stabile company's theatre season begins in Turin's various theatres, including the Carignano and the Gobetti.
Mystery of the Iron Mask

The logo of the Salone del Gusto

(beginning Oct), Pinerolo. This event commemorates one of Louis XIV's subjects, who spent 16 years in the city's prisons. Dancing, games, competitions, mock duels and parades.
Festival Cinema delle Donne, Turin. A unique event in Italy dedicated to women's role in the cinema.
Opera season *(until Jun)*, Turin. A dozen great productions are staged at Teatro Regio.
Cinemambiente, Turin. A week of films with an environmental theme.

NOVEMBER

Artissima *(beginning Nov)*, Turin. Exhibition of international contemporary art dedicated to new and up-and-coming art galleries.
Salone del Vino, Turin. Wine producers and buyers meet at this trade fair. Not open to the public.
Torino Film Festival, Turin. Italy's major film event after Venice. The festival launches many film directors.
Sottodiciotto Film Festival, Turin. A film competition dedicated to the under-18s.
Luci d'Artista e Arte Contemporanea (ManifesTO) *(until mid-Jan)*, Turin. The Christmas season sees the city decorated with artistic light installations and huge posters, turning the city centre into an atmospheric open-air gallery. Guides are available for tours.

The Mystery of the Iron Mask

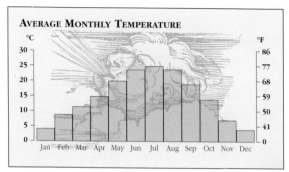

AVERAGE MONTHLY TEMPERATURE

Temperature
Temperature variations are very noticeable through the year. In December and January it can get very cold, typical of continental Europe, while the summers can be hot and sultry. The weather in the spring and autumn is very pleasant, however.

WINTER

T HE TURINESE WINTERS can be very cold (heavy snowfalls are not uncommon). There are, however, many cultural events and important festivals. Exhibitions, the theatre and concert seasons, artistic events, contemporary art activities and Luci d'Artista are all on-going events. At the weekends, the ski resorts are full of people attracted not only by the snow, but also by the many events which are organized there.

DECEMBER

Christmas Markets. Of the many markets held in the city's squares selling handicrafts, local wine and food products, the market of Borgo Dora, in the beautiful Maglio courtyard, is a particular attraction.

Waldensian emblem

Christmas and New Year, Turin. Nativity scenes are set up around the city and New Year's Eve is celebrated in its squares and open spaces.

JANUARY

Danza degli Spadonari *(22 Jan)*, Giaglione. An ancient pagan ritual celebrated on the local patron saint's day which is repeated again the following Sunday, during Corpus Domini, on 7 October and on 22 November.
Sintonie *(Jan–Feb)*, Turin. Music, visual arts, theatre and cinema in various locations, including the famous Agnelli Auditorium.

FEBRUARY

L'Orso della Candelora *(first Sun in Feb)*, Urbiano di Mompantero. An ancient ceremony; a masked man

Walking with snow shoes – *ciaspole* – in Pragelato

leads a bear around the streets of the town.
Racchettinvalle *(end Feb)*, Pragelato. An international sporting event of snow shoe *(ciaspole)* racing.
Carnivale. Events, parades and shows in the districts of Turin, Rivoli and Ivrea, where the "battle of the oranges" takes place.
Torino Danza *(until Oct)*. Every month the dance performances focus on a different theme.
Festa dei Valdesi *(16–17 Feb)*. Bonfires and fireworks in the Waldensian valleys on the 16th, followed by a day of worship, a community lunch and a parade in costume. The event commemorates religious rights granted in 1848.
AutomOtoretrò, Turin. This event at Lingotto is for car and motorbike enthusiasts: vintage spare parts and accessories for sale.

One of Turin's squares lit up during the Luci d'Artista event

THE HISTORY OF TURIN

EW ARCHAEOLOGICAL TRACES *remain of Turin's remote past, or of the ancient history of the surrounding valleys which climb up towards the Alps. It would appear that during the prehistoric age, the areas closer to the coast were more appealing. However, in the last centuries before the birth of Christ, the entire Piedmont area was inhabited by groups of Celtic origin.*

Apart from a few archaeological remains – mostly places of worship – the history of the people who inhabited the Turinese area can only be reconstructed from notes and descriptions left to us by Roman historians. The Taurini tribe, whose presence gave rise to the city's Roman name of Augusta Taurinorum, fought against Hannibal who, in 218 BC, crossed the Alps at Monginevro with his army. According to Pliny, the Taurini came from Liguria and were part of a large civilization which, in around the 1st century BC, began to make use of iron. A century later, the Taurini clashed with the advancing Gauls, who came down the Dora Baltea valley.

Dancer in bronze, **Museo di Antichità, Turin**

Julius Caesar crossed the plain and the valleys during his successful military campaigns, and his experiences, which he described in *De Bello Gallico* (Gallic Wars), convinced Rome that it was necessary to control the alpine pass in order to guarantee safety in the Po river valley. However, it was only during Augustan rule that Roman expansion was really consolidated in Piedmont and along the alpine range.

In 28 BC the city of Augusta Taurinorum was founded, but it is not known whether it was built on an earlier settlement. The Kingdom of Donno, which included Val di Susa, was allied with Caesar, and Donno's son Cozio I, who became a prefect under Augustus, built a triumphal arch dedicated to the Roman emperor in 9 BC. Augusta Praetoria – present-day Aosta – was also founded in the same era, to control the Piccolo and Gran San Bernardo.

Turin, protected by the Dora and Po rivers, was at the centre of a network of Roman routes to Gaul and became increasingly rich and important. With the shifting of Roman interests towards the Po river valley in the late Imperial era, the city extended outside its original boundaries. Roman Turin is thought of as the city's historic centre. The ancient Roman *decumanus* (main street) survives in the layout of what is now Via Garibaldi.

TIMELINE

Hannibal

300 BC The first Taurini, descendants of the Ligurian-Celts and Gallic races, settle along the Po	**218 BC** Taurasia, the city of the Taurini, resists Hannibal's troops which crossed at Monginevro	**9 BC** An arch is built in Susa to commemorate the alliance between the valley tribes and Rome	**AD 312** Constantine destroys Susa, which is guilty of an alliance with Maxentius

300 BC	250 BC	100 BC	AD 1	AD 100	300

Bust of Caius Julius Caesar

58 BC Julius Caesar founds the *castrum* that would become the city of Augusta Taurinorum	**28 BC** Augusta Taurinorum is founded	**AD 69** During the civil wars which followed Nero's death, Turin is burned and almost completely destroyed.

◁ **Part of the fresco cycle depicting San Nicola in the Abbey of Novalesa, in Val di Susa**

THE FALL OF THE EMPIRE

After the fall of the Roman Empire, Piedmont was ruled by the Lombards. Key figures at the time were the dukes of Turin: Agilulfo, husband of Teodolinda, and Ariperto. They owed their status and importance to the strategic position of their lands, which controlled the mountain passes to France.

Meanwhile, in Turin, the political and spiritual role of the bishops was growing. The bishops introduced the cult of St John the Baptist and built a basilica and the monastery of San Solutore, which was later demolished in 1536 to make way for the building of the Cittadella.

After lengthy disputes, in 773 the Franks defeated the Lombards at the foot of the Sacra di San Michele and put an end to their reign. The feudal system was spreading in Piedmont in this period and some families were becoming increasingly politically important. The region was also divided into three *marche* or

Votive cross of Agilulfo, Teodolinda's husband

marches: Arduinica (Turin, Alba and Ventimiglia), Aleramica (Monferrato and Savona) and Obertenga (Genoa, Pavia and Milan). However, political instability quickly brought about the break-up of these areas and Olderico Manfredi became the first marquis of Turin, taking up residence in Palazzo di Porta Segusina (near Porta Garibaldi). In the same era, the basis for the Savoy dynasty was being laid: Umberto Biancamano, feudal lord of Burgundy, received land in Maurienne from the Emperor and became Count of Savoy. The family's domains spread into Piedmont with the marriage of Oddone of Savoy to Adelaide, daughter of the marquis of Turin.

BISHOPS AND FEUDAL LORDS

Thanks to their great estates and their control of the forts and main roads, the bishops of Turin dominated the city for a long time. In around the middle of 1100, Bishop Claudio acquired the status of a prince.

The city's economic growth and the increase in power of Turin's most important families also brought about growth in the city's power. In 1193 the commune gained the use of the fortresses should it need them and, a few decades later, this was stipulated in treaties with other nearby cities. While in Turin the commune dominated the scene, with the support of the bishops, in the rest of the region the two most important feudal states were those of the counts of Savoy and the marquises of Monferrato. In this period, Charles of

Porta Palatina in Turin (1st century AD)

TIMELINE

773 With victory over the Lombards at Chiusa di San Michele, Charlemagne opens the road to Italy

Sacra di San Michele

10th century First known construction at Sacra di San Michele

Oddone with his wife Adelaide in an ivory relief

700	800	900	1000	1050

888 End of Carolingian power: county of Turin becomes part of the Italic kingdom of Berengarius

1046–91 Adelaide of Susa becomes the wife of Marquis Oddone: expansion of Savoy estates in Piedmont

Anjou came to Italy and founded a state made up of a number of cities, including Turin, which feared the power of the marquises of Asti. In 1280, at the end of the Angevin episode, Turin was conquered by the Savoys. Upon taking possession of the city, Count Tommaso III made a pledge to destroy irrevocably the foundations of the commune's power.

THE SAVOY DYNASTY IN TURIN

Having lost its legislative power and the chance to nominate a chief magistrate, the Turinese commune soon lost its influence and left the city in the hands of the Savoy family. With the failure of the anti-Savoy revolt of 1344, the power of Turin's main aristocratic families soon diminished.

Monument to Amedeo VI, the Green Count, Turin

However, on the borders of Piedmont a new great regional power was closing in: the Visconti family of Milan. Amedeo VI of Savoy – known as the "Green Count" – used military skill and cunning against them and managed, together with his successor Amedeo VII (the "Red Count"), to resist pressure from the Viscontis and even enlarged Savoy dominions, gaining Nice and access to the sea.

Amedeo VII went down in history as the last count and the first duke of Savoy; during his reign Piedmontese estates extended towards Biella, Ossola and Vercelli. After years of uncertainty, Italy found itself vulnerable to invasion in the battle between the major European powers and, unable to oppose the army of Francis I of France, the Savoys were left without a state to govern at the beginning of the 1500s.

THE WALDENSIANS

Condemned as heretics by the Council of Verona (1184) and the Fourth Lateran Council (1215), the followers of Waldes, a preacher from Lyon, had scattered throughout Europe, settling in Piedmont's western valleys, Milan, France, Switzerland and parts of eastern Europe (Poland, Bohemia and Hungary). However, in only a couple of centuries, the Church eradicated Waldensian presence almost everywhere, except for the valleys between Italy and France. Despite often brutal repression, the original Waldensian community coexisted here with the Catholic faith but had no particular structure until its adherence to the Reformation in 1532. Persecution intensified in 1555, when Waldensians refused to participate in Catholic services and founded their own specific style of worship.

Stone stele at Chanforàn in Val d'Angrogna

	1100		1200		1300		1400		1500	

1140 Lyon-born Waldes dedicates his life to Waldensian preaching

13th century Waldensian presence grows in the Piedmontese valleys

1491 The Florentine architect Meo del Caprino begins building the cathedral

1506 Erasmus of Rotterdam obtains a degree in theology from the University of Turin

1149 The first city consuls are nominated in Turin

1248 Turin is granted in fief by Frederick II to Thomas II of Savoy

1404 Founding of the University of Turin by Ludwig of Savoy-Acaja

University of Turin

1532 Adherence of Waldensians to Reformation, Council of Chanforàn

The House of Savoy

THE SAVOY FAMILY, originally from Burgundy in France, became counts in the 10th century. Their estates grew from the time of Amedeo I and later expanded into parts of Piedmont and Liguria. In the 16th century, Emanuele Filiberto consolidated the family possessions and in 1563 moved the Savoy capital from Chambéry to Turin. Vittorio Amedeo II became king of Sicily and other territories following the Treaty of Utrecht of 1713, and the royal title came to Turin. The last king of Italy reigned until 1946. The Savoys left an indelible imprint on Turin by introducing the Piedmontese Baroque style.

Umberto I Biancamano,
the first Savoy count

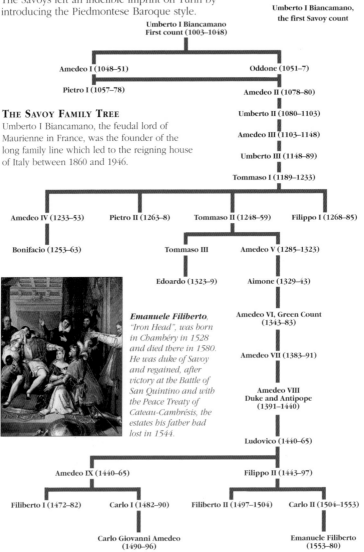

Umberto I Biancamano
First count (1003–1048)

Amedeo I (1048–51)　　　　**Oddone (1051–7)**

Pietro I (1057–78)　　　　**Amedeo II (1078–80)**

THE SAVOY FAMILY TREE

Umberto I Biancamano, the feudal lord of Maurienne in France, was the founder of the long family line which led to the reigning house of Italy between 1860 and 1946.

Umberto II (1080–1103)

Amedeo III (1103–1148)

Umberto III (1148–89)

Tommaso I (1189–1233)

Amedeo IV (1233–53)　　**Pietro II (1263–8)**　　**Tommaso II (1248–59)**　　**Filippo I (1268–85)**

Bonifacio (1253–63)　　　　**Tommaso III**　　　　**Amedeo V (1285–1323)**

Edoardo (1323–9)　　　　**Aimone (1329–43)**

Emanuele Filiberto,
"Iron Head", was born
in Chambéry in 1528
and died there in 1580.
He was duke of Savoy
and regained, after
victory at the Battle of
San Quintino and with
the Peace Treaty of
Cateau-Cambrésis, the
estates his father had
lost in 1544.

Amedeo VI, Green Count
(1343–83)

Amedeo VII (1383–91)

Amedeo VIII
Duke and Antipope
(1391–1440)

Ludovico (1440–65)

Amedeo IX (1440–65)　　　　**Filippo II (1443–97)**

Filiberto I (1472–82)　　**Carlo I (1482–90)**　　**Filiberto II (1497–1504)**　　**Carlo II (1504–1553)**

Carlo Giovanni Amedeo
(1490–96)

Emanuele Filiberto
(1553–80)

The Savoy Dynasty in Turin and Italy
From the 14th century the family acquired large parts of
Piedmont (Canavese, Cuneo and Biella). Later Emanuele
Filiberto, known as Iron Head, transferred the capital to Turin.

Emanuele Filiberto, Duke (1553–80)

Carlo Emanuele I (1580–1630)

Vittorio Amedeo I (1630–37)

Tommaso Francesco (1596–1656)

Francesco Giaciato (1637–38)

Carlo Emanuele II (1638–75)

Emanuele Filiberto Amedeo (1628–1709)

Vittorio Amedeo II (1675–1730)

Vittorio Amedeo I (1690–1741)

Carlo Emanuele III (1730–73)

Luigi Vittorio (1721–78)

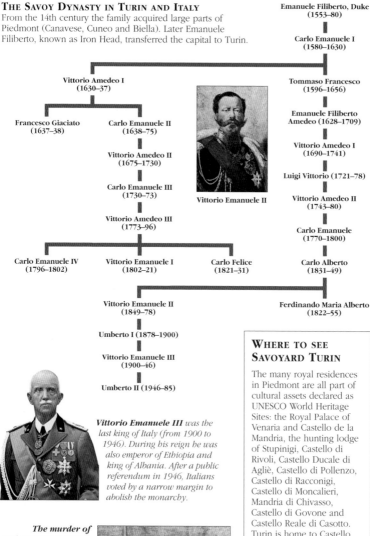

Vittorio Emanuele II

Vittorio Amedeo III (1773–96)

Vittorio Amedeo II (1743–80)

Carlo Emanuele (1770–1800)

Carlo Emanuele IV (1796–1802)

Vittorio Emanuele I (1802–21)

Carlo Felice (1821–31)

Carlo Alberto (1831–49)

Vittorio Emanuele II (1849–78)

Ferdinando Maria Alberto (1822–55)

Umberto I (1878–1900)

Vittorio Emanuele III (1900–46)

Umberto II (1946–85)

Vittorio Emanuele III was the last king of Italy (from 1900 to 1946). During his reign he was also emperor of Ethiopia and king of Albania. After a public referendum in 1946, Italians voted by a narrow margin to abolish the monarchy.

The murder of Umberto I in Monza in 1900 brought the "end-of-century crisis" to a close and ushered in a period of renewal and democratization. Umberto I was born in Turin and became king of Italy in 1878 after taking part in the Battle of Custoza in 1866. He was an authoritative figure, but took no active part in politics.

Where to see Savoyard Turin

The many royal residences in Piedmont are all part of cultural assets declared as UNESCO World Heritage Sites: the Royal Palace of Venaria and Castello de la Mandria, the hunting lodge of Stupinigi, Castello di Rivoli, Castello Ducale di Agliè, Castello di Pollenzo, Castello di Racconigi, Castello di Moncalieri, Mandria di Chivasso, Castello di Govone and Castello Reale di Casotto. Turin is home to Castello del Valentino, Villa della Regina, Palazzo Reale, Basilica di Superga, Palazzo Madama, Palazzo Carignano and the keep.

Throne Room, Palazzo Reale

BETWEEN FRANCE AND ITALY

The turning point of the 1500s was Emanuele Filiberto's victory at the battle of San Quintino (1557) and the treaty of Cateau-Cambrésis, which redrew the map of Europe and returned the duchy to the Savoys. The duke began to rebuild the state: he transferred the capital to Turin, liberated Piedmont from foreign invaders and reorganized the army and education system. Pinerolo, Santhià, Asti and Turin returned to the Savoys, as did the county of Tenda, consolidating access to the Mediterranean.

With the duchy divided between France and Italy, the next duke, Carlo Emanuele I, faced an important decision. Politically, France provided few opportunities for the Savoy family, and with the Treaty of Lyon (1601) the duke ceded estates between Geneva and Lyon in exchange for the marquisate of

Duke Emanuele Filiberto in the new Cittadella

Saluzzo. The Savoys were now the ruling family in the Italian peninsula.

TURIN CHANGES

The 1600s began with the Spanish and then the French in Piedmont. Wars at Monferrato were followed by battles which brought about, with French control of Pinerolo and the alpine passes, dependence on France.

Meanwhile Turin was changing. Considering it impossible to defend, the French had built walls around the city, and Emanuele Filiberto built the Cittadella fort in 1564. The architect Vitozzi devised a new urban scheme which included Porta Nuova, a new district and Piazza Castello. Owners of houses in the square were ordered by

An ancient cannon, Museo di Artiglieria, Turin

Carlo Emanuele I "to align the façades of the houses so as to conform to the design given you by our engineer Ascanio Vitozzi".

THE SAVOY MONARCHY

Shifting between factions, after more wars between France and Spain, Vittorio Amedeo II won back Pinerolo (1696) and Monferrato, and Turin was saved from French siege in 1706 by the intervention of the Austrian army, led by Eugenio of Savoy. With the subsequent Treaty of Utrecht (1713), the title of king of

The fortifications of the Cittadella in Turin (1564–77) in an old print

TIMELINE

Palazzo Carignano

1536–61 Turin and much of the duchy are under French control

1631 At the end of the war of Monferrato, cession of Pinerolo to France

1655 Carlo Emanuele orders massacre of Waldensians: the massacre begins on Holy Saturday, which becomes known as Piedmont Easter

1550	1600	1650	1700

1557 Emanuele Filiberto is victorious at the Battle of San Quintino

1564 Emanuele Filiberto orders construction of the Cittadella and transfers the capital from Chambéry to Turin

1666 The architect Guarino Guarini begins construction of San Lorenzo, the Consolata, Palazzo Carignano and the Chapel of the Holy Shroud

1686 The Waldensians are attacked and persecuted and flee to Switzerland. They return to Val Pellice *en masse* during the Glorious Repatriation (1689)

The giant steps at the Fenestrelle Fort

Sicily was gained (the island was exchanged in 1720 for Sardinia), and the royal title came to Turin, where it stayed until 1946. Lombardy was also in the sights of the Savoys and the political moves of the 18th century aimed at gaining this objective. French armies penetrated the Susa and Chisone valleys on various occasions, leading to the construction of the Fenestrelle and Exilles forts. On 19 July 1747 the battle of Assietta was fought. The French army could not break through Savoy lines and the Savoys gained lands in Novara, Vigevano, Voghera and Pavia.

BETWEEN REVOLUTION
AND RESTORATION

Vittorio Amedeo III waged war early against revolutionary France: in 1792 the armies of the Directory occupied Savoy and Nice. In 1796 Bonaparte defeated the Savoys and, with the Paris Peace Treaty, Savoy, Nice and the alpine forts passed to France. In 1798 French troops invaded the

Piedmont region and, despite Austrian and Russian counter-attack, Carlo Emanuele IV fled to Sardinia. In 1801 Piedmont was annexed to France. Napoleon's decision to dismantle all the forts "so as to make it impossible to rebuild them" began Turin's transformation from a fortified city, symbol of Savoy power, into a monumental metropolis inspired by enlightened principles. Military structures were turned into civic facilities, and this led to the building of wide avenues around the city. A stone bridge was built over the Po, as was a road up to Monginevro and a main road through Val Chisone. After the defeat of Napoleon at Waterloo, the Treaty of Paris took away part of Savoy from the Kingdom of Savoy. This was later returned with the Congress of Vienna, which also gave Turin the Genoa Republic.

Prince Eugenio of Savoy

The battle of Assietta (1747) in an old print

1706 Heroic deeds performed by Pietro Micca during the French siege of Turin	**1717–31** Juvarra constructs the Basilica di Superga and the Stupinigi hunting lodge outside the city walls	**1798** Turin is occupied by the French troops of the Revolution. After victory at Marengo (1800) Napoleon annexes Piedmont to France		*Napoleon at Marengo*

1750	**1800**	**1850**

| **1713** After the Treaty of Utrecht, Vittorio Amedeo II becomes king of Sicily. In 1720 the island is exchanged for Sardinia. Enlargement of the Fenestrelle fort begins | *Vittorio Amedeo III* | **1824** The Museo Egizio is founded in Turin | **1836** Restorations complete, Carlo Alberto entrusts Sacra di San Michele to Rosminian fathers | **1848** Carlo Alberto grants Statute that gives emancipation to Jews and Waldensians |

The Risorgimento

The Italian flag from 1848

PIEDMONT AND THE HOUSE OF SAVOY played a key role in Italy's unification in the period between the Congress of Vienna (1815) and the taking of Rome in 1870. After the first revolts in 1821, which caused Vittorio Emanuele I to abdicate in favour of his brother Carlo Felice, the Savoys steered a middle course between family interests, territorial aims and democratic concessions. In 1848, Carlo Alberto granted a Statute which gave Waldensians and Jews freedom of worship. After wars with Austria, Garibaldi's expedition and the breach of Porta Pia in Rome, the Savoys found themselves at the head of a united Italy.

Carlo Felice, who was almost blind, became king of Sardinia (1821–31) following the revolts which forced his brother Vittorio Emanuele I to abdicate.

Carlo Alberto declared war on Austria in 1848 (left, the manifesto), but hesitated too long and was forced to return Milan to Radetzky. A month earlier he had granted religious rights to the Waldensians.

Via Garibaldi was straightened in the 18th century by the architect Plantery. The street was formerly called Via Dora Grossa.

TURIN THE CAPITAL

Between 1849 and 1859, Turin was the centre of political life in the kingdom. The Siccardi laws on the abolition of ecclesiastical privileges were promulgated, the railway to Genoa was built and the Frejus tunnel was started. This economic and political fervour was interrupted when the capital was transferred to Florence in 1864.

The Battle of Bezzecca, 21 July 1866, was the only Italian victory in the field in the third war of independence. Ordered to cease fire following the armistice with the Austrians, Garibaldi answered "obbedisco" (I obey).

Camillo Benso, Count of Cavour and prime minister of Sardinia from 1852, united the forces of the Risorgimento in a moderate programme. He died three months after the creation of the Kingdom of Italy.

Giuseppe Garibaldi (1807–82) and the Savoys *had a stormy relationship. First Cavour, and then Vittorio Emanuele II, was forced to restrain Garibaldi, the "hero of the two worlds" and the driving force behind the Red Shirts military force. This painting depicts a meeting in 1875.*

Alfonso Ferrero of the Marmora, *a Turinese citizen, was prime minister in 1859 following Cavour's resignation after the armistice of Villafranca. In 1855 he commanded an expedition to the Crimea after the reorganization of the troops.*

The buildings along the street were rebuilt, avoiding creating new façades on old constructions, in line with Plantery's project (1736).

Carlo Alberto *of Carignano ascended to the Savoy throne in 1831 and reigned until 1849. Mazzini invited him to "create Italy". After defeat at Novara, Carlo Alberto abdicated and fled to Oporto. He promulgated a number of reforms and was considered a liberal sovereign.*

Procession of Corpus Domini in Via Dora Grossa (1847) in Turin, in a painting by Carlo Bossoli (1815–84).

The Waldensians *were granted the right to practise their religion in Carlo Alberto's Statute of 17 February 1848, which had been fought for by Vincenzo Gioberti and other Piedmontese liberals.*

Sitting of the first Italian Parliament in 1861

TOWARDS A UNITED ITALY

With the Napoleonic wars over, Vittorio Emanuele I, Carlo Felice, Carlo Alberto and then Vittorio Emanuele II succeeded in turn to the throne. The first, faced with the Carbonari revolts of 1821, abdicated in favour of Carlo Felice who did little more than control the political situation in his ten-year reign. Carlo Alberto, who followed, was a king with an aura of liberalism to whom patriots in Italy looked with hope, which was often unfounded. Driven by the views of Mazzini, D'Azeglio and Gioberti, and following the example of other European sovereigns, the king granted religious rights in his 1848 Statute and set himself at the forefront of the Risorgimento movement, which sought the unification of Italy. He intervened in the war against Austria on the occasion of the Milanese

The monument to Vittorio Emanuele II in Turin

revolts and was succeeded by Vittorio Emanuele II who, after the wars of independence, became king of Italy on 14 March 1861. After Garibaldi's expedition in 1870, Rome joined a united Italy. The capital, which had been transferred to Florence in 1864, was moved south, for the last time.

A UNITED KINGDOM

Although no longer the capital of Italy, Piedmont did not lose its importance. Together with Lombardy, it became a centre of industry and the city changed radically. The bureaucratic red tape which had dogged the royal capital disappeared.

Between 1881 and 1911 the population grew from 250,000 to 415,000. This was mainly due to industrial growth, which already employed 90,000 workers in the 1880s. The city's appearance also altered, and there was a divide between areas inhabited by the middle classes and those occupied by the workers, which had been built with bank investments and private enterprise. The old city centre was rebuilt and became the business and banking district.

In 1899 Fabbrica Italiana Automobili Torino (FIAT) was founded and its history would reflect that of the city. The workers'

FIAT trademark

TIMELINE

			LA STAMPA		
1853 Turin's population is 160,000. The new railway line to Genoa is opened	**1859** Second war of independence. Piedmont acquires Lombardy and cedes Nice and Savoy to France	**1871** Work is completed on the Frejus tunnel	*La Stampa* **1895** *La Stampa* is founded		**1922** Piero Gobetti founds the *Rivoluzione Liberale*

1850	1860	1870	1880	1920

| **1857** Building of Via Cernaia in Turin. In 1864 Piazza Statuto is also created | **1861** Vittorio Emanuele II becomes king of Italy | **1862** Work begins on the construction of the Mole Antonelliana, designed originally as a synagogue | **1881** Turin, with 250,000 people, is the fourth city in Italy after Naples, Milan and Rome | **1899** Fabbrica Italiana Automobili Torino, FIAT, is founded | **1928** The ski resort of Sestrière opens |

movement, organized with the founding of the Italian Socialist Party in Genoa in 1892, became increasingly important. In the early 1900s, workers' disputes with Rome often disrupted Italy's tranquillity.

THE TWO WORLD WARS

After the growth of the arms industry and the economic and human sacrifices of World War I, problems re-emerged, culminating in the so-called Two Red Years (1920–21) with the occupation of factories and the founding of the Italian Communist Party. Violent official responses to the demands of factory and farm workers marked the start of the Fascist movement which, aided by a deal with the House of Savoy, led to 20 years of Fascism and World War II.

After the armistice in 1943, with Mussolini's escape from prison and the founding of the Republic of Salò allied with the Nazis, the Resistance developed into a mass movement, which was particularly strong in Piedmontese and Lombard valleys. While allied bombers sought to destroy Turinese industry and

March on Rome, G Balla, Pinacoteca Agnelli, Turin

Piedmontese cities, in Val d'Ossola and Alba the first regions were being liberated from the Nazi-Fascists. In 1943 there were strikes in the Turinese factories by the same workers who, a year later, defended the firms from German destruction.

A student protest in the 1960s

FROM 1945 TO THE PRESENT

The referendum of June 1946 ended royal rule and set up the Republic of Italy. The post-war period saw the rebuilding of infrastructure and bombed districts. The boom years coincided with a great flow of migrants from southern Italy, social tension and the growth of small and large industries. The end of the 1960s saw an explosion in protests from students and workers, conflicts that only came to an end in the 1970s.

The slow decline in heavy industry gradually changed the social and physical make-up of the region. No longer the workers' capital, the city discovered tourism. In the valleys, the increasing popularity of winter sports coincided with the setting up of parks and reserves to protect the environment, and restrain exploitation of the Alps, a tourist resource but also a precious legacy for the future.

1937 The first Topolino cars leave the FIAT factory

FIAT Topolino

1961 Turin exceeds 1 million people

1997 Fire breaks out inside the Cappella Guarini in the Duomo of Turin

1999 Turin is awarded the 2006 Winter Olympics

2003 Death of FIAT's Giovanni Agnelli

Senator Agnelli

1940	1960	1980	2000	2005

1945 Turin liberated by partisans, but is badly damaged by the war

1949 A plane carrying the Turin football team crashes into the Superga hill

1973 The rebuilt Teatro Regio opens to the public

1998 The Holy Shroud is displayed

2000 Display of the Holy Shroud for the jubilee year; the Museo del Cinema opens in the Mole

2006 The 20th Winter Olympic Games and the 9th Paralympics Winter Games take place

Turin
Area by Area

Central Turin 50-61
Around Piazza San Carlo 62-75
Quadrilatero Romano 76-83
Along the Po 84-91
Further Afield 92-105

CENTRAL TURIN

Detail of the entrance to Palazzo Reale

PIAZZA CASTELLO, the heart of Turin, has witnessed the unfolding of the history of the city, from a Roman encampment in the 1st century BC to the capital of Italy in 1861. The square was transformed radically with the urban projects of the 17th century. Where Palazzo Madama now stands there was once one of the four gateways in the city walls, Porta Pretoria. But with the transfer of their capital from Chambéry to Turin, the institutions of Savoy power were built around the square: the Royal Palace (Palazzo Reale), the Armoury and the Library. Leading from the same square are streets lined with porticoes and shops which seem to come from another age. Via Po is one typical street, connecting the centre of political power to the soul of the city, the great river Po. From any point in this area, the monumental Mole Antonelliana can be seen. This extraordinary building was erected in 1863–89, when the city was beginning to take on an important industrial role. Today it stands as a symbol of Turin in Italy and the world.

SIGHTS AT A GLANCE

Museums, Galleries
Armeria Reale ❷
Mole Antonelliana,
  Museo Nazionale
  del Cinema
  pp60–61 ❸
Museo della Radio e
  della Televisione
  ❿
Museo di Antichità ❽
Museo di Arti
  Decorative ⓮
Pinacoteca
  dell'Accademia
  delle Belle Arti ⓫

Monuments and Historic Buildings
Complesso della
  Cavallerizza
  Reale ❼
Palazzo Madama ❻

Palazzo Reale ❶
Porta Palatina ❹

Streets and Squares
Piazza Carlo
  Emanuele II ⓬
Piazza Vittorio
  Veneto ⓯
Via Po ❾

Churches
Duomo *pp56–7* ❸
San Lorenzo ❺

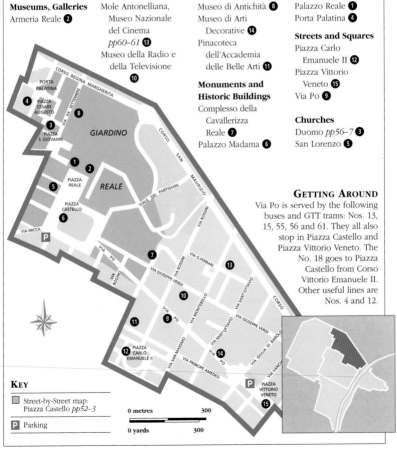

GETTING AROUND
Via Po is served by the following buses and GTT trams: Nos. 13, 15, 55, 56 and 61. They all also stop in Piazza Castello and Piazza Vittorio Veneto. The No. 18 goes to Piazza Castello from Corso Vittorio Emanuele II. Other useful lines are Nos. 4 and 12.

KEY

▢ Street-by-Street map: Piazza Castello *pp52–3*

P Parking

0 metres   300
0 yards   300

◁ **The intertwined arches of the Baroque dome by Guarini in the church of San Lorenzo**

Street-by-Street: Piazza Castello

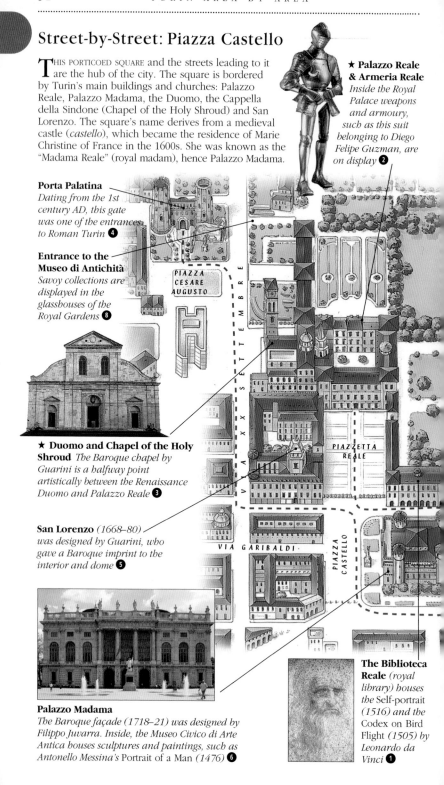

THIS PORTICOED SQUARE and the streets leading to it are the hub of the city. The square is bordered by Turin's main buildings and churches: Palazzo Reale, Palazzo Madama, the Duomo, the Cappella della Sindone (Chapel of the Holy Shroud) and San Lorenzo. The square's name derives from a medieval castle (*castello*), which became the residence of Marie Christine of France in the 1600s. She was known as the "Madama Reale" (royal madam), hence Palazzo Madama.

★ **Palazzo Reale & Armeria Reale**
Inside the Royal Palace weapons and armoury, such as this suit belonging to Diego Felipe Guzman, are on display ❷

Porta Palatina
Dating from the 1st century AD, this gate was one of the entrances to Roman Turin ❹

Entrance to the Museo di Antichità
Savoy collections are displayed in the glasshouses of the Royal Gardens ❽

★ Duomo and Chapel of the Holy Shroud *The Baroque chapel by Guarini is a halfway point artistically between the Renaissance Duomo and Palazzo Reale* ❸

San Lorenzo *(1668–80) was designed by Guarini, who gave a Baroque imprint to the interior and dome* ❺

Palazzo Madama
The Baroque façade (1718–21) was designed by Filippo Juvarra. Inside, the Museo Civico di Arte Antica houses sculptures and paintings, such as Antonello Messina's Portrait of a Man *(1476)* ❻

The Biblioteca Reale *(royal library) houses the* Self-portrait *(1516) and the* Codex on Bird Flight *(1505) by Leonardo da Vinci* ❶

PIAZZA CESARE AUGUSTO

PIAZZETTA REALE

VIA GARIBALDI

PIAZZA CASTELLO

VIA XX SETTEMBRE

In the Giardini Reali (*royal gardens*), *designed by Le Nôtre, the architect of the gardens at Versailles in France, stands this* Fountain of Triton and the Nereids *by Simone Martinez (1750).*

LOCATOR MAP
See Street Finder Map 3

QUADRILATERO ROMANO

CENTRAL TURIN

AROUND PIAZZA SAN CARLO

ALONG THE PO

River Po

KEY

- - - - Suggested route

0 metres   100
0 yards   100

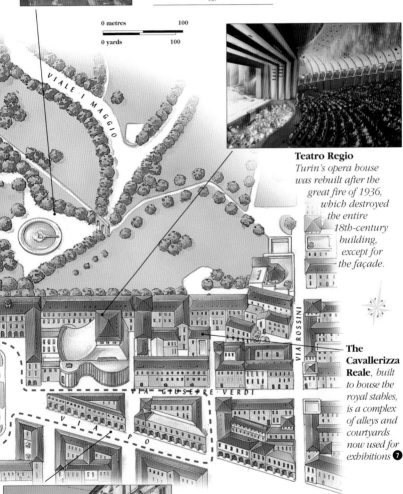

Teatro Regio
Turin's opera house was rebuilt after the great fire of 1936, which destroyed the entire 18th-century building, except for the façade.

VIALE I MAGGIO

VIA ROSSINI

VIA GIUSEPPE VERDI

VIA PO

The Cavallerizza Reale, *built to house the royal stables, is a complex of alleys and courtyards now used for exhibitions* ❼

Via Po
Porticoes line this street, famous for its shops and antique book shops. Highlights are Palazzo degli Stemmi and Palazzo dell'Università ❾

STAR SIGHTS

★ **Duomo and Chapel of the Holy Shroud**

★ **Palazzo Reale and Armeria Reale**

Façade of the Palazzo Reale, with statues of the Dioscuri

Palazzo Reale ❶

Piazzetta Reale. **Map** 3 B4.
C 011 436 14 55. ☐ 8.30am–
7.30pm Tue–Sun. ● Mon, 1 Jan, 25
Apr, 2, 24 Jun, 25 Dec. 🎫 ⬛ ♿
partially accessible. 🎫
W www.ambienteto.arti.beniculturali.it

THIS WAS THE House of
Savoy's official Royal
Palace until 1865. It was built
on the site of Palazzo
Vescovile (Bishop's Palace) in
1646 and completed 14 years
later. The leading architects
and artists of the age were
commissioned to put this
enormous residence on an
equal footing with other
European palaces. The
internal **gardens** were laid
out in 1697–8 by André Le
Nôtre, who also created the
gardens for the Palace of
Versailles near Paris. Apart
from the original façade, built
in 1658 to a design by
Amedeo di Castellamonte,
reconstruction continued until
the 20th century.
    The palace was sacked by
Napoleon's troops, but
regained its former splendour
under Carlo Alberto. The
private apartments of the king
and Queen Maria Teresa are
open to the public, as are the
state rooms on the first floor,
the Audience Hall, the Hall of
the Servants and Pages, and
the small Court Pharmacy.
    Luxurious furnishings and
decoration abound in the
official rooms, such as the
Alcove Room and the King's
Throne Room, which has its
original tapestry with the
royal insignia. Of special note
are the inlaid floors, the
crystal chandeliers, mirrors,
painted coffered ceilings, art

galleries and collections of
Chinese vases. Don't miss the
Queen's Throne Room, the
dining room with its smoking
room and the Galleria del
Daniel, with portraits of the
Savoys, from Umberto I
Biancamano to Emanuele
Filiberto. The Ballroom,
supported by 20 columns,
could accommodate up to
2,000 people. This room gives
access to the Scala delle
Forbici, a striking
staircase designed
by Filippo
Juvarra, who
also created the
decorations in the
Chinese Studio.
    The **Biblioteca
Reale** (Royal Library),
in restored Neo-
Classical chambers,
was founded by Carlo Alberto
in 1832. It contains 185,000
volumes (the oldest dates
from the 11th century), 4,300
manuscripts, parchments and
incunabula, and 2,000
drawings, including the
famous *Self-portrait* and the
Codex on Bird Flight by
Leonardo da Vinci.

Armeria Reale ❷

Piazza Castello 191. **Map** 3 B4.
C 011 543 889.
● for restoration.
W www.artito.arti.beniculturali.it

THE ROYAL ARMOURY was
opened in 1837 by Carlo
Alberto, and the associated
collections are displayed at
the Palazzo Reale, in an area
reached via porticoes and a
staircase by Benedetto Alfieri
(1700s). The armoury comes
from the arsenals of Turin
and Genoa and collectors.
    The series of military and
civil arms from different
periods by Lombard,
Venetian, German, Spanish
and Flemish gunsmiths is
remarkable. The Rotonda has
18th–20th-century weapons,
Napoleonic memorabilia, the
Risorgimento and the Savoy
rulers: Napoleon's sword,
Prince Eugenio's personal
weapons, Vittorio Emanuele
II's uniform, and
flintlocks and
pistols by various
gunsmiths. Suits
of armour,
including a large
2-m (6.5-ft) one
belonging to Diego
Felipe Guzman and
another used by
Emanuele Filiberto
II, are in the Galleria
Beaumont. Also of note is the
oriental weapons collection
(Turkish, Arab, Chinese,
Persian, Indonesian), in the
Saletta del Medagliere.

**Emanuele Filiberto's
helmet**

Duomo ❸

See pp56–7.

A group of Tritons decorating the fountain in the Giardini Reali

Porta Palatina ❹

Piazza Cesare Augusto. **Map** 3 B3.

THE ARCHAEOLOGICAL area in Piazza del Duomo has remains of the old Roman walls and sections of the original paving around Porta Palatina (1st century AD), the gateway into the Roman *castrum* from the Po valley.

Two bronze copies of the statues of Julius Caesar and Augustus face this red brick construction, which has four openings below and a double row of windows in the upper sections. To the sides are two towers 30 m (98 ft) high. Despite the damage it has suffered over the centuries, it is one of the best examples of a Roman city gate. On the site of the present-day Palazzo Madama is another gateway, the Pretoria, the most easterly of the gates.

The dome of San Lorenzo, by Guarino Guarini

San Lorenzo ❺

Via Palazzo di Città. **Map** 3 B4.
📞 *011 43 61 527.* 🕐 *7.30am–12 noon, 4–7.30pm Mon–Fri (3–7.15pm Sat); 9am–1pm, 3–7.15pm, 8.30–10pm Sun.*

THIS CHURCH WAS the first work by architect Guarino Guarini for the Savoys. It was originally the royal chapel. Guarini began work in 1666, and left a clear Baroque imprint on the interior and dome. The façade dates from the 19th century. The church was built to fulfil a vow made

by Emanuele Filiberto at the battle of San Quintino in 1557, but work only began in 1634.

The rectangular Addolorata Oratory leads into an area animated by arches, columns, colourful decorations, stucco and gilding. The dome is decorated with oriental Gothic motifs. Inside, on the first altar on the right, is a *Crucifixion* by Andrea Pozzo.

Palazzo Madama ❻

Piazza Castello. **Map** 3 B4.
📞 *011 44 29 912.* 🕐 *10am–8pm Tue–Sun; 10am–11pm Sat.* ⚫ Mon.
Museo Civico di Arte Antica
🕐 *from 2005.* ♿
🌐 www.comune.torino.it/ palazzomadama

THE MASSIVE STRUCTURE in the centre of Piazza Castello, a combination of various styles and periods, is like a resumé of Turin's 2,000 years of history. The two oldest towers incorporate the ruins of the Roman gate, Porta Pretoria. In the 1200s the towers were incorporated into the Porta Fibellona fort, later enlarged by the Savoy-Acaja dynasty. In 1350, the marriage of Galeazzo Visconti and Bianca of Savoy was celebrated here. The building was initially renovated to allow visits to the medieval castle via a double-ramp staircase by Juvarra and a vaulted stairway.

Since 1934, the upper floor apartments have housed the **Museo Civico di Arte Antica**. Exhibits include *Portrait of a Man* by Antonello da Messina (1476), a *Madonna and Child* sculpture by Tino da Camaino (1312), and canvases by Tanzio da Varallo and other Piedmontese masters. The 28,000 exhibits date from the early Middle Ages to the 1700s. The collections also include stained glass, majolica, porcelain, gold and medals.

The staircase in Palazzo Madama, by Filippo Juvarra

Complesso della Cavallerizza Reale ❼

Via Verdi 5–7. **Map** 3 B5.
🕐 *for events.*

THIS LARGE COMPLEX in the heart of Turin's historic centre is now used for temporary exhibitions and cultural events, while some of the courtyards are still inhabited. It was conceived as part of the project for Turin's second town-planning expansion scheme towards the river Po (1673) and was part of a large group of buildings for use by the royal family. This so-called "area of command", designed by Amedeo di Castellamonte, was completed the following century. The Royal Stables and the Equestrian Centre (1739–40) were designed by Benedetto Alfieri.

The complex housed archives, a mint, secretaries' offices, and an academy, and were connected to the main floor of the palace by a network of passages, which enabled the royal family to get to all parts of the building without going outside.

***Portrait of a Man* by Antonello da Messina**

Duomo & Cappella della Sindone ❸

THE CATHEDRAL was built by Meo del Caprino for Cardinal Domenico della Rovere in 1491–8 and is Turin's only Renaissance religious building. It has a white marble façade and three fine doorways, and the chapels house interesting paintings and sculptures. The bell tower of Sant'Andrea from 1465 stands to one side. The Sacra Sindone (Holy Shroud) has been kept in the Duomo since 1587. The Cappella della Sindone, designed by Guarino Guarini to house this precious holy relic, was completed in 1694, and could be reached from the presbytery and Palazzo Reale. On the night of 11 July 1997 the chapel was damaged by fire.

The Holy Shroud
This linen sheet came to Turin in 1578 and was housed in Guarini's chapel until 1997. In 2002 delicate restoration work began on the shroud and it will probably not be displayed again until 2025.

The Bell Tower
(1400s) was extended by Filippo Juvarra in 1720.

★ Renaissance Polyptych
Attributed to Defendente Ferrari and Giovanni Martino Spanzotti (16th century), this work is in the Cappella dei Santi Crispino e Crispiniano. Another 18 panels narrate the story of the two saints.

★ Mausoleum of Giovanna d'Orlier de la Balme
This Burgundian-style funerary monument stands in the area behind the façade, on the right-hand side of the entrance.

STAR SIGHTS

★ Mausoleum of Giovanna d'Orlier de la Balme

★ Renaissance Polyptych

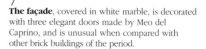

The façade, covered in white marble, is decorated with three elegant doors made by Meo del Caprino, and is unusual when compared with other brick buildings of the period.

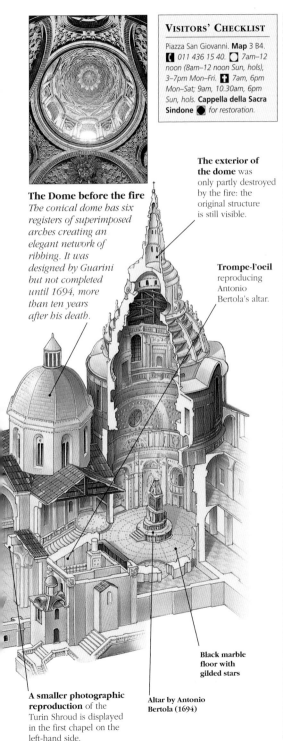

The Dome before the fire
The conical dome has six registers of superimposed arches creating an elegant network of ribbing. It was designed by Guarini but not completed until 1694, more than ten years after his death.

The exterior of the dome was only partly destroyed by the fire: the original structure is still visible.

Trompe-l'oeil reproducing Antonio Bertola's altar.

A smaller photographic reproduction of the Turin Shroud is displayed in the first chapel on the left-hand side.

Altar by Antonio Bertola (1694)

Black marble floor with gilded stars

Visitors' Checklist

Piazza San Giovanni. **Map** 3 B4.
011 436 15 40. 7am–12 noon (8am–12 noon Sun, hols), 3–7pm Mon–Fri. 7am, 6pm Mon–Sat; 9am, 10.30am, 6pm Sun, hols. **Cappella della Sacra Sindone** for restoration.

Museo di Antichità ⑧

Via XX Settembre 88/c. **Map** 3 B4.
011 521 11 06. 8.30am–7.30pm Tue–Sun. Mon, 1 Jan, 1 May, 25 Dec.
w www.museoantichita.it

SINCE 1989 this museum has been housed in the remodelled glasshouses of the Royal Gardens (Giardini Reali). A new section has 8,000 finds from excavations in the region, making up a comprehensive overview of the history of Piedmont from the Paleolithic era to the early Middle Ages.

The museum's exhibits, which cover the main periods of ancient history, originated with the Savoy collections, started in the 1500s.

Treasure discovered in 1928 at Marengo includes silver pieces from the 2nd century AD, such as the bust of Lucius Verus. The bronze statuettes from the same era, such as *Dancer* (*see p37*), come from the Roman city of Industria, on the river Po. The mosaic of Orpheus (3rd century AD) was found in 1762 near Cagliari in Sardinia. Small bronzes represent the bull, symbol of the Taurini people. There are also statues of Roman emperors from Susa.

The Greek and Italic pottery, Etruscan bronzes from Vulci and the Cypriot vases from the 3rd millennium BC to the Hellenistic age, are all of high quality.

The mosaic of Orpheus (3rd century AD), discovered in 1762

The long porticoes lining Via Po

Via Po ❾

Map 3 B5.

THIS STREET, with 1,250 m (4,100 ft) of porticoes, links Piazza Castello with Piazza Vittorio Veneto and was part of the enlargement scheme planned by Amedeo di Castellamonte in 1673, which was only completed in the 1700s. One side houses shops and cafés, including Caffè Fiorio. On the side of the Mole (No. 1) is Italy's oldest jeweller's (1707), along with **Palazzo dell'Università** by Michelangelo Garove (1713), **Palazzo degli Stemmi** and numerous second-hand book stalls. This side, where the porticoes are continuous thanks to terraces built in the early 1800s, was reserved for the royal family.

Museo della Radio e della Televisione ❿

Via G Verdi 16. **Map** 3 C5.
📞 011 810 49 27. ◯ 9am–5pm Mon–Fri by appt. @ info-cpto@rai.it

THE IDEA for this collection arose in 1939, when Turin was the centre of Italian broadcasting. Since then, RAI, the Italian broadcasting corporation, has been archiving all kinds of material relating to the history of radio and television. The 1,500 exhibits here include documents, recordings and technical equipment, displayed in chronological order with a theme for each decade: wireless, radio, audio-video recording, telephones and television.

Pinacoteca dell'Accademia delle Belle Arti ⓫

Via Accademia Albertina 6. **Map** 3 B5. 📞 FAX 011 817 7862. ◯ 9am–1pm, 3–7pm Tue–Sun. ● Mon, Easter, 25 Dec. ♿ 🗹 @ info@accademialbertina.torino.it 🅦 www.accademialbertina.torino.it

TURIN'S IS THE SECOND oldest academy of art in Italy. It was founded in 1678 as the Accademia dei Pittori, Scultori e Architetti and the greatest masters of the time taught here. Its usual name, Albertina, derives from its "refounding" in 1833 by Carlo Alberto of Savoy. The richly-endowed art gallery annexed to the Academy since 1824 originally had a educational role, but is now used as exhibition space. Twelve large rooms house 300 paintings, sculptures and drawings, including a unique collection of 60 cartoons by Gaudenzio Ferrari and his school, donated by Carlo Alberto in 1832.

In each of the renovated rooms, visitors can admire paintings dating from the 15th to the 18th century: panels by Filippo Lippi (*Fathers of the Church: Augustine and Ambrose*; *Fathers of the Church: Gregory and Jerome*), by Spanzotti (*St Francis, St Agatha and a Donor*), by Defendente Ferrari (*Adoration of the Magi*), paintings by the Genoese school from the early 17th century and late Lombard and Piedmontese Mannerist works. There are also Caravaggesque, Dutch and Flemish works, and some by the masters of the late 18th century and the Vedutisti. There is also a plaster cast gallery and library. Today, the Academy also contributes to Turin's role as the Italian capital of contemporary art.

Piazza Carlo Emanuele II ⓬

Map 7 B1.

EVEN THOUGH Giovanni Dupré's statue of Camillo Benso, Count of Cavour (holding a scroll with the words "a free Church, in a free state") has stood in the centre of this square since 1872, the Turinese still call it Piazza Carlina. The statue replaced a guillotine, which made its chilling appearance during the Napoleonic

Lamentation of the Dead Christ, Gaudenzio Ferrari, Pinacoteca Albertina

Looking towards Piazza Vittorio Veneto with Vittorio Emanuele I bridge

period. In the original design, the square was to have been hexagonal in shape.

In 1678 a wine market was moved here and the important buildings around the square had side entrances added. Facing the square are **Palazzo Roero di Guarene**, with an attractive 18th-century façade, and the church of **Santa Croce**. Antonio Gramsci, the famous Italian exponent of communist politics, lived at No. 15 in 1919–1921. In the same square, on the corner of Via Des Ambrois, traces of the former Jewish ghetto are still visible.

Mole Antonelliana, Museo Nazionale del Cinema ⓭

See pp60–61.

Museo di Arti Decorative – Fondazione Pietro Accorsi ⓮

Via Po 55. **Map** 7 C1. *011 812 9116.* FAX *011 815 0770.* ◯ *10am–8pm Tue–Sun; 10am–11pm Thu.* @ info@fondazioneaccorsi.it w www.fondazioneaccorsi.it

THE DECORATIVE ARTS MUSEUM originated from a rich legacy left by Pietro Accorsi (Turin 1891–1982), one of the most important European antiquarians of the 20th century. The 30 rooms of the museum house a rich collection of works of art, which originally furnished Accorsi's own home.

Thousands of objects, mainly 18th century, are on exhibit: a famous dresser in rare wood with ivory and tortoiseshell made in 1738 by Pietro Piffetti (1701–77), a dresser covered in majolica tiles by Pesaro, a rare, elegant Venetian bedroom, French furniture, Meissen, Ginori, Frankenthal and Sèvres porcelain and Baccarat crystal.

Fine paintings include a series of six hunting scenes by Vittorio Amedeo Cignaroli (1730–1800) and *Pleasures of Country Life*, a variant of the famous work by François Boucher, now in the Louvre, Paris. Accorsi collaborated with other Turin museums, acquiring works such as *Portrait of a Man* by Antonello da Messina and the Duc de Berry's Book of Hours illuminated by Jan van Eyck.

Piazza Vittorio Veneto ⓯

Map 7 C1.

THIS SQUARE, one of the largest in the world, was laid out in 1825–30 to a design by Giuseppe Frezzi. Its rectangular plan is 360 m by 111 m (1,180 by 365 ft). The square is bordered on three sides by porticoes and the end of Via Po. Beyond the square, the Napoleonic stone bridge, which drops down 10 m (33 ft) in height, crosses the river over to the massive church of the Gran Madre.

Today, Piazza Vittorio Veneto is a venue for open-air shows as well as being a large parking area. It is particularly convenient for the clubs, bars and other nightspots in the area. The square is also part of a scheme for improving the area, which also includes the construction of a large underground car park.

Piedmontese furniture in Louis XV parlour, Museo di Arti Decorative

Mole Antonelliana, Museo Nazionale del Cinema **⑬**

THIS MUSEUM IS UNIQUE IN ITALY and one of the most important specialist collections on the subject worldwide. It is housed in the Mole Antonelliana, which has been transformed into a spectacular vertical museum using architect François Confino's interior designs. Next door is the Cinema Massimo, an avant-garde multi-screen complex which hosts film festivals (Torino Film Festival, CinemAmbiente, Sottodiciotto) and special events, previews and interviews with personalities from the world of cinema and culture. The Mole was designed by Alessandro Antonelli and was originally planned as a synagogue. It was completed in 1889 and is 167.5 m (550 ft) high.

Level 18
Poster Gallery
This section takes visitors on an exciting tour through the history of film advertising.

★ Level 5 The Archaeology of Cinema
This rich collection of documents and materials shows the phases which preceded the birth of cinema: the study of movement, photography, the stereoscope, chronophotography and the cinema from its origins to the present day.

The Dome
The shell of the dome, set on a square base 30 m x 30 m (98 x 98 ft) and 50 m (164 ft) high, is made up of two walls, less than 2 m (6 ft) apart, held together by iron tie beams and a network of brick arches. Inside is a zig-zag staircase which affords access to the spire for maintenance purposes.

Level 15
The Cinema Machine
This section is dedicated to the various phases of film-making, with objects, sketches and costumes, showing the complexities of cinema.

STAR SIGHTS

★ **The Panoramic Lift**

★ **Level 5**

The Mole's squared dome

MOLE ANTONELLIANA

Originally intended as a synagogue for the Jewish community following the emancipation granted by Carlo Alberto, the design was entrusted to Alessandro Antonelli, a professor at the Accademia Albertina. Work began in 1863, but as the original scheme expanded and became more expensive the Mole was taken over by the town council. It was finally completed in 1889, a year after Antonelli's death. Since then, its unique outline has become the symbol of Turin, with its large dome crowned by a small columned temple and thin spire. Until a high wind in 1953 broke off 47 m (154 ft) of the original spire, the Mole was Europe's highest brick building at 167.5 m (550 ft). The spire was rebuilt with a metal frame covered in stone. Initially the home of the first Museo del Risorgimento, it now houses the Museo del Cinema: a unique vertical museum.

★ The Panoramic Lift
*The lift stops at the small temple at the top
of the Mole from which there is a stunning
360-degree view of the city and the
surrounding hills and mountains.*

Inside the dome
there are some 3 km (2 miles)
of gilded decorations.

FLOORPLAN

Level 18 – Poster Gallery

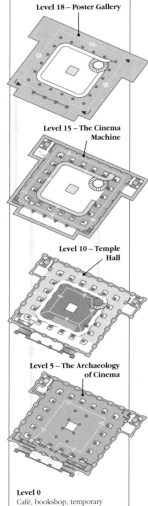

Level 15 – The Cinema Machine

Level 10 Temple Hall
*From the reclining seats in this
large hall on the tenth floor,
surrounded by ten anterooms
dedicated to major themes of the
cinema, you can comfortably
view the projections inside the
dome. The floor also affords
access to a helical ramp.*

Level 10 – Temple Hall

Level 5 – The Archaeology of Cinema

GALLERY GUIDE
*Level 0 houses the café, the
bookshop, temporary exhibitions
and the ticket office. On this
floor, a cinematographic
"experience", designed by
François Confino, creates a
unique atmosphere, recreating
the excitement of the cinema. A
lift takes visitors from here to the
various levels. A light and sound
show is projected onto the dome
at intervals, and is visible from
the 10th and 18th floors.
Individual or group guided tours
of two hours are available.*

Level 0
Café, bookshop, temporary
exhibitions and access to the
gardens.

AROUND PIAZZA SAN CARLO

WHEN ONE OF THE CITY'S football teams wins the championship, fans celebrate in the elegant Piazza San Carlo, which is divided into two by Via Roma, Turin's main shopping street. A short distance from the shops and the historic cafés are open squares named after members of the House of Savoy and the city's prestigious museums. The paintings in the Galleria Sabauda,

Café sign, Piazza San Carlo

the collections in the Museo Egizio and the memorabilia in the Museo del Risorgimento all testify to Turin's rich cultural inheritance. The 19th-century buildings, which bear traces of the French style, in Piazza Carlo Alberto, Piazza Maria Teresa and Piazza Cavour are evidence of the city's glorious past, which owes much to the extended presence of the Savoy dynasty (*see pp40–41*).

GETTING AROUND

To get to this area, it is best to use the buses and trams that stop in Piazza Castello or in Corso Vittorio Emanuele II. The buses and trams that serve this district are numbers 4, 18, 61, 63 and 68.

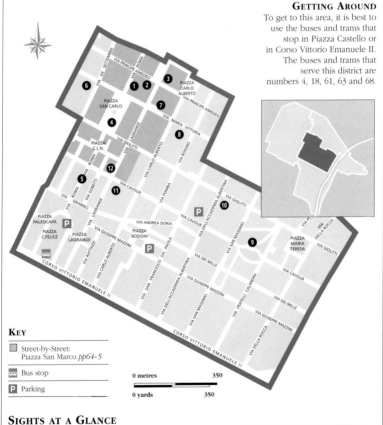

KEY

Street-by-Street: Piazza San Marco *pp64–5*

Bus stop

P Parking

0 metres 350
0 yards 350

SIGHTS AT A GLANCE

Museums and Galleries
Galleria Sabauda *pp70–71* ❷
Museo della Marionetta ❻
Museo Regionale di Scienze Naturali ❿
Museo Egizio *pp66–9* ❶
Palazzo Bricherasio ⓬

Palazzo Carignano, Museo del Risorgimento *pp72–3* ❸

Monuments and Buildings
Palazzo Cavour ⓫
Palazzo Dal Pozzo della Cisterna ❽

Streets and Squares
Piazza Cavour ❾
Piazza San Carlo ❹
Via Roma ❺

Churches
San Filippo Neri ❼

◁ **Detail of a family funerary stele with the god Osiris, in the Museo Egizio**

Street-by-Street: Piazza San Carlo

Piazza San Carlo was designed in the 17th century by Carlo di Castellamonte. It has two symmetrical wings of elegant buildings and is regarded as the city's drawing-room. The old cafés under the porticoes evoke the atmosphere of the ancient capital. In the centre of the square stands an equestrian statue of Emanuele Filiberto, which the Turinese call *caval 'd brôns* (the bronze horse). Around the square are some of the city's major museums: the Museo Egizio, the Galleria Sabauda and the Museo del Risorgimento. This area is also popular for the numerous shops along the porticoed, and more modern, Via Roma.

Via Roma
One of the most exclusive streets in the city: a place to stroll, shop, or meet in the cafés under the porticoes **5**

The Museo della Marionetta
Housed in the Teatro Gianduja, this museum exhibits a collection of costumes and 5,000 puppets made over the last two centuries. **6**

Church of Santa Teresa

Caffè San Carlo (1822) was once the favourite haunt of the writers Alexandre Dumas and Edmondo De Amicis, and the philosopher Benedetto Croce.

Piazza San Carlo
In the centre of the square stands an equestrian monument of Emanuele Filiberto, designed by Carlo Marocchetti in 1838 and made at a Parisian forge. Juventus fans celebrate their club's victories in this square **4**

The Confetteria Stratta has made a wide variety of traditional cakes and sweets since it opened in 1836.

The twin churches on the south side of the square have a 17th-century look, but were completed later. San Carlo's façade was rebuilt in the 1800s, that of Santa Cristina is by Juvarra (1715–18).

VIA MONTE DI PIETA

VIA XX SETTEMBRE

BERTOLA

VIA ROMA

VIA SANTA TERESA

PIAZZA SAN CARLO

VIA XX SETTEMBRE

VIA ALFIERI

★ **Palazzo Carignano**
Originally the home of the Subalpine Parliament, this building, by Guarino Guarini, now houses the Museo del Risorgimento. The Baroque façade and large courtyard are striking. The façade at the back faces Piazza Carlo Alberto ❸

LOCATOR MAP
See Street Finder Map 3

La Galleria Subalpina *is an elegant covered passage in glass and iron built in 1873, which connects Piazza Carlo Alberto and Piazza Castello.*

★ **Museo Egizio**
This collection, one of the richest in the world of Egyptian antiquity, covers a period of almost 5,000 years and documents the history, religion, art and everyday life at the time of the Egyptian pharaohs ❶

Palazzo dal Pozzo della Cisterna
is now the offices of the Province of Turin. Maria Vittoria, Queen of Spain from 1871 to 1873, was born in this building ❽

| 0 metres | 100 |
| 0 yards | 100 |

KEY

- - - - Suggested route

Church of San Filippo Neri
Begun in 1675, it was completed in 1730 to a design by Juvarra ❼

★ **Galleria Sabauda**
This major collection of 12th–18th-century Italian painting, holds 700 works in seven sections. Exhibits include The Children of Charles I of England *by Flemish painter Jan Van Dyck* ❷

STAR SIGHTS

★ **Galleria Sabauda**

★ **Museo Egizio**

★ **Palazzo Carignano**

Museo Egizio ❶

Founded in 1824 by Carlo Felice of Savoy with the purchase of 8,000 pieces from the collection of Bernardino Drovetti, this is the most complete Egyptian museum in the world after Cairo. Its collections share the impressive Baroque Accademia delle Scienze (from 1678, attributed to Guarino Guarini) with the Galleria Sabauda (see pp70–71), and have been enriched over the last century, thanks in particular to the work of Ernesto Schiaparelli and his successor, Giulio Farina of the Missione Archeologica Italiana. Today the museum has around 30,000 exhibits documenting religion, art and the daily life of the pharaohs, covering 5,000 years of history.

The Isiac Table is a bronze altar panel with Isis and other divinities. Probably a Roman copy, it was purchased by the Savoys in the 1600s.

★ Tomb of Kha and Merit
The complete set of burial goods found in the intact tomb of the architect Kha and his wife Merit (c.1430 BC) includes perfectly preserved everyday objects, including a beautiful casket for cosmetics and a wig.

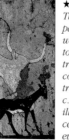

★ Paintings of Iti
The tempera paintings on plaster were removed from the tomb of Iti, the king's treasurer and commander of the troops (XI dynasty, c.2100 BC). The scenes illustrate funeral ceremonies and everyday life.

Entrance to the museum and the Galleria Sabauda

KEY

☐ Paintings	☐ Funerary Articles
☐ Religion	☐ Steles and Small Statues
☐ Writing	☐ Statuary
☐ Textiles, Art and Trades	☐ Nubia
☐ Cultural Materials	☐ New Rooms

STAR SIGHTS

★ Paintings of Iti

★ Statue of Ramses II

★ Temple of Ellesiya

★ Tomb of Kha and Merit

VISITORS' CHECKLIST

Via Accademia delle Scienze 6.
Map 3 B5. 011 561 77 76.
011 440 69 03.
8.30am–7.30pm Tue–Sun.
Mon, 1 Jan, 25 Dec.
combined ticket with the
Galleria Sabauda. no flash.
special routes for
the blind or disabled.
www.museoegizio.org;
www.museitorino.it

Book of the Dead
*This sacred text has magic formulas, scenes of everyday
life, spells and prayers for the dead person's
journey to the other world. The image shows the
psychostasis, or weighing of the soul.*

★ Statue of Ramses II
*This statue in black granite
represents the great
pharaoh of the XIX
dynasty, seated on a
throne and holding the
sceptre of power (the
heka). He is wearing
a crown with a cobra
ready to attack (the
ureo). At the sides,
the bas reliefs
represent his
wife and son.*

**Two sandstone
sphinxes** from the
New Kingdom
(1186–55 BC), at the
entrance to the
statuary section, are
the museum's
symbol.

**★ Temple
of Ellesiya**
*Built by Pharaoh
Thutmose III in
around 1430 BC,
this was brought
from Egypt in 1965
and reassembled.*

**In the
basement** are the
burial goods of the
officials of the southern
provinces and objects
found in the necropoli of
the same area.

GALLERY GUIDE
*The museum is on three levels. In the basement
are finds from the excavations at Gebelein, Asyut
and Qau El-Kebir. On the ground floor, after the
entrance, are the Statuary Room and the Temple
of Ellesiya. The other collections are in the rooms
on the first floor: funerary steles and offering
tables; burial goods, sarcophagi and mummies;
examples of weaving and spinning; papyrus and
writing; tools for arts and crafts; religious objects
and animal mummies; and paintings.*

Visiting the Museo Egizio

Plate with the figure of the goddess Hathor

CONSIDERED SECOND only to that in Cairo, the Egyptian Museum of Turin houses an enormous collection covering all aspects of Egyptian civilization, from its origins in the 4th millennium BC up to the 5th and 6th centuries AD. The richly varied exhibits include, along with everyday objects, reconstructions of temples and tombs, large statuary celebrating the pharaohs, paintings and sacred objects for the cult of the dead, papyri and vases.

Sarcophagus with the mummy of a child named Petamenofi

One of the two sandstone sphinxes, the symbol of the museum

collection. The sarcophagi section has the mummiform sarcophagus of the vizier Gemenef-Har-Bak and painted wooden sarcophagi, made for the priests of the temple of Amon at Karnak from the XXI dynasty to the first centuries after Christ.

STATUARY

IN THE ROOMS DEDICATED TO large statuary, the group depicting Ramses II between Queen Nefertari and the heir stands out: it is smaller in size as a sign of respect to the pharaoh. This masterpiece was greatly admired by the French Egyptologist Champollion, and is one of the symbols of the museum.

Next to the sculpture of Princess Redi (c.2800 BC), the oldest piece, are many other monuments testifying to the power of the pharaohs and the skill of Egyptian craftsmen in their working of stone (sandstone, basalt, limestone, diorite, granite): Ramses II between Amon and the goddess Mut; a group with Tutankhamun and the god Amon on the throne from Thebes; a statue of Amenhotep II from the temple of Karnak, with the names and titles of the pharaoh written in hiero-glyphics on the belt; one of his father Thutmose III, the great Egyptian military commander; and a colossal figure of Sethos II. The two giant sphinxes at the entrance were part of the Drovetti

STELES AND SMALL STATUES

THE VOTIVE and funerary steles are exhibited in a separate room from the other statuary, along with bas reliefs, plaques, and cult figures in painted wood or limestone. These emphasize the importance of the divinities, often female, such as the snake goddess Mertseger, stylized on an arched stele from the XX dynasty, or the Syrian goddess Kadesh, represented on a XIX-dynasty stele. A cast of the famous Rosetta Stone is also on display (the original is in London's British Museum).

The stele of goddess Kadesh with the royal scribe Ramosi and wife

FUNERARY ARTICLES

NEXT TO THE SARCOPHAGI and mummies is a range of objects and ritual items: canopic vases for the preservaton of the internal organs of the dead, amulets which decorated and protected the mummies, papyri from the Book of the Dead, and small statues charged with providing food for the dead in the next world. The rituals and spells contained in the Book of the Dead were used to help the dead pass to the next world.

Of particular interest is a sarcophagus with the mummy of a child, Petamenofi, with its Greek inscription dating from the Hadrian period (123 AD). The Greek transcription of hieroglyphics confirmed theories regarding ancient Egyptian writing.

NUBIA

IN THIS ROOM, a passage leading to the basement, the stone temple of Ellesiya, made for Pharaoh Thutmose III in about 1430 BC, has been reconstructed. The building is an example of Egyptian architecture in Nubia and was donated by the Egyptian government in 1965 (on condition that it was shown in Turin's Museo Egizio) for help given in saving monuments from Lake Nasser, during the building of the Aswan dam. The ancient monument was dismantled to save it from the water, and reassembled.

CULTURAL MATERIAL

THE TOMB OF MAIA and the funeral chamber of Kha are must-see exhibits in this section. The tomb of Maia stands in a small, barrel-vaulted room. Maia was a painter of royal tombs during the XVIII dynasty, and he probably also decorated his own death chamber. On the side walls, which are divided into panels, are paintings of ritual scenes; the coloured stele from the Drovetti collection is at the back.

Of particular interest is the complete set of articles recovered from the tomb of the architect Kha and his wife Merit: numerous objects and furnishings document daily customs and uses.

Many other finds are displayed in this section of the museum, including the famous Isiac Table and the model reconstruction of the tomb of Queen Nefertari, the wife of Ramses II. The tomb is particularly notable for the splendid relief discovered by Schiaparelli in the Valley of the Queens in 1903. The museum displays sections of the sarcophagus cover and the few remaining articles.

WRITING

THIS PART of the collection includes various examples of writing dating from the New Kingdom: the royal papyrus (or royal canon) with a list of pharaohs from the XVII dynasty; the papyrus of mines, with a map of the gold deposits of the Wadi Hammamat; the judicial papyrus containing the proceedings against the conspirators who assassinated Ramses II. The *Acrobatic Figure of a Dancer* is an extraordinary example of a design on a fragment of limestone, a material which was often used for writing.

Acrobatic Figure of a Dancer (XVIII dynasty), drawing on limestone

WEAVING, CRAFTS AND TRADES

TWO MORE ROOMS ARE dedicated to various everyday objects: fabrics, objects and utensils for hunting, fishing, games, study and domestic life.

RELIGION

AMONG THE OBJECTS used for magic and the statuettes of divinities, is the section of mummies of sacred animals used in the cults of the divinities: falcons of Horus, bulls of Hapi, fish of the goddess Neith, cats of the goddess Bast, crocodiles of Sobek, the ibis and baboons of Thoth.

Gilded statuette, falcon of Horus

PAINTING

THE CYCLE OF PAINTINGS of Iti's tomb dates from around 2000 BC, and is worth seeing for its depiction of everyday life. The museum preserves numerous fragments of colourful wall decorations: most of the scenes show farm and manual work, such as carrying sacks of wheat, butchering and cutting trees.

PROVINCIAL SITES

ON A NUMBER OF OCCASIONS Ernesto Schiaparelli and Giulio Farina explored the necropoli of provincial towns which flourished during the so-called "feudal" period between 2150 and 1750: Asyut, Qau El-Kebir and Gebelein. Of note among the exhibits displayed in the rooms in the basement are the wooden models of Asyut, examples of the rock tombs of the dignitaries (Wahka I and II, Ibu) of Qau el-Kebir. The paintings of Iti and the burial goods of the so-called "tomb of the unknown" (c.2400–2300 BC) found in the area of Gebelein are displayed on the first floor.

The cycle of paintings in the tomb of Maia, XVIII dynasty

Galleria Sabauda ❷

THE GALLERIA SABAUDA, one of Italy's major art galleries, was founded in 1832 by Carlo Alberto with the Savoy collections. Since 1865 it has occupied the second and third floors of the Accademia delle Scienze building (also home to the Museo Egizio). From 2007 it will be housed in the Manica Nuova of the Palazzo Reale. The gallery contains works by Italian masters and Piedmontese schools, Flemish and Dutch works.

Portrait of a Lady, a Mannerist work by Bronzino (1555)

St Francis Receiving the Stigmata, by the Flemish artist Jan Van Eyck

SECOND FLOOR

THIS IS THE first floor of the gallery, home to works of the Piedmontese school, 14th–16th-century Italian masters and works by Flemish and Dutch artists.

PIEDMONTESE SCHOOL

In the five rooms dedicated to the Piedmontese school (entrance on the same floor) visitors can admire works by Giovanni Martino Spanzotti, Giovanni Canavesio, Macrino d'Alba, Gandolfino da Roreto, Defendente Ferrari, Ottaviano Cane, Pietro Grammorseo, Gerolamo, Giuseppe and Raffaele Giovenone, Eusebio Ferrari and Bernardino Lanino. There are also a number of paintings by the major Piedmontese artist of the 16th century, Gaudenzio Ferrari (1475–1546). In his *Crucifixion* from 1535, as often occurs in his paintings, the pathos of the scene is rendered through varied gestures and the careful arrangement of the figures.

ITALIAN MASTERS

In the six rooms (to the left of the entrance) housing works by masters of the Tuscan, Venetian, Piedmontese and Lombard schools, visitors can also admire *Angels, Madonna and Child* by Fra Angelico, an *Archangel Raphael and Tobias* by the Pollaiolo brothers and *Three Archangels and Tobias* by Filippino Lippi.

Of particular note among the Mannerist works is the *Portrait of a Lady* by the noted Florentine artist Bronzino, from 1555. In this work the bright colours and the extraordinarily detailed draughtsmanship combine to evoke a sense of the aristocratic.

FLEMISH AND DUTCH PAINTING

The gallery also has a large collection of important Dutch and Flemish works, many of which came from the collection of Prince Eugenio of Savoy-Soissons. These include paintings by Gerard Dou, Van Dyck, Van der Werff, Jan Brueghel de Velours, Teniers and Jan Griffier. The gallery also has several fine acquisitions, including Hans Memling's *Passion of Christ*, a *Last Judgment* by Bartholomaeus Spranger and a *Portrait of an Old Man Sleeping* attributed to Rembrandt. Also included in this group are several important works by the great master of 15th-century Flemish painting, Jan Van Eyck. In *St Francis Receiving the Stigmata*, the background landscape is rendered with masterful precision and a strong sense of perspective.

Crucifixion, one of the last masterpieces by Gaudenzio Ferrari

Palazzo Reale in Turin, one of two landscapes painted by Bellotto

THIRD FLOOR

THE SECOND LEVEL of the gallery houses the dynastic collections, divided into three chronological periods, and the Gualino collection. The dynastic collections, from the patronage and purchases of the Savoy dukes and sovereigns, cover the periods 1550–1630 (from Emanuele Filiberto to Carlo Emanuele I), 1630–1730 (from Vittorio Emanuele I to Vittorio Amedeo II) and 1730–1831 (from Carlo Emanuele III to Carlo Felice).

DYNASTIC COLLECTIONS 1550–1630

Among the most interesting works from the first period of the House of Savoy collections are a *Madonna and Child with Saints* by the famed Italian artist Andrea Mantegna, *Worshipper in Prayer* and *Visitation* by the Flemish Rogier van der Weyden, a *Trinity* by Tintoretto and a large canvas, *Feast in the House of Simon* (dated 1560), by Paolo Veronese, in which the religious theme is transposed into the period of its painter. This painting is part of Veronese's series of "Feasts" which represent the apogee of his theatrical style.

There are further works by Guercino, Peter Paul Rubens, and Anthony van Dyck, while an entire room is dedicated to work by the Venetian masters of the second half of the 16th century.

DYNASTIC COLLECTIONS 1630–1730

The second period numbers many works by Guercino and the Lombard artist Francesco Cairo, court artist from 1633 onwards. In the collection of paintings of fruit and flowers, by the Italian and Flemish schools, the favourite subject matter of the first "Madama Reale" (royal madam), Marie Christine of France, is evident. However, each of the works on display reflects the taste of the royals of the time.

Many foreign artists contributed to the international atmosphere of the Savoy court, such as Gaspard van Wittel, Charles Dauphin and Jan Miel. In *The Children of Charles I of England* (*see p65*) from 1635, the great portraitist Van Dyck, who studied with Rubens, shows interest in the individual psychology of the subjects, typical of Flemish painting.

DYNASTIC COLLECTIONS 1730–1831

The period 1730–1831 shows an interest in theatrical settings, as shown by the sketches for theatre sets and some of the frescoes on the vaults of the Palazzo Reale. Striking works are two views of Turin painted in 1745 by Bernardo Bellotto, the great interpreter of 18th-century Vedutism, and nephew and pupil of Canaletto. Bellotto's *Palazzo Reale in Turin*, one of two large views of Turin in the gallery, shows the minute descriptive details accentuated by the contrast of light and shade. On the left of the picture, the Cappella della Sindone is visible.

GUALINO COLLECTION

The Gualino collection is displayed in seven rooms with a separate nucleus which includes paintings, sculptures, furniture, gold objects, fabrics and art set up in a house-museum. Of great interest are the *Madonna and Child Enthroned between two Angels* by Duccio and *Venus* from the studio of Botticelli.

THE NEW VENUE

TRANSFER of the collections to the Manica Nuova of Palazzo Reale is planned for 2007. The exhibition space will increase from 5,070 sq m (54,575 sq ft) to more than 12,000 sq m (129,165 sq ft). The columned staircase in the centre of the Manica Nuova will be the entrance, with access from the courtyard of the Reggia and Via XX Settembre.

Feast in the House of Simon, part of Paolo Veronese's "Feast" series

Palazzo Carignano, Museo del Risorgimento ❸

T HE PALACE of the Savoia Carignano princes was the birthplace of Carlo Alberto and Vittorio Emanuele II. The building was also the seat of both the National and Subalpine parliaments, and the Kingdom of Italy was proclaimed here in 1861. Built in 1679–85 to a design by Guarino Guarini, it originally had a single brick façade and two wings. Since 1934, the main floor has housed the Museo del Risorgimento Italiano, which has the fullest documentation of the history of the unification of Italy, from 1706, the year of the French defeat at the siege of Turin, until 1946. You can visit a reconstruction of Cavour's study and the room where Carlo Alberto was exiled, and it is possible to visit the apartments with 18th-century frescoes by Legnanino. Reorganization of the rooms is planned for 2006.

Bronze Cartouche
This cartouche commemorates the birth of Vittorio Emanuele II (1820), who, like Carlo Alberto, was born in this palace.

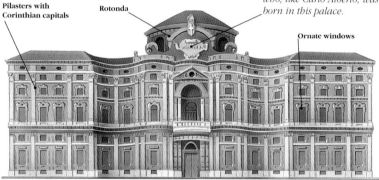

Pilasters with Corinthian capitals

Rotonda

Ornate windows

17th-century façade, overlooking Piazza Carignano
The impressive curved brick façade by Guarini is lightened by concave sections and decorative relief features. When it was the only existing façade, the back of the building opened onto the gardens and the stables of Prince Tommaso. In the centre of Piazza Carignano stands a monument dedicated to Gioberti (1859).

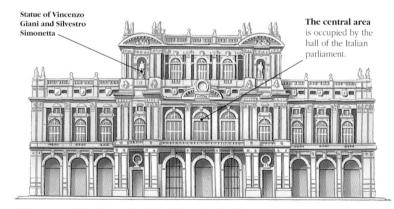

Statue of Vincenzo Giani and Silvestro Simonetta

The central area is occupied by the hall of the Italian parliament.

19th-century façade, overlooking Piazza Carlo Alberto
This wing was built by Giuseppe Bollati in 1864–72, to a design by Gaetano Ferri, during work to enlarge the building so as to house the national parliament. It replaced the original garden area. The Biblioteca Nazionale in front stands on the site of the stables.

Hall of the Subalpine Parliament
The hall has remained as it was at the last session in 1860; the seats of Cavour, Garibaldi and D'Azeglio are marked with red, green and white cockades.

VISITORS' CHECKLIST

Via Accademia delle Scienze 5.
Map 3 B5.   011 56 21 147.
9am–7pm Tue–Sun.
Mon, 1 Jan, Easter, 1 May,
25, 31 Dec.   guides in
braille for the blind.

Giuseppe Mazzini
One section is dedicated to the Giovine Italia (Young Italy) movement, revealing the life of the nationalist leader who fought for a unified Italian republic.

Giuseppe Garibaldi
Room 19 documents one of Italy's best-known leaders. Exhibits include the red shirts of the volunteer force he commanded.

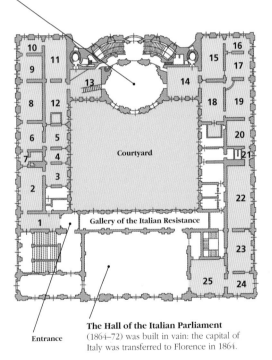

Entrance

Gallery of the Italian Resistance

Courtyard

The Hall of the Italian Parliament
(1864–72) was built in vain: the capital of Italy was transferred to Florence in 1864.

KEY

1	Old Piedmont
2–3	French Dominion
4	Napoleonic Period
5	Restoration Period
6–7	Secret Societies
8	Mazzini
9–10	Liberal Reforms
11–14	1848–9
15	European Nationalism
16	The Crimean War
17–18	1859 War
19	Garibaldi
20–23	Unification of Italy
24–25	1915–18

Battle of Sommacampagna
Felice Cerruti Bauduc's work depicts a crucial moment in the history of the 19th-century European independence movements.

Piazza San Carlo, with the equestrian statue of Emanuele Filiberto

Piazza San Carlo ❹

Map 3 A5.

THE "DRAWING ROOM" of Turin, this square is distinguished by fine façades and porticoes with 19th-century cafés and *pasticcerie*, along with prestigious clubs and institutions, such as the Philharmonic Academy.

In the centre is an equestrian statue known locally as "*l caval 'd brons*" (the bronze horse). Made by Carlo Marocchetti in 1838, it represents Emanuele Filiberto sheathing his sword after victory at San Quintino (1557). The square, once called Piazza Reale, was laid out in 1640–50 on the site of old Roman walls, to a design by Carlo di Castellamonte (1637). It has witnessed historic events; in 1864, a protest broke out against the transfer of the capital to Florence. On the south side stand the Baroque churches of **Santa Cristina** and **San Carlo**.

Via Roma ❺

Map 3 A5.

THE MODERN APPEARANCE of this wide street is evident, not only in the succession of fashion boutiques along the 750 m (2,460 ft) of porticoes, but also because of the rebuilding work carried out in 1931–7. This shopping street connects Piazza Castello in the north to Piazza San Carlo and continues on to Piazza Carlo Felice and the Porta Nuova railway station.

Beyond Piazza San Carlo is a square dedicated to the Committee of National Liberation. Fountains depict the rivers Po and Dora.

Museo della Marionetta ❻

Via Santa Teresa 5. **Map** 3 A5.
☎ 011 530 238. ◯ Sep–Jul:
9.30am–1pm Mon–Fri, 2.30–5.30pm
by appt; Sat, Sun by appt. ◖ 25 Apr,
1 May, 2 Jun, 24 Dec–6 Jan. ♿
@ museomarionettelupi@tin.it

THE BASEMENT of the church of **Santa Teresa** (1642–74), which holds the ashes of Marie Christine of France and has two chapels by Juvarra, houses the **Teatro Gianduja** and **Museo della Marionetta** with 5,000 puppets and stage scenery. The oldest piece is an 18th-century Harlequin.

The collection belongs to the Lupi family, puppeteers who came to Turin in the early 1800s and who made the character of Gianduja, a Commedia dell'Arte figure, a popular symbol of Turin.

San Filippo Neri ❼

Via Maria Vittoria 5. **Map** 3 B5.
☎ 011 538 456. ◯ 8am–12 noon,
5.30–7pm Mon–Fri; 10am–12 noon
Sun, hols.

TURIN'S LARGEST church also bears Juvarra's imprint. In 1714 the dome, begun in 1675 by Antonio Bettini, collapsed and the project for rebuilding it was entrusted to Juvarra who was called to court by Vittorio Amedeo II in the same year. However, the Neo-Classical façade was completed in 1824 by Giuseppe Talucchi.

The interior of the church is 69 m (226 ft) long with a single nave and six side chapels. The main altar has a canvas by Carlo Maratta of the Virgin Mary and Child. The oratory is used for events.

In front of the church is **Palazzo Carpano**, home to the company that produces a famous vermouth, made from wine and herbs. The courtyard is worth a visit.

Palazzo Dal Pozzo della Cisterna ❽

Via Maria Vittoria 12. **Map** 3 B5.
☎ 011 535 101. ◯ 9am–12 noon
Sat; the art gallery and gardens can
be visited. ◖ only.

THIS FINE 17th-century residence, home to the Dal Pozzo family and later the dukes of Aosta, was the birthplace of Maria Vittoria, the duke of Aosta's wife who was queen of Spain for a short time. In 1714 the number of servants employed

The twin churches of Santa Cristina and San Carlo flanking Via Roma

The Palaeontology Section of the Museo Regionale di Scienze Naturali

here was surpassed only by the Royal Palace.

Additions gave the building a Tuscan-Renaissance and Neo-Baroque look: the stucco is from the 1600s, the façade 18th century. Many frescoes and staircases date from the 1800s and the courtyard and gardens are 18th–19th century. Since 1940 it has housed the provincial government.

Piazza Cavour **9**

Map 7 B1.

THIS IS ONE OF THE LOVELIEST of Turin's squares. Built in 1835, this small green hill is surrounded by elegant villas with typical sloping roofs in the French style and Baroque-style brick façades. Nearby is **Piazza Maria Teresa**, with a statue of patriot Guglielmo Pepe and a number of period buildings.

Museo Regionale di Scienze Naturali **10**

Via Giolitti 36. **Map** 7 B1.
011 432 073 33. 10am–7pm Wed–Mon. Tue; 1, 2, 6 Jan, 25, 26 Dec.
www.regione.piemonte.it/ museoscienzenaturali

TURIN'S Natural History museum, opened in 1980, is housed in the former Ospedale San Giovanni Vecchio, a charitable institution. Built at the end of the 17th century by Amedeo di Castellamonte, it was later completed by illustrious architects. The exhibition space (1,000 sq m/10,765 sq

ft) is divided into sections on botany, petrography, entomology, mineralogy, geology, zoology and palaeontology. The fossil collections include the almost complete skeleton of a rhinoceros and an aquatic animal found near Asti. The museum also hosts temporary shows, and cultural events are held in the courtyard in summer.

Palazzo Cavour **11**

Via Cavour 8. **Map** 7 A1. 011 530 690. 10am–7.30pm Tue–Sun (10pm Thu).
www.palazzocavour.it

THIS FINE EXAMPLE of 18th-century Piedmontese Baroque was built by engineer Giacomo Plantery in 1729 for Cavour's grandfather, Michel Antonio. Part of the statesman's life was spent in these rooms: he was born here on 10 August 1810, it was here that he founded the newspaper *Il Risorgimento*, and he died here in 1861, just after unification. After his death the building was used, in part, by the Banca di Napoli and it was bought by the Fascist Federation of Commerce in 1928. Today, it is used as exhibition space.

The vestibule affords access to the courtyard and staircase. The architectural features are refined by decorations on the

doors. The columns support Ionic capitals.

The staircase leads to the main floor where the entrance of honour is the White Room, named after the colour of the walls, decorated with capitals, volutes, shells, leaves and cornices. This room leads to Cavour's small study, in Empire style, with silk-covered walls. Three corner rooms follow, the first with a marble fireplace. The Sala Magnifica is almost square. A small room with decorated doors gives on to the rest of the floor, used for exhibitions.

Palazzo Bricherasio **12**

Via Lagrange 20. **Map** 7 A1.
011 571 1811. for exhibitions. Mon.
www.palazzobricherasio.it

BUILT IN 1636, this property has passed through the hands of several noble families. Cavaliere Luigi Cacherano di Bricherasio bought it in 1855, and in 1871 it became a meeting place for artists thanks to the cosmopolitan friendships of his daughter, Countess Sofia. His son, Count Emanuele, had a great interest in cars and on 1 July 1899, the documents of incorporation of FIAT, founded by the count together with industrialists and bankers, were signed here. Since its restoration in 1995, major exhibitions have been held here.

An exhibition at Palazzo Bricherasio

QUADRILATERO ROMANO

TRACES OF TURIN'S PAST are concealed in this district, made up of narrow streets and squares alongside Via Garibaldi, the city's oldest street. This was the *decumanus maximus* or main road, which, along with the *cardus maximus* (Porta Palatina and Via San Tommaso), made up the main thoroughfares in Roman Turin. The remains of medieval

The market at Porta Palazzo

towers, beams, pilasters and Romanesque and Gothic architecture can be seen in this district, known as the Quadrilatero Romano. Today the district is renowned for its nightlife. Nearby is the multicultural heart of Turin: the large market at Porta Palazzo. The Town Hall, Piazza Savoia and the Museo della Sindone are all found in this less well-known district.

SIGHTS AT A GLANCE

Museums and Galleries
GAM – Galleria Civica d'Arte Moderna e Contemporanea ⑫
Museo Civico Pietro Micca ⑪
Museo della Sindone ⑨
Museo Storico Nazionale di Artiglieria ⑩

Monuments and Buildings
Palazzo Faletti di Barolo ⑤
Palazzo Saluzzo Paesana ⑦

Streets and Squares
Piazza Consolata ⑧
Piazza Palazzo di Città ③
Piazza Savoia ⑥
Via Garibaldi ①

Churches
San Domenico ②
Santissimi Martiri e Cappella della Pia Congregazione ④

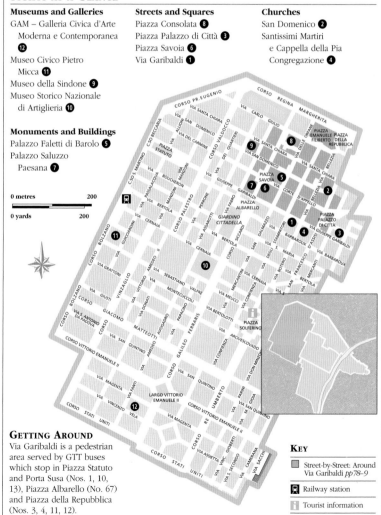

0 metres 200
0 yards 200

GETTING AROUND
Via Garibaldi is a pedestrian area served by GTT buses which stop in Piazza Statuto and Porta Susa (Nos. 1, 10, 13), Piazza Albarello (No. 67) and Piazza della Repubblica (Nos. 3, 4, 11, 12).

KEY

　Street-by-Street: Around Via Garibaldi *pp78–9*

　Railway station

　Tourist information

◁ **Monument to Amedeo VI, the Green Count, in Piazza Palazzo di Città**

Street-by-Street: Around Via Garibaldi

L EAVING PIAZZA CASTELLO and taking the perfectly straight Via Garibaldi, you enter a fascinating network of alleys and small squares. It is here that the large metropolis takes on a more human dimension with numerous churches, traditional shops, street markets and night spots. Don't miss the area around the church of the Consolata and Piazza Palazzo di Città. Turin's largest open-air market is held nearby. There are also many traces of the city's history in the area, such as Piazza Savoia and numerous fine buildings.

Al Bicerin
Opened in 1763, this café is famous for its bitter-sweet drink, bicerin. *Its 19th-century atmosphere evokes a time when Cavour was one of its regular customers.*

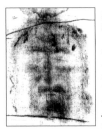

Museo della Sindone
The crypt of the church of the Santissima Sudario houses this museum, which documents the history of the famous Turin Shroud **9**

Piazza Savoia
The obelisk in the centre commemorates the Siccardi laws of 1850 which abolished ecclesiastical privileges **6**

Palazzo Saluzzo Paesana
This is one of the most luxurious 18th-century residences in the Baroque style **7**

Palazzo Faletti di Barolo
This museum covers Turin life from 1600 onwards. The ground and first floors, and cellars, can be visited. The writer Silvio Pellico lived and died here **5**

Via Garibaldi
This pedestrian shopping street is directly aligned with the façade of Palazzo Madama **1**

Cappella dei Banchieri e dei Mercanti
The Baroque chapel of bankers and merchants (1600s), next to the church of Santissimi Martiri, is an example of Piedmontese Mannerism **4**

★ Santuario della Consolata

This church, which is much loved by the Turinese, has a Neo-Classical façade, which was added in 1860, and an 11th-century red brick bell tower. There are numerous bars, cafés and eating places nearby **8**

LOCATOR MAP
See Street Finder Maps 2–3

Cafés and wine bars, Via Sant'Agostino

Porta Palazzo

The largest market in Europe sells products from Italy's regions and elsewhere. On Saturdays there is a flea market, and the Gran Balôn (antiques market) takes place once a month.

San Domenico

This church, a rare survivor from the Middle Ages, contains the only 14th-century frescoes in the city **2**

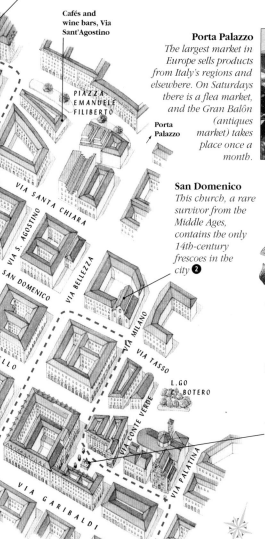

★ Piazza Palazzo di Città

This monument in front of the Town Hall represents Amedeo VI of Savoy, known as the Green Count **3**

KEY

– – – – Suggested route

STAR SIGHTS

★ Piazza Palazzo di Città

★ Santuario della Consolata

PIAZZA EMANUELE FILIBERTO

Porta Palazzo

VIA SANTA CHIARA

VIA S. AGOSTINO

SAN DOMENICO

VIA BELLEZZA

VIA MILANO

VIA TASSO

L.GO E. BOTERO

VIA CONTE VERDE

VIA PALATINA

VIA GARIBALDI

0 metres 100

0 yards 100

Porta Palazzo market

FROM PORTA PALAZZO TO BALÔN

The Balôn flea market began life in the mid-19th century and is still held in the streets around Piazza della Repubblica every Saturday. Its name may derive from the fact that in the late 18th century there was a spheristery here. This was where the ancient ball games of *pallone a bracciale* (played in Turin since Roman times) were held. On the second Sunday of every month the Gran Balôn is held, an antique market with hundreds of stalls. Porta Palazzo is the largest outdoor market in Europe. It is held in Piazza della Repubblica every morning except Sunday and offers a striking diversity of products. The glass and metal pavilion in the square dates from 1916; the futuristic building is by Fuksas. There is also a plaque dedicated to the "patron" of plum tomatoes, the Piedmontese Francesco Cirio.

Logo of the Balôn market

Via Garibaldi ❶

Map 3 A4.

THE pedestrian zone linking Piazza Castello to Piazza Statuto is a pleasant area for strolling. Along Turin's oldest street, the *decumanus maximus* of the Roman era, Porta Segusina once stood.

This typical shopping street was straightened in 1775 by the architect Plantery. It was planned in such a way as to line up neatly with the façade of Palazzo Madama.

At one time the street was called Via Dora Grossa and there was a channel for water runoff. The street today features many places of artistic interest.

San Domenico ❷

Via San Domenico. **Map** 3 A4.
📞 011 522 97 11. ○ 7am–12 noon, 4–6.30pm. ✝ 7.30am Mon–Fri, 10am hols, 6pm.

THIS CHURCH and monastery, begun in 1260, when they stood on the site of the present-day sacristy, are the only examples of the Gothic style in Turin. A bell tower was a later addition.

In the early 20th century Riccardo Brayda and Alfredo d'Andrade uncovered the original 14th-century Gothic features which had been concealed by 18th-century alterations. In the three-aisle interior is a carved pulpit.

The Cappella del Rosario, from the second half of the 1700s, contains Guercino's Madonna of the Rosary and saints Dominic and Catherine of Siena (1637). In the left aisle, level with the bell tower, is a fresco cycle (1360) attributed to the master of San Domenico, the only one from this period in Turin.

The monastery was the seat of the Inquisition in the 13th century, and one of the rooms was used as a prison.

Piazza Palazzo di Città ❸

Map 3 A4. **Corpus Domini**, Piazza Corpus Domini. 📞 011 436 60 25. ○ 7.30–11.30am, 3–6pm. ✝ 7.30am Mon–Fri, 10am Sat, Sun, hols, 5.30pm Thu.

THIS SQUARE was once the site of the Roman forum.

In the 14th century a fruit and vegetable market was held here and the piazza became home to the Town Hall in 1663. In the 18th century, the square was redesigned by the architect Benedetto Alfieri, who created its current look. From 1300 to 1801 a tower stood here but it was razed because it did not align with nearby Via Garibaldi.

The statue by Pelagio Pelagi in the centre of the square represents the **Green Count**, Amedeo VI, battling with two Saracen warriors during the 1366 crusade. It is said that green was this popular legendary figure's lucky colour, hence his nickname.

A narrow porticoed street leads to the charming Piazzetta **Corpus Domini**, home to *Piercing*, a steel ring attached to the corner of the top floor of an 18th-century building. This original

Statue of the Green Count with the Town Hall in the background

Piercing, **an example of urban art in Piazzetta Corpus Domini**

example of urban art (1996) was made by Corrado Levi and a group of young artists called Cliostraadt.

Santissimi Martiri e Cappella della Pia Congregazione ❹

Via Garibaldi 25. **Map** 3 A4.
Church ☎ *011 562 25 81.*
○ *7am–12 noon, 4.30–7.30pm.*
🔲 *9am, 6pm, Mon–Fri.*
Chapel ☎ *011 562 72 26.*
○ *3–6pm Sat; 10am–noon Sun.*
🔲 *11am Sun.* ● *Jul, Aug.*

THIS BUILDING, completed by the Jesuits in 1612 and dedicated to the martyrs Solutore, Avventore and Ottavio, is Mannerist in style. Inside, behind the organ, are frescoes by Andrea Pozzo; *St Paul, San Saverio and other Saints* by Federico Zuccari; the main altar is by Juvarra (1730). The church houses the relics of Santa Giuliana and San Solutore.

The adjacent **Cappella dei Banchieri e dei Mercanti**, commissioned by the lay Congregation of Bankers and Merchants, is a Baroque chapel from 1692 (restored in 1957). It affords access to the 18th-century courtyard of the House of the Jesuits. In the chapel, the 11 canvases above the choir by Andrea Pozzo, Sebastiano Taricco and Luigi Vannier represent the themes of the Three Kings and the Epiphany. The vault fresco, with Paradise, prophets and sybils, is attributed to Legnanino.

Palazzo Faletti di Barolo ❺

Via delle Orfane 7. **Map** 3 A3.
⧉ *011 436 03 11.* 𝖥𝖠𝖷 *011 431 03 32.* ○ *Sep–Jul: 10am–12 noon, 3–5pm Mon, Wed, 10am–12 noon Fri; Aug: 10am–12 noon Mon, Wed, Fri.* ● *Tue, Thu, Sat, Sun; 1, 6 Jan, Easter, 25 Apr, 1 May 2, 24 Jun, 8 Dec, 24–26, 31 Dec.* 🏷
🆆 *www.palazzobarolo.it*

THIS patrician residence was the venue for an important cultural salon during the mid-19th century, which was patronized by Cavour on his visits to the Marchesa Giulia di Barolo. Author and patriot Silvio Pellico also lived and worked here as the family librarian from 1830 until his death in 1854. The old apartments, which have remained almost unchanged, are open to the public and afford an intriguing journey back in time.

The building was constructed at the end of the 17th century following a design by Gian Francesco Baroncelli and was enlarged in 1743 by Benedetto Alfieri. The building boasts a splendid monumental staircase, fine stuccowork and frescoes and period furniture.

The last owner was Giulia Colber, the wife of Marquis Tancredi Faletto di Barolo, the founder of the Opera Pia, a charity organization. In 1864, the entire building was donated to this same charity.

The monumental staircase leading to the main floor of Palazzo Barolo

It is now used as a venue for cultural events.

Further along the same street stands the church of **Santa Chiara**, designed by Bernardo Vittone and dating from 1745. It has an octagonal plan and curved corners with small balconies and an eight-cornered dome.

The obelisk in Piazza Savoia

Piazza Savoia ❻

Map 2 F4.

IN THIS LIVELY square, which marked the limits of Roman-era Augusta Taurinorum, you cannot miss the obelisk commemorating the abolition of the ecclesiastical courts which the Siccardi Laws promulgated in 1850. The obelisk was erected with public donations and commemorates the anti-clerical victory with the inscription: "The law is the same for everyone". Completed in 1853, it bears the names of the communes that participated in the collection, launched by the newspaper *La Gazzetta del Popolo*. A box buried at the base of the obelisk contains the Nos. 141 and 142 editions of the newspaper from 1850, a bottle of Barbera wine, *grissini* (bread sticks) and rice.

Palazzo Saluzzo Paesana **❼**

Via della Consolata 1 bis. **Map** 3 A3.

T HIS BUILDING is one of 18th-century Turin's most luxurious mansions. It was built in the Baroque style, to a design by the architect Gian Giacomo Plantery (1715–18), in 1730. The grand entrance leads to a large courtyard, with loggias and staircases set at the four corners. The private apartments on the main floor are particularly elegantly decorated. Within the building is a guesthouse called Ai Savoia, where the six bedrooms bear the names of members of the House of Savoy.

At No. 3 Via Consolata stands another similarly elegant 18th-century residence, **Palazzo Martini di Cigala** (1716). The wide entrance doorway is flanked by half-columns and surmounted by a balcony.

The Consolata church

THE "BICERIN"

A *bicerin* is a hot drink, first fashionable in the 18th century, made by mixing espresso coffee, hot chocolate and cream to an ancient recipe. The name derives from the glass in which the drink is traditionally served. It is also the name of a famous café (Al Bicerin), which stands opposite the church of the Consolata, and still has its original 18th-century furnishings. Among its famous customers were Alexandre Dumas, Puccini and Cavour.

The famous Al Bicerin café

Piazza Consolata **❽**

Piazza della Consolata. **Map** 3 A3.
Church 011 436 32 35.
6.30am–7.30pm.
6.30am–12 noon, 4–6.30pm, every hour.

T HIS SMALL, CHARMING square, today set among Turin's lively nightlife area, is home to Al Bicerin, one of the city's most famous cafés. This establishment opened in 1763 and is famous for a drink made of coffee, milk and chocolate, the *bicerin*.

Also facing the square is the church of the **Consolata**. It was designed by Guarini in 1678, replacing an earlier church, Sant'Andrea, erected during the 10th century. Today's visitors can still see the original Romanesque bell tower. The church's central oval presbytery was designed in 1729 by Filippo Juvarra while the Neo-Classical façade dates from 1860. Further embellishments

were added during work carried out by Carlo Ceppi in 1899–1904.

Inside, the large high altar, with two white marble angels and the image of Maria Consolatrice, is by Juvarra. The church of the Consolata is probably one of Turin's best-loved churches.

Museo della Sindone **❾**

Confraternità del SS. Sudario di Torino, Via San Domenico 28. **Map** 2 F3. 011 43 65 832. 9am–12 noon, 3–7pm. 1 Jan, 25 Dec. @ sindone@tin.it www.sindone.it

T HE MUSEUM OF THE HOLY SHROUD was founded by the Centro Internazionale di Sindonologia, and since 1998 it has occupied the crypt of the Santissimo Sudario.

The museum was founded in 1936 in order to document the history of the Holy Shroud (*sindone*) and the scientific research which has been carried out on the revered image, gathering together the finds preserved by the Confraternità del Santissimo Sudario.

The museum provides visitors with information about the shroud's history from the 1500s to the present day, covering the historical, scientific, devotional and artistic aspects of this image.

Restoration of the crypt itself uncovered particular structural aspects of this evocative underground room,

THE HOLY SHROUD

This linen sheet is 4.37 m (14 ft) long by 1.11 m (3.6 ft) wide and bears the image of a crucified man. According to Christian tradition, it is the shroud in which Christ's body was wrapped after his descent from the Cross. In 1578 it was placed in Guarini's chapel, where it stayed until the fire in 1997.

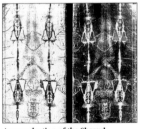

A reproduction of the Shroud, positive and negative

Cannons in the Museo Storico Nazionale di Artiglieria

which is now enlivened with virtual frescoes of the Passion of Christ, projected onto the vault and in the niches. These images slowly but regularly change and accompany visitors on their tour.

Also on display are the casket used to transfer the shroud from Chambéry to Turin in 1578 and the camera which, for the first time in 1898, produced a negative photographic image of the shroud. In addition, life-size photographic reproductions allow visitors to examine the images on the shroud in greater detail.

Museo Storico Nazionale di Artiglieria ⑩

Corso Galileo Ferraris. **Map** 2 F4.
[011 562 92 23.] for exhibitions. W www.artiglieria.org

FIVE CENTURIES of military history, beginning in the 15th century, are documented by the firearms, bayonets and assorted equipment displayed in this museum, which was set up in 1731 by Carlo Emanuele III to train young artillerymen at a school founded by Ignazio Bertola. In 1893 the museum was transferred to its present location in the keep, which is all that remains of the fortified Cittadella built for Emanuele Filiberto.

The museum has around 11,500 exhibits which also include military documents, publications and iconographic collections.

Museo Civico Pietro Micca ⑪

Corso Guicciardini 7a. **Map** 2E 4.
[011 546 317.] 9am–7pm Tue–Sun. ● Mon, 1 Jan, Easter, 1 May, 25, 31 Dec. 🦽 🖭
W www.comune.torino.it/musei/civici/pietromicca

THIS MUSEUM IS dedicated to Pietro Micca, the patriot who ended the French siege on 29–30 August 1706, and has models, prints and memorabilia from the period. Micca's heroic deed took place in underground tunnels where his mining experience was crucial. Only around 8 km (5 miles) of the 14 km (9 miles) of tunnels which existed then remain and only a few hundred metres are open to the public.

Pietro Micca, A. Gastaldi, 1858

GAM – Galleria Civica d'Arte Moderna e Contemporanea ⑫

Via Magenta 31. **Map** 6 E1. [011 562 99 11.] 9am–7pm Tue–Sun.
● Mon, 1 Jan, Easter, 1 May, 25, 31 Dec. 🦽 🖭 🎟 🖭 🖭
W www.gamtorino.it

RENAMED GAM, this gallery reopened in 1993 in this modern, restructured venue, close to the 19th-century avenues of Corso Galileo Ferraris and Corso Vittorio Emanuele II.

In 1863 Turin was the first Italian city to have a public exhibition of modern art. The collection now boasts 15,000 works which includes sculptures, drawings and etchings. A multipurpose centre, GAM has permanent exhibitions, hosts temporary shows, and has a book-shop, conference room, photo library and café.

The gallery, one of the best in Italy, covers the last two centuries of visual arts, with the masters of the 19th century (Fontanesi, Pellizza da Volpedo, Fattori, Medardo Rosso), the 20th century (Casorati, Martini, Morandi, De Pisis, Manzù, Melotti, Fontana), and historic avant-garde and contemporary art.

***Execution of Partisans (Small Execution)*, Renato Guttuso, GAM**

ALONG THE PO

Vintage tourist tram

THANKS TO the river Po, which crosses the city, Turin has large green areas right in the city centre. The large number of Turinese who flock to the Murazzi riverside terraces and the Parco del Valentino on spring and summer evenings shows the great attraction that the Po has for the city's people. Also popular in the summer is the Monte dei Cappuccini, one of the city's closest panoramic viewpoints.

During the 19th century, new architectural works were begun in this area. They included the Vittorio Emanuele II bridge, the Neo-Classical church of the Gran Madre and the reconstruction of the Borgo Medioevale. Behind the Parco del Valentino, towards Porta Nuova railway station, is the district of San Salvario, an interesting melting pot of ethnic groups and religions. This area is home to a synagogue, a Waldensian temple and meeting places for the many immigrants from Arab and African countries. This is also a good place to try ethnic food. Visitors can also make use of tourist transport services, such as the boats that cruise the river or the antique trams that crisscross the historic centre of Turin.

KEY

- 🔲 Street-by-Street map *pp86–7*
- 🚆 Railway station
- ℹ️ Tourist information

GETTING AROUND

Piazza Vittorio Veneto and the Gran Madre are good reference points for arriving or changing buses or trams. The Nos. 13, 53, 56, 61 and 66 buses and trams all stop here. Nos. 9, 16 and 52 run alongside the Parco del Valentino.

SIGHTS AT A GLANCE

Museums and Galleries
Museo Nazionale
della Montagna ②

Monuments and Buildings
Borgo and Rocca Medioevale
⑥
Castello del Valentino ④
Villa della Regina ③

Parks and Gardens
Orto Botanico ⑤

Streets and Squares
Quartiere di San Salvario ⑩

Churches
Chiesa della Gran Madre ①
Chiesa Valdese ⑧
Synagogue ⑨

Tour
Tour of the Parco del Po ⑦

| 0 metres | | 150 |
| 0 yards | | 150 |

◁ **The River Po from the Murazzi riverside terraces at sunset**

Street-by-Street: Parco del Valentino

BETWEEN THE UMBERTO I and Principessa Isabella bridges on the Po, lies the city's largest park (550,000 sq m/ 5,920,200 sq ft), designed in the mid-19th century by the landscape artist Barillet-Deschamps. The entire area, with intriguing spots such as the Rocca and Borgo Medioevale, is crossed by tree-lined avenues and cycle paths. Along the banks of the river are famous boat clubs and atmospheric cafés and bars. In summer, the area is crowded until late into the night.

Giardino Roccioso
Laid out in 1961 to celebrate the 100th anniversary of the unification of Italy, the rock garden has fine roses and colourful flower beds.

Principessa Isabella bridge

The Fontana dei Mesi
Designed by Carlo Ceppi in 1898, the basin is surrounded by an array of Art Nouveau statues representing the months and the seasons.

CORSO MONCALIERI

Torino Esposizioni, the work of Pierluigi Nervi, is a large single hall measuring 10,000 sq m (107,640 sq ft).

★ **Rocca and Borgo Medioevale**
This faithful reproduction of Piedmontese houses and shops was conceived by the architect D'Andrade and the poet Giacosa. The complex was built for the 1884 Esposizione Generale ❻

Houses in the Borgo Medioevale
These dwellings were inspired by houses in Alba, Avigliana, Cuorgnè, Mondovì, Frossasco and Pinerolo. There are also streets, shops, squares and churches.

FURTHER AFIELD

URIN expanded enormously during the last century and today some of these outlying districts are home to important galleries and museums, including the Fondazione

Nude by Modigliani, Pinacoteca Giovanni e Marella Agnelli

Sandretto Re Rebaudengo in Via Modane and the Pinacoteca Giovanni e Marella Agnelli at Lingotto. The city is also taking on a new look thanks to its increasing importance in the field of contemporary art and the emphasis on innovative architecture. The Winter Olympics have also accelerated the transformation of suburban areas. However, traces of the era when Turin was the capital of the car industry are

still evident in the more than 170 cars on display in the museum and complex of Lingotto, a fine example of post-industrial transformation. Closer to the centre, visitors should not miss the splendid view from the Superga, or the Castello di Rivoli, a major site for contemporary art and formerly a Savoy residence. The Savoy family has also given Turin some splendid parks, such as Parco della Mandria and Castello di Moncalieri. A few kilometres from Turin there are other attractions, such as many fine examples of the Piedmontese-Gothic and Romanesque style of architecture.

SIGHTS AT A GLANCE

Museums and Galleries
Fondazione Sandretto
  Re Rebaudengo ❶
Museo dell'Automobile ❸
Pinacoteca Giovanni
  e Marella Agnelli ❷

Historic Buildings
Lingotto ❹
Palazzina di Caccia
  di Stupinigi ❼

Churches and Sanctuaries
Abbazia di Vezzolano ❸

Basilica di Superga ❺
Sant'Antonio di Ranverso ❽

Parks and Gardens
Parco Regionale La Mandria ❿

Towns
Chieri ❿
Moncalieri ⓫
Rivoli ❾

Tour
The Savoy Residences ❻

KEY

⬜	Turin centre
⬜	Urban area
═	Motorway
▬	Main road
═	Minor road
—	Railway line
✈	Airport

0 kilometres 8

0 miles 4

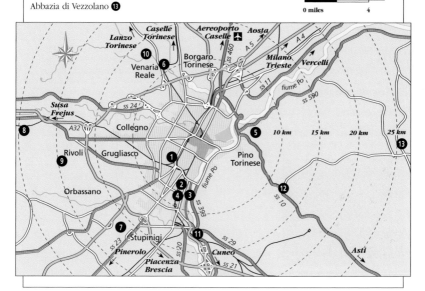

A temporary exhibition at the Fondazione Sandretto Re Rebaudengo

Fondazione Sandretto Re Rebaudengo ❶

Via Modane 16. **Map** 5 B3.
(011 198 316 00. **FAX** 011 198 316 01. **ℹ** 011 198 316 16 (24 hr).
◯ Jan–Jun, Sep–Dec: 12 noon–8pm Fri–Wed, 12 noon–11pm Thu; Jul, Aug: 12 noon–8pm Tue–Sun. **●** Mon, Easter, 2 Jun. **🎫** free 20–23 Jun. **♿ 🚻 @** info@fondsrr.org **W** www.fondsrr.org

I N 2002 THE Fondazione Sandretto Re Rebaudengo opened this contemporary exhibition area outside the historic centre of Turin in order to promote the visual arts. The aim of this new cultural centre is to bring the public closer to a new generation of artists.
Designed by the architect Claudio Silvestrin and the engineer James Hardwick on the site of the former Fergat factory, the centre covers an area of 3,500 sq m (37,675 sq ft), which includes a video room and auditorium, a cafeteria (designed by Rudolf Stingel), and a bookshop, a restaurant and an internet room. The building, which resembles a large box laid horizontally, is functional and

A corner of the cafeteria in the Fondazione Re Rebaudengo

is designed to house large installations and host contemporary art events. The building blends in with its modern urban surroundings and is close to some of the art installations recently placed along the route of Turin's suburban railway.
Much more than a museum, the Fondazione Sandretto Re Rebaudengo centre is an observatory of international avant-garde trends in art, as well as being a source of reference for experts and enthusiasts of modern art.

The futuristic structure of the Pinacoteca Agnelli at Lingotto

Pinacoteca Giovanni e Marella Agnelli ❷

Lingotto, Via Nizza 230 (entrance from Centro Commerciale 8Gallery).
Map 7 A5 off map. **(** 011 006 27 13. **FAX** 011 006 27 12.
◯ 9am–7pm Tue–Sun. **●** Mon, 1 Jan, 24, 25, 31 Dec. **🎫 🚻** **W** www.pinacoteca-agnelli.it **@** pinacoteca.agnelli@palazzograssi.it

T HIS EXHIBITION SPACE at Lingotto, which houses 25 exhibits from the private collection donated to the city by Giovanni and Marella Agnelli, was designed by the architect Renzo Piano. The suspended building, lit

only by a glass roof with blinds which filter the sunlight, was named the Scrigno (casket) and was opened to the public in 2002 with the aim of offering the people of Turin "pleasure, beauty and joy". The building stands at the same height as its similarly avant-garde neighbour, the "Bolla", a futuristic conference hall built of glass and steel.
The works in the gallery are displayed with no particular academic criteria, but according to the taste of Marella Agnelli. The 18th, 19th and 20th-century pictures include works by painters such as Canaletto, Renoir and Matisse. Of particular note is a panel from a painting by Gian Battista Tiepolo, *Halberdier in a Landscape* (1736), as well as one of six views of Venice by Canaletto, *The Bucentaur at the Wharf on Ascension Day* (c.1726). There are also two plaster statues of dancers sculpted by Antonio Canova between 1809 and 1814: one touching her chin with her finger, the other hand on hip.
As well as Matisse and Picasso, the 20th century is represented by works by the Italian artists Modigliani, Balla and Severini. Visitors can also admire *La Négresse* (1862–3) by Manet and Modigliani's famous *Nu couché* (1917).
Beneath the Scrigno are another five levels which are used for temporary exhibitions, education, offices and a shop which can be reached from the Lingotto shopping centre.

Museo dell'Automobile ❸

Corso Unità d'Italia 40. **Map** 7 A5 off map. 011 677 666. FAX 011 664 7148. 10am–6.30pm Tue–Sat (10pm Thu); 10am–8.30pm Sun. Mon, 25 Dec, 1 Jan. @ museoauto.centrodoc@tin.it W www.museoauto.org

THIS MUSEUM is housed in an interesting building in modern Turin and is easily recognizable by its long curved façade: the only one of its type in Italy. The 170 vehicles displayed on the three floors along the 1-km

(half-a-mile) route document over a century in the history of the car. Visitors can admire one of the largest collections of vehicles in Europe, which includes a replica of the first propelled vehicle, dating from 1769, and a solar powered model built in 1990.

Around 80 makes of vintage and modern car are shown, from Italy, France, the UK, Germany, the Netherlands, Spain, the US and Poland.

The museum also has sections dedicated to racing cars, the evolution of the pneumatic tyre and the history of the Italian Automobile Club (ACI).

A collection of vintage cars at the Museo dell'Automobile

The "Bolla", conference hall

Lingotto ❹

Via Nizza 280. **Map** 7 A5 off map. 011 664 41 11 (Lingotto Fiere, Auditorium). W www.8gallery.it

LINGOTTO WAS ORIGINALLY one of FIAT's car factories. It was designed by Giacomo

Mattè Trucco. Building began in 1917 and by 1918, 40,000 workers were employed on the assembly line.

In the 1980s the architect Renzo Piano transformed the factory into a multipurpose centre, able to accommodate international events such as the Book Fair, the Salone del Gusto food fair and the Salone dell'Automobile (until 2000), as well as international conferences.

The exhibition area consists of galleries and

pavilions with facilities for visitors and exhibitors on several levels. The complex also includes an auditorium, a conference centre, the Agnelli art gallery, an exhibition centre, a modern restaurant called vll Posto2 and Turin's only five-star hotel, Le Meridien Art+Tech, with a restaurant, Torpedo. The gardens are also open to the public, as is the FIAT test track on the roof, from which there are fine views of the Alps on clear days.

Lingotto logo

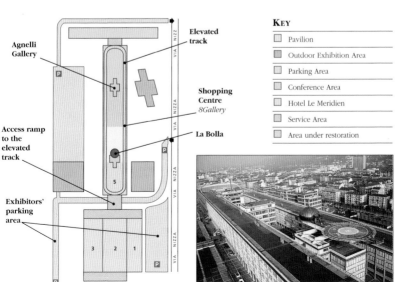

View over the former FIAT factory at Lingotto

KEY
- Pavilion
- Outdoor Exhibition Area
- Parking Area
- Conference Area
- Hotel Le Meridien
- Service Area
- Area under restoration

Agnelli Gallery · Elevated track · Shopping Centre 8Gallery · La Bolla · Access ramp to the elevated track · Exhibitors' parking area

Basilica di Superga ❺

Cappella del Voto, detail

THIS BAROQUE CHURCH by Filippo Juvarra stands proudly on a hill at a height of 669 m (2,195 ft), in line with Castello di Rivoli. Tradition has it that Vittorio Amedeo II vowed to build the church if Turin were to be successfully liberated from the French siege in 1706. The building of the basilica (1717–31) meant reducing the height of the hill by 40 m (130 ft). The basilica has a striking dome and two bell towers. To the rear is the cloister of the adjacent monastery. Inside the awe-inspiring circular interior are a main altar, the Cappella del Voto and a crypt with the tombs of members of the Savoy dynasty.

The cross on the lantern stands at 75 m (245 ft).

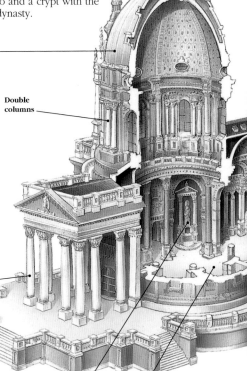

Double columns

★ The dome
The large double-vaulted octagonal dome rises 65 m (213 ft) above the central circular area. It is supported by eight columns and lit by eight large windows. A staircase, with 137 steps, leads to a panoramic balcony.

The pronaos
by Gassino, with eight marble columns, blends well with the church's curved lines.

★ Cappella del Voto
The chapel houses a 17th-century painted wooden statue of the Madonna and commemorates the spot where Vittorio Amedeo II made his vow to the Virgin Mary during the siege of Turin in 1706. It is reached via a short corridor to the left of the main altar.

The luminous interior
has two main chapels and four minor chapels which house important works of art by Claudio Francesco Beaumont, Sebastiano Ricci, Bernardino Cametti and Giovan Battista Bernero.

Façade
The large façade, preceded by a pronaos with Corinthian columns, is surmounted by a striking dome and flanked by twin bell towers 60 m (197 ft) in height.

VISITORS' CHECKLIST

Strada Basilica di Superga 73.
Map 8 F1 off map. 011 89 97 456. 9am–12 noon, 3–6pm (5pm Nov–Mar).
Crypt Apr–Oct: 9.30am–1.30pm, 2.30–5.30pm Mon–Fri, 9.30am–7.30pm Sat, Sun; Nov–Mar: 9.30am–1.30pm, 2.30–6.30pm Sat, Sun.

Symmetrical bell tower with balustrade

The monastery, designed by Juvarra, was the home of the Congregation of Regular Monks, to whom Vittorio Amedeo II entrusted the training of senior clergy.

★ **The Savoy Tombs**
The crypt houses 58 tombs of the Savoy kings, queens and princes, from Vittorio Amedeo II to Carlo Alberto. Vittorio Amedeo II's tomb (above), was made by Francesco Martinez (1777).

THE MUSEO DEL GRANDE TORINO

On 4 May 1949, a plane flying from Lisbon to Turin crashed into the rear wall of the Basilica di Superga in bad weather. On board was the Turin football team (champions of the Italian football league for five consecutive years). In all, 31 people died: all the team officials, the reserves, captain Valentino Mazzola, managers, journalists and crew members. A plaque with a marble cross behind the basilica commemorates this tragic event and the **Museo del Grande Torino** exhibits the team's memorabilia, including football boots, the entire changing room from the Filadelfia stadium, contracts, and the postcards sent from Lisbon, all of which fondly commemorate the glory of the *granata* football team.
4.30–6.30pm daily.

Logo of Torino Calcio 1906

STAR SIGHTS

★ **The Dome**

★ **The Savoy Tombs**

★ **Cappella del Voto**

The dramatic profile of the Basilica di Superga at sunset ▷

The Savoy Residences ❻

**Bronze stag,
Stupinigi**

BETWEEN THE 17th and 19th centuries, the Savoy family built a number of sumptuous residences and castles around Turin as symbols of power: Venaria, Stupinigi, Rivoli, Moncalieri and, further out, Racconigi and Agliè. Usually surrounded by large parks, they were used for hunting parties and the recreation of the monarchs and the court. They were designed by the best architects of the day, such as Amedeo di Castellamonte, Benedetto Alfieri, Michelangelo Garove, Pelagio Palagi and Filippo Juvarra. In 1997, UNESCO declared the Savoy residences and their collections World Heritage Sites.

0 kilometres 10

0 miles 5

Reggia di Venaria Reale ②
This group of buildings at Carlo Emanuele II's hunting ground was designed to rival the splendour of Versailles. Various architects, including Juvarra, worked here from 1661 to 1767. Today, the nearby La Mandria estate, built for Vittorio Amedeo II as a stud farm, is a regional park.

Castello di Rivoli ③
In 1718 Vittorio Amedeo II commissioned Juvarra to build this palace, but the great project remained incomplete. A wooden model of the first design is displayed in one of the castle rooms. Since 1984, and after careful restoration, the castle has housed the Museo di Arte Contemporanea.

The Palazzina di Caccia di Stupinigi ④
Vittorio Amedeo II commissioned Juvarra to build this hunting lodge (*see pp102–3*) in 1729. The bronze stag on the roof makes the palace distinctive from a distance. The Stupinigi now houses a museum of decorative arts.

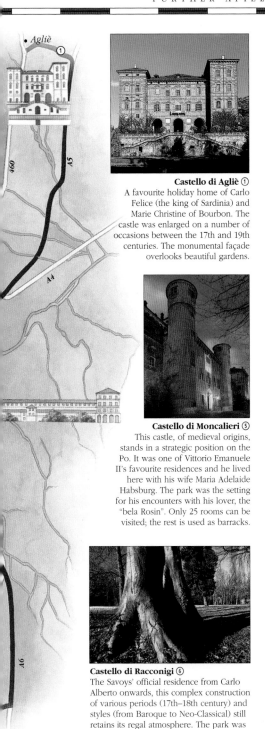

Agliè

Castello di Agliè ①

A favourite holiday home of Carlo Felice (the king of Sardinia) and Marie Christine of Bourbon. The castle was enlarged on a number of occasions between the 17th and 19th centuries. The monumental façade overlooks beautiful gardens.

Castello di Moncalieri ⑤

This castle, of medieval origins, stands in a strategic position on the Po. It was one of Vittorio Emanuele II's favourite residences and he lived here with his wife Maria Adelaide Habsburg. The park was the setting for his encounters with his lover, the "bela Rosin". Only 25 rooms can be visited; the rest is used as barracks.

Castello di Racconigi ⑥

The Savoys' official residence from Carlo Alberto onwards, this complex construction of various periods (17th–18th century) and styles (from Baroque to Neo-Classical) still retains its regal atmosphere. The park was laid out in the 1600s by André Le Nôtre.

VISITORS' CHECKLIST

Castello di Agliè, Piazza del Castello 2, Agliè (To). 012 433 01 02. **Park** Aug–Oct: 9am–1pm, 2–6pm Tue–Sun.
Reggia di Venaria Reale, Piazza della Repubblica 4, Venaria Reale (To). 011 459 36 75. 9.30–11.30am, 3–6pm Tue, Thu, Sat, Sun, hols; Mon, Wed, Fri by appt. 1 hr 30 mins. Evening visits: Sat 9pm by appt. www.lavenariareale.it
Parco Regionale La Mandria, Viale Carlo Emanuele II 256, entrance Ponte Verde, Venaria Reale (To). 011 499 33 81. 8am–6pm daily (summer: 8am–8pm). www.parks.it/parco.mandria
Castello di Rivoli, Museo di Arte Contemporanea, Piazza Mafalda di Savoia, Rivoli (To). 011 956 52 22. 10am–5pm Tue–Thu; 10am–9pm Fri–Sun. www.castellodirivoli.org
Palazzina di Caccia di Stupinigi, Piazza Principe Amedeo 7, Stupinigi, Nichelino (To). 011 358 12 20. Apr–Oct: 10am–6pm Tue–Sun; Nov–Mar: 9.30am–5pm; last adm. 1 hour before closing. Mon, 1 Jan, 1 Nov, 25 Dec. www.mauriziano.it
Castello di Moncalieri, Piazza Baden Baden 4, Moncalieri (To). 011 881 645 42. 8.30am–6.30pm Thu, Sat, Sun. groups. www. ambienteto.arti.beniculturali.it
Castello di Racconigi, Via Morosini 1, Racconigi (Cn). 017 284 005. 8.30am–7.30pm Tue–Sun. Mon, 1 Jan, 25 Dec. **Park** groups.
Centro Cicogne (Nature reserve). Via Stramiano 206, Racconigi (Cn). 017 283 457. www.cicognaracconigi.it
Castello di Govone, Piazza Roma 1, Govone (Cn). 0173 58 103. 10am–noon, 3–6pm Sun. groups.

KEY

Tour route

Other roads

Palazzina di Caccia di Stupinigi ❼

The young duke of Aosta

THE PALAZZINA DI CACCIA DI STUPINIGI, in a large park 9 km (6 miles) from the city, is a Rococo masterpiece. Designed by Filippo Juvarra in 1729 for the shooting parties of Vittorio Amedeo II, it became a royal palace and the stag on the roof testifies to its use as a hunting lodge. The layout is original: four wings in the form of a St Andrew's cross radiate from the main building and the apartments lead off from the elliptic central reception room, in which court celebrations and important weddings were held. Displayed in the frescoed rooms is the furniture of the Museo dell'Arte e Ammobiliamento, with masterpieces by Piedmontese master cabinet makers. The park is also home to Castelvecchio, a well-preserved medieval manor house.

★ Museo di Arte e Ammobiliamento
A compendium of 18th-century decorative arts, with chests of drawers, desks, sofas, tables, stools and paintings from other royal residences.

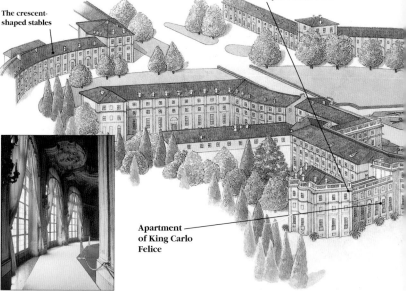

The crescent-shaped stables

Apartment of King Carlo Felice

Side Corridors
Curved corridors link the apartments of the king and queen with the central reception room where important feasts were held.

STAR SIGHTS

★ The Stag

★ Museo di Arte e Ammobiliamento

★ Reception Room

The Exterior
The upper section of the central building supports a dome, with a marble balustrade featuring statues of hunting trophies. The central façade is curved. Large windows illuminate the upper part.

★ The Stag
The original stag on the dome by Francesco Ladatte (1766) was replaced by a copy. The original is located at the entrance to the Palazzina.

VISITORS' CHECKLIST

Piazza Principe Amedeo 7, Stupinigi, Nichelino.
011 35 81 220.
Apr–Oct: 10am–6pm Tue–Sun; Nov–Mar: 9.30am–5pm; last admission 1 hr before closing. Mon, 1 Jan, 1 Nov, 25 Dec.
www.mauriziano.it

The Portraits Room includes a series of portraits of young princes and the future kings of the House of Savoy.

★ Central Reception Room

This elliptical room is embellished with Roman Baroque decorations. The wall frescoes (Triumph of Diana) and 36 "appliqués" with stags' heads, designed by Juvarra, confirm the palace's use as a hunting lodge.

Copy of Ladatte's stag

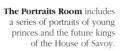

The renovated Games Room

The Queen's Apartments
The period furnishings in the queen's bedroom are perfectly preserved. The ceiling frescoes are by Carlo Andrea Van Loo (The Repose of Diana, 1733). The door panels have fanciful stucco decorations.

Hunting Scene
Four pictures painted by the Turinese landscape painter Vittorio Amedeo Cignaroli (1773–8) decorate the walls of the central section of the king's apartments. They depict oak woods, fields, hunting scenes, wide open spaces and rivers and streams.

Sant'Antonio di Ranverso **8**

SS25 Rivoli-Avigliana, Buttigliera Alta (To). **Road Map** D3. 011 936 74 50. Nov–Mar: 9am–12.30pm, 2–5pm Tue–Sun; Apr–Oct: 9am–12.30pm, 2.30–6pm Tue–Sun. Mon, 1 Jan, 1 Nov, 25, 31 Dec.

THE ABBEY COMPLEX (a church, hospital and monastery) was founded in 1188 by Umberto III of Savoy, who was known as the "Blessed". The Antonian monks who built the abbey came from Vienne in the Dauphiné region of France and dedicated their lives to healing sicknesses such as leprosy and shingles, which is also known as "St Anthony's fire". The hospital also had a shelter for pilgrims travelling on the pilgrim route from Canterbury to Rome, the Via Francigena.

Over the centuries, the abbey grew in importance and in 1470 the apse was enlarged. Three Gothic pediments on the façade create a feeling of upward movement. The Romanesque bell tower was made taller.

The three-aisle interior, with pointed arches and ribbed vaults, has numerous frescoes (*Life of St Barbara, St Anthony, St Blaise, Christ, Madonna and Child*) painted in the early 1400s by Giacomo Jaquerio (his signature can be seen in the presbytery). The abbey is considered a masterpiece of the Piedmontese Gothic style.

The church of the abbey of Sant'Antonio di Ranverso

A work by Maurizio Cattelan in a historic room of the Museo di Arte Contemporanea, Rivoli

Rivoli **9**

14 km (9 miles) from Turin. **Road Map** D3. 49,900. 36 from Turin; shuttle bus Turin–Castello di Rivoli, Sat, Sun. **FS** Alpignano, then the Satti bus. **Turismovest** Via Frejus 40bis, 011 956 10 43. Tue–Sat. Antiques, 3rd Sun in month; Spring Festival, 25 Apr; Festival of Santa Caterina, 23 Nov.

THE TOWN STANDS at one end of the Val di Susa on the banks of the Dora Riparia river: the medieval meaning of the name is "elevated place on the riverbank". Its history is linked to that of Roman Augusta Taurinorum.

In the 1200s the increasingly powerful local families formed the representative assemblies of the municipality. In the 1300s the influential Savoy family set up a residence at Castello di Rivoli. The castle's golden age coincided with the heyday of the Green Count, Amedeo VI, until the wars with the French when it was subject to sacking. After the Treaty of Utrecht (1713) Rivoli became important once again and a road was built to Turin and a more sumptuous palace was designed. The castle dominates the town from the hilltop. In the 11th century it was a fortified manor house and was gradually transformed into a magnificent residence by the royal family. Since 1984 it has housed a

fine **Museo di Arte Contemporanea**. The museum has a collection of international acclaim and a full calendar of events and temporary exhibitions. From up high you can make out the ancient bell tower of Santa Maria della Stella, in one of the town's most evocative spots. The 14th-century bell tower is all that remains of the 13th–14th-century church.

The church of Santa Croce (17th–18th-century) preserves traces of a medieval confraternity. In Via Piol, with its traditional paving, is the house of the Green Count, the brick façade decorated with tiled motifs. The building, once used as an inn and later as a Casa del Popolo (communist meeting place), now hosts exhibitions.

Museo di Arte Contemporanea
Piazza Mafalda di Savoia. 011 956 52 22. 10am–5pm Tue–Thu; 10am–9pm Fri–Sun. Mon, 1 Jan, 1 May, 25 Dec.
www.castellodirivoli.org

Parco Regionale La Mandria **10**

10 km (6 miles) from Turin. **Road Map** D–E 2–3. 72 from Turin (stops 2.5 km from park). **Borgo Castello**, 011 499 33 81. 1 Jan–15 Feb, 16 Oct–31 Dec: 8am–5pm; 16 Feb–start of summer time, start of standard time–15 Oct: 8am–6pm; summer: 8am–8pm.

THE PARK, a short distance from the city centre, is all that remains of the oak and ash forest which covered the Po river valley thousands of years ago. In the 16th century it was used by the Savoys as a hunting reserve and a stud farm. Since 1978 it has been a regional park. The wooded areas alternate with pastures, small lakes and farmland. The

Parco della Mandria

park includes important architecture, with numerous farmhouses, villas and reservoirs at Borgo Castello, a complex of over 35,000 sq m (376,737 sq ft), and at Castello dei Laghi. Visitors can walk or cycle here; there are picnic areas, horse riding, carriage rides, exhibitions and events.

Moncalieri ⓫

8 km (5 miles) from Turin. **Road Map** E3. 🏠 53,500. 🚌 67, 45, 40, 70, 39 from Turin. 🚉 ℹ **Pro Loco** Via Real Collegio 20, 011 640 74 28. 📅 Tue. 🎭 Carnival; Fera dij Subiét, Oct.

MONCALIERI GREW UP around the 12th-century Benedictine monastery of Sant'Egidio and became a free town in 1230. From the 14th century it was a busy trading town and this formed the basis of the merchant classes. Today the town is spread over a large area at the edge of Turin. The **castello**, now a museum with antique furniture, dominates the town. The various phases of its construction can be seen in the contrast between its

round medieval towers and its square Baroque ones.

Piazza Maggiore is the centre of the town. Porticoes border three sides and there are some fine buildings. The Osservatorio Meteorologico Real Collegio Carlo Alberto was founded in 1859 and holds a fine collection of antique instruments.

♣ Castello di Moncalieri
Piazza Baden Baden 4. ℹ 011 640 28 83. 📅 Thu, Sat, Sun: 9am–6pm. 🔲 📷

Chieri ⓬

13 km (8 miles) from Turin. **Road Map** F3. 🏠 32,800. 🚌 30, 70, 170, 175 from Turin. 🚉 Piazza Don Bosco. ℹ Via Palazzo di Città 10, 011 947 33 11. 🎭 Primavera della Collina, 3 days in Apr; Santi Giuliano e Basilissa, 21 May; Fiera San Martino, 8–16 Nov.

OF PARTICULAR NOTE among the many churches in the old part of this town is the Piedmontese-Gothic style Duomo (1405–35). It has a brick façade and the interior boasts a fine baptistery, with frescoes by Guglielmetto Fantini, and a crypt, which is beneath the main altar. The history of Chieri is bound up with that of the textile trade and the **Museo del Tessile** (textile museum), in the former convent of Santa Chiara, has instruments used for dyeing cloth.

ENVIRONS: the **Museo Martini di Storia dell'Enologia**, in the small village of Pessione, explains the various processes

involved in wine-making. The exhibits are on display in the cellars of the first Martini & Rossi factory, which dates from the 18th century.

🏛 Museo del Tessile
Via G Demaria 10. ℹ 011 942 74 21. 📅 by appt. 🔲 ♿
🏛 Museo Martini di Storia dell'Enologia
Piazza L Rossi 1, Pessione. ℹ 011 941 91. 📅 Sep–Jul: 2–5pm Tue–Fri, 9am–12 noon, 2–5pm Sat, Sun. ● Mon, 11, 25 Apr, Aug. 🔲 ♿ 📷

Romanesque Abbey of Vezzolano

Abbazia di Vezzolano ⓭

34 km (21 miles) from Turin. **Road Map** F3. ℹ 011 992 06 07. 📅 summer: 2pm–6pm Tue–Sun; winter: 9.30am–1pm; 2–5pm Tue–Sun.

THIS ABBEY, which stands at the foot of the hill below the small town of Albugnano, enjoyed a golden age in the 12th–13th century. The present church, built over a pre-existing building in 1110–89, has a Romanesque brick and sandstone façade divided in three by two buttresses. A mullioned window with two lights in the upper section is decorated with statues.

The interior, with two aisles and two apses with pointed arches and cross vaults, has frescoes and reliefs from the 12th, 13th and 14th centuries. A particular feature is the narthex, a porticoed atrium supported by five arcades which crosses the full length of the main aisle, on which there is a bas relief (1189) with the 35 patriarch forefathers of the Virgin Mary.

Antique instruments in the Osservatorio Meteorologico at Moncalieri

THE VALLEYS
AREA BY AREA

THE VALLEYS AT A GLANCE 108-109
VAL DI SUSA 110-133
THE CHISONE AND GERMANASCA VALLEYS 134-153
VAL PELLICE 154-171

The Valleys at a Glance

JUST A SHORT DISTANCE FROM TURIN lies a series of valleys whose history and development have always been linked to the city. Many important defensive structures, such as the forts of Exilles and Fenestrelle, were built in the area. Since Roman times Val di Susa and Val Chisone have been thoroughfares for traders, travellers and pilgrims. This led to the building of large abbeys and places of worship – such as San Michele. Many small frescoed chapels dot Val di Susa. The populating of the valleys dates from ancient times and there is still a strong Waldensian community in Val Pellice. Various eco-museums have been set up in recent years to display the crafts and traditions which are deeply rooted in the local culture. Summer is the time to explore the parks, while winter is the time for skiing at one of the resorts in the Chisone and Susa valleys. The well-equipped towns of Sestrière, Cesana, Sauze d'Oulx, Pragelato and Bardonecchia have been chosen to host the 2006 Winter Olympic Games.

Parco Naturale Orsiera-Rocciavré *(pp120–21)*

The Parco del Gran Bosco di Salbertrand (pp126–7) *covers the right slopes of Val di Susa at a height of between 1,000–2,600 m (3,280–8,530 ft). The reserve was founded in 1980 to protect the lush vegetation, and particularly the forests of fir and larch. Many bird species come to this area to nest and there are also deer, roebuck and chamois.*

THE CHISONE AND GERMANASCA VALLEYS *(pp134–53)*

The Forte di Fenestrelle *(pp142–3) is one of the most impressive military structures in Europe. It was built for Vittorio Amedeo of Savoy and construction began in 1728. The fort was never attacked and at the end of the 18th century it was converted into a jail for high-ranking prisoners. Forte San Carlo, just above the valley floor, can be visited, as well as Forte Tre Denti and Forte delle Valli, higher up.*

◁ The Monti della Luna group, Valle del Thuras, Alta Val di Susa

The Sacra di San Michele (pp116–19) *was probably founded by the Lombards. It was an important, influential centre for study and had a famous library. The church, dating from the 12th century, stands at the top of Monte Pirchiriano, supported by impressive buttresses. The terraces offer splendid views of the lower valley and the surrounding mountains.*

| 0 kilometres | 10 |
| 0 miles | 10 |

VAL DI SUSA
(pp110–33)

Pinerolo
(pp158–9)

VAL PELLICE
(pp154–71)

Alta Val Pellice
(pp164–5), *reached from Bobbio Pellice, is a paradise for hikers and mountaineers and there are plenty of refuges in the area. Monviso's massive form is clearly visible from panoramic viewpoints. The Conca del Prà and the Valle dei Carbonieri are some of the most charming spots.*

Torre Pellice
(pp160–61) *is the heart of the Waldensian museum network. This church was built just after the Waldensians gained relicious freedom in 1848, but there are older ones in the valley. The statue of pastor Arnaud commemorates the Great Repatriation of 1689, after exile abroad.*

VAL DI SUSA

V AL DI SUSA *runs from the outskirts of Turin to the Alps, and has always been one of the most populated valleys in Piedmont. The main reason for this is its wide, almost flat, open spaces which make the valley easily accessible. Since Roman times it has been used as a highway to France, and many important traces of the valley's eventful history can still be seen in the area.*

Val di Susa is the result of erosion by the Dora Riparia river, which flows into the river Po in the city of Turin. The valley begins to close in beyond the morainic amphitheatre of Rivoli and, from here, continues on to the foot of the Monginevro and Moncenisio mountain passes.

Val di Susa's varied history is clearly evident: the Romans left important traces of their achievements and government in Susa. Dating from the Middle Ages are the frescoed vaults in dozens of chapels, such as in the impressive Sacra di San Michele.

The period of the great conflicts for rule over Europe is remembered in the impressive structure of Forte di Exilles which, like the Fenestrelle fort in the nearby Val Chisone, testifies to the continuing passage of armies who fought for these regions lying around the present-day borders of Italy and France. The lower and wider part of the valley, which is also known as Comba di Susa, boasts many places of cultural interest, chief of which are the Sacra di San Michele, Susa, the abbey of Novalesa and the Forte di Exilles.

During the 20th century, the higher part of the valley, once used for mountain crops and summer pastures, became one the most important skiing areas in the western Alps, with the ski resorts of Bardonecchia, Oulx and Cesana. These towns are connected by state-of-the-art ski lifts to the slopes of Sestrière, at the end of Val Chisone.

A number of important motorways and railway lines with international links run through Val di Susa. Work is currently under way on a modern, high-speed rail track which, in around 2010, will connect the city of Turin to Lyon in France, passing through what will be one of the longest tunnels in the world.

Fresco in the Abbey of Novalesa, showing St Eldradus working the land so as to better serve the pilgrims

◁ The area of Moncenisio viewed from Forte Varisello

Exploring Val di Susa

THE VALLEY OF SUSA offers visitors a variety of historical places of interest and areas of natural beauty to visit. The most important sights, apart from the Sacra di San Michele, are the Charterhouse of Monte Benedetto, the Roman and medieval remains in the town of Susa and the fresco cycles in the abbey of Novalesa. The impressive, even sinister structure of Forte di Exilles is also of interest for the exhibitions that are held there. The natural landscape in the upper valleys is varied, and the Parco Naturale Orsiera Rocciavré and the Parco Naturale del Gran Bosco di Salbertrand are especially charming in the summer. There are interesting traces of religious culture and country life in the small towns in the valley, particularly in Bardonecchia. The ski slopes in the highest part of the valley are popular in the winter season.

The parish church at Salbertrand, with 16th-century frescoes

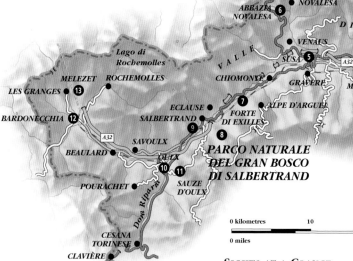

0 kilometres   10

0 miles   10

SIGHTS AT A GLANCE

Abbazia di Novalesa **6**

Avigliana **1**

Bardonecchia **12**

Certosa di Monte Benedetto **4**

Forte di Exilles **7**

Parco Naturale del Gran Bosco di Salbertrand pp126–7 **8**

Melezet **13**

Oulx **10**

Parco Naturale Orsiera – Rocciavré pp120–21 **3**

Sacra di San Michele pp116–17 **2**

Salbertrand **9**

Sauze d'Oulx **11**

Susa pp122–4 **5**

Fir trees in the Parco del Gran Bosco di Salbertrand

GETTING AROUND

It is very easy to get to Val di Susa from Turin. The A32 motorway links Turin with Bardonecchia (72 km/45 miles) and has exits for Rivoli, Avigliana, Borgone, Chianocco, Susa and Oulx. The SS25 road through Val di Susa runs alongside the motorway and is more convenient for getting to the various tourist attractions in the valley. All the main towns in Val di Susa are served by the railway which connects Turin with Bardonecchia. From here you can reach France by going in the direction of Modane. The nearest airport is that of Caselle in Turin, from which a short ring road joins up to the A32 motorway.

The Sacra di San Michele, dominating the top of Monte Pirchiriano, at the mouth of Val di Susa

SEE ALSO

• *Where to Stay* p178

• *Where to Eat* p190

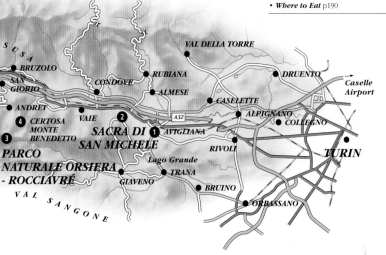

VAL DELLA TORRE
SUSA
BRUZOLO
SAN GIORIO
CONDOVE
RUBIANA
DRUETO
Caselle Airport
ANDRET
ALMESE
CASELETTE
VAIE
ALPIGNANO
COLLEGNO
4 CERTOSA MONTE BENEDETTO
2
A32
AVIGLIANA
3
SACRA DI SAN MICHELE
1
RIVOLI
TURIN
PARCO NATURALE ORSIERA - ROCCIAVRÉ
Lago Grande
TRANA
GIAVENO
BRUINO
VAL SANGONE
ORBASSANO

The stone houses of Moncenisio, the first stopping place in Italy for travellers on the Via Francigena pilgrim route

KEY

▬	Motorway
▬	Major road
▬	Minor road
—	Other roads
—	River
▬	Provincial border
▬	International border
▬	Railway line

One of the two lakes of Avigliana, depressions at the entrance to Val di Susa

Avigliana ❶

Turin. **Map** D3. ⚒ *11,200.*
🚃 *Turin–Modane line.*
ℹ **Town Hall** Piazza Conte Rosso 7,
011 976 91 11; **Montagnedoc**
Corso Torino 6, *011 936 60 37.*
🏛 *Thu am.* 🎪 *Flea market, 2nd
Sun in month.*
🆆 www.montagnedoc.it,
www.comune.avigliana.to.it

A VIGLIANA is a
busy, lively
town with an
ancient heart. The
original nucleus of
the town, perched
on the northern
slopes of Monte
Pezzulano at 400 m
(1,310 ft), deserves
a leisurely visit –
many traces of the
Middle Ages can
still be seen. Casa di Porta
Ferrata, a 13th-century house,
is one example, providing
useful evidence of the
decorative architectural
elements used at the time,
with arches, corbels and
fantasy figures.

Casa Senore, also known as
the bishop's house, has a
characteristic portico with
pointed arches, brick cornices
and stone capitals which also
date from the 13th century.

A castle stood on the top of
the small hill of Pezzulano,
but it was destroyed by
Maresciallo Catinat in 1691.
The building seen on the site
today dates from just after the
year 1000. It is known that it

**Logo of the Parco
dei Laghi di Avigliana**

was used by the House of
Savoy from 1137 and was a
court residence. Today it
offers a splendid panoramic
view over the lakes and town.

A visit to the town should
include Piazza Conte Rosso,
where you can see the
various styles of construction
used over the years. Around
the asymmetrical square there
are pointed arches and
sculpted capitals dating from
the Middle Ages
and buildings from
the 17th and 18th
centuries. Of
particular interest
is the church of
San Giovanni
which dates from
the 13th century.
Originally it
probably had a
Latin cross plan and
the side chapels were added
to the single nave in the 17th
century. The interior houses a
16th-century pulpit, as well as
paintings by Defendente
Ferrari and other works from
his studio.

Just outside the town are
the two lakes of Avigliana,
Riss and Würm (the latter was
formed 120,000 years ago),
which were created during
the last glaciations. The
definitive receding of the
glaciers dates from around
10,000 years ago when water
covered the entire area,
including that between the
moraines. Later, four lake
basins were formed: one of
which became the peat bog

of Trana; another is in the
area known as the Mareschi
marsh. Today, much of the
area, which also includes
these two lakes, is protected
by the **Parco Naturale dei
Laghi di Avigliana**.

In the park there are seven
marked trails, such as the
Sentiero Lungo Lago
(lakeside path), the Sentiero
della Palude (marsh path)
and the Sentiero Collinare
(hill path). A stretch of the
Via dei Pellegrini (pilgrims'
way) runs along what was
once the bank of the ancient
post-glacial lake, which
covered the entire area. The
road begins at Castello di
Rivoli, passes through
Avigliana and goes on to the
Sacra di San Michele, which
stands at the top of Monte
Pirchiriano, at over 1,000 m
(3,280 ft).

The route through the
lower valley takes in the
towns of Rivoli, Rosta, Trana,
Reano, Buttigliera Alta,
Avigliana and Sant'Ambrogio.
The numerous boulders that

**Fungi growing on the plain
around the town**

dot the area reveal the power and extent of the glaciers.

🍀 **Parco Naturale dei Laghi di Avigliana** *Via Monte Pirchiriano 54, Avigliana.* 📞 *011 931 30 00.* **Visitors' Centre** 🕐 *8.30am–12 noon, 2.30–4.30pm Mon–Thu (3.30pm Fri).*

Sacra di San Michele ❷

See pp116–17.

Parco Naturale Orsiera-Rocciavré ❸

See pp120–21.

Certosa di Montebenedetto ❹

Turin. **Map** *C3.* 🚆 *Borgone station, Turin–Modane line.* 🏠 **Comune di Villar Focchiardo** *Via Carroccio 30, 011 964 50 25;* **Parco Orsiera–Rocciavré** *Via San Rocco 2, Bussoleno, 0122 470 64;* **Associazione Cartusia** *011 964 65 64.* 🕐 *Summer: 2pm–6pm Sat & Sun.* 🎟 *11am, 2 & 4pm Sun, bookings on 011 964 60 57.*

I**N THE EARLY PART OF** 1200 a community of Carthusian monks settled in this sheltered valley in the Villar

The Romanesque Charterhouse of Montebenedetto

Focchiardo mountains. The monastic order was founded in 1084 by St Bruno at Chartreuse in France and gradually expanded. The location of the charterhouse was carefully chosen to fit in with the Carthusian ideal of a "desert": a place for monks to live in solitude suitable for prayer and meditation.

The monastery of Montebenedetto was used until the end of 1400, when it was abandoned by the monks, who moved to a charterhouse at Banda, lower down in the valley. The church, one of the few to retain its original features, is well preserved thanks to restoration work funded by the park.

Inside, the park authorities have set up a permanent exhibition about the Carthusian religious order and the charterhouses of Montebenedetto and Banda.

A short walk around the area will take you to the evocative ruins of the "lower house" (a separate part of the monastery used by lay brothers who did the manual work) and the remains of the cells. The charterhouse can be reached from Villar Focchiardo, and the hamlet of Castellaro, 632 m (2,075 ft), can be reached by car. From here, a winding road leads to the charterhouse.

A fresco in the Charterhouse of Montebenedetto

An explosion in 1900 at the Dinamitificio Nobel

INDUSTRIAL ARCHAEOLOGY

The museum of Dinamitificio Nobel (Nobel dynamite factory) stands in a wood at the edge of Avigliana and was created with the aim of preserving this historically interesting production site. The factory was built in 1872, and was operative until 1965. It employed over 200 workers who produced dynamite (600 kg/1,325 lb a day), and various by-products. By the end of the 19th century the factory had electricity, an internal railway which linked it to Avigliana and a chemical laboratory. Expansion, mostly facilitated by excavating part of the hillside, also made the production of acids and phosphates possible. After the two world wars, when production was at its peak, work at the factory declined and it began producing explosives for mining work, construction and road building. In the 1960s, Dinamitificio was closed and the abandoned buildings were in part converted to other uses or demolished. The museum was opened in 1999 in order to make use of the abandoned section, which has unusual features peculiar to the production of explosives. Guided tours must be booked ahead; contact the Parco Naturale dei Laghi di Avigliana for information. 🕐 *by appt Mon–Fri, 2–6pm Sun.* 📞 *011 93 41 405 (9am–12 noon, Mon–Fri).*

Sacra di San Michele ❷

THE SACRA DI SAN MICHELE, or Abbazia della Chiusa (962 m/3,155 ft), was probably founded by the Lombards and the cult of the Archangel Michael became widespread here. History, however, tells that at the end of the year 900 a disciple of San Romualdo founded the oldest church on the mountain, thanks to a donation by the nobleman Ugo di Montboissier. Built by the road used by pilgrims on their way to Rome and the Italian shrines, the Sacra soon became an important study centre, with a large library crowded with copyists: it was also fortified. Its influence and power grew until it controlled 176 churches and abbeys in Italy, France and Spain. The present-day basilica, supported by impressive buttresses, dates from the 12th century.

The capitals of the Porta dello Zodiaco
The symbolic figures represent women tearing out their hair or breast feeding serpents, and lions with dragons' heads and tails. The biblical ones represent Cain and Abel and Samson and Delilah.

The Sacra by night
At night, the illuminated Sacra can be seen from a great distance. On Saturday evenings in August there are night visits to the churches, new monastery, the monks' workshop and Torre della Bell'Alda.

A triptych by Defendente Ferrari, depicting the Madonna, St John and St Michael (16th century), can be seen on the west wall of the old choir.

STAR SIGHTS

★ **Porta dello Zodiaco**

★ **Scalone dei Morti**

★ **Torre della Bell'Alda**

The Exterior
The building, damaged in local wars, took on its present appearance at the end of the 1800s following restoration work by the Portuguese architect Alfredo d'Andrade for Carlo Felice and Carlo Alberto. The complex was later entrusted to the Rosminian fathers.

★ Porta dello Zodiaco

The marble bas reliefs on the door, with biblical stories and allegorical representations, are the work of the architect and sculptor Nicolao (12th century).

VISITORS' CHECKLIST

Via Sacra di S. Michele 14, SS589 from Avigliana, or on foot from Sant'Ambrogio. **Map** D3.
📞 *011 939 130.* ⏰ *16 Oct–15 Mar: 9.30am–12.30pm, 2.40–5pm Mon–Fri, 9.30am–12 noon, 3–5pm Sat, Sun, hols; 16 Mar–15 Oct: 9.30am–12.30pm, 3–6pm Mon–Fri, 9.30am–12 noon, 2.40–6pm hols.* ⏺ Mon. 🎦 🅿
✝ *8.15pm Wed; 12 noon, 6.30pm Sun, hols; 9pm Fri.*
🌐 www.sacradisanmichele.com

The Belvedere terrace

★ Torre della Bell'Alda

Legend has it that Alda, who threw herself from the tower to escape a soldier of fortune, was miraculously saved by angels. She died when she jumped a second time, while attempting to demonstrate the truth of her story.

The Loggia dei Viretti is a crown of arches which rests on 16 columns, each with capitals decorated with friezes.

★ Scalone dei Morti

This steep, dark staircase, known as the Staircase of the Dead, leads to the church and the Porta dello Zodiaco. At one time the tombs of the monks were placed here (hence its name); today only five can be seen (until recently it was also possible to see the skeletons). A pillar 18 m (60 ft) high, on the left after the initial steps, supports the church above.

A footpath from Colle della Croce Nera leads up to the Sepolcro dei Monaci. Having passed the fortified guest quarters and the Porta di Ferro, you reach the complex itself. From the entrance doorway there is a long monumental staircase leading up to the splendid Porta dello Zodiaco.

An atmospheric sunset over Monte Pirchiriano and the Sacra di San Michele ▷

Parco Naturale Orsiera-Rocciavré ❸

T HIS PARK WAS FOUNDED IN 1980. It covers an area of 11,000 ha (27,180 acres) on the massif that divides Val di Susa from Val Chisone and surrounds the top of Val Sangone. The park is named after two massif peaks: Orsiera (2,878 m/9,445 ft) and Rocciavré, which is the only peak common to all three valleys. The natural environment is wild and has seen little interference by man. However, civic, religious and military settlements from the past can be found as well as forts, chapels and archaeological sites with prehistoric remains. Cars should be parked at one of the entrances and visitors then continue along the marked trails. Mountin refuges and other kinds of accommodation are available.

Monte Orsiera
This is the highest mountain in the park (2,878 m/9,445 ft), while Rocciavré is a major peak between three valleys.

Chamois
It is common to see chamois, deer, roebuck, wild boar and moufflon in the area. Higher pastures are home to marmots, stoats, mountain pheasants and hares. At the lower levels are badgers, martens, foxes, squirrels, jays and wall creepers.

0 kilometres   2.5

0 miles   2

• Meana

Mattie

M. Pintas
2,543 m/
8,345 ft

M. Boulian
2,001 m/
6,565 ft

Torr. Scaglione

Rio Arneirone

Rio Gorreite

M. Carlei
2,441 m/
8,010 ft

M. Rognone
2,354 m/
7,725 ft

Rio Orsiera

M. Francaise Pelouxe
2,736 m/8,890 ft

M. Pelvo
2,770 m/
9,090 ft

Lago Clardonnet

Lago Gayia

M. Rocciavré
2,778 m/
9,115 ft

GTA

GTA

A small museum is dedicated to the park's wildlife.

Visitors' Centre at Pra Catinat

Chisone   23

• Villaretto

Forte di Fenestrelle
The park also boasts important examples of military architecture, such as the impressive fort of Fenestrelle (see pp142–3), which rises from 1,150 m (3,770 ft) at Fenestrelle to almost 2,000 m (6,560 ft) at Prà Catinat.

Park Wardens
Alpine guides and park wardens protect the safety of the park's visitors and its fauna, and also lead excursions within the park.

Chianocco

The Riserva dell'Orrido di Chianocco protects the only area in Piedmont where holm oak grows wild. It covers 26 ha (65 acres) in an area separate from the park as a whole. The orrido *referred to in the name is a gorge eroded by the river Prebèc, 50 m (165 ft) deep and 10 m (33 ft) wide.*

VISITORS' CHECKLIST

Turin. **Map** C3.

🚉 Bussoleno station, then by bus. ℹ️ **Val Susa** Via San Rocco 2, frazione Foresto, Bussoleno, 0122 47 064.

ℹ️ **Val Chisone** Prà Catinat 2, Fenestrelle, 0122 837 57.

Ⓦ www.parco-orsiera.it

Lago Paradiso delle Rane

San Giorio

Dora Riparia

24

Villar Focchiardo

Torr. Gravio

GTA/SF

M. Cormetto
2,050 m/
6,725 ft

GTA/SF

M. Salancia
2,088 m/
6,850 ft

GTA/SF

M. Villano
2,663 m/
8,735 ft

M. Muretto
2,277 m/
7,470 ft

Lago Rosso

Roccia Rossa
2,397 m/
7,865 ft

Lago Blu

M. Pian Real
2,617 m/8,590 ft

M. P. del Lago
2,632 m/8,635 ft

Rio Rocciavré

Rio della Balma

Lago Soprano

Segnale Carasa
2,035 m/6,680 ft

Lago Sottano

Lago Rouen

GTA

Certosa di Monte Benedetto

This charterhouse (1200) was abandoned in favour of Banda, at lower altitude. The church houses an exhibition about Carthusian monks and two charter-houses (see pp114–15).

Cappella della Madonna della Neve at Pian dell'Orso

KEY

▬▬▬ Scenic route

▬▬▬ Minor road

░░░░ Other roads

▬■▬ Paths

ℹ️ Information

Monte Robinet

From Monte Robinet (2,679 m/8,790 ft) you can enjoy a marvellous view of Val Sangone. The chapel on the summit has a small room which is used as a refuge. An easy route to the top (four hours) starts at the Sellerie refuge (2,023 m/6,640 ft).

Susa ❺

FOUNDED BY LIGURIANS AND CELTS, Susa was a major town on the way to Gaul, the capital of the kingdom of Donno, and was allied with Caesar. Independence ended in Nero's reign and the town, then Segusia, was given a commemorative arch, gates and a theatre. Despite its fortifications, it was destroyed by Constantine in 312 and in around 900, it was controlled for over 50 years by Arabs from the Moorish kingdom of Albenga and Provence. It was given in dowry to Oddone by Adelaide and was a stopping place for people on the Via Francigena pilgrim route. Part of the Savoy estates, Susa controlled roads to Monginevro and Moncenisio.

Arch built in 8 BC in honour of Emperor Augustus

Exploring Susa

The most important monuments in the town, which is dominated by the peak of Rocciamelone, date from the time of the Roman era and from the Middle Ages. The old centre of Susa is Piazza San Giusto, which is overlooked by Porta Savoia and the town's cathedral.

On the other side of the river Dora is the Chiesa del Ponte, home to the Museo Diocesano d'Arte Sacra. The church, founded in the 1400s, was completely renovated in 1597 to house the confraternity of Spirito Santo.

🏛 Arco di Augusto and Anfiteatro

Amphitheatre ⬚ *7.30am–8pm daily.*
Cozio I built the Arch of Augustus between 9 and 8 BC. The arch stands in the park of the same name, not far from the old town centre. Made of local white stone, it is decorated with a series of interesting friezes, including a bas relief of a sacrificial ritual and the alliance between

Cozio I and the Roman emperor. This area was once the site of the *castrum* (on which the castle of the Arduinici was later built); the ruins of a small Roman amphitheatre can still be seen here. This structure later provided the building materials for the nearby church of San Francesco.

🏠 Cattedrale

Piazza San Giusto 6.
📞 *0122 622 053.*
⬚ *9am–6.30pm daily.*
The church, dedicated to San Giusto, was built for Olderico Manfredi in the first half of the 11th century and bears traces of many different styles with Gothic and Graeco-Byzantine influences. The church has a curious form: at one time its façade stood outside the town walls; this was then walled up but later reopened.

The large Romanesque bell tower, 50 m/165 ft high, has a bas relief on the plinth

Wooden statue, 12th century

and its six storeys are decorated with arches.

The cathedral's three-aisle interior is supported by pilasters and has an exceptional wooden choir (1300s) from the nearby church of Santa Maria Maggiore, access to the baptistry, and a Baroque altar decorated with a triptych, probably by Borgognone.

🏛 Porta Savoia

This gateway is joined to the church of San Giusto. Built in the late Imperial period, it has two large cylindrical towers, probably originally higher than they are now. Openings allowed the gate to be defended on all sides.

🏛 Museo Diocesano di Arte Sacra di Susa

Via Mazzini 1. 📞 *0122 622 640.*
⬚ *Oct–Jun: 2.30–6.30pm Sat, Sun; Jul–Sep: 9.30am–12 noon, 3.30–7pm Tue–Sun (book in advance).* ⬤ *Mon (except Aug).*
✉ @ museo@centro culturalediocesano.it
🌐 www.centroculturale diocesano.it
This museum is a fundamental source of information for understanding the history of religious art in the Val di Susa. It is housed in part of the church of the Madonna del Ponte. Built in the mid-13th century, the church was completely restructured in the 17th century and became the seat of the confraternity of Spirito Santo. The museum has three sections: the first

View of Susa with the bell tower of the church of San Giusto on the left

The Roman arch between the towers of Porta Savoia

includes the treasury of the cathedral of San Giusto, the second houses works usually kept in the church of the Madonna del Ponte, and the third has objects from churches and chapels around the diocese of Susa.

Passing through the room that houses the treasury of San Giusto (where a Lombard casket is one of the highlights), decorations from the portal and lovely frescoes from the abandoned church

of Santa Maria Maggiore, you come to the most important and evocative work in the museum. This is a 12th-century Pyrenean wooden statue of the *Madonna del Ponte* which has become the symbol of the museum.

In the old sacristy are more statues and a collection of sacred vestments, while on the floor above you can admire the triptych of the *Madonna del Rocciamelone*, a work in bronze dated 1358 which, according to legend, was carried by a knight to the top of the mountain of Susa to fulfil a vow. This section of the museum has displays of wooden statues from various periods which testify to the great creativity and craftsmanship found in the valley from the 15th to 18th centuries.

🔒 Chiesa di San Francesco
Piazza San Francesco 3. 📞 0122 622 548. ⏱ 9am–6.30pm Mon–Sun.
Material to build the church of San Francesco, founded in 1244 by Beatrice of Geneva, was taken from the Roman amphitheatre. Although the exterior is very simple, as

VISITORS' CHECKLIST

Turin. **Map** B2. 🏠 6,600. 🚉
Turin–Lyon line. 🚌 *SAPAV, 800 801 901.* 🏢 **Assessorato Turismo e Cultura** *0122 622 694;* **Pro Loco** *Corso Inghilterra 39, 0122 622 470.* 🗓 *Tue.* 🎪 *Tournament, Jul.* 🌐 *www.prosusa.it, www.montagnedoc.it*

required by Franciscan rules, the church has Gothic and Romanesque features and is worth visiting for the fragments of fresco cycles from the 15th century.

♜ Castello
Courtyard ⏱ 10am–6pm. **Museum** ⬤ *for restoration.* 🏢 **Associazione Amici del Castello**, at the library, Via al Castello 16. 📞 0122 622 694.
Built on the site of King Cozio I's palace, this castle, which dominates Susa, was the seat of government and a military garrison. Only the courtyard is open to visitors. The castle now houses an eclectic Museo Civico (founded 1884) with historic collections and a room of Egyptian exhibits.

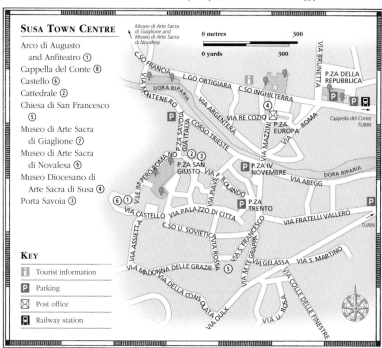

SUSA TOWN CENTRE

Arco di Augusto
  and Anfiteatro ①
Cappella del Conte ⑧
Castello ⑥
Cattedrale ②
Chiesa di San Francesco
  ⑤
Museo di Arte Sacra
  di Giaglione ⑦
Museo di Arte Sacra
  di Novalesa ⑨
Museo Diocesano di
  Arte Sacra di Susa ④
Porta Savoia ③

KEY

🏢	Tourist information
🅿	Parking
✉	Post office
🚉	Railway station

0 metres   300
0 yards   300

Museo di Arte Sacra di Giaglione and Museo di Arte Sacra di Novalesa

P.ZA DELLA REPUBBLICA
VIA BRUNETTA
Cappella del Conte TURIN
C.SO FRANCIA
L.GO ORTIGIARA
VIA MONTENERO
DORA RIPARIA
C.SO INGHILTERRA
VIA ARGENTERA
VIA RE COZIO
P.ZA SAVOIA
CORSO TRIESTE
GIA ITALIA
P.ZA EUROPA
VIA MAZZINI
VIA ROMA
VIA IMPERO ROMANO
P.ZA SAN GIUSTO
VIA F. ROLANDO
VIA PIAVE
P.ZA IV NOVEMBRE
VIA ABEGG
DORA RIPARIA
VIA CASTELLO
VIA PALAZZO DI CITTA
P.ZA TRENTO
VIA FRATELLI VALLERO
TURIN
VIA ASSIETTA
C.SO U. SOVIETICA
VIA ROSSA
VIA S. FRANCESCO
VIA MTE GRAPPA
VIA GELASSA
VIA S. MARTINO
VIA MADONNA DELLE GRAZIE
VIA DELLA CONS.LATA
VIA COLLE DELLE FINESTRE
VIA OULX
VIA U. ROSA

⛪ Museo di Arte Religiosa Alpina di Giaglione

Via Sant'Andrea 1, Giaglione. ☎ 0122 622 640. ◯ bookings at the Museo di Susa, 0122 622 640. ♿ Ⓦ www.centroculturalediocesano.it
Housed in the parsonage next to the parish church of San Lorenzo Martire, this museum contains an exceptional range of the valley's wooden statuary art, with works from the surrounding towns but also from the more distant French Maurienne. Of particular note are the statues made by the Clappier di Bessans family of wood carvers, which cover a period of almost three centuries.

🔓 Cappella del Conte

Piazza della Chiesa, San Giorio di Susa. ☎ 0122 647 459. ◯ Apr–Jun, Sep: 3.30–6pm Sun; Jul, Aug: 4–7pm Sun; other times by appt. ☎ 0122 622 640. ♿ Ⓦ www.centroculturalediocesano.it
This chapel is part of the diocesan museum system and was built next to the old pilgrim route, the Via Francigena, on a site where chapels hewn from the rock confirm the presence of a Celtic place of worship.

Built in its present form in 1328 for Lorenzetto Bertrandi, the lord of the castle of San Giorio, the Cappella del Conte boasts a fine fresco cycle. Painted by a French-Piedmontese master in around the third decade of the 14th century, the frescoes (restored in 2000) narrate the legend of three living knights and three deceased, stories of the life of San Lorenzo and other images clearly aimed at promoting a life of faith.

San Lorenzo, Giaglione

⛪ Museo di Arte Religiosa Alpina di Novalesa

Via Maestra 19. ◯ by appt at the Museo Diocesano di Arte Sacra di Susa, 0122 622 640. ♿ Ⓦ www.centroculturalediocesano.it
This museum in Novalesa, not far from the abbey of the same name, forms part of the confraternity chapel of the Santissimo Sacramento, next to the parish church of Santo

---

THE DIOCESAN MUSEUMS IN VAL DI SUSA

The tradition of frescoing chapels in the valley of Susa is very old and closely correlated to the frequent passing of pilgrims who, having crossed the alpine passes, continued on down to Rome along the old trading routes. Many small churches boast a fresco or a valuable statue. A new initiative for visitors and art enthusiasts is the founding of a network of museums, which makes it possible to comfortably and easily view the valley's entire treasury of religious art.

Detail of a fresco (1328), Cappella del Conte, San Giorio

Stefano. Of particular interest among the objects on display, mementoes of the passage of pilgrims from the nearby Moncenisio Hospice, are a Lombard casket and various objects of worship from the Carolingian period, as well as a 12th-century silver urn, made to contain the remains of St Eldradus, the abbot of Novalesa.

The museum also has some good paintings, including a *Crucifixion of Peter* in the Caravaggesque style, an *Adoration of the Magi* from the school of Rubens and a *Deposition of Christ* by Daniele da Volterra, which Napoleon had transferred to the hospice and then on to Novalesa.

Fresco in the chapel of Sant'Eldrado, showing the saint receiving a habit

---

Abbazia di Novalesa ⑥

Borgata San Pietro. **Map** B2. ☎ 0122 653 210. **Church** ◯ 9–12 noon, 3.30–5.30pm Mon–Sat; 9am–12 noon Sun. **Chapels** ◯ 🎟 only, 10.30am, 4.30pm Mon–Sat; 9–11.30am Sat, Sun. Ⓦ www.abbazianovalesa.org

AT THE BEGINNING of the 8th century, Val di Susa contained the borders of the Lombard dominions and also provinces controlled by the Franks. On 30 January 726 the Frankish nobleman Abbone decided to found an abbey at Novalesa, not far from the Moncenisio pass. The monastic Benedictine settlement grew and became so important that it acquired numerous estates in the Kingdom of the Franks, and even Charlemagne himself was one of its guests. In 906, a raid by Saracens from Provence destroyed the abbey and much of the library. Novalesa was restored and used again, but the abbey never really regained its former glory and remained subject to the monastery at Breme.

Closed as a place of worship by the Savoys in 1855, the abbey then became a boarding school. It was again entrusted to Benedictine monks in the 1970s.

The abbey is dedicated to the saints Peter and Andrew. In front of the façade is a courtyard dating from 1715, which gives access to the church. The circular apse is a later addition to the original simple rectangular-shaped church. On the left-hand side of the church, level with the present-day floor and lower, are frescoes dating from the 11th century, depicting the stoning of St Stephen.

The abbey cloister, also altered on various occasions, retains only two sides of the original portico. The frescoes here were only recently discovered, and have just been restored.

Outside the abbey are the chapels of Salvatore (dating from the 11th century) and San Michele, founded in an earlier period. There is also a small church, dedicated to St Eldradus, the abbot of Novalesa, where there are some splendid frescoes from the 11th century. In the church's apse is a Byzantine-style Christ Pantocrator, flanked by St Eldradus and St Nicholas of Bari: legend has it that a crusader returning from the Holy Land left a relic of the latter saint, who came from Asia Minor, here at Novalesa.

The nave is divided into two sections: in the first are scenes depicting the life of St Eldradus, while the second section, nearer the altar, has representations of the life and works of St Nicholas, including his election as bishop of Myra, in Asia Minor.

The atmospheric Forte di Exilles

Forte di Exilles ❼

Map B3. **[** 0122 582 70.
☐ 15 Apr–30 Sep: 10am–7pm;
1 Oct–14 Apr: 10am–2pm. **●** Mon.
w www.comune.exilles.to.it

THIS FORT STANDS proudly at the beginning of Alta Val di Susa and was a point of contention between the Savoys and the Dauphins. The structure, greatly altered over the centuries, is thought to have very old origins, possibly Roman, although the first known documents date back to 1155. By the 1400s the fort was already a complex structure and from 1681 to 1687 the mysterious "Man in the Iron Mask" (see p34) resided here. However, most of the present-day structure dates from the 1800s.

The steep Royal Stairs lead to the Royal Doorway which leads to the First Tenailles. At the Second Tenailles is a well dug in the 1700s which is around 70 m (230 ft) deep.

Next is the Knights' Courtyard and the centre of the fort; the chapel facing it is used for concerts, meetings and exhibitions. After this is the stables from where a steep staircase leads to the Lower Fort. Continuing along the Great Moat, over which the Royal Battery looms, you come to the Staircase of Paradise, which leads to the Prison Courtyard.

The fort is a museum in itself and models, maps, sketches and drawings reveal the fortress and its ancient history. An exhibition is dedicated to alpine troops.

The fort can be reached from the main road alongside. The turning for the fort is signposted and there is a parking area below the walls.

The town of Exilles boasts late medieval origins. After a fire in 1593, its original layout was changed. The town has been restored with care and there are splendid views of the lower valley.

MONCENISIO

After Novalesa the climb up to Moncenisio continues along a series of hairpin bends until you reach the upland plain of San Nicolao where there is a small lake. Beyond this is the

Forte Varisello, Moncenisio

plain of Moncenisio (2,048 m/6,720 ft). The artificial lake here (used by French and Italian electricity companies) flooded the old Moncenisio Hospice, which stood at the foot of the Moncenisio hills (Roman Mons Cinerum). Forte Varisello stands on a rise in the centre of the depression. It was built in 1870 and later partly demolished. After the pass, the road descends into France towards Lanslebourg Mont-Cenis, at the foot of the Vanoise massif, which is part of a national park. Information: Casa Comune Colle del Moncenisio **[** 0033 4790 52636.

Parco Naturale del Gran Bosco di Salbertrand ⓼

THE TOWN OF SALBERTRAND is the starting point for visiting the Parco Naturale del Gran Bosco. This vast area of unspoilt vegetation around the Gran Bosco covers over 3,774 ha (9,325 acres) and boasts 700 ha (1,730 acres) of mixed forest with silver and spruce firs, the only one of its type in Piedmont. This woodland has been carefully cultivated since the 18th century. At that time, the wood from here was used in a variety of construction projects, including the building of the military arsenal of Turin, the Castello di Venaria and the Basilica di Superga (see pp96–7).

San Giovanni
The late-Gothic-style parish church of Salbertrand (14th–15th century) is one of the finest in the valley, and contains frescoes from the 16th century.

Ecomuseo Colombano Romean
Twelve museum sections (including a water mill, an ice house, a bakery, a charcoal kiln, a stone quarry and a seasonal cod factory) show the traditional trades. The museum route runs around the edge of town (see p128).

The Daniele Arlaud refuge

Monfol, in the district of Sauze d'Oulx, is a good starting point for excursions to the Gran Bosco.

Sauze d'Oulx is an important resort for winter sports.

| 0 kilometres | 1.5 |
| 0 miles | 1.5 |

Salbertrand

Gr. Himbert

Grange Seu

Sersaret

GRAN BOSCO

Monfol

Gad

C.le Blegier 2,381 m/7,812 ft

M. Genevris 2536 m/8,320 ft

Sauze d'Oulx

Gran Bosco
The heart of the park is this 700-ha (1,730-acre) wood, with silver and spruce firs. These trees, rare in the Western Alps, grow here thanks to the particularly humid microclimate.

Flora
Besides rare species such as Cortusa matthioli, *the lovely dogtooth violet also grows here.*

Wildlife
The varied fauna includes goshawks, buzzards, kestrels, rock ptarmigans, eagle owls and mountain pheasants. Besides small mammals such as hares, squirrels and foxes, there are chamois, deer, roebuck and wild boar. Wolves also live in the park.

VISITORS' CHECKLIST

Turin. **Map** B3. ◻ *Turin–Modane line.* ◻ *SAPAV, Turin–Briançon.* ◻ **Parco Naturale del Gran Bosco di Salbertrand** *Via Monginevro 7, Salbertrand, 0122 854 720.* **Ecomuseo Colombano Romean** ◻ *Bookings: 0122 85 47 20.* ◻◻

At the Forte di Exilles the original nucleus is from 1100, although its present appearance dates back to the early 1800s *(see p125).*

• Exilles

Deveys

Grampra •
Gr. Godisard •

• Alpe Arguel

• Clot des Anes

BOSCO DEL PINO

• Gr. Ruine

P.ta del Gran Serin
2,589 m/8,495 ft ▲

PICCOLO BOSCO

Testa dell'Assietta
2,547 m/8,355 ft ▲

M. Gran Costa
2,615 m/8,580 ft ▲

USSEAUX

Piccolo Bosco
In the lovely Piccolo Bosco the Swiss stone pine is present in its wild form: a rarity in the western Alps. The photo above shows monkshood in flower.

Monte Gran Costa
is the highest peak in the park.

KEY

▬	Motorway
▬	Major road
▬	Scenic route
▬	Minor road
▬	Other roads
▬	GTA route
▬	SF route

Passage to France
Historically, Val di Susa was the main route between Italy and France. The natural landscape is dotted with castles, abbeys and churches which witnessed the passing of merchants, pilgrims and soldiers.

A 16th-century fresco in the parish church of Salbertrand

Salbertrand 9

Turin. **Map** B3. 450. *Turin–Bussoleno–Bardonecchia line.* **Pro Loco** *Via Roma 59, 0122 854 558.* *Sun.* *Marchà d'oc, handicrafts market, Jun, Aug.* www.comune.salbertrand.to.it, www.montagnedoc.it

THIS SMALL VILLAGE, lying at 1,032 m (3,385 ft), owes its fame to the park of Gran Bosco that takes its name. However, the natural wildness of the park is not Salbertrand's only attraction. Visitors will find a number of ancient fountains in the village, including one in Piazza San Rocco, in the centre, which bears the date of 1524.

The history of Salbertrand goes back as far as the 11th century. Like other towns in the area, Salbertrand was for many years part of the Dauphiné, and then France, until 1713 when the Treaty of Utrecht granted the town to the House of Savoy.

The 16th-century frescoes in the parish church of San Giovanni Battista are one of Salbertrand's main attractions. The Romanesque-Gothic church is a fine example of French art in the valley and dates from the 14th and 15th centuries. It has an elegant entrance porch, which is the only one of its kind found in Piedmont. Inside, light plays on the stone capitals carved with fleur-de-lys, dolphins and Celtic-inspired subjects.

The hamlets of Salbertrand are typical examples of alpine architecture with wood and stone houses, an old water-mill, a communal oven, a charcoal kiln and a stone quarry. The various sections of the **Ecomuseo Colombano Romean**, set up in both Salbertrand itself and in the park, show the trades and traditions of Alta Val di Susa. Inside the old buildings visitors can see the tools and everyday implements once used by the people of the area. Of particular note are an ancient water mill, a stone quarry, an ice house and a communal bakery. The mill dates from 1200 and still contains the original machinery and an old grinding stone.

Wooden churn, Ecomuseo Colombano Romean

Oulx 10

Turin. **Map** B3. 2,630. *Turin–Lyon line.* **Pro Loco** *Via Vittorio Emanuele 24, 0122 831 895;* **Montagnedoc** *0122 831 596.* *Wed.* *Fiera Franca, Oct; Flea market, Jul, Aug.* www.montagnedoc.it

THE TOWN OF OULX lies at 1,100 m (3,610 ft) above sea level and is a crossroads in the Alta Val di Susa. The route connecting the Rodano plain with the Po river valley passes through the hills of Monginevro, and since prehistoric times this area has been a meeting point of cultures and civilizations. Archaeological exploration has uncovered a tomb covered with a stone slab; a large bronze pin found in the tomb was discovered to date from between 800 and 500 BC.

Roman occupation transformed the settlement of Oulx into a town with public buildings and even a police force to control local brigands. However, after the emperors, the area saw the arrival of the Huns, Goths, Lombards and Franks. Towards the end of the first millennium, the Saracens also raided the region and this is reflected in the name of the Torre Saracena (Saracen tower): a construction whose origins go

FOLKLORE IN ALTA VAL DI SUSA

Since 2001, the Aoute Doueire folk group has sought to preserve the traditional costumes, music and dance of the towns that were once part of Escarton d'Oulx. The costumes date from different periods. For example, the men's white shirts and the knee-length trousers were worn until the 18th century, while long black trousers with a more classic-style jacket date from the late 19th century when the railway arrived in the area. The only change to the women's costumes is the way the bonnet or shawl is worn. Typical dances performed by the group are Filandole, Carnevale a Salbertrand, the dance of Santa Caterina and the Festa del Fieno.

The folk group Aoute Doueire in performance

back to the Dark Ages. The tower may have been built as a look-out post against the last barbarian raids, or may have been part of the castle of the old Dauphiné. During the centuries of invasions pilgrims and missionaries also passed through the area.

After having suffered a great deal of destruction, Oulx was given a new lease of life thanks to the provostship of San Lorenzo which bishop Cuniberto had built here in 1065.

In the 15th century, Carlo VIII and his army were given food and shelter by the local inhabitants. In gratitude, Carlo VIII granted Oulx town status, with the added concession that it had the right to hold an annual *fiera franca* (tax-free fair), an event that is still held.

With the Treaty of Utrecht, the area became part of the Savoy duchy. What follows is recent history: the railway tunnel of Frejus transformed the lives of the people in the valley, and after the two world wars, the area gradually adapted its economy to mass tourism.

In Oulx today attractions include the Gothic-style parish church of Santa Maria Assunta, which bears the date 1676 on the door. The Casa des Ambrois is a lovely building from the 15th century, with an interior courtyard, the birthplace of Louis des Ambrois de Névache, minister to Carlo Alberto. The fountain of Vière dated 1504, near the Casa Gally is also of interest.

Skiing near Oulx, with Monte Niblè in the background

Sauze d'Oulx, called the "Balcony of the Alps"

Sauze d'Oulx ⓫

Turin. **Map** B3. 🚶 1,060. 🚉
Turin–Lyon line and then bus from Oulx. 🛈 **Montagnedoc** *Piazza Assietta 18, 0122 858 009.* 🛒 *Fri.* 🎿 *The Via dei Saraceni by mountain bike, Jul; Trophy of the Mountain Race, Sep.* Ⓦ *www.montagnedoc.it, www.comune-sauzedoulx.to.it*

KNOWN AS "the balcony of the Alps", Sauze stands at 1,510 m (4,955 ft) on a sunny plain on the slopes of Monte Genevris. The area has been inhabited since ancient times, and tombs have been found dating from the Roman era. Near Richardet, a store of votive objects with hundreds of terracotta vases, bronze goblets and coins dating from between the 1st and 4th centuries AD was found.

In the medieval period, Sauze was part of the Abbazia della Novalesa's estates and it followed the same political destiny as the abbey. Linked to the Dauphiné, it remained French territory until 1713 and then became part of the Kingdom of Savoy. The town played a particular role in the war for Austrian Succession. When the Austro-Piedmontese and the Franco-Spanish armies clashed in the famous Battle of Assietta (July 1747), the Piedmontese victory, which in fact ended the war, left 5,300 soldiers and 430 French officers dead. The bodies were buried in Sauze, some at the church, and some in an area which is named after this fact: Le Fosse (the graves). The remains of the fortifications and the road leading to Assietta, above Sauze, still bear witness to the battle. During the Fascist era the name of Sauze d'Oulx was changed to Salice d'Ulzio, but the old name was taken up again after World War II.

Until the 1930s, Sauze's economy was still based on agriculture, but it was in this period that tourism, especially skiing, began to emerge as a new economic area. Sauze is the venue for the freestyle competitions in the 2006 Winter Olympics and is one of the best equipped resorts in the area. Apart from skiing facilities, there are also opportunities for playing tennis, hiking, horse riding and fishing.

Next to the church of San Giovanni Battista is an octagonal fountain, erected in the 16th century. Originally it stood in the small square next to the old communal bakery, near the chapel of San Rocco e San Giuseppe, but was later moved by the inhabitants. The church of San Giovanni Battista was consecrated in 1538 and is of great artistic interest. The fresco of the *Last Judgment* on the façade is by the workshop of Bartolomeo and Sebastiano Serra di Pinerolo. Carved on the baptismal font is the Dauphin coat-of-arms. The pseudo-Romanesque bell tower ends in a pinnacle and four triangular spires.

In the village of Jouven-ceaux there is a lovely stone fountain, with a mitre on the coat-of-arms, which originally stood in the courtyard of the provostship in Oulx.

Bardonecchia ⑫

Turin. **Map** A3. 🏠 3,070. 🚊
Turin–Lyon line. 🛈 **Town Hall**
Piazza De Gasperi 1, 0122 999 988;
Montagnedoc *Viale Vittoria, 0122
990 32.* 🚌 *Thu, Sun.* 🛍 *Flea
market, Jul, Aug.*
🆆 www.montagnedoc.it,
www.bardonecchia.to.it

The Vallonetto and Sommelier peaks seen from Bardonecchia ski slopes

BARDONECCHIA'S
geographical location is
somewhat curious, as can be
seen by glancing at a map.
The town, which stands at
1,312 m (4,305 ft) altitude, is
the westernmost municipality
in Italy and is almost
completely surrounded by the
French border. Its name also
raises some curiosity.
Although numerous
hypotheses have been put
forward, no definite
conclusions have been
reached as to its origins.
Some have linked its name to
the presence of the
Lombards, and in the diploma
of Emperor Ottone (the year
1001) the area was called
Bardisca, which then became
Bardonisca in the *Chronicon
Novalicense*. Other authorities
claim the name derives from
the word *bard*, meaning
saddle, thus connecting it to
the transport of goods using
beasts of burden. Another
possibility is that it derives
from the root of the Celtic
word *bard*, meaning barrier
or bulwark.

The history of this area is
also extremely complex and
its exact origins have been
lost in time. The first definite
account of the area dates
from 58 BC, the year when

the Roman legions of Julius
Caesar passed through here
on their way to conquer Gaul.
Very soon the Belaci, the
inhabitants of the valley
where the town of
Bardonecchia now stands,
were governed by a prefect
and subject to Rome. After
the barbarian invasions, the
name of a certain Vitbaldo
emerges from the mist of
local history. Vitbaldo was the
founder of the family of the
viscounts of Bardonnèche, a
noble family whose coat-of-
arms (interwoven nailed
strips) is still used by the
municipality. The Bardonnèche
family dominated the upper
and lower valley as far as
Exilles until, on the death of
Contessa Adelaide di Susa,
the estates were divided, and
the upper valley as far as
Chiomonte became prey to
the counts of Albon. In this
way Bardonecchia became
part of the Dauphiné, and
remained so until 1349.

After the religious wars,
which brought about the
passage of armies and

consequent destruction, the
valley of Bardonecchia had to
wait until the Treaty of
Utrecht to enjoy relative
peace. The area's extreme
isolation ended only with the
opening of the Frejus railway
tunnel, which was begun in
1857 and completed in 1870.

Bardonecchia has
encouraged winter sports
since the early 20th century –
the Bardonecchia ski club
was founded in 1908. Today,
Bardonecchia is the largest
resort in Val di Susa with
around 30 ski lifts and 150
km (93 miles) of ski slopes,
artificial snow, cross-country
trails, ice rinks and indoor
swimming pools. The resort is
the venue for the snow-
boarding events in the 2006
Winter Olympics.

The town's **Museo Civico
Etnografico** is of interest.
The museum was founded in
1953 and aims to preserve the
traditions of this town and
the mountains, for a society
undergoing slow, but
inexorable, transformation.
The museum contains an
impressive collection of
everyday objects from the
past: carved furniture,
wooden tools and hand-made
lace. A section on traditional
women's costumes also
shows the traditional
agricultural trades and the
tools used for working the
land, made from larch or
Swiss stone pine.

Museo Civico Etnografico
Via des Geneys 6. 📞 *0122 999 350
(contact Noemi Grisa).* ⏰ *Jul, Aug:
3–7pm Mon–Fri; 9.30–12.30pm,
3–7pm Sat, Sun; by appt at other
times.* 📷 *on request.*

Bardonecchia in winter

ENVIRONS: the **chapels in the valley of Bardonecchia**, around the town and in the hamlets, are well worth visiting. Near Les Arnauds is Notre Dame di Coignet, known to exist by 1496, which has frescoes by the Maestro di Coignet. Near Melezet is the chapel of Nostra Signora del Carmine, with a bell tower from 1600 and, a little further on, the parish church of Sant'Antonio.

At Pian del Colle, near the road for the Colle della Scala, is the small 16th-century chapel of San Sisto. Here an unknown master painted a *History of Pope Sixtus and his Deacon Lawrence*, an *Annunciation* in which the colours are still visible, a *Martyrdom of St Sebastian* and a *St Christopher*, the patron saint of travellers.

In the village of Rochemolles is the small church of San Pietro (1456); the font in the parish church of Sant'Andrea in Millaures is also of note. In Les Horres, the chapel of the same name has frescoes depicting a *Cavalcade of Vices and Virtues*. The paintings on the façade have been ruined by

Modern residential building near the slopes of Campo Smith in Bardonecchia

time and weather, but those inside are well preserved.

On the external walls of many buildings in Borgo Vecchio you can see various sundials and interesting decorations and mottoes. The loveliest ones are in Piazza Suspize, Via Herbarel, Via Fiume and in Via Pasubio. There are many others in less obvious spots; a stroll around the area is an ideal way to discover them.

Melezet ⓭

Turin. **Map** A3.
🚉 **Bardonecchia Town Hall** *Piazza De Gasperi 1, 0122 999 988;* **Montagnedoc** *0122 990 32.*

MELEZET IS ONE of six outlying hamlets that form part of Bardonecchia and it is named after the stream running through it. In the centre of the village stands the spired bell tower of the church of Sant'Antonio Abate, where visitors can admire the 16th–17th-century painted and gilded wooden carvings known as the "Melezet bunches": cascades and garlands of fruit and flowers decorating the apses and altars.

Just 100 m (328 ft) from the church is the 17th-century del Carmine chapel, home to the **Museo di Arte Religiosa Alpina** with works from local chapels and churches. Of interest are the wooden icon of San

Wooden carving and decoration from the school at Melezet

Sisto, a silver cross by Yppolite Borrel (1530) and painted panels by the Maestro di Notre Dame du Coignet (15th century). The wood carving school of Melezet in the church square teaches young people this old craft.

Today Melezet is also very popular with snowboarders. The piste is 1,619 m (5,310 ft) long and starts at over 1,700 m (5,580 ft) above sea level, dropping to 1,370 m (4,495 ft). In winter, the area is also popular with skiers. The newest facility, built for the 2006 Winter Olympics, is a chair lift between Melezet and La Selletta (2,230 m/7,315 ft), and an Olympic stadium. In winter, there are good cross-country ski trails on Pian del Colle, while in summer there is a nine-hole golf course.

🏛 **Museo di Arte Religiosa Alpina**
📞 *0122 622 640.* ⏰ *Jul, Aug: 3.30–6pm Sun, by appt at other times.* ♿

WOOD CARVING AT MELEZET

To fully understand the ancient tradition of wood carving in Melezet, visitors only need to go to the village's parish church; at the sides of the columns of the main altar there are impressive bunches of coloured fruit and flowers. Here, and in the chapels in the valley of Bardonecchia, wood is used for building and as decoration, as well as for making tools and other implements. Wood is a living, sustainable resource and, thanks to the artisans' skill, has become a prestige product.

A Melezet wood carving

There are no known records about the existence of a recognized school as such in Melezet, but generations of wood carvers and sculptors have lived and worked in the village. Some of the oldest pieces of work are the lecterns in the parish church of Millaures (1508), the doors of the churches in Salbertrand and Bousson (1512–14) and the font in the parish church in Bardonecchia (1513). Today the school at Melezet is an institution and an association that teaches young people this ancient craft.

Skiing Facilities at Bardonecchia

THE CLOSEST SKIING AREA to Turin is that of Coazze and Pian Neiretto, in Val Sangone. From Susa, you can climb up to Pian del Frais, with its 22 km (14 miles) of cross-country ski trails, 18 km (11 miles) of slopes and six ski lifts. The ski circuit of Bardonecchia, not far from the Frejus tunnel, includes the Jafferau lift (2,807 m/9,210 ft), the Colomion (2,100 m/6,890 ft) and the Melezet lift, linked to Punta della Mulattiera at 2,400 m (7,875 ft). The 23 ski lifts serve 140 km (87 miles) of pistes: 5 black, 25 red and 21 blue.

Snowshoe tracks in the snow

Two chair lifts go from Campo Smith up to Pian del Sole, giving access to Monte Colomion and then the lower slopes at Les Arnauds and adjacent Melezet. The 22 km (14 miles) of slopes connecting Sauze d'Oulx to Valle Stretta are for more expert skiers.

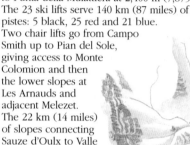

Melezet
This is the snowboarding capital with a slope 1,619 m/ 5,310 ft long starting at 1,820 m/5,970 ft. The Half Pipe slope is 120 m (395 ft) long, with an average gradient of 16 per cent.

Bardonecchia

Melezet

Mountaineering
The first international competition was held in 1985 a few kilometres from Bardonecchia in Valle Stretta. Towards Colle della Scala is the Parete dei Militi rock face.

Pian del Colle

Colomion
The Colomion "sledgeway" (1934) was the first lift built in Bardonecchia. Today a lift goes from Pian del Sole (1,554 m/5,100 ft) up to 2,100 m (6,890 ft) on Colomion.

Bardonecchia

With four ski schools and 140 instructors, this is a good place to learn to ski or improve technique. New facilities include three chair lifts (at Melezet and Colomion) and the Olympic stadium at Melezet.

Rochemolles

0 kilometres 6

0 miles 4

Off-piste Skiing

The Rochemolles valley is a favourite spot for this sport until late in the season, as well as for excursions to Monte Niblé, Punta Sommeiller and Cima del Vallonetto.

Borgo Nuovo

T4

Royeres

335

Puys

Beaulard

OULX

Monte Jafferau

The Testa del Ban chair lift reaches the highest point of the ski circuit at 2,694 m/8,840 ft. The Jafferau lift goes up to 2,650 m (8,695 ft). In summer the mountain can also be reached by mountain bike.

Castello

Chamois

Thanks to its proximity to the Gran Bosco di Salbertrand (at over 2,000 m/6,560 ft) and the Frejus valley, it is common to see herds of chamois in search of the first grass shoots of the spring.

THE CHISONE AND GERMANASCA VALLEYS

IT WAS NAPOLEON WHO *wanted to make the road running through the valley of the Torrente Chisone safer and more modern, and today it is one of the most convenient routes between Piedmont and France. The natural environment is of great interest and the valleys also preserve important traces of their past, with large military fortresses, small traditional hamlets and deep mines.*

The natural environment is the essence of these valleys and it is no accident that on these mountain slopes, which make up the natural arc of Val Chisone, are the entrances to the Parco dell'Orsiera-Rocciavré and the Parco Naturale della Val Troncea. Nearby, there are also splendid trails through the Gran Bosco di Salbertrand. From the Chisone valley you can also reach Perrero and Prali in Val Germanasca, which is less crowded than Val di Susa. This area, along with nearby Val Pellice, was once a refuge for persecuted followers of the Waldensian religion. Today, the area is appreciated for its tranquillity and its cross-country skiing.

For centuries the valley has been a mining area for talc, the *peiro douço* (sweet stone) used in pharmacy, cosmetics and industry. The golden age of mining is over, although some work still continues lower down the valley. The opening of old mines to the public has created a new interest in the splendid, but isolated, Val Germanasca.

Along the Chisone valley the focal point is the impressive Fenestrelle fortress, built to bar the way to Savoy holdings such as the Forte di Exilles, which guarded the nearby Val di Susa. Before reaching Sestrière, one of the most renowned skiing resorts in the western Alps, there are other attractions of note such as Roure, with its theme murals and sundials, or Usseaux with its typical 18th-century farmhouses, Tyrolean-style parish church and murals. At Pragelato the main valley divides and a steep climb leads up to the lively town of Sestrière, while Val Troncea is the place to enjoy the natural environment and cross-country skiing.

Mural in Usseaux, Val Chisone

◁ **A waterfall near Perrero, in Val Germanasca**

Exploring the Chisone and Germanasca Valleys

THE VALLEY SPANS 50 km (30 miles) and runs from Pinerolo to the ski resorts around Sestrière. To the north are the slopes of the Orsiera, Rocciavré and Genevris mountains, all of which are around 3,000 m (9,845 ft) in height. The lower valley has broad meadows and pastures while after Perosa the slopes rise more steeply and are dominated by the impressive Fenestrelle fort. Val Germanasca begins on the valley floor in the area of Perosa and runs southwest towards Val Pellice. The valley is known for its mining industry and for mines open to the public, and ends in Prali which, together with its outlying hamlets, is popular with cross-country skiers. Beyond Fenestrelle the Valle del Chisone rises towards Usseaux and then Pragelato, where the plains are bordered by woodlands. From the small Val Troncea (where there is also a nature reserve) a road climbs up the Colle del Sestrière (2,035 m/6,675 ft): an area famous for its skiing facilities.

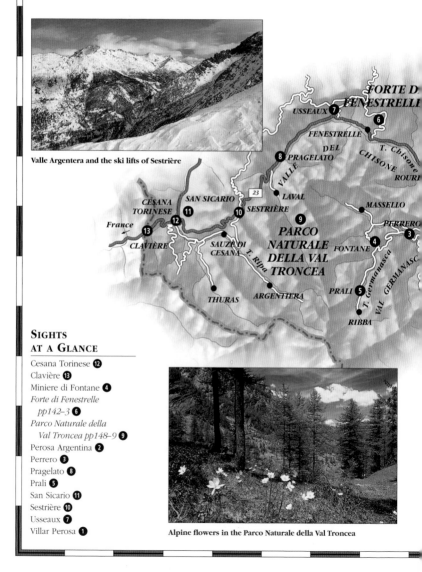

Valle Argentera and the ski lifts of Sestrière

FORTE D FENESTRELLI

USSEAUX **7**

6

FENESTRELLE

DEL

T. Chisone

PRAGELATO **8**

CHISONE

VALLÉ

ROURE

CESANA TORINESE **11**

SAN SICARIO

23

LAVAL

SESTRIÈRE **10**

MASSELLO

France

12

13

CLAVIÈRE

SAUZE DI CESANA

T. Ripa

9

PARCO NATURALE DELLA VAL TRONCEA

FONTANE **4**

PERRERO **3**

VAL GERMANASC

THURAS

ARGENTERA

PRALI **5**

T. Germanasca

RIBBA

SIGHTS AT A GLANCE

Cesana Torinese **12**
Clavière **13**
Miniere di Fontane **4**
Forte di Fenestrelle pp142–3 **6**
Parco Naturale della Val Troncea pp148–9 **9**
Perosa Argentina **2**
Perrero **3**
Pragelato **8**
Prali **5**
San Sicario **11**
Sestrière **10**
Usseaux **7**
Villar Perosa **1**

Alpine flowers in the Parco Naturale della Val Troncea

The village of Usseaux,
in Alta Val Chisone

GETTING AROUND

The only train station for the Chisone and Germanasca
valleys is at Pinerolo; after this point connections must
be made by SAPAV buses (which operate from Pinerolo
and Perosa Argentina). To reach the valleys from Turin
by car, either take the road to Pinerolo from the south
ring road, or the SS23 which leads to Pinerolo. From
here the SS23 continues into Val Chisone, passing Villar
Perosa and Perosa Argentina. A road to the left of the
main valley leads towards Val Germanasca and the towns
of Perrero and Prali, which are about 8 km (5 miles) and
19 km (12 miles) from the turn-off respectively. The SS23
continues towards the Colle del Sestrière and Fenestrelle
and then Pragelato (turning off for Val Troncea).

| 0 kilometres | 8 |
| 0 miles | 5 |

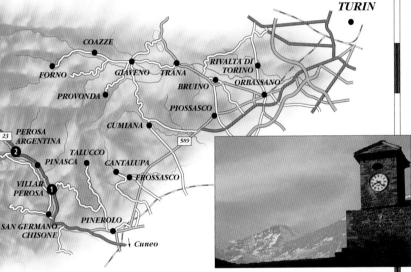

TURIN

COAZZE

FORNO   GIAVENO TRANA

PROVONDA

RIVALTA DI
TORINO

BRUINO   ORBASSANO

PIOSSASCO

CUMIANA

PEROSA
ARGENTINA

TALUCCO   CANTALUPA

PINASCA

FROSSASCO

VILLAR
PEROSA

PINEROLO

SAN GERMANO
CHISONE

↓ Cuneo

The tower in Piazza d'Armi at Forte di Fenestrelle

SEE ALSO

• *Where to Stay* pp179–80

• *Where to Eat* p191

KEY

━━ Motorway

━━ Main road

━━ Minor road

━━ Other roads

— River

▬▬ International border

╍╍ Railway line

Inside the Fontane talc mine, near Prali

The church of San Pietro in Vincoli in Villar Perosa

Villar Perosa ❶

Turin. **Map** C4. 🏚 4,200.
🚌 🚉 Turin–Pinerolo. 🛈 **Town Hall**
Piazza Centenario 1, 0121 313 234.
🔄 Tue. 🎪 Patron saint's Day, 29
Jun. W www.montagnedoc.it

H ALF WAY ALONG the road
from Turin to Sestrière,
at a height of 498 m (1,635
ft), lies Villar Perosa. This
town takes its name from the
word *villar* meaning "village",
and *perosa* (from the nearby
town of Perosa Argentina),
which means stony and refers
to the cobblestone road that
climbs the entire Val Chisone.
The two parts of Villar Perosa
are located along this road.
One part was built quite
recently, while the older one
dates from the Middle Ages
and mention of it can be
found in documents dating
from as far back as 1064.
Little is known about the
years following, but it is
documented that in 1580 the
local community was entirely
Waldensian. The Edict of
Nantes guaranteed the
Waldensians freedom until
Louis XIV's revocation of this
provision. This brought about
dreadful consequences for the
inhabitants, who then also
faced the persecutions of
1686. Giovanni Agnelli, the
founder of FIAT, Italy's main
car producer, was born in
Villar Perosa in 1866.

The parish church of San
Pietro in Vincoli, in the
Piedmontese-Baroque style, is
of great interest. The **Museo
della Meccanica e del
Cuscinetto**, housed in a
factory from 1906, offers a
journey into the history of
technology. The museum is
dedicated to ball bearings, a
fundamental innovation
making much machinery
possible, and there are
reconstructions of two mills, a
section on the lathe and its
development, and a collection
of precision instruments.

🏛 Museo della Meccanica e del Cuscinetto
Via Nazionale 14. 🛈 **Ente Gestore
Consorzio Interaziendale** 0121 31
60 11. ⏱ 9am–12 noon, 2–4pm
Mon–Fri, 9am–12 noon Sun (by appt).
🎫 ♿

Perosa Argentina ❷

Turin. **Map** C3. 🏚 3,850. 🚌 🚉
Turin–Pinerolo. 🛈 **Comunità
Montana** Via Roma 22, 0121 802
524. 🔄 Thu (fish), Sun. 🎪 Spring
Fair, Jun; Autumn Fair, Oct; Historical
Commemoration, 3rd Sun in Sep. W
www.montagnedoc.it, www.perosa.it

P EROSA ARGENTINA, in Bassa
Val Chisone at the
beginning of Val Germanasca,
is an industrial town in a
pleasant spot at a height of
610 m (2,000 ft). The origins
of its name are interesting:
Perosa derives from the word
petrosa, meaning stony, and
mention of the town is found
in medieval documents from
1064. The name probably
refers to the cobblestone road
passing through it, while the
adjective *argentina* (meaning
silver), added by royal decree
in 1863, refers to the silver
mines once found in the area.
The town began to become
industrialized in the 19th
century with the growth of
the textile trade. The first
manufacturer was the
Bolmida mill, followed by
Abegg, Gütermann, and Jenny
& Ganzoni. Some of the
factories were created from
existing mills by modifying
the production methods, thus
increasing the work output.
The transition from being a
community based on
agriculture to one based on
industry was not easy for the
population, and it was also
necessary to make various
alterations to the urban layout
to meet these new needs.
Many of the buildings from
this period have now been

Perosa Argentina, at one end of Val Germanasca

A combing machine, Ecomuseo dell'Industria Tessile, Perosa

abandoned, and the Associazione Ecomuseo di Perosa has set up an industrial archaeological tour, called "**Di Filo in Filo**" to celebrate the textile industry of Perosa Argentina. The museum, consisting of the building itself and a walking route with nine stopping places around the town, preserves the history of the century-old local textile industry. By means of panels and photographs, the museum explains the various production processes. The walking route goes to factories, and the houses, boarding schools and nurseries built for the workers and their families, and documents the history of the town's transformation.

Despite its ancient origins, few traces of the town's more remote past have been preserved. Only a few ruins remain of the castle which belonged to the princes of Acaja, which is thought to have stood on the rise of the redoubt surrounded by walls.

The church of San Genesio is mentioned in documents dating from 1239 and was virtually rebuilt in the mid-17th century. It was constructed in the medieval period by Benedictine monks and had a portico. The original bell tower was probably destroyed in the 13th century in the period of conflict between Tommaso of Savoy and the Pinerolo militia, but the church did not suffer any serious damage until the 17th century, when it fell into ruin after religious wars provoked episodes of intolerance and vandalism. The most recent restorations date from the 1980s.

🏛 "**Di Filo in Filo**" **Ecomuseo dell'Industria Tessile di Perosa Argentina**
Via Chiampo 16. *By appt.*
📞 0121 82 105 (Valter Bruno). 🏢

Perrero ❸

Turin. **Map** C3. 🏘 760. 🚌 *Via Perosa Argentina.* 🚆 *Turin–Pinerolo.*
ℹ️ **Town Hall** 0121 808 758.
🌐 www.montagnedoc.it

T HE NAME of this village derives from the medieval Latin word *pererium*, meaning a stony place. In times past, Perrero, which lies at 850 m (2,790 ft) above sea level, was a trading town. In the medieval period it was defended by fortifications and small castles, the residences of the local squires. Between 1704 and 1708 it was even the capital of the Venetian Republic of Val San Martino, a free zone protected by the king of France for political reasons.

The valley where the various hamlets lie is narrow and twisting initially but soon widens out to form flat grassy plains. The area suffered from depopulation at the end of the last century and is now looking for a new identity in the tourist sector.

Near Perrero, the mining area in the large valley of Maniglia is an interesting spot worth visiting. In the area between Massello and Maniglia is the Arturo Genre

Gianavello, Museo della Balsiglia

Meadows in the valley of Massello, near Perrero

path, named after a local linguist and historian. The route is indicated with yellow and red markers.

ENVIRONS: the hamlet of Balsiglia, in the district of Massello, is infamous for a number of attacks on the Waldensians during religious wars waged by Franco-Piedmontese troops. The **Museo Storico Valdese della Balsiglia** documents crucial points in the resistance of 300 Waldensians in the Balsiglia hills where, in 1689–90, they had taken refuge with their leader, Gianavello, on their return from exile in Switzerland. The Waldensian church in Ciaberso has a Baroque façade.

🏛 **Museo Storico Valdese della Balsiglia**
Balsiglia, Massello. ⏰ *By appt.*
📞 0121 932 179.

The Waldensian church at Massello

Miniere di Fontane **❹**

Turin. **Map** B3. 🚌 *SAPAV, from Turin, Pinerolo, Perosa, Prali.*

AT THE BEGINNING of the 20th century the area of Prali, not far from Villar Perosa, was important economically because of its talc mines. Talc from Val Germanasca is considered the best in the world thanks to the absence of metallic or abrasive contaminants, and its natural whiteness. Talc is used in the paper-making, car and food industries, in pharmacy, for cosmetics, and in the production of ceramics, plastics and paints.

The mining of copper and graphite, as well as talc, began at the end of the 18th century when the tunnels were much smaller and the working conditions were extremely poor.

Production peaked in the decades between the 1930s and 1950s, but after this period their importance slowly declined until most of the mines were closed.

The idea of making the mines into a tourist attraction was first mooted in 1994 and after three years of work to make the areas below ground safe for visitors, the first mining tour became available in 1998.

Today the talc mines are run by Scopriminiera. The tour begins in a small museum dedicated to talc and the history of its extraction, and then continues with a

EXPLORING THE TALC MINE

Today the largest talc mine in Europe is open to the public, with underground tours and a museum exhibition. It is possible to visit over 3 km (2 miles) of the tunnels where, from the late 18th century, talc was extracted. About 50 miners still work at the extraction site, while work in the

Entrance to one of the tunnels, 1940

mine that is open to the public ceased in 1995. The Paola mine can be visited in complete safety aboard a small train and then on foot along the extraction site. Visitors pass through the explosives deposit, the canteen, the talc face and various other parts of the mine. A visit lasts around two hours and it is advisable to wear warm clothing because of the cool temperatures deep in the mine. The Gianna mine tour takes place on foot and walking shoes and warm jackets should be worn. Visitors are taken through the side tunnels, the explosives deposit and the slant (an inclined shaft). The museum has an educational workshop and archives. The site is popular with school groups and it is advisable to book in advance.

🏛 **Ecomuseo Scopriminiera**
Paola, Prali. ☎ *0121 806 987.*
🕐 *Oct–Feb: 9.30am–12.30pm, 1.30–5pm Thu–Mon.*
Mar–Sep: 9.30am–12.30pm, 1.30–6pm Wed–Mon.
● *9 Dec–31 Jan.* ✔ *Paola tunnel: 2–3 hrs; Gianna tunnel 2–3 hrs (no children under 14).* 🌐 *www.scopriminiera.it*

visit to the mine itself along the Paola and Gianna underground tunnels. The Gianna tunnel is 40 m (130 ft) lower than the Paola. After a journey of about 1 km (half a mile) on one of the old trains used in the mines, visitors are shown the various mining techniques and the lives and living conditions of generations of miners.

Prali **❺**

Turin. **Map** B4. 🏔 *320.*
🚉 *Turin–Pinerolo.* 🚌 *Via Perosa Argentina.* 🏛 **Town Hall** *0121 807 513/361 111;* **Pro Loco** *Borgo Ghigo 1 bis, 0121 807 418.* 🗓 *Fri (not in winter).* 🌐 *www.montagnedoc.it, www.praly.it*

PRALI IS MADE UP OF various outlying districts (Ghigo, Malzat, Prali Villa, Rodoretto) in the Val Germanasca, a secondary valley to the Chisone. The area lies at an altitude of 1,455 m (4,775 ft) near the borders of the French regional park of Queyras. The town hall is in Ghigo, the administrative centre of the district.

The name of the area is thought to derive from the Latin word *pratalia*, meaning meadows or pastureland, after the green fields at the foot of the mountains which rise up to 3,000 m (9,845 ft).

The first mention of this district dates back to 1462

Touring the talc mines on a small train

when there was already a considerable Waldensian presence. For a short time, Prali was also part of the Republic of San Martino and was annexed to the Savoy state in 1815.

The oldest building in Prali is the Waldensian church (1556), which is now home to the main museum. This building is also one of the oldest Protestant places of worship in these valleys and the only one to have escaped the destruction of the Waldensian culture which occurred during the 17th century. This was because it was used as a Catholic church between 1686 and 1689.

The **Museo di Prali e della Val Germanasca** inside the old church illustrates the history of the valley's Waldensian community through that of its places of worship. The museum, founded to document the history of the valley from the prehistoric era of rock carvings to the present day, has numerous exhibits on the local history of Waldensian Protestantism. The area has retained many rural features, but has also built facilities for winter

Prali in winter

Waldensian coat-of-arms, Museo di Prali

sports. Seven ski lifts are used to reach the 35 km (22 miles) of slopes. In winter there is also a cross-country ski circuit, 15 km (9 miles) long. The circuit of the 13 lakes is popular. This trail starts at the arrival point of the chair lift at Ghigo (Bric Rond) and takes in the lakes in the valley and goes down into the Larhe valley. This valley lies parallel to Vallone del Clapou which is a plateau with clear lakes, dominated by Monte Cournour (2,868 m/9,410 ft).

The **Museo di Rodoretto** is in Villa di Rodoretto, an outlying ward of Prali. This museum opened in 1973 and documents local life. There are displays of the tools used for working the mines and the old measures for cereals. There are also some reconstructions of traditional living and working areas.

🏛 Museo di Prali e della Val Germanasca
Former Waldensian church in Prali, Borgo Ghigo 27. 📞 *0121 950 203, 0121 807 519.* 🕐 *Jul: 4–6.30pm Thu–Sat; 11.45–12.45pm, 4–6.30pm Sun; Aug: 4–6.30pm Mon–Fri; 10–12 noon, 4–6.30pm Sat, 11.45–12.45pm, 4–6.30pm Sun.* 🏷 📷 *by appt.* 🆆 *www.fondazionevaldese.org*
🏛 Museo di Rodoretto
Villa di Rodoretto, Prali. 📞 *0121 807 450, 0121 374 782.* 🕐 *Easter–mid-Oct, by appt.* 🏷 🆆 *www.fondazionevaldese.org*

CROSS-COUNTRY SKIING IN VAL CHISONE

Skiing in the Parco Naturale della Val Troncea

Cross-country skiing is a good way to escape the busy pistes. In Val Chisone there are trails through some very beautiful landscapes. The Prali trail in Val Germanasca runs 15 km (9 miles) around the bottom of the valley and this is where many champions train. There are trails for all levels of skill. Ascending Val Chisone you come to the district of Villaretto, part of the commune of Roure, where there is a FISI (Italian Winter Sports Federation) approved trail, usually only prepared for diagonal cross-country skiing. The trail has three circuits of varying lengths and winds through the woods and along the River Chisone. However, Pragelato boasts some of the best trails in the entire Piedmont region. The Val Troncea trail is famous and the 15-km (9-mile) route runs through one of the area's most beautiful parks. This track is an alternative to the Alta Val Chisone trail, which is 30 km (19 miles) long and has three circuits, one a tourist circuit and two FISI-approved.

Cross-country skiers should respect the codes: take care not hinder or harm other skiers; respect the signs; choose the right-hand track and stay in line if you are in a group; overtake on the right or the left without hindering or harming others; keep to the right at crossroads; those descending have precedence over those ascending; keep ski sticks close to your body while overtaking and at crossroads; adapt your skiing techniques to the snow conditions, your ability and how crowded the trails are; leave the trail immediately if you stop; give assistance in the event of accidents; give your personal details if there is an accident, even if you are only a witness.

Forte di Fenestrelle 6

EVEN THOUGH not a single shot has been fired from this fort in battle, it is one of the most impressive military structures in Europe. Its walls, batteries and covered stairway guard Val Chisone from the bottom of the valley up 635 m (2,085 ft) to the redoubts of Forte delle Valli. Begun in 1728 for Vittorio Amedeo, building of the great wall was only completed 122 years later. In the meantime, part of the casemates had become a prison. Xavier de Maistre was imprisoned here in 1790 and it was here that he drafted *Voyage Autour de ma Chambre*. Cardinal Bartolomeo Pacca, secretary to Pius VII, was also held prisoner here. The fort fell into disuse, was later restored, and is today open to visitors.

★ Scala Coperta and Scala Reale
The open-air Royal Staircase made for Carlo Emanuele III is 2 km (half a mile) long and flanked by a covered stairway with 4,000 steps.

Panorama
This impressive military structure climbs up along 3 km (2 miles) of the ridge of Orsiera. The three forts, seven redoubts, the powder magazines, batteries and warehouses are linked by 4,000 steps.

The Beato Amedeo bastion

★ Piazza d'Armi
This square in Forte San Carlo is overlooked by the Palazzo del Governatore, the church, the Padiglione degli Ufficiali and cells.

Entrance to the fort

Bridge with a caponiere
At the top of Forte delle Valli the three redoubts, Belvedere, Sant'Antonio and Elmo, are separated by two pairs of bridges with caponieres.

STAR SIGHTS

★ **Padiglione degli Ufficiali**

★ **Piazza d'Armi**

★ **Scala Coperta and Scala Reale**

The Church

This austere building was, among other things, an arms depot and a prison. The bare interior has three aisles and there is a lovely half dome in brick with stone arches above the apse. The date of its construction is not known.

The Sant'Ignazio powder magazine

The barracks

are three long parallel buildings. They were used by troops and prisoners and had latrines connected to a drainage system.

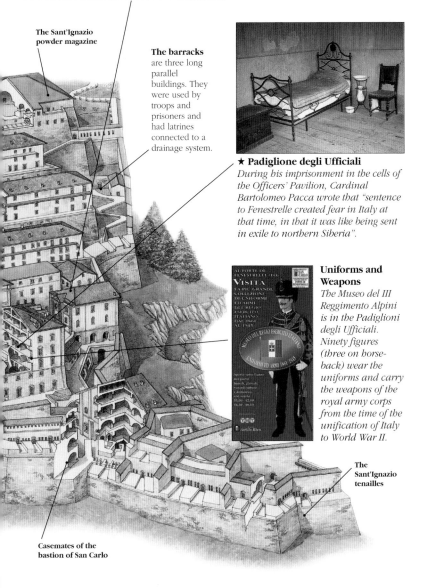

★ Padiglione degli Ufficiali

During his imprisonment in the cells of the Officers' Pavilion, Cardinal Bartolomeo Pacca wrote that "sentence to Fenestrelle created fear in Italy at that time, in that it was like being sent in exile to northern Siberia".

Uniforms and Weapons

The Museo del III Reggimento Alpini is in the Padiglioni degli Ufficiali. Ninety figures (three on horseback) wear the uniforms and carry the weapons of the royal army corps from the time of the unification of Italy to World War II.

The Sant'Ignazio tenailles

Casemates of the bastion of San Carlo

Bird's-eye view of Usseaux, a well preserved mountain village

Usseaux ❼

Turin. **Map** B3. 🏠 *219.* 🚌 *SAPAV,
line 275 from Pinerolo and Sestrière.*
🛈 **Town Hall** *Via Conte Eugenio
Brunetta 53, 0121 884 400, 0121
839 09.* 📷 *San Pietro, 29 Jun;
Commemoration of the Battle of
Assietta and Festival of Piedmont,
mid-Jul; Zootechnic Fair of Balboutet,
23 Aug.* 🆆 *www.montagnedoc.it*

USSEAUX LIES AT 1,416 m
(4,645 ft) in the heart of
the Alta Valle Chisone. The
commune consists of five
villages lying between 1,210
m and 2,890 m (3,970–9,480
ft): Usseaux (the administrative
centre), Laux, Balboutet,
Pourrieres and Fraisse. The
parks of Gran Bosco di
Salbertrand and Orsiera-
Rocciavré also lie within the
municipality. The local rural
architecture is striking – the
villages have characteristic
wood and stone houses. The
villages of Usseaux represent
some of the best examples of
alpine architecture, with
fountains, communal bakeries,
stables, mills and terracing.
    The area also boasts one of
the oldest churches in the
valley. Founded in 1098, its
history dates from at least
1068 when Contessa Adelaide
di Susa, widow of Oddone of
Savoy, founded the abbey of
Santa Maria di Pinerolo and
filled it with treasures from
these areas. Usseaux later
became part of the Escartons,
autonomous areas set up in
1343, and for centuries both
Catholics and Waldensians
lived here. Usseaux also has
interesting murals.
    In Laux there is a pretty
village by a lake, and at

Balboutet there are 20 or so
sundials. Other options for
trips include: the Napoleonic
road, the hills of Assietta,
rock carvings at Rocca, Colle,
Pian dell'Alpe, and the
Sentiero del Pensiero with
fountains and picnic areas.

Pragelato ❽

Turin. **Map** B3. 🏠 *438.*
🚊 *Turin–Pinerolo.* 🚌 *for Colle del
Sestrière.* 🛈 **Town Hall** *0122 785
98 (Ruà); Montagnedoc Piazza
Lantelme (Ruà) 0122 788 44.*
🛍 *Sun.* 📷 *Fiera di Ferragosto, Aug.*
🆆 *www.montagnedoc.it*

FIRST MENTION of Pragelato is
found in a document
dated 8 September 1064, in
which Contessa Adelaide di
Susa donated the land of the
commune to the abbey of
Santa Maria in Pinerolo. The
locality, at 1,550 m (5,085 ft),
became part of plans to
expand the territory of the
Dauphiné, and clashed with
the House of Savoy.
    In 1349 Humbert III, the last
lord of the Dauphiné, left the
land to the king of France on
condition that the heir to the
throne held the title of
Dauphin. And so for a further
350 years, the valley in which
Pragelato lies remained a
French enclave right in the
middle of the region ruled by
the House of Savoy. It was
only with the Treaty of
Utrecht that Pragelato became
part of the House of Savoy's

**Musician in Val Chisone playing
the *ghironda*, or hurdy-gurdy**

THE VILLAGE MURALS

In many villages in the Chisone and Germanasca valleys
the external walls of the traditional stone houses are
decorated with murals. They can be seen particularly in
Salza di Pinerolo, Roure and Usseaux. In Usseaux, these
colourful murals represent scenes of daily and country life.
One example is a series of murals representing the making

**A mural painted on the wall
of a house in Usseaux**

of bread, depicting the seasons
with ploughing, sowing,
harvesting and threshing, and
ending with breadmaking. The
theme of the 32 murals in Salza
di Pinerolo are the words from
songs by the singer-songwriters
who have performed in the
area. In Balma, at Roure, 33
murals depict the work that was
carried out in the talc mines
when they were still active. In
other places there are pictures
of old crafts, the history of
bread and cattle farming. In
Usseaux, guided tours tell the
visitor more about this unusual
aspect of the region's villages.

Overlooking Pragelato, which lies at 1,550 m (5,085 ft) above sea level

possessions. The Napoleonic period brought about important developments in the area, however, chief of which was the construction of the main road.

The 19th and 20th centuries saw an increase in migration towards France and in the same period the mines of Beth were opened. Today these mines are remembered, sadly, for a tragic avalanche which killed 81 miners in 1904. With time the mines were closed and the valley fell into decline.

After World War II, which saw particularly difficult partisan struggles in this zone, the area underwent various changes as a result of the growth in tourism. The first pistes and lifts were set up in the 1960s. Pragelato is one of the venues chosen for the 2006 Winter Olympics and will host the cross-country, Nordic Combined and ski jump events.

The municipality of Pragelato is made up of around 20 hamlets. La Ruà, home to the town hall, is the chief village. Its parish church, the Assunzione di Maria Vergine, was built for Louis XIV between 1686 and 1689. Louis also built the church of San Lorenzo in Traverses, in 1698. This church stands on the site of

an earlier church, used between 1560 and about 1685 as a Waldensian church. In order to build San Lorenzo, Louis had the previous church demolished.

In Souchères Basses the interesting **Museo dell'Osservatorio di Apicoltura** exhibits a collection of objects used for beekeeping and has exhibits illustrating traditional methods. Objects from the alpine valleys are displayed here, while those from other sources are exhibited in the branch museum in Reaglie on the slopes of the hill of Turin.

The **Museo del Costume e delle Tradizioni delle Genti Alpine** in Rivet offers an insight into a way of life

The bell tower of the church of San Lorenzo in Traverses

which has characterized these valleys for centuries. Reconstructions of rooms, the handicrafts and the tools on display here testify to the hard life that local people led until relatively recently.

In La Ruà, next to the church of the Assunzione di Maria, is the **Centro di Documentazione delle Meridiane**, which contains a good collection of sundials, the earliest dating from the 1600s. Using lighting and sound effects, a series of panels illustrates the history of the measurement of time. Visitors can see various models of sundials, accompanied by images and sound effects.

🏛 **Museo dell'Osservatorio di Apicoltura**
Loc. Souchères Basses, Via Nazionale 12. ☎ 0122 78 038.
◯ by appt.

🏛 **Museo Etnografico del Costume e delle Tradizioni delle Genti Alpine**
Via San Giovanni, Rivet. ☎ 0122 78 800. ◯ 8am–12 noon Wed, 8am–12 noon 3–6pm Sat, Sun; by appt at other times. 🎫 🖼

🏛 **Centro di Documentazione delle Meridiane**
Viale Cavalieri di Vittorio Veneto, La Ruà. ☎ 0122 78 800, 0122 741 728. ◯ 3–6pm Sat; 10am–12.30pm Sun, by appt. 🖼 ♿ 🎫 1 hr.

Parco Naturale della Val Troncea ●

VAL TRONCEA WAS ONCE PART of the ancient kingdom of the Cozii. It is a narrow, sunny valley at 1,650–3,280 m (5,415–10,760 ft), the height of Monte Rognosa. Since 1980 the park has covered 3,250 ha (8,030 acres). There are small areas of isolated woodland, mainly larch, often mixed with Swiss stone pines. At Seytes there is an almost intact forest of Swiss stone pine, while there are some birch and aspen woods in Valle del Chisone. In Laval there are mountain pines. The spring and summer flowers are spectacular and include rare species. The park is home to chamois, deer, wild boar and steinbocks, which were reintroduced in 1987. There is also a pair of golden eagles.

In **Laval** there is a small museum about the park.

Duc
Joussand

Borgata Sestrière

23

Laval

Via Lattea, the lifts of the ski circuit of Sestrière.

Sestrière

La Tuccia

M. Banchetta
2,823 m/9,260 ft   La Grangia

P.so Banchetta
2,679 m/8,790 ft

P. ta Rognosa
3,280 m/10,760 ft

Lago Rouit

An Alpine House
These rural houses date from the 18th and 19th centuries and have large stables with cross vaults and stone-tiled trussed roofs.

M. Platasse
3,149 m/10,330 ft

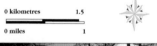

| 0 kilometres | 1.5 |
| 0 miles | 1 |

M. Giornalet
3,063 m/10,050 ft

Brusà Des Planes

T. Ripa

Skiing facilities
In winter the park can be toured on skis along a magnificent cross-country trail. The trail runs from Laval to La Tuccia. A cross-country biking trail goes from La Tuccia to Berg. Mey. Skis can be hired in Pragelato.

Argentiera

Chamois
In the early 1950s only chamois inhabited the area, but today it is home to deer, roebuck and about 80 alpine ibex as well as over 550 chamois.

◁ **A larch wood in the Parco Naturale della Val Troncea**

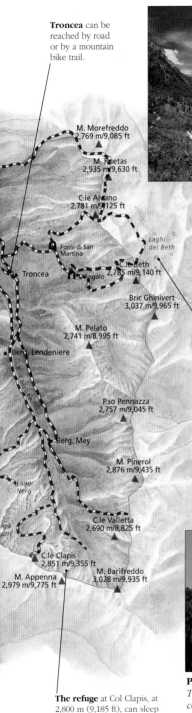

Troncea can be reached by road or by a mountain bike trail.

M. Morefreddo
2,769 m/9,085 ft

M. Ruetas
2,935 m/9,630 ft

C.le Arcano
2,781 m/9,125 ft

Forni di San Martino

Laghi del Beth

Troncea

L'Angolo

C.le Beth
2,785 m/9,140 ft

Bric Ghinivert
3,037 m/9,965 ft

M. Pelato
2,741 m/8,995 ft

Berg. Lendeniere

P.so Pennazza
2,757 m/9,045 ft

Berg. Mey

M. Pinerol
2,876 m/9,435 ft

Lago Nero

Lago Lauri

C.le Valletta
2,690 m/8,825 ft

C.le Clapis
2,851 m/9,355 ft

M. Appenna
2,979 m/9,775 ft

M. Barifreddo
3,028 m/9,935 ft

The refuge at Col Clapis, at 2,800 m (9,185 ft), can sleep four. Another refuge can be found at Colle del Beth.

VISITORS' CHECKLIST

Turin (SS23 to Traverses).
Map B3. 🚌 *SAPAV from Turin and Pinerolo.* 🛈 *Via della Pineta 2, outlying hamlet of Ruà, Pragelato, 0122 788 49.*

Flowers
Alpine pasque flower, tufted leopardsbane and edelweiss grow in Val Troncea, which is also known as the "valley of flowers".

KEY

▰▰	Scenic route
▰▰	Minor road
⚊⚊	Other roads
▰◼▰	Paths
🛈	Information
⋔	Ruins
🅿	Parking

Small Lakes
On Colle del Beth (2,785 m/ 9,140 ft), at the entrance to the copper mines, there are seven glacial lakes known as the "lakes of Beth", which are a characteristic deep blue colour.

Panorama
The park, located in the heart of the Alpi Cozie, covers the upper part of the valley of the Torrente Chisone. Much of its perimeter is bordered by peaks of 3,000 m (9,845 ft) above sea level.

Sestrière ⑩

Turin. **Map** B3. ⚑ 870.
🚉 Oulx, Turin–Lyon line. 🚌 SAPAV
bus from Oulx, 800 801 190.
ℹ **Montagnedoc** Piazza Fraiteve 1,
0122 755 444. 🔺 Tue.
🌐 www.montagnedoc.it

Sestrière, with its famous 1930s tower hotels

T HE NAME SESTRIÈRE, thought to derive from *ad Petram Sextariam* or *Sextera*, is thought to be a reference to the existence of a Roman milestone in the hills. The history of Sestrière dates from that of the two oldest villages, Champlas du Col and Borgata, which were small hamlets inhabited by communities of woodsmen and shepherds. As in other places, this area also saw the arrival of Vandals and Saracens, followed by the invasions of the Dauphins in the battles against the Savoys.

The pioneer of Sestrière's development was Paolo Vincenzo Possetto, who was born in the area. Possetto came from a family of roadsmen which was the only family actually living in Sestrière before 1930. In around 1920, with great foresight, Possetto built a small hotel with 20 rooms and a restaurant, thus earning himself the title of the area's first tour operator. However, in 1930 it was Senator Giovanni Agnelli, together with his son Edoardo, who created the Società Incremento del Sestrière and, thanks to the assistance of the skilled engineer Bonadè Bottino, the present-day town was created.

The church of San Restituto, a few minutes from Sauze di Cesana

The Principi di Piemonte hotel and the two-part cableway of Alpette and Sises were inaugurated in 1932. The famous towers and the Monte Banchetta and Fraiteve cableways were built later. Very soon what had been a bare hill lying at 2,035 m (6,680 ft), used for summer pasture, became a large winter resort with hotels to suit all budgets. The new middle classes arrived in FIAT Balilla cars, while lorries and buses brought groups of skiers from the city: the forerunners of the skiing clubs.

The Kandahar event in 1951 has gone down in skiing history, recording the triumph of Zeno Colò in the downhill competition. Since that time Sestrière has become a renowned ski resort, with famous names such as Schranz and Killy competing here, and in recent decades it has also hosted World Cup skiing events. Sestrière was an obvious choice to host skiing events in the 2006 Winter Olympics.

The town is linked to other skiing areas, such as San Sicario and Clavière, which are also connected to the Via Lattea circuit. For non-skiers, or during the summer, there is a wide range of other facilities to choose from: heated open-air swimming pools, tennis, volleyball, basket ball, squash, horse

Emblem of the commune of Sestrière

riding and archery. Sestrière also boasts the highest 18-hole golf course in Europe.

The parish church of Sant'Antonio Abate is in Champlas du Col and dates from the 17th century. It was rebuilt in 1839 and underwent radical renovation in the last century. The church houses a precious 17th-century wooden *retable* and a pulpit from 1747, the year of the Battle of Assietta. A few minutes' walk from Sauze di Cesana, and also reached via a path from Champlas du Col, is the church of San Restituto, whose simple lines testify to an ancient faith. It dates from the early Middle Ages and was enlarged by Louis XIV. The church was later remodelled to repair the damage caused by time.

Despite its strong walls, which protected it during the many religious wars fought in these parts between the 15th and 18th centuries, the church was looted on several occasions and finally closed. It is documented that a silver reliquary of the patron saint, a gilded cross, chalices and other sacred objects were stolen from the church. However, other items have been rediscovered, including brocaded silk stoles, a baptismal font, candlesticks in bronze with floral motifs, an ornamental angel, and 17th- and 18th-century prayer books.

San Sicario

Turin. **Map** A3. 🏘 100. 🚉 Oulx, Turin–Lyon line. 🚌 SAPAV bus from Oulx, 800 801 190. 🛈 **Montagnedoc** Cesana T., 0122 89 202; **Town Hall** 0122 89 114. 🎿 torchlight procession in the snow, 30 Dec. 🅦 www.montagnedoc.it

S‍AN SICARIO is an outlying district of the commune of Cesana and stands at 1,700 m (5,580 ft) above sea level. The area began to develop in the late 1960s, when there was a noted increase in the number of skiing enthusiasts visiting the region. The mountain slopes best suited to the sport were chosen and various ski slopes were laid out, connected by lifts.

Today, this resort is being relaunched and is an important part of the Via Lattea, the large ski circuit that stretches from Sestrière to Monginevro. San Sicario is the venue for the biathlon and women's skiing events in the 2006 Winter Olympics.

Cesana Torinese

Turin. **Map** A3. 🏘 980. 🚉 Oulx, Turin–Lyon line. 🚌 SAPAV bus from Oulx, 800 801 190. 🛈 **Montagnedoc** Piazza Vittorio Amedeo 6, 0122 892 02; **Town Hall** 0122 891 14. 🛒 Thu am. 🅦 www.montagnedoc.it

T‍HE COMMUNE INCLUDES the outlying districts of Bousson, Champlas Séguin, Colle Bercia, Fenils, Mollières, Pian Gimont, Rhuilles, Sagna

Cesana Torinese, a few kilometres from the border with France

Longa, San Sicario, Thures, Désertes and Solomiac, which were united into one municipality during the Fascist era. The town lies just 6 km (4 miles) from the French border at 1,354 m (4,440 ft) at the foot of Monti della Luna and the confluence of the rivers Dora and Ripa. From this point on, the river becomes the Dora Riparia, one of the largest tributaries of the river Po.

Ancient documents mention a place called Goesao on the road to Gaul, and it is possible that this is present-day Cesana. The town boasts some attractions of artistic interest such as the church of San Giovanni Battista, where you can still see some original 11th-century features, and the church in Bousson, built in the 16th century in the late-Gothic style. Also of interest in Bousson is the Casa delle Lapidi, whose outer walls are decorated with stone tablets with moral sayings and curious decorations.

Clavière

Turin. **Map** A3. 🏘 170. 🚉 Turin–Lyon. 🚌 bus from Oulx. 🛈 **Montagnedoc** Via Nazionale 30, 0122 878 856; **Town Hall** 0122 878 821. 🛒 Fri pm (summer only). 🅦 www.montagnedoc.it

C‍LAVIÈRE IS ONE of the venues for the 2006 Winter Olympics and will host the downhill and cross-country skiing events. This small village lies at 1,760 m (5,775 ft) above sea level, immediately after the Monginevro pass. Its name is thought to derive from the Latin word clavis (key), which aptly states its strategic position. Before the 1713 Treaty of Utrecht, the area lay within French territory. The village was practically razed to the ground during World War II and with the Treaty of Paris (1947), half of the territory was given up to the French. Today it is a sunny resort with various facilities, as well as a good golf course.

San Sicario in the district of Cesana, with its renowned skiing facilities

Skiing Facilities on the Via Lattea

Snowboarding, a young sport

IN 1934, JOURNALIST GUIDO TONELLA penned the following about Sestrière: "this impressive complex and the great commotion it creates – lorries coming and going up and down the slopes, the cablecars in a continuous line along the taut cables crossing the mountains, lines of cars winding their way up the steep slopes along the tracks made by the snow ploughs – these things strike the visitor's imagination...". Since then, a lot has changed in these mountains lying between Val di Susa and Val Chisone. Today, the Via Lattea (Milky Way) ski circuit includes the skiing areas of Sestrière, Cesana, Clavière, San Sicario and Sauze d'Oulx, and Montgenèvre in France. The 211 slopes are all connected. The full circuit covers over 400 km (250 miles) of slopes which are served by 91 lifts rising from 1,350 m (4,430 ft) at Cesana to 2,800 m (9,190 ft) at Motta. Many of these facilities will be used for the 2006 Winter Olympics events, including the biathlon at Cesana and San Sicario, cross-country events at Pragelato, downhill at Sestrière and freestyle at Sauze d'Oulx.

Monte Chaberton
This wide peak at 3,130 m (10,270 ft) has eight regular points, or "teeth", and dominates the town of Cesana Torinese. There is also a fort with a battery for cannons. It can be reached from Clavière.

Fenils

San Sicario

Cesana Torinese

Clavière

Monginevro

0 kilometres 3

0 miles 2

Clavière
Thanks to the town's position, snow is guaranteed on the numerous slopes and off-piste routes. You can also get to the French slopes of Montgenèvre from here.

KEY

▬▬	Motorway
▬▬	Major road
▬▬	Minor road
▬▬	Other roads
▬▬	Lifts

Capanna Mautino
This private refuge (2,150 m/7,055 ft) in the Monti della Luna group near Lago Nero is a starting point for excursions for people arriving by chair lift from Cesana.

Sauze d'Oulx
This sunny, sheltered resort, known as the "balcony of the Alps", has broad slopes and trails through the woods. Italian skiing was first practised here in 1899.

Sestrière
Italy's most modern ski resort even offers night skiing on floodlit slopes. The Kandahar Banchetta (downhill) and the Sises-Cit Roc and Giovanni Alberto Agnelli (slalom) slopes are renowned.

Bousson
Part of the winter routes network in Val Thuras and Monti della Luna, Bousson is good for cross-country, with trails for snow shoes, and off-piste skiing.

Thures
The nearby cross-country trail on the Rhuilles plain is 7 km (4 miles) long and 4 m (13 ft) wide and is suitable for skiers with visual impairment. There is a parallel track for snow shoes and dog sledges.

VAL PELLICE

*V*AL PELLICE *is one of the shortest and most secluded of the Piedmontese valleys. Just 28 km (17 miles) to the divide of the Alps, the valley was for centuries home to the Waldensians and thus the stage for their terrible persecution as well as their glorious deeds. This particular history has deeply influenced the character of the valley, especially its rich and interesting cultural life.*

In response to a yearning for social justice that was widespread among Christian nations, the Protestant preacher Waldes began to preach and convert in Lyon in around the middle of the 11th century. His ideal of poverty, which led him to follow St Francis in giving away all his worldly goods, went hand in hand with the spread of evangelism. Very soon his followers – known from the 12th century on as Waldensians (Valdesi in Italy) – spread into France, Spain, Italy and eastwards into Hungary, Poland and Bohemia. Reaction from the Catholic church was violent, and brought about the extermination of the "heretics" who managed to hold out in just a few of the Piedmontese valleys. Despite persecution, Waldensian presence (the most important Protestant community in Italy) has survived to the present day and is now a characteristic of this small alpine valley. The spread of this popular culture was so vast in

the 19th century that, on arriving in Torre Pellice, writer Edmondo De Amicis wrote "We get off at the station and go into the square: where the devil are we? Are we in Italy or in a town in somewhere in Switzerland or on the Rhine?". Today these traditions and frequent contact with the Protestant communities of northern Europe mean that Torre, Bobbio and Villar Pellice have numerous museums, theatres and festivals.

However, the valley does not only look to its difficult past. The working of Luserna stone still flourishes and a network of museums illustrates the area's history. Val Pellice is also a good starting point (together with the nearby Valle Po) for exploring Monviso or the peaks of the French Alpi Cozie, and is a popular area with hikers and nature lovers. In winter, cross-country skiing and excursions on snow shoes are popular rather than downhill skiing, for which there are few facilities.

The church of San Loreto at Angrogna

◁ **The scenic landscape of the Val Pellice**

Exploring Val Pellice

AFTER THE AGRICULTURAL towns of Pinerolo and Bricherasio, onward travellers leave the Piedmontese plain behind and go right into the heart of Val Pellice. This short valley was isolated for many centuries but it boasts many places of interest. Torre Pellice is the historical centre of Waldensian culture in the valley but the other villages in the area also have small museums and important places recalling the long history and trials of the Waldensians. These include the old textile mill of Crumière at Villar Pellice, the museum of stone at Rorà and the old Santa Margherita mill (near Torre Pellice).

For those who love the mountains, Val Pellice is an interesting starting point: from Bobbio a detour leads to the Barbara Lowrie refuge, one of the possible starting points for the "Giro del Monviso" excursion *(see pp168–71)*, while from the last villages beyond Villanova you can climb up to the Willy Jervis refuge at Prà.

View of the small town of Luserna San Giovanni and Monte Frioland

SIGHTS AT A GLANCE

Alta Val Pellice ⑩
Angrogna ⑥
Bobbio Pellice ⑨
Bricherasio ②
Cavour ③
A Tour of Monviso pp168–71 ⑪
Luserna San Giovanni ④
Pinerolo ①
Rorà ⑦
Torre Pellice ⑤
Villar Pellice ⑧

France

VILLAR PEROSA
SAN GERMANO CHISONE
PRADELTORNO
ALTA VAL PELLICE ⑩
ANGROGNA ⑥
BOBBIO PELLICE
TORRE PELLICE ⑤
VILLANOVA
VILLAR PELLICE
CARBONERI
RORÀ
LUSERN. SAN GIOVANN
VAL PELLICE
BORGO
VALLE DEL PO
⑪ MONVISO
CHIANALE
PONTECHIANALE

0 kilometres   10
0 miles   5

The picturesque Piano del Prà and the Willy Jervis mountain refuge

GETTING AROUND

Val Pellice is not far from Turin. To get out of the city drivers can choose between the Pinerolo turn-off from the ring road south of the city or take the SS23 road which passes the Stupinigi and the park, and continues on to Pinerolo. After passing the village of Bricherasio, the road enters the valley and ends at Villanova at the foot of the mountains on the border with France. Pinerolo can also easily be reached by train. Buses to Val Pellice leave from the square in front of Pinerolo train station.

TURIN

BEINASCO

ORBASSANO

PIOSSASCO

STUPINIGI

NICHELINO

E70

CANTALUPA

T. Chisola

589

VOLVERA

CANDIOLO

PISCINA

Rio Torto

NONE

23

AIRASCA

PINEROLO

CASTAGNOLE PIEMONTE

SCALENGHE

SAN SECONDO DI PINEROLO

BURIASCO

T. Lemina

OSASCO

VIGONE

GARZIGLIANA

PANCALIERI

BRICHERASIO

T. Pellice

CAMPIGLIONE FENILE

Po

VILLAFRANCA PIEMONTE

BIBIANA

CAVOUR

589

BAGNOLO PIEMONTESE

Cuneo

An *Ara ararauna*, one of the hundreds of macaws in the Parco Ornitologico Martinat, near Pinerolo

SEE ALSO

• *Where to Stay* p181

• *Where to Eat* p191

The Waldensian church in Torre Pellice

KEY

▬▬▬	Motorway
▬▬	Major road
▬▬	Minor road
═══	Other roads
—	River
▬▬▬	Provincial border
▬▬▬	International border
▬•▬	Railway

The Romanesque church of San Maurizio in Pinerolo

Pinerolo ❶

Turin. **Map** C4. 🏛 *35,110.* 🚉
Turin–Pinerolo. **Montagnedoc** *Viale
Giolitti 7, 0121 795 589.* 🗓 *Wed,
Sat, Fri (fish).* 🎪 *Handicrafts Fair,
Aug; Fungo d'oro, Oct; Organic-
natural foods market, 3rd Sat in
month (except Aug); national and
international horse race, 2nd and 3rd
weekend of Sep.*
Ⓦ *www.montagnedoc.it*

IN ROMAN TIMES, the main
town of the area was
Cavour (then called
Caburrum), and what is now
Pinerolo was simply a wood
of conifers with a minor
settlement. The name of the
town is thought to derive
from this: *pinariolum* is in
fact a diminutive of *pinarium*,
meaning "pine wood".

The first document that
mentions the existence of a
town here dates from 995:
this is the diploma of Ottone
III (or possibly Ottone II,
which would give it a date of
981). In 1064, Adelaide di
Susa founded the Benedictine
monastery of Santa Maria. In
1078, Adelaide donated to the
monastery the whole of
Pinerolo, including its castle,
to consolidate its power and
importance.

The town's history from this
date on is one of feuds and
wars, various dominations
and restoration, until Vittorio
Emanuele I's return to
Piedmont. From this point in
time Pinerolo's history goes
hand in hand with that of the
kingdom of Sardinia.

Today, Pinerolo is a lively
town in a splendid position
and it has been chosen to
host the curling events in the
2006 Winter Olympics.

One of the town's many
points of interest is the
cathedral of San Donato. This
was built in the second half
of the 14th century on the site
of an earlier building which
dated from at least 1044.
After various alterations
carried out in the
15th, 18th and 19th
centuries, San Donato
has regained its
original simple lines.

In Piazza San
Donato, home to
some very good pastry
shops, are a churchyard
and numerous
medieval houses;
the writer Silvio
Pellico lived in one
of these. The market
of the "madames" is held
beneath the porticoes,
commonly known as Portici
Vecchi, and women from the
surrounding countryside and
valleys come here to sell their
produce. There is also,
unusually, an anchovy seller.

*Man from Similaun,
Museo di Arte
Preistorica*

Also of interest is the church
of San Maurizio, at the top of
the town, which dates from at
least 1078. It was rebuilt on
the same spot in the 15th
century in the Romanesque
style, increasing the size to
five aisles. The church houses
the remains of the Acaja
princes, who were previously
buried in the church of San
Francesco. On the counter-
façade there are some
medieval frescoes.

The Piedmontese cavalry
occupies a special place in
the history of Pinerolo and
there is an important military
school here. The **Museo
Nazionale dell'Arma della
Cavalleria** documents its
history in 33 rooms arranged
over three floors. The
museum displays memorabilia
of the Scuola di Cavalleria
saved from the spoils of war
or given as donations. On the
ground floor are a
number of wagons
and a reconstruction
of the farriers' school.
On the first floor are
paintings, prints,
bronzes, silver,
standards and flags.
There is also a large
collection of uniforms
and decorations from
the period between the
Risorgimento and
the present day. The
second floor is
dedicated to the
history of the
colonial campaigns and the
two world wars.

The **Centro Studi e Museo
di Arte Preistorica** promotes
research into human
spirituality and the evolution
of the prehistoric and
protohistoric population of

Medieval houses and porticoes in Piazza San Donato in Pinerolo

ROCK CLIMBING AT ROCCA SBARUA

Climbing the rock face at Rocca Sbarua

Rocca Sbarua, 1,445 m (4,740 ft) high, lies in the area of San Pietro Val Lemina, and is part of the divide between Val Sangone and Val Noce. This impressive wall of gneiss rock with veins of white quartz is the winter "practice wall" for climbing in Piedmont. Well-known climbers such as Ellena, Bianciotto, Cinquetti, Rivero, Rossa, Motti and Grassi have trained here, and it is still used by young climbers today. The wall has hundreds of routes (from 20 m/65 ft to 200 m/655 ft) of varying difficulty. Rocca Sbarua is reached from Pinerolo by ascending towards San Pietro Val Lemina and then going in the direction of Talucco.

the Western Alps through the study of cultural material. It also has a library, an archaeological laboratory and it regularly organizes exhibitions, meetings and conferences.

🏛 **Museo Nazionale dell'Arma della Cavalleria**
Via Giolitti 5. 📞 0121 376 344.
⏰ 9–11.30am, 2–4pm Tue, Thu, 9am–11.30pm Sat, Sun.

🏛 **Centro Studi e Museo di Arte Preistorica**
Via Brignone 5. 📞 0121 794 382.
⏰ 10.30–12 noon, 3.30–6pm Sun; educational activities daily, booking required.

ENVIRONS: the **Parco Ornitologico Martinat** covers an area of 80,000 sq m (861,120 sq ft) on the hill between Pinerolo and San Pietro Val Lemina. Despite the fact that Piedmont is relatively cold, the climate here is mild and olives, holm oaks and oleanders grow here. It was therefore a suitable area for large aviaries (one is 13,000 sq m/139,930 sq ft, and is the largest in the world).

The main aim of the park is to protect endangered species and to promote their breeding in captivity. The park also offers visitors an ideal opportunity to see and learn about the tropical species that risk extinction in an almost natural environment. The bird species here include colourful

Pelican in the Parco Ornitologico Martinat, near Pinerolo

parrots, macaws, cranes, flamingoes, ibis, storks, pelicans and great bustards.

🦅 **Parco Ornitologico Martinat**
Via Petrarca 6, San Pietro Val Lemina.
📞 0121 303 199. ⏰ daily, 10am–dusk.

Bricherasio ❷

Map C4. 🏘 4,000. 🚌 🚉 Turin–Pinerolo. 🏛 **Town Hall** Piazza Santa Maria 11, 0121 591 05.
📅 Thu. 🍇 Grape Festival, Oct.
🌐 www.montagnedoc.it

THIS TOWN IS THE gateway to Val Pellice. Founded by the Ligurian people long before the arrival of the Roman legions, Bricherasio originally lay in the valley of Torrente Chiamogna. It moved to its present site in around the 14th century, to be in a better position for trading along the main roads to Val Pellice.

The town's history is complex, featuring feudal events, the Waldensians and the House of Savoy. After 1860 its fortunes followed those of Piedmont. The parish church of Santa Maria Assunta has an unusual bell tower.

ENVIRONS: the **Ecomuseo della Resistenza** in Angrogna (Val Pellice), Coazze (Val Sangone) and Colle del Lys (Valli di Lanzo), documents the contribution made by the local people to the Resistance and the places where the partisan struggle was most fierce. As well as the museum, people can also visit the places where the events of 1943–5 took place.

✊ **Ecomuseo della Resistenza**
San Michele, Bricherasio. **AGESS Val Pellice** 📞 0121 934 907. 🏛 Coazze, Via Matteoli 77, 011 934 9681. ⏰ all year, by appt. 🗒

A quiet, secluded side valley near Bricherasio

Luserna San Giovanni and the Waldensian church

Cavour ❸

Turin. **Map** D4. 👥 5,200. 🚊
Turin–Pinerolo. 🛈 **Pro Loco** Via
Roma 3, 0121 681 94;
Montagnedoc Viale Giolitti 7, 121
794 003. 🗓 Tue. 🎪 Apple Festival,
Nov. 🌐 www.cavour.info,
www.montagnedoc.it

THIS TOWN, centred around
the Rocca di Cavour, has
Celtic and Ligurian origins
and was inhabited by the
Romans in the 1st century BC.
It stands at the entrance to
Valle Po between the Turin
and Cuneo provinces and was
the birthplace of politicians
Camillo Benso di Cavour and
Giovanni Giolitti. Cavour is
renowned for its quality meat
and salamis and has excellent
butchers' shops. It is famous
in the field of gastronomy for
its "Cena dei Grassoni", a
special dinner held annually
at the Posta restaurant.

The abbey of Santa Maria is
worth a visit. It was built in
around 1037 on the site of an
earlier building dating from
the 8th century, of which only
the crypt remains.

The **Rocca di Cavour** has
been a nature reserve since
1980 and stands on a rise
which is effectively an alpine
peak on the Dora-Maira
massif. The peak was isolated
by alluvial deposits which
covered much of the Po river
valley in the quaternary
period. The reserve protects
varied vegetation (from caper
bushes to birch trees), various
bird species (from kestrels to
the great spotted wood-
pecker) and important rock
paintings dating from the
post-Neolithic period.

Luserna San Giovanni ❹

Turin. **Map** C4. 👥 7,990. 🚊
Turin–Pinerolo. 🛈 **Town Hall** Via
Roma 31, 0121 954 114; **Pro Loco**
Via Trieste 15, 0121 902 441. 🗓 Fri.
🎪 Book Fair, May; Fair of the Saints,
Nov. 🌐 www.montagnedoc.it,
www.comune.luserna.to.it

THE VALLEY'S MOST populous
commune is made up
of Alta Luserna, Cattolica
and San Giovanni and
is inhabited mainly by
Waldensians. The
three areas were united
in 1871, and the village
of Airali became the
administrative centre.

Fortified by the
11th century,
between 1400 and
the Napoleonic
campaigns it was an
important town in the
valley (formerly Val
Lucerna), partly
because of its
geographical position.
A variety of gneiss, known
as Luserna stone, is still
quarried in this area.

**Monument
to Arnaud,
Torre Pellice**

Borgo Vecchio, once the
residence of the Luserna
lords, is on the far side of the
river Pellice and is connected
by a stone bridge (1600) at
Lusernetta. Airali stands on
the road to Torre Pellice, and
San Giovanni is on the left of
the valley. Medieval buildings
in the Borgo Vecchio include
the palazzo of the Luserna
counts, the church of San
Giacomo, the Ala Pubblica
(the site of the market), the
monastery of San Francesco
and that of the Serviti, and
the former Mauritian hospital.

Torre Pellice ❺

Turin. **Map** C4. 👥 4,600.
🚊 Turin–Pinerolo. 🛈 **Pro Loco** Via
Repubblica 3, 0121 953 221;
Comunità Montana Corso
Lombardini 2, 0121 952 411. 🗓
Wed, Fri. 🎪 Organic market, 2nd Sat
in month. 🌐 www.montagnedoc.it

MENTION of this town is
found in documents of
1186 and its name probably
refers to the defensive
tower (torre) built on
the hill where the
Pellice and
Angrogna rivers
meet. The oldest part
of the town probably
stood near the old
cemetery in Via del
Forte. This charming
spot is the capital of
the Waldensian
community.

The town began to
grow in the early
19th century and
saw important
developments thanks to the
denominational solidarity of
English travellers of the

Val Pellice viewed from Lusernetta, at 500 m (1,640 ft) above sea level

The town of Torre Pellice and the surrounding valley

Anglican faith. Two exponents of the British pro-Waldensian movement, General Charles Beckwith and the Reverend Stephen Gilly, encouraged education and the construction of some of the buildings, still important components of Protestant Torre Pellice today: the church, the presbytery and the house of the professors. Carlo Alberto had the Mauritian Catholic church and the adjacent fountain built in 1845. Until the early 1960s Torre Pellice was home to the Mazzonis factory and was an important industrial town.

Torre Pellice has a long tradition in ice hockey and has an excellent ice rink. The ice hockey teams will train and compete here during the 2006 Winter Olympics.

The valley's most important **Museo Valdese** (Waldensian museum) is also in Torre Pellice, in Via Beckwith. The historical section is of great interest, illustrating the entire Waldensian history, from its origins until 1948. Apart from an impressive amount of documentation about the religion, the institution also has a copy of the Olivetan Bible (the first Bible in French, translated in 1532 not from Latin, but from the Greek and Hebrew originals, by Pietro Robert, known as Olivetan), the culverin (a type of gun) of Capitan Giosuè Gianavello and various

memorabilia of the English general Charles Beckwith.

The ethnographic section illustrates aspects of mountain life with reconstructions of typical rooms showing the everyday and religious life of the past. The same building also houses a library with over 100,000 books, the archive of the Waldensian Table, the Waldensian Study Society and a Cultural Centre.

Torre Pellice is also home to the **Galleria Civica d'Arte Moderna "Filippo Scroppo"** which has around 400 paintings, sculptures and drawings by Italian post-war artists including Carena, Cherchi, Cordero, Galvano, Garelli, Griffa, Levi, Mastroianni, Menzio, Merz, Pistoletto and Ruggeri. Filippo

Scroppo, a painter and journalist, began to collect the works in 1949 and his exhibitions included many artists who later exhibited at the Venice Biennale.

🏛 **Museo Valdese**
Fondazione Centro Culturale Valdese, Via Beckwith 3. 📞 0121 932 179. FAX 0121 932 566. ⏰ 3–6pm Thu, Sat, Sun (4–7pm daily, Aug). ⬤ Dec, Jan. 📷 🚻 ♿ ✉ contact the Il Barba association, 0121 950 203. @ il.barba@tin.it, centroculturale valdese@tin.it W www.fondazionevaldese.org

🏛 **Galleria Civica d'Arte Moderna "Filippo Scroppo"**
Via M D'Azeglio 10. 📞 0121 932 530. ⏰ 3.30–6.30pm Tue–Thu, Sun; 10.30am–12.30pm Fri; 10.30am–12.30pm, 3–6.30pm Sat.

Paese Alpino **(1961) by Daphne Casorati, Galleria Scroppo**

Angrogna ❻

Turin. **Map** C4. 🏔 759. 🚌 *Torre
Pellice.* 🏠 **Town Hall** *Piazza Roma
1, 0121 944 153.* 🎨 *Autumn Fair,
Oct.* 🅆 *www.montagnedoc.it*

Angrogna, with its
characteristic hamlets, is
the most widespread of Val
Pellice's communes and has
preserved many traces of its
history. The Synod, in which
the Waldensians joined the
Protestant Reformation and
came out from under cover,
was held in Chanforàn in
1532. A memorial stele marks
the site and commemorates
this important date.

The Coulege del Barba, once used by future Waldensian clergymen

The oldest
Waldensian church
is in Angrogna, as
well as the Gheisa
d'la Tana, a
concealed grotto
where secret
meetings were
probably held.

Another attraction
is the Coulege del
Barba in Pra del
Torno, a rustic
country house
similar to an alpine
hut with stone walls
and stone-tiled
roofs. This
secluded spot was
used by those
preparing to become
ministers and for Bible
courses. Also within the
territory of the commune are

**A stone stele recording
the Synod of 1532**

a section of the Ecomuseo
della Resistenza walking tour,
a rock with the profile of a
prophet (on Colle
Vaccera), a
stopping place
along the Grande
Traversata delle
Alpi route through
the mountains, the
Museo dei Pons, set
up to preserve
traces of country
life, and prehistoric
rock carvings.

The **Museo della
Donna** (Museum of
Womankind), in the
hamlet of Serre di
Angrognas, is part
of the museum
network of the
Waldensian valleys.
The museum is housed in a
"Beckwith school", one of
many small schools built by
Charles Beckwith in the

1800s. The museum looks at
the role of Protestant women
in an international context
and how this intertwines with
the role of Waldensian
women in the valleys.

Not far away, in the village
of Odin-Bertot, in another
small Beckwith school, is the
Museo Odin-Bertot. The
museum covers Waldensian
education of the last century
and shows the importance
attached to the reading and
writing skills of children who,
from an early age, were able
to read Bible texts.

🏛 **Museo della Donna**
Serre. 📞 *0121 944 182.* 🕐 *by
appt.* 🔳 *Il Barba, 0121 950 203.*
🅆 *www.fondazionevaldese.org*
@ *il.barba@tin.it*
🏛 **Museo Odin-Bertot**
Località Odin. 📞 *0121 944 144,
0121 950 203 (Il Barba).* 🕐 *by appt.*
🅆 *www.fondazionevaldese.org*

The stone profile known as the "face of the prophet" on Colle Vaccera, near Angrogna

The Waldensian Community

THE WALDENSIAN MOVEMENT began in Lyon in around 1180 when Pierre Waldes, a rich merchant who gave away his worldly goods, started to preach the gospel and gather around him the so-called followers of the "Poor of Lyon". His public preaching provoked the reaction of the Church and persecution soon began. Two and a half centuries of repression reduced the movement, which remained active only in Bohemia, the Dauphiné, the Pellice, Chisone and Germanasca valleys, and Calabria (until the 1561 massacre). At the Synod of Chanforàn in 1532, medieval Waldensianism

Henri Arnaud, Museo Valdese, Balsiglia

adhered to the Reformation begun by Luther and became a Protestant church. No longer a secret cult, the first churches were built, itinerant preachers *(barbas)* became resident ministers, and the community was modelled on the Calvinist church. Persecution by the Savoys began in the second half of the 1500s, and the 1600s saw many attacks against European Protestants. Religious conflict in the Waldensian valleys provoked military campaigns and massacres (that of 1655 was particularly bloody). It wasn't until 17 February 1848 that the Waldensians gained civil and political freedom.

THE EXODUS AND GLORIOUS REPATRIATION

In 1685, in the wake of the revocation of the Edict of Nantes (which guaranteed Huguenots religious freedom), Vittorio Amedeo II's edict was issued. Months of terror and violence ensued, forcing Waldensians to forsake their beliefs or seek exile in Switzerland or southern Germany. In summer 1689, the establishment of the Savoy duchy created a new political situation, and a military expedition (the Glorious Repatriation) led by pastor Henri Arnaud brought around 1,000 Waldensians and Huguenots back to the valleys.

Resistance in Vallone degli Invincibili (1686)

A Waldensian minister leads the group

On the eve of 17 February numerous "bonfires of joy" burn in the valley, recalling those of 1848 which sent the message from village to village that civil and religious rights had been recognized with Carlo Alberto's 1848 Statute.

Women *are part of the pastoral staff and hold important roles in the social sector. Typical costume, consisting of a long skirt, shawl and embroidered bonnet, is worn on 17 February and for confirmation and baptisms.*

The Centro Culturale Valdese, founded in Torre Pellice in 1989 on the 300th anniversary of the Glorious Repatriation, houses a museum, library, documentation centre, photographic archives, an archive of the Waldensian Tablet and a study society.

The interior of the Crumière mill in Villar Pellice

Rorà ❼

Turin. **Map** C4. 👥 *261*. 🚌
Luserna–Torre Pellice. 🏛 **Town Hall**
Vía Duca Amedeo 18, 0121 931 02.
📅 *Fri.* 🎭 *Festa di Giari, end
May–beginning Jun.*
🆆 *www.montagnedoc.it*

THIS SMALL COMMUNE, whose
name means "oak wood"
in dialect, extends to the foot
of Monte Frioland. In the
Middle Ages the Waldensian
community came under the
feudal rule of the lords of
Luserna and during the
Waldensian resistance, Vallone
di Rorà was an important
centre for the groups led by
Giosuè Gianavello (1655).
Stone quarrying has long been
an important source of income
for the local people, and the
Bounet quarries are still in
operation today.

Of particular interest is the
Museo Valdese in the village
centre. The museum, laid out
on two floors, displays old
farm implements and those of
the quarrymen who extracted
Luserna stone (gneiss), as
well as various objects used
in everyday life.

In an old gneiss quarry,
1 km (half a mile) from the
village in the area of Fournais
(meaning "furnaces"), you
can visit the **Ecomuseo della
Pietra**. Here, life-size models
and tools displayed along a
walking route show how
stone was extracted in the
19th century and the various
phases of its production. Two
sites can be visited, one
where the Ecomuseo stands
in the centre of the village,
the other at the Tulipet
quarry, which can be toured

with a guide. The quarries
still in production are on the
road to Mugniva.

🏛 **Museo Valdese di Rorà**
Via Vittorio Amedeo II 11. 📞 *0121
931 02, 0121 950 203 (Il Barba).* 🕐
9–12 noon, 4–7pm Sun, Jun–Sep. ✉
🆆 *www.fondazionevaldese.org*
🏛 **Ecomuseo della Pietra**
Fournais. 📞 *0121 952 411, 0121
934 907 (AGESS, Piazza Jervis 1, Villar
Pellice).* 🕐 *Mar–Oct by appt.*

Villar Pellice ❽

Turin. **Map** C4. 👥 *1,215*. 🚌 *from
Pinerolo.* 🏛 **Town Hall** *Viale
I Maggio, 0121 930 712.* 📅 *Thu.*
🆆 *www.montagnedoc.it*

VILLAR PELLICE is the second-
last inhabited village in
the valley. It dominates the

middle part of the river
Pellice basin. During the
centuries when the
Waldensians were under
persecution, the village was
at the heart of the conflict,
but it enjoyed a period of
peace from the 18th century
on, apart from a bloody battle
between the Piedmontese
and French in 1794.

In the former **Crumière**
factory, which dates from the
early 20th century, there is an
interesting industrial museum
documenting the history of
the textile industry, with
exhibits of machinery.

Bobbio Pellice ❾

Turin. **Map** C4. 👥 *600*. 🚌 *from
Pinerolo.* 🏛 **Town Hall** *Piazza Caduti
per la Libertà 7, 0121 957 882;* **Pro
Loco Bobbio Pellice** *Via Maestra 25,
0121 957 989.* 📅 *Tue.*
🎭 *Blood sausage Fair, Oct.*
🆆 *www.montagnedoc.it*

THIS IS THE highest
commune in Val Pellice.
Although the administrative
area is large, there are few
inhabitants. Overlooked by
the peak of Bariùnt and
framed by wonderful
mountain scenery, its history
is closely linked to that of the
Waldensian community. In
the past it was subject to
disastrous flooding, and in the

Bobbio Pellice, surrounded by mountains

Panorama of Valle Carbonieri in Alta Val Pellice

19th century it was protected by a dam (the so-called Cromwell dam) built at the western end of the village, still partly visible.

A 15-minute walk from the square leads to the Sibaud monument, erected in 1899 on the site where returning Waldensians of the Glorious Repatriation swore to keep their faith alive in the future.

The centre of Bobbio Pellice in winter

floods the Maritime Alps, but neither are there the severe cliffs and glaciers that characterize the ridge further north. Monviso is not far away as the crow flies; it is enough to climb one of the many peaks in the valley to see this majestic mountain. The upper part of Val Pellice is a world of green meadows and wide valleys, offering splendid views. It is a good area for climbers in search of routes of medium difficulty.

From Bobbio Pellice a road leads to Villanova (1,223 m/ 4,010 ft), from where a dirt track (closed to private traffic) gives access to the wide valley of Prà and the Willy Jervis refuge (1,732 m/5,680 ft). This is an excellent base for excursions towards the Colle della Croce (2,298 m/7,540 ft; 1 hr 20 mins), a pass giving access to Vallée du Guil, Queyras, Monte Palavas (2,929 m/9,610 ft; 3hr 45 mins), Colle Barant (2,373 m/7,785 ft), home to the Bruno Pyronel botanical

garden (tel. 0121 953 547) or, further on, the Battaglione Monte Granero refuge (2,377 m/7,800 ft) and the peak of Granero (3,171 m/10,405 ft), which is the highest point in the valley. However, by passing Villanova and re-ascending the valley of Crosenna, you reach the Colle Boucie (2,630 m/8,630 ft). Experienced climbers can get to the top of Bric Boucie (2,998 m/9,835 ft) from here.

A turning off the main road in the upper valley, 1 km (half a mile) before Bobbio Pellice, crosses a bridge over a stream, and climbs the Valle dei Carbonieri up to the Barbara Lowrie refuge (1,753 m/5,750 ft).

Valle Angrogna can be reached by car from Piazza Pietro Micca (just as you enter Torre Pellice) and by turning right a few metres before Torrente Angrogna. The road leads up to Pradeltorno (1,024 m/3,359 ft), an old Waldensian stronghold and the site of a temple, the historic Collegio dei Barba (for the itinerant preachers of medieval Waldensianism), and a Catholic church.

Descending to Chiot dl'Aiga, it is worth climbing up to Serre (847 m/2,780 ft) to see the Waldensian church and an old Beckwith school. You can also go on foot along the *Sentiero Storico* which passes Chanforàn (where the Waldensians joined the Reformation in 1532), the Beckwith school in Odin, and the Ghieisa d'la Tana, said to have been used as a place of Waldensian worship when it was a secret cult.

Alta Val Pellice ⑩

Turin. **Map** B4. 🚠 *261*. 🇮
Comunità Montana Val Pellice
Via J Lombardini 2, Torre Pellice, 0121 952 411; **Pro Loco Bobbio Pellice**
Via Maestra 25, 0121 957 989;
Gruppo Guide Alpine *c/o Willy Jervis Refuge 0121 932 755.*
W www.montagnedoc.it,
www.valpellice.to.it

T HE VILLAGES of Alta Val Pellice do not enjoy the Mediterranean light that

Hikers at the Pis waterfalls, near Villanova

A Tour of Monviso ⑪

Signposts on the path

THE "Giro del Monviso" does not require special climbing skills and takes five days, staying overnight in refuges in good weather. A round trip, it starts and ends at the Lowrie refuge (1,753 m/ 5,750 ft), passing the Jervis (1,750 m/5,740 ft) and Granero (2,377 m/ 7,800 ft) refuges. From Colle Selliere the route descends to the Refuge du Viso (2,460 m/ 8,070 ft) in France. After the Vallanta pass (2,811 m/9,220 ft), you come to the Vallanta refuge. From the Colle di San Chiaffredo (2,764 m/9,070 ft) and Colle Gallarino (2,728 m/8,950 ft) you reach the Sella refuge on the Grande di Viso lake (2,640 m/8,660 ft). The route then traces the source of the Po, Pian del Re, and Col d'Armoine (2,689 m/8,820 ft).

Willy Jervis Refuge
This refuge in the lovely valley of Prà, at 1,732 m/5,680 ft, near a practice wall and Barant, is reached from Villanova along a mule track in 80 minutes, or from the Barbara Lowrie refuge along an old military road in under three hours.

Passo di Vallanta
At 2,811 m/9,220 ft this hill leads to splendid views overlooking the western slope of Monviso. From the pass you descend towards the Vallanta refuge (2,450 m/8,040 ft) and then along the wide valley towards Castello.

The regional nature park of Queyras, in France

Alpine valley with typical stone houses

KEY

═══	Minor road
═══	Other roads
━━━	Main path
━━━	Minor path
▪ ▪	Other paths
ⓐ	Refuge

Map labels:
Barant, Jervis al Prà, Pellice, CONCA DEL PRA, Lago Mal Consej, Granero, Lago Lungo, MONTE GRANERO, COL SELLIERE, 2,834 m/9,300ft, 3,171 m/10,405 ft, Bergerie du Grand Vallon, COLLE DELLE TRAVERSETTE, 2,950 m/9,680 ft, VALLE DEL GUIL, Caf Viso, Giacometti, VALLONE DI VALLANTA, Vallanta, Chianale, VAL VARAITA, Pontechianale, Maddalena, Lago di Castello, Castello

◁ **Snow-clad Monviso seen from Ostana, near Crissolo, in the province of Cuneo**

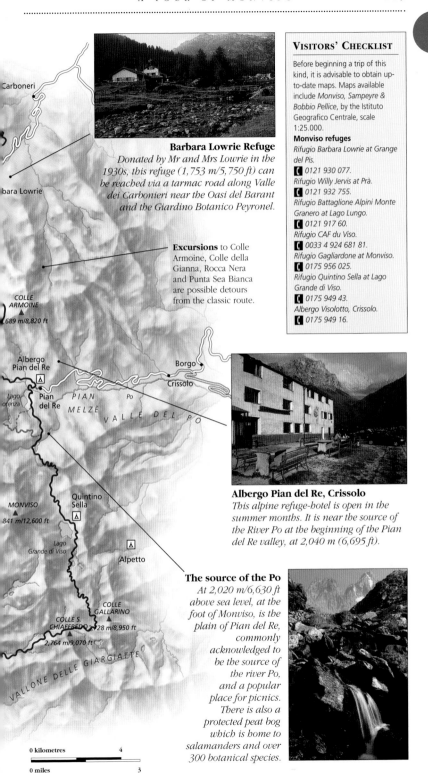

Barbara Lowrie Refuge
Donated by Mr and Mrs Lowrie in the 1930s, this refuge (1,753 m/5,750 ft) can be reached via a tarmac road along Valle dei Carbonieri near the Oasi del Barant and the Giardino Botanico Peyronel.

Excursions to Colle Armoine, Colle della Gianna, Rocca Nera and Punta Sea Bianca are possible detours from the classic route.

Albergo Pian del Re, Crissolo
This alpine refuge-hotel is open in the summer months. It is near the source of the River Po at the beginning of the Pian del Re valley, at 2,040 m (6,695 ft).

The source of the Po
At 2,020 m/6,630 ft above sea level, at the foot of Monviso, is the plain of Pian del Re, commonly acknowledged to be the source of the river Po, and a popular place for picnics. There is also a protected peat bog which is home to salamanders and over 300 botanical species.

0 kilometres   4

0 miles   3

Monviso

T HE "VISO", as it is often referred to in Piedmont, is a constant presence and its white snowfields in winter or the darkening rocks in the summer are a familiar everyday sight. For centuries the surrounding valleys were part of the small alpine state of the Escartons Republic. Later, with the birth of centralized states, Monviso was no longer the centre of a country but a border. Lying among the mountains of the Alpi Cozie, Monviso is the most impressive, the most visible and the most famous peak. The river Po starts here and then flows across northern Italy. The mountain was climbed for the first time in 1861 by the British climbers Matthews and Jacomb.

The unmistakeable triangular form of Monviso

Quintino Sella, a statesman and scientist, participated in the first Italian ascent of Monviso (August 1863). He founded the Club Alpino Italiano two months later.

The Alpi Cozie range

Monviso is 3,841 m/ 12,600 ft high

THE GIANT OF THE ALPI COZIE

Monviso lies entirely within Italy and is surrounded by peaks at least 500 m/1,640 ft lower. It is visible from the nearby valleys and the distant plain. The valleys are all different: the wide Val Varaita, the steep Valle Po, the French valley of Guil and the long Vallone di Vallanta.

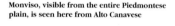

Monviso, visible from the entire Piedmontese plain, is seen here from Alto Canavese

The wildlife *is varied and increasingly protected. For example, deer have been reintroduced in the Po valley. Alpine salamanders of Lanza inhabit the peat bog of Pian del Re and the wet areas.*

Refuges
Many of the dozen or so refuges are run by CAI (Italian Alpine Club). A useful map is Carta dei Sentieri e dei Rifugi del Monviso. *There are also bivouacs and stopping places. In Alta Valle Po, the Alpetto refuge was reopened next to a historic bivouac in 2003. The oldest refuge is on Monte Granero (2,377 m/7,800 ft).*

The alpine ibex has been introduced into the protected area of Monviso. The first four were introduced into Val Pellice in 1978. Alpine ibex can be seen near the Colle delle Traversette and the Giacoletti and Quintino Sella refuges and also sometimes as high up as 3,200 m/10,500 ft.

Off-piste skiing enables you to admire Monviso from every possible angle. There are numerous trails with refuges and stopping places. It is also possible to contact local alpine guides. At Pian della Regina di Crissolo and Pian Munè di Paesana there are lift facilities.

In France, the Aiguillette group in the Parc Regional du Queyras is an exceptional viewpoint from which to admire the steep slopes of the northwest face of Monviso.

The source of the Po at Pian del Re is a depression of glacial origins lying at 2,020 m/6,630 ft. The numerous springs fed by the glaciers collect into streams which then run down towards the plain.

THE GREAT ITALIAN RIVER

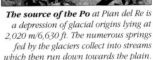

Mallard

After the steep climb along the twisting hairpin bends of the Po valley, the plain of Pian del Re at the foot of the Monviso peak, with its peat bog scored with winding rivulets, is an unexpected sight. From this altitude, at a little over 2,000 m (6,560 ft) above sea level, the longest river in Italy begins to flow eastwards over a distance of 652 km (405 miles) to the broad delta south of Venice, on Italy's Adriatic coast. The Po river basin is the most important in Italy, measuring a little less than 75,000 sq km (29,000 sq miles), some of which lies in Switzerland. The maximum capacity of the river can reach 8,940 cu m (315,580 cu ft) of water per second.

The river Po crossing the Piedmontese plain

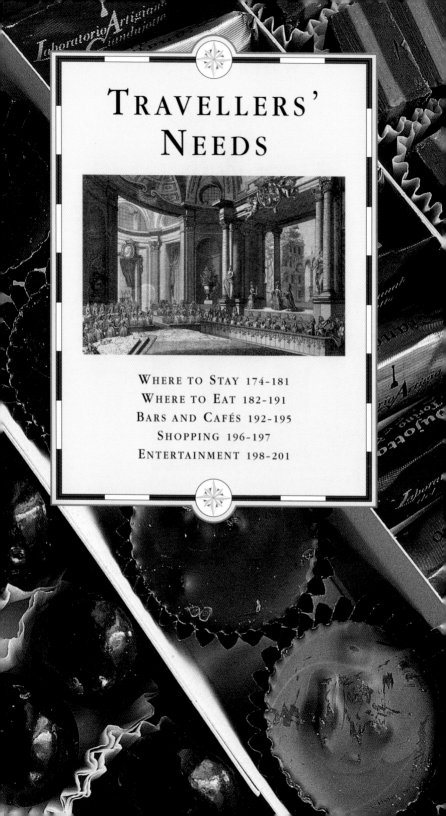

TRAVELLERS' NEEDS

WHERE TO STAY 174–181

WHERE TO EAT 182–191

BARS AND CAFÉS 192–195

SHOPPING 196–197

ENTERTAINMENT 198–201

WHERE TO STAY

TURIN AND THE VALLEYS are preparing to host a major event: the 2006 Winter Olympics. The city of the Savoys has a long tradition of hospitality, and some of the hotels in business today date from around the mid-19th century. This important and prestigious event is certain to attract a large number of visitors and many hoteliers have set about renovating their premises in order to meet high international standards. This has often meant the complete re-styling of the external architecture, the hotel's public areas and the bedrooms themselves, in which you will often find the latest technological facilities, such as satellite TV, computer points, fax machines and modems. There is a wide choice of hotels in the city itself, ranging from luxury hotels designed to cater for a large number of guests, with conference facilities, to smaller and more intimate family-run hotels. Guesthouses provide a personal service but do not usually offer meals. The surrounding valleys also offer many accommodation options for skiers and mountain lovers, and visitors can choose between the elegant luxury hotels, a simple alpine hut or one of the agritourism centres.

Weekend a Torino logo

The hall of the Grand Hotel Sitea in Turin

HOTELS

HOTEL FACILITIES in Turin fall into the medium to high category. Service is very professional and facilities are good quality. Many of the hotels cater particularly for the business sector and therefore have large well-equipped meeting rooms with all the latest technology.

The importance of tourism to the city can be seen by the presence of the major international hotel chains, including Jolly Hotels, Best Western and Starhotels. Turin's own hotel group, Turin Hotels International (THI) was founded in 1991 by Amato Ramondetti, owner of the Turin Palace Hotel and the Ristorante Del Cambio (*see p187*).

The Turismo Torino information points (*see p175*) offer a free hotel booking service for Turin and the surrounding area in the 48 hours prior to arrival. The *Weekend a Torino* deal offers two nights in a double room (free for children under 12 years old) with breakfast, plus the Torino Card (*see p205*) and a special gift.

BOUTIQUE AND HISTORIC HOTELS

MANY HOTELS have preserved the charm and elegance of the city's fine 19th-century buildings, sometimes with frescoed ceilings, detailed stuccowork and antique furniture. These unusual and characterful establishments aim to provide a friendly, personal service. In many, modern facilities have been installed without compromising the charm of the historic buildings in which they are located.

AGRITOURISM

FARMHOUSE ACCOMMODATION, or *agriturismo*, has developed greatly over the years in the province of

Farmhouse accommodation, a popular option in the province of Turin

◁ **A selection of home-made chocolates from the *pasticceria* Gobino in Turin**

Overlooking the resort of Sestrière with its modern hotels

Turin. Most holiday farms are in the mountains and provide simple, but clean and functional accommodation. Genuine home-made food is served, specializing in the typical, traditional dishes of the valleys. Many of these farms also run summer courses aimed at encouraging children and young people to take part in outdoor activities.

Another country option that is becoming more widespread in the region is staying in an inn, or *locanda*. This old type of hotel, which historically provided food and shelter for travellers, has become very popular. This is partly thanks to the success of theme holidays offering wine and gastronomy tours. Options range from simple, family-run inns to upmarket *relais gourmand* restaurants.

BED AND BREAKFAST

P ROVIDING a restaurant service is often considered an uneconomic enterprise, and many hoteliers prefer to offer a more simple solution such as bed and breakfast accommodation. In Turin and the valleys, many places offer bed and breakfast only, but the owner will often recommend places to eat out.

In Turin itself there are about 40 bed and breakfast places, some located in historic buildings. Some 20 of these are conveniently located in the city centre.

ACCOMMODATION IN THE VALLEYS

T HE VIA LATTEA, or Milky Way, is a paradise for skiers with its network of 400 km (250 miles) of ski slopes for all levels. The hotel facilities on offer in the ski areas are already very good, but have been augmented for the Winter Olympics and many new hotels, often with elegant, well-equipped spas, have been built.

An alternative is a traditional family-run alpine guesthouse with rustic decor. In the more popular places you can also rent a studio or apartments for short periods. Other accommodation on offer in the valleys includes agritourism, bed-and-breakfast, rented rooms, holiday flats and camping sites.

The Willy Jervis refuge in Val Pellice

DIRECTORY

Turismo Torino
Atrium, Piazza Solferino, Turin.
(011 53 51 81/53 59 01.
FAX 011 883 426.
W www.turismotorino.org
@ info@turismotorino.org

Montagnedoc Incoming
Piazza Garambois 2,
Oulx (To).
(0122 831 596.
FAX 0122 831 880.
W www.montagnedoc.it
@ incoming@montagnedoc.it

IAT Avigliana
Piazza del Popolo 2,
Avigliana (To).
(011 936 60 37.
FAX 011 936 82 92.
W www.montagnedoc.it
@ avigliana@montagnedoc.it

IAT Bardonecchia
Viale della Vittoria 4,
Bardonecchia (To).
(0122 990 32.
FAX 0122 980 612.
W www.montagnedoc.it
@ bardonecchia@
montagnedoc.it

IAT Clavière
Via Nazionale 30, Clavière (To).
(0122 878 856.
FAX 0122 878 888.
W www.montagnedoc.it
@ claviere@montagnedoc.it

IAT Fenestrelle
Piazza della Fiera 1,
Fenestrelle (To).
(0121 836 17.
FAX 0121 830 82.
W www.montagnedoc.it
@ fenestrelle@montagnedoc.it

IAT Pinerolo
Viale Giolitti 7/9, Pinerolo (To).
(0121 795 589.
FAX 0121 794 932.
W www.montagnedoc.it
@ pinerolo@montagnedoc.it

IAT Sauze d'Oulx
Piazza Assietta 18,
Sauze d'Oulx.
(0122 858 009.
FAX 0122 850 700.
W www.montagnedoc.it
@ sauze@montagnedoc.it

IAT Sestrière
Via Louset 14, Sestrière (To).
(0122 755 444.
FAX 0122 755 171.
W www.montagnedoc.it
@ sestriere@montagnedoc.it

Choosing a Hotel

THESE HOTELS have been selected across a wide price range,
for their good facilities or their location. They are listed
according to the area divisions used in this guide. The colour
code for Turin is red while the other areas follow the colours
used throughout this book. For the Road Map references see
the inside back cover and the Turin Street Finder.

	CREDIT CARDS	GARDEN OR TERRACE	SWIMMING POOL	PARKING	RESTAURANT OR BAR

TURIN

Amadeus e Teatro €€
Via Principe Amedeo 41 bis. **Map** 3 A5. 011 817 49 51. FAX 011 817 49 53.
www.turinhotelcompany.com amadeus_hotel@libero.it
This small hotel is housed in a 19th-century building near the Mole Antonelliana.
The rooms are tastefully furnished. A buffet breakfast is served
in the former winter garden. TV Rooms: 28. Aug.

| | ■ | | | ● | ■ |

Aprile €
Via delle Orfane 19. **Map** 3 A3. 011 436 01 04. www.aprile.to.it info@aprile.to.it
A delightful bed and breakfast in the heart of old Turin, the Quadrilatero
Romano. Three tastefully decorated rooms, all with private bathroom.
A good-value option. Rooms: 3. 3 wks Jan; Jul, Aug–11 Sep.

Aston €€€
Strada Mongreno 23. **Map** 4 F5 off map. 011 899 87 33. FAX 011 89 89 472.
www.astonhotel.it info@astonhotel.it
Situated at the foot of the Turinese hills but only 5 km (3 miles) from the
centre. Modern, comfortable rooms. Free parking and conference centre,
restaurant and American-style bar. TV Rooms: 40. 2 wks mid-Aug.

| | ■ | | | ● | ■ |

Boston €€€€
Via Massena 70. **Map** 6 F1. 011 500 359. FAX 011 599 358.
www.hotelbostontorino.it direzione@hotelbostontorino.it
Elegant hotel with a gallery of contemporary art in the upmarket district of
Crocetta. Comfortable rooms and fine suites. The restaurant, Casa Vicina,
offers excellent Piedmontese cuisine. TV small breeds. Rooms: 87.

| | ■ | ● | | ● | ■ |

Chelsea €€€
Via Cappel Verde 1/d. **Map** 3 B4. 011 436 01 00.
FAX 011 436 31 41. www.hotelchelsea.it prenotazioni@hotelchelsea.it
A traditional, family-run hotel in a central location. Comfortable rooms and
meeting facilities for business travellers. The restaurant, La Campana, serves
typical Mediterranean dishes. TV Rooms: 15. Aug.

| | ■ | | | ● | ■ |

Atahotel Concord €€€€€
Via Lagrange 47. **Map** 7 A1. 011 517 67 56. FAX 011 517 63 05.
www.hotelconcord.com prenotazioni@hotelconcord.com
This modern, functional hotel in a 19th-century building is ideal for business
travellers. It has a conference centre, garage and laundry. The Le Lanterne
restaurant serves Piedmontese cuisine. TV small breeds. Rooms: 139.

| | ■ | | | ● | ■ |

Conte Biancamano €€€
Corso Vittorio Emanuele II 73. **Map** 1 A4. 011 562 32 81. FAX 011 562 37 89.
www.hotelcontebiancamano.it cbhtl.to@iol.it
A small, aristocratic hotel in a late 19th-century building with stuccowork and
frescoes. Sound-proofed rooms. TV small breeds. Rooms: 24. Aug, Christmas.

| | ■ | | | ● | ■ |

Crimea €€€€
Via Mentana 3. **Map** 7 C3. 011 660 47 00. FAX 011 660 49 12. www.hotelcrimea.it
A comfortable hotel from the 1960s in a quiet position near the Parco del
Valentino. Elegant public areas and well-furnished rooms. Buffet breakfast.
TV small breeds. Rooms: 49. Aug.

| | ■ | | | ● | ■ |

Des Artistes €€€€
Via Principe Amedeo 21. **Map** 3 A5. 011 812 44 16. FAX 011 812 44 66.
www.desartisteshotel.it info@desartisteshotel.it
Professional staff and comfortable, sound-proofed rooms. Des Artistes numbers
film and TV celebrities among its guests. TV Rooms: 22. Aug.

| | ■ | | | ● | ■ |

Price categories are per night for two people, occupying a standard double room, with tax, breakfast and service included:
€ under 75 euros
€€ 75–125 euros
€€€ 125–175 euros
€€€€ 175–225 euros
€€€€€ over 225 euros

CREDIT CARDS
Major credit cards are accepted.

GARDEN OR TERRACE
Park, garden or a panoramic terrace.

SWIMMING POOL
Unless otherwise specified, the swimming pool is open-air.

RESTAURANT
Good restaurant, also open to non-residents.

	Credit Cards	Garden or Terrace	Swimming Pool	Parking	Restaurant or Bar
Diplomatic €€€€€ Via Cernaia 42. **Map** 2 E4. **C** 011 561 24 44. **FAX** 011 540 472. **W** www.hotel-diplomatic.it This hotel, near Porta Susa station, is in a six-storey building and has well-furnished rooms with satellite TV and safes. As well as the Crimea restaurant, the hotels also has conference facilities and a laundry. 目 TV ⛄ 🛁 Rooms: 126.	■			●	■
Dogana Vecchia €€€ Via Corte d'Appello 4. **Map** 3 A4. **C** 011 436 67 52. **FAX** 011 436 71 94. **W** www.hoteldoganavecchia.it **@** info@hoteldoganavecchia.it Part of a gracious old palazzo in the heart of the Quadrilatero Romano. Central, but quiet, with good size rooms. TV ⛄ Rooms: 64. ● Aug.	■			●	
Genio €€€€ Corso Vittorio Emanuele II 47. **Map** 6 F1. **C** 011 650 57 71. **FAX** 011 650 82 64. **W** www.hotelgenio.it **@** info@hotelgenio.it Near Porta Nuova railway station, this hotel has rooms and suites of varying types with satellite and pay TV. Buffet breakfast. 目 & TV ⛄ Rooms: 120.	■			●	■
Genova e Stazione €€€€ Via Sacchi 14/b. **Map** 6 F2. **C** 011 56 29 400. **FAX** 011 562 98 96. **W** www.albergogenova.it Each of the rooms in this late 19th-century building near Porta Nuova railway station has different furnishings and decor. 目 & TV ⛄ Rooms: 78.	■				■
Giotto €€ Via Giotto 27. **Map** 6 F5. **C** 011 663 71 72. **FAX** 011 663 71 73. **W** www.turinhotelcompany.com **@** giottohotel@libero.it A modern hotel towards Lingotto. The rooms are comfortable, and each is equipped with its own water massage tub. 目 TV ⛄ Rooms: 50.	■			●	■
Grand Hotel Sitea €€€€€ Via Carlo Alberto 35. **Map** 3 B5. **C** 011 517 01 71. **FAX** 011 548 090. **W** www.thi.it A historic hotel behind Piazza San Carlo, offering elegant rooms with classic decor and marble bathrooms. The hotel restaurant is the Carignano. Conference facilities are also available. 目 & TV ⛄ Rooms: 114.	■	●		●	■
Holiday Inn Turin Centre €€€€ Via Assietta 3. **Map** 6 F1. **C** 011 516 71 11. **FAX** 011 516 76 99. **W** www.holiday-inn.com/turin-cityctr **@** hi.torit@libero.it A modern hotel in a 19th-century building: comfortable rooms, water massage tubs, satellite TV and conference facilities. 目 & TV ⛄ small breeds. Rooms: 57.	■			●	■
Jolly Hotel Ambasciatori €€€€ Corso Vittorio Emanuele II 104. **Map** 1 A4. **C** 011 57 52. **FAX** 011 544 978. **W** www.jollyhotels.it **@** torino_ambasciatori@jollyhotels.it A modern hotel near Porta Susa. Popular with business professionals, it has conference facilities equipped with the latest technology. Il Diplomatico restaurant is elegant. 目 & TV ⛄ Rooms: 199.	■				■
Liberty €€ Via Pietro Micca 15. **Map** 3 A5. **C** 011 562 88 01. **FAX** 011 562 81 63. **W** www.hotelliberty-torino.it **@** info@hotelliberty-torino.it A historic building in the city centre in the Art Nouveau style. The pleasant, comfortable rooms have antique furniture. 目 TV ⛄ Rooms: 35.	■				■
Le Meridien Lingotto €€€€€ Via Nizza 262. **C** 011 664 20 00. **FAX** 011 664 20 01. **W** www.lemeridien-lingotto.it A modern hotel which is a model for the city's projects for the future. An example of 1920s industrial architecture, it was redesigned by Renzo Piano, and combines the best of modern design and tradition. Luxurious rooms. Torpedo restaurant. 目 & TV ⛄ small breeds. ⛄ Rooms: 240.	■	●		●	■

For key to symbols see back flap

Price categories are per night for two people, occupying a standard double room, with tax, breakfast and service included:
€ under 75 euros
€€ 75–125 euros
€€€ 125–175 euros
€€€€ 175–225 euros
€€€€€ over 225 euros

CREDIT CARDS
Major credit cards are accepted.

GARDEN OR TERRACE
Park, garden or a panoramic terrace.

SWIMMING POOL
Unless otherwise specified, the swimming pool is open-air.

RESTAURANT
Good restaurant, also open to non-residents.

	CREDIT CARDS	GARDEN OR TERRACE	SWIMMING POOL	PARKING	RESTAURANT OR BAR
Le Meridien Lingotto Art + Tech €€€€€	■			●	■
Pacific Hotel Fortino €€€€	■	●		●	■
Piemontese €€€€	■			●	■
Starhotel Majestic €€€€€	■			●	■
Turin Palace Hotel €€€€€	■			●	■
Victoria €€€	■	●	●	●	■
Villa Sassi €€€€€	■	●		●	■
AVIGLIANA (To): *Chalet del Lago-La Magnolia* €	■	●		●	■
BARDONECCHIA (To): *Bucaneve* €	■	●		●	■
BARDONECCHIA (To): *Des Geneys-Splendid* €€€	■	●		●	■

Le Meridien Lingotto Art + Tech   €€€€€
Via Nizza 230. 011 664 20 00. FAX 011 664 20 01. W www.lemeridien-lingotto.it
The only five-star hotel in Turin, this luxury accommodation stands out for its design and modern technology, offering guests well designed, relaxing surroundings. *small breeds.* **Rooms: 142.**

Pacific Hotel Fortino   €€€€
Strada del Fortino 36. **Map** 2 F1. 011 521 77 57. FAX 011 521 77 49.
W www.pacifichotels.it @ hotelfortino@pacifichotels.it
A modern hotel near the city centre, suited to business professionals. The Teorema restaurant is excellent. **Rooms: 100.**

Piemontese   €€€€
Via Berthollet 21. **Map** 7 A2. 011 669 81 01. FAX 011 669 05 71. W www.hotelpiemontese.it
Located in a late 19th-century Art Nouveau building. Sound-proofed rooms, air conditioning, satellite TV and water massage tubs. **Rooms: 33.**

Starhotel Majestic   €€€€€
Corso Vittorio Emanuele II 54. **Map** 6 F1. 011 539 153. FAX 011 534 963.
W www.starhotels.com @ majestic.to@starhotels.com
An elegant hotel near Porta Nuova, good for business people, families and tourists. Le Regine restaurant. *small breeds.* **Rooms: 158.**

Turin Palace Hotel   €€€€€
Via Sacchi 8. **Map** 6 F1. 011 562 55 11. FAX 011 561 21 87.
W www.thi.it @ palace@thi.it
This charming, traditional hotel opened in 1872 near Porta Nuova station. The luxurious rooms have satellite TV and modem points. The Vigna Reale restaurant serves high quality cuisine. *small breeds.* **Rooms: 125.**

Victoria   €€€
Via Nino Costa 4. **Map** 7 B1. 011 561 19 09. FAX 011 561 18 06.
W www.hotelvictoria-torino.com @ reservation@hotelvictoria-torino.com
Popular with those who appreciate fine things, the bedrooms have canopied beds and antique furniture. Elegant public areas and professional service. In summer, breakfast is served under the gazebo outside. **Rooms: 100.**

Villa Sassi   €€€€€
Strada Traforo del Pino 47. **Map** 4 F3 off map. 011 898 05 56. FAX 011 898 00 95.
W www.villasassi.com @ info@villasassi.com
This 17th-century villa is set in a lovely garden. Romantic rooms and good service. Elegant restaurant with excellent wines. **Rooms: 16.**

VAL DI SUSA

AVIGLIANA (To): *Chalet del Lago-La Magnolia*   €
Via Monginevro 26. **Road Map** D3. 0119 369 225. FAX 0119 369 281.
W www.chalet-del-lago.it @ dellago@tin.it
A cosy chalet, with wood decor and terraces overlooking the lake. It has a gym and a beach with water skiing, sailing and canoeing facilities. **Rooms: 15.**

BARDONECCHIA (To): *Bucaneve*   €
Viale della Vecchia 2. **Road Map** A3. 0122 999 332. FAX 0122 999 980.
W www.hotelbucanevebardonecchia.it @ info@hotelbucanevebardonecchia.it
A chalet near woodlands and ski facilities. Rooms with natural wood furnishings. Reading room with a piano; restaurant. **Rooms: 22.** ● Sep–Nov.

BARDONECCHIA (To): *Des Geneys-Splendid*   €€€
Via Einaudi 21. **Road Map** A3. 0122 990 01. FAX 0122 999 295. W www.desgeneys.com
Hotel with a long tradition located in wooded area. Large functional rooms. Typical restaurant. **Rooms: 57.** ● 16 Apr–20 Jun, 16 Sep–15 Dec.

BARDONECCHIA (TO): *La Nigritella* €
Via Melezet 96. **Road Map** A3. 0122 980 477. FAX 0122 980 054.
A small hotel in a peaceful wood with seven pleasant, comfortable rooms. The restaurant is for hotel residents only. TV Rooms: 7. ● May, Jun, Oct, Nov.

GIAVENO (TO): *La Patuana Agriturismo* €
Via S Francesco d'Assisi 178, loc. Sala. **Road Map** D3. 0119 37 71 82. FAX 0119 377 182.
A farm holiday centre on a hilltop surrounded by woods and pastures where cows and pigs graze. Linen is provided and the rooms have central heating. Home cooking with typical dishes and regional wines. Courses are organized for children and it is possible to go riding in a gig. Rooms: 3. ● varies.

MATTIE (TO): *Il Mulino Agriturismo* €
Via Giordani 52. **Road Map** C2–3. FAX 0122 381 32. W www.mulinomattie.it
The guestrooms, in a converted early 20th-century mill, have fireplaces, stone walls, wooden furniture and rooms with bunk beds. Horse riding and holidays for youngsters can be organized. Home cooking. Rooms: 13. ● Jan.

OULX (TO): *Residence La Genzianella* €
Via Cazzettes 2. **Road Map** B3. FAX 0122 832 119.
W www.cascinagenzianella.it
An old converted farmhouse surrounded by a large garden, this place has one- or two-room accommodation with hand-made pine furniture. TV Rooms: 9.

SAUZE D'OULX (TO): *Grand Hotel Besson* €€€
Via del Rio 15. **Road Map** B3. 0122 859 785. FAX 0122 859 515.
W www.sauze2006.it/martini @ grandhotelbesson@sauze2006.it
In a converted historic building from the 1950s, the former Martini holiday centre, this is a very comfortable hotel with two restaurants, a spa and the latest technological facilities. The rooms and suites, with wood and stone decor, have LCD wall screens and Internet connections. TV Rooms: 50.

SAUZE D'OULX (TO): *Gran Baita* €
Via Villaggio Alpino 21. **Road Map** B3. 0122 850 183. FAX 0122 858 439.
W www.club2006.com
A comfortable hotel with rustic-style furnishings in a quiet position in the town centre, near the ski lifts. There are lovely views of the mountains from the garden. The restaurant offers typical regional dishes and special children's menus. TV Rooms: 32. ● Apr–Jun, Sep–mid-Dec.

SAUZE D'OULX (TO): *Il Capricorno* €€€
Via Case Sparse 21, loc. Les Clotes. **Road Map** B3. 0122 850 273.
FAX 0122 850 055. W www.chaletilcapricorno.it
Romantic wood-and-stone alpine hut in a pine forest at 1,800 m (5,900 ft). The wood-furnished rooms have splendid views. The restaurant's specialities include roast rabbit. TV Rooms: 7. ● 15 May–15 Jun, 15 Sep–1 Dec.

SUSA (TO): *Napoleon* €€
Via Mazzini 44. **Road Map** B2. 0122 622 855. FAX 0122 319 00. W www.hotelnapoleon.it
Hotel built in the 1970s in the centre of Susa. The rooms are comfortable and have wood furnishings. TV Rooms: 62.

THE CHISONE AND GERMANASCA VALLEYS

CESANA TORINESE (TO): *Chaberton* €€
Via Roma 10. **Road Map** A3. 0122 891 47. FAX 0122 897 163.
W www.hotelchaberton.com @ info@hotelchaberton.com
Family-run hotel at the centre of the Via Lattea ski complex with comfortable rooms and shuttle bus service to ski lifts. TV Rooms: 27. ● May, Nov.

CLAVIÈRE (TO): *Pian Del Sole* €€
Via Nazionale 26. **Road Map** A3. 0122 878 085. FAX 0122 878 731.
A small hotel in the centre, with eight well-furnished rooms. Good facilities. Near ski lifts, golf course and stables. TV Rooms: 8. ● 1 May–15 Jun, Oct.

FENESTRELLE (TO): *Meizoun Blancho Agriturismo* €
Via Granges 10, loc. Mentoulles. **Road Map** B3. FAX 0121 839 33.
A farm offering accommodation in the French-speaking area of the mountains, near the Parco Orsiera, with comfortable rooms. Linen is provided and there is central heating. Traditional cooking and home-made wines are on offer. Rooms: 5. ● varies.

For key to symbols see back flap

Price categories are per night for two people, occupying a standard double room, with tax, breakfast and service included:
€ under 75 euros
€€ 75–125 euros
€€€ 125–175 euros
€€€€ 175–225 euros
€€€€€ over 25 euros

CREDIT CARDS
Major credit cards are accepted.
GARDEN OR TERRACE
Park, garden or a panoramic terrace.
SWIMMING POOL
Unless otherwise specified, the swimming pool is open-air.
RESTAURANT
Good restaurant, also open to non-residents.

	CREDIT CARDS	GARDEN OR TERRACE	SWIMMING POOL	PARKING	RESTAURANT OR BAR
PRAGELATO (To): *Albergo Passet* €	■	●		●	■
PRALI (To): *Hotel delle Alpi* €	■	●		●	■
SESTRIÈRE (To): *Il Fraitevino* €€	■	●		●	■
SESTRIÈRE (To): *Grand Hotel Sestrière* €€	■	●	■	●	■
SESTRIÈRE (To): *Miramonti* €€	■	●		●	■
SESTRIÈRE (To): *Sud-Ovest* €€	■			●	■
USSEAUX (To): *Albergo Lago Laux* €€	■	●		●	■
VILLAR PEROSA (To): *Bianconero Hotel Meublé* €	■			●	■

PRAGELATO (To): *Albergo Passet*   €
Via Nazionale 5, Grange. **Road Map** B3. 0122 789 48. @ albergo.passet@tiscalinet.it
This long-established hotel is close to the centre of Pragelato, and has a popular restaurant and bar attached. The Passet is run by a local family. All rooms have en suite bathrooms and satellite TV. Lovely views of the surrounding countryside. TV Rooms: 12.

PRALI (To): *Hotel delle Alpi*   €
Via Roma 9, frazione Ghigo. **Road Map** B4. 0121 807 537. FAX 0121 807 615.
W www.hoteldellealpi.it
A family-run hotel at 1,445 m (4,740 ft) in the centre of Ghigo di Prali, near the ski lifts. Ideal for skiing holidays, the Alpi has comfortable rooms with telephone and television. In summer there are many opportunities for excursions on foot or by mountain bike. TV ⬛ ⬛ ⬛ ⬛ Rooms: 15. ● Oct.

SESTRIÈRE (To): *Il Fraitevino*   €€
Piazza Fraiteve 3/bis. **Road Map** B3. 0122 760 22. FAX 0122 763 55.
W www.hotelilfraitevino.it @ info@hotelilfraitevino.it
This hotel, in a two-storey building in the town, is close to the main facilities and ski lifts. It has well-furnished rooms with balconies affording splendid views of the mountains. Guest facilities include a bar, roof terrace and laundry service. ⬛ TV ⬛ Rooms: 20. ● Apr–15 Jun, end Aug–Nov.

SESTRIÈRE (To): *Grand Hotel Sestrière*   €€
Via Assietta 1. **Road Map** B3. 0122 764 76. FAX 0122 767 00.
W www.grandhotelsestriere.it
A large but welcoming resort hotel with a swimming pool, spa and gym. The superior rooms have balconies and lovely views. The two restaurants serve typical mountain fare and the wine cellar is excellent.
☰ ⬛ Rooms: 100. ● May, Sep–Nov.

SESTRIÈRE (To): *Miramonti*   €€
Via Cesana 3. **Road Map** B3. 0122 755 333. FAX 0122 755 375.
W www.miramontisestriere.com @ info@miramontisestriere.com
In a good position by the ski slopes and golf course, this hotel is family-run. The spacious rooms are furnished in the style typical of the mountains and the terraces have splendid views. ☰ ⬛ TV ⬛ Rooms: 30.

SESTRIÈRE (To): *Sud-Ovest*   €€
Via Monterotta 17. **Road Map** B3. 0122 755 222. FAX 0122 755 166.
W www.hotelsud-ovest.it @ hotelsud-ovest@tin.it
This hotel is in a quiet location near the centre of cross-country skiing. It has comfortable rooms and apartments. Good buffet breakfast and a restaurant serving typical cuisine. Free use of mountain bikes and a shuttle bus service to the slopes. ☰ TV ⬛ ⬛ ⬛ Rooms: 23. ● May & Jun, Sep–Nov.

USSEAUX (To): *Albergo Lago Laux*   €€
Via Al Lago 7. **Road Map** B3. FAX 0121 839 44. W www.hotellaux.it @ laux@mclink.it
Situated by the side of a lake at 1,381 m (4,530 ft), this hotel is an ideal place for fishing and excursions to the Val Troncea Nature Park, Rocciavré and the Fenestrelle fort. It is completely furnished in wood, and has a typical restaurant offering excellent ravioli, Savoy salad and tongue *alla piemontese*. TV ⬛ Rooms: 7. ● 4–14 May, 20 Sep–15 Oct.

VILLAR PEROSA (To): *Bianconero Hotel Meublé*   €
Viale Giovanni Agnelli 11. **Road Map** C4. 0121 515 879. FAX 0121 515 536.
W www.hotelbianconero.it
A new, comfortable guesthouse, near the Museo della Meccanica e del Cuscinetto and Giovanni Agnelli's birthplace. It makes a good base for visiting the Chisone and Germanasca valleys and the Pinerolo area. TV Rooms: 12.

VAL PELLICE

BIBIANA (TO): *Il Frutto Permesso* €
Via del Vernè 16. **Road Map** C4. **C FAX** *0121 553 83.* **W** www.fruttopermesso.it
Located at the mouth of Val Pellice, this holiday guesthouse is made from three
converted farm buildings. In summer it is reserved for children attending theme
holidays. Excellent cooking with typical traditional dishes, including *bagna
cauda* and *supa mitunà* (bread-based soup). **Rooms:** *12.*

CANTALUPA (TO): *Locanda della Maison Verte* €€
Via Rossi 34. **Road Map** D4. **C** *0121 354 610.* **FAX** *0121 354 614.*
W www.maisonvertehotel.it **@** information@maisonvertehotel.it
A charming hotel in a converted 19th-century farmhouse surrounded
by a large park with beech and chestnut trees. The public areas and
rooms are tastefully decorated with period furniture and elegant fabrics.
The restaurant serves local dishes accompanied by a good choice of
Piedmontese wines. Guests have the use of a spa offering restorative and
relaxing treatments based on natural products. **Rooms:** *28.*

CAVOUR (TO): *Locanda La Posta* €
Via dei Fossi 4. **Road Map** D4. **C** *0121 699 89.* **FAX** *0121 697 90.*
W www.locandalaposta.it **@** posta@locandalaposta.it
This old post house, which has been in business since 1682, is now a pleasant
inn that has been run by the same family for many years. The well-furnished
rooms have period furniture and look onto a lovely hanging garden. The
restaurant, with its large fireplace and a beamed ceiling, offers typical
Piedmontese cooking. **Rooms:** *20.* *25 Jul–10 Aug.*

PINEROLO (TO): *Regina* €€
Piazza Luigi Barbieri 22. **Road Map** C4. **C** *0121 322 157.* **FAX** *0121 393 133.*
@ hotel.regina@noicom.net
A small, traditional hotel offering a friendly service in the heart of this small
town. The rooms are fitted with double glazing. The restaurant has an
old-fashioned atmosphere and offers traditional Piedmontese specialities.
Rooms: *15.* *1–2 wks in Aug.*

PINEROLO (TO): *Il Torrione Agriturismo* €€€
Strada Galoppatoio 20. **Road Map** C4. **C** *0121 322 616.* **FAX** *0121 323 358.*
W www.iltorrione.com **@** prenotazioni@iltorrione.com
Surrounded by 20 ha (50 acres) of land, this agritourism centre began with the
conversion of the main house, from which four elegant and comfortable
rooms were made. There is a swimming pool and tennis courts, and bicycles
are available to visit the parks and castles in the area. The farm specializes
in breeding sheep for wool. **Rooms:** *4.*

RORÀ (TO): *Sibourgh Agriturismo* €
Via Fornaci 4. **Road Map** C4. **C FAX** *0121 931 05.*
For a totally relaxing holiday, this agritourism centre offers comfortable rooms in
an old converted building. It is surrounded by a 20-ha (50-acre) estate planted
with wheat, vegetables and fruit trees. The restaurant offers typical Waldensian
cooking and wines produced on the farm. Excursions to the surrounding areas
can be made by bicycle or on horseback. **Rooms:** *4.*

TORRE PELLICE (TO): *Filipot* €€
Corso Gramsci 17. **Road Map** C4. **C** *0121 953 465.* **FAX** *0121 912 36.*
W www.filipot.com **@** filipot@filipot.com
An elegant hotel with only eight rooms and a good restaurant. The
building, a mid-18th-century farmhouse, has preserved the ancient and
romantic atmosphere of an inn. Good service and the chance to try
genuine Waldensian cooking. Specialities include: *salmerino* river fish cooked
on Luserna stone, *agnoli* filled with snails flavoured with rue and veal's liver
with onion confit. **Rooms:** *8.* *24 Dec–10 Jan, 15–30 Jun.*

TORRE PELLICE (TO): *Gilly* €€
Corso Lombardini 1. **Road Map** C4. **C** *0121 932 477.* **FAX** *0121 932 924.*
W www.gillyhotel.it **@** mail@gillyhotel.it
In a quiet position surrounded by greenery, this hotel has spacious, elegant
rooms and public areas. There are facilities for meetings and a large restaurant
which is also used for dances. Popular with cyclists.
small breeds. **Rooms:** *31.* *Jan.*

For key to symbols see back flap

WHERE TO EAT

Turin is one of Italy's most important gastronomic cities. It could be said that the solid, practical appearance of the metropolis is softened by the gentle rolling hills and the winding rivers around the city. The same analogy can be made with its cuisine, where the simple, satisfying ingredients of traditional dishes are flavoured with the aromas of the Mediterranean. Oil, anchovies and capers are widely used

Bagnet vert is a herb sauce served with meat

thanks to the centuries-old trade with nearby Liguria. The 20th century saw a large influx of migrants and some regional Italian dishes have also become part of the Piedmontese tradition. More recently, ethnic food has become popular. However, the philosophy and style of the local cuisine is still based on fresh produce from the surrounding areas of Langa, Monferrato, Canavese and much of the Piedmontese province.

TRADITIONAL DISHES AND TYPICAL PRODUCE

Turinese cuisine is satisfying and well-presented and much of the produce used in the city restaurants comes from the local area. The most famous salami, from Langhe, is the *salamin d'la duja*, which is stored in an earthenware jar *(duja)* filled with lard. Other Piedmontese delicacies include alpine cheeses from Cesana, mushrooms and cow and goat cheeses from Pinerolo, tench from Avigliana, cherries from Perosa, *cavourrini* with rum from Cavour, honey from Pragelato, and *grissini*, the breadsticks said to have been made especially for Vittorio Amedeo II in the late 1600s. The truffle is supreme in

The Cavour Room in Turin's Del Cambio restaurant

Piedmontese cuisine, lending its unmistakeable fragrance to many dishes.

Antipasti are an important part of a meal and are taken very seriously. Salads may appear, particularly *capricciosa*, with pickled meat, ham and mushrooms. Chicken salad is made with chicken breasts dressed with oil, lemon and anchovies, and white truffles when in season. *Carne cruda* (raw meat) is also of very good quality; minced Fassone beef dressed with oil, garlic and lemon juice, for example.

Tasty stuffed onions are made using a filling of Parmesan cheese, eggs, butter and herbs. Stuffed peppers are filled with rice, butter, oil, anchovies and garlic. These are cooked in an oven but served cold.

Vitello tonnato (veal with tuna sauce) is another good

dish, made with topside of veal simmered with herbs. When it has cooled, it is thinly sliced and covered with a smooth tuna sauce with anchovies and capers.

First courses include pasta dishes such as *agnolotti* (ravioli) filled with meat, eggs and cheese, and *tajarin*, thin strips of pasta dressed with the juices from roast meat or butter, sage and Parmesan. *Finanziera* (chicken crests and giblets) or truffles are often added to risottos. A popular dish is *fonduta*, a "cream" made with melted fontina cheese and milk, and flavoured with white truffles.

A convivial dish is *bagna cauda* (a sauce of melted butter flavoured with garlic, anchovies and oil, kept warm on a burner) into which raw vegetables such as peppers, carrots or celery sticks are dipped and eaten.

A display of typical dishes in a restaurant in Sestrière

Meat braised in Barolo is meltingly tender. *Fritto misto*, or mixed fried meat and/or vegetables, may be made with up to ten different ingredients. Hare (*lepre*) is served *in civet*, with mushrooms, or *alla vignarola*. It is said that the famous chicken *alla Marengo* was invented by a cook in Napoleon's entourage at the battle of Marengo.

Zabaione, filled peaches or *marrons glaçés* complete the meal. Turin is also famous for its fine quality chocolate, named after the theatrical character of Gianduja.

The region of Piedmont produces some of Italy's finest red wines, including Barolo and Barbaresco.

OPENING HOURS AND PRICES

LUNCH is eaten at around 1pm and dinner from 8pm. Service is available until midnight in wine bars and *piole*, or small taverns, and the bill generally amounts to 15–25 euros. Restaurant prices vary from 35–70 euros.

RESTAURANTS

THERE IS a wide choice of eating options in the city, from simple, unassuming trattorie to top class dining. There are also many restaurants in the city offering good ethnic cuisine.

BARS AND CAFÉS

TURIN'S HISTORIC CAFÉS are good places to try snacks, cakes and chocolates in an old-world atmosphere. Try a *bicerin* drink at the café of the same name (*see p192*).

Turin's oldest restaurant, still serving traditional food

Piero Chiambretti, the owner of Birilli restaurant

TRATTORIAS AND AGRITURISMO

TRADITIONAL PIEDMONTESE dishes can be sampled in the many authentic trattorias which can still be found in the city. However, just a few kilometres from Turin it is also possible to enjoy the rural hospitality of Piedmont by staying on one of the region's farms. Farm holidays are an excellent way of discovering traditional culture, typical cuisine and the rhythms of the changing seasons. Accommodation is available in restored farm buildings set deep in countryside, and meals are provided by the owners. These places make a good starting point for making the most of the various opportunities which the area has to offer. Particular attention is given to activities for young people. Cooking, gardening and guided visits can also be organized.

Consorzio Agriturismo Piemonte (To). ☎ 011 534 918. FAX 011 535 916. @ info@agriturismopiemonte.it

FESTIVALS AND FAIRS

THE Salone del Gusto (Food and Wine Fair), held in Turin, is an international affair, but local food and wine festivals and fairs are held all over the province. Every season a variety of events celebrates the varied local gastronomic traditions.

FESTIVALS AND FAIRS

Turin
CioccolaTO, Feb–Mar.
Salone del Gusto, Oct (even years), Lingotto Fiere.

Bobbio Pellice
Festa della Pouia e Sagra del Sirass, May.
Festa della Cala e Sagra della Mustardella, Oct.

Carema
Grape and Carema Wine Festival, Sep.

Cavour
Settimana della Carne (Meat Week), Mar.

Chieri
Chestnuts and promotion of typical local products, Oct.

Ciriè
Mushroom Festival, Sep.

Coassolo Torinese
Apple Festival, Oct.

Condove
Toma Cheese Fair, Oct.

Corio
Cheese Festival, May.

Lanzo Torinese
Sagra del Torcetto, Grissino & Toma, Jul.

Maglione
Peach Festival, Jul.

None
None al Cioccolato: chocolate, sweets, Nov.

Perosa Argentina
Medicinal Herbs and New Wine, Mar.

Pinerolo
Food and Wine Fair, May.

Poirino
Asparagus and Tench Fair, Apr.

Pragelato
Fiera di Ferragosto, Aug.

Rivalba
White Truffle Fair, Nov.

Rivalta di Torino
Tomino Cheese, Sep.

San Pietro Val Lemina
Mushroom Fair, Oct.

Torre Pellice
Flowers-Food-Wine Fair, Apr.

Trofarello
Sour Cherry Fair, Jun.

Val della Torre
Wild Boar Salami Fair, Mar.

Villar Perosa
Summer Festival, Jul.

What to Eat and Drink

Giandujotti chocolates

THE VAST PLAINS surrounding Turin provide a plentiful supply of fresh vegetables and meat; cheeses come from mountain pastures and fish from neighbouring Liguria. Although Turin now has a wealth of excellent restaurants, typical dishes such as *bagna cauda* and *bollito misto* reflect an impoverished past where creativity in the kitchen was essential.

Mustardela, *blood sausage from Val Pellice, is a pork sausage flavoured with spices. It is sliced and eaten raw.*

ANTIPASTO

Hors d'oeuvres form an important prelude to a meal in Piedmont. Savoury and tangy, they may consist of cooked or pickled vegetables or different kinds of meat, salami and cheese. *Bagna cauda* is a ritual in which everyone can share: sliced raw vegetables are dipped into a warm sauce made with anchovies, oil and garlic. Carmagnola peppers are particularly prized.

Piedmontese antipasto *may include a variety of pickled or cooked vegetables, including carrots and cauliflower.*

Peperoni ripieni *are small, often fiery peppers stuffed with anchovies, capers and tuna and stored in oil.*

FIRST COURSES (PRIMI)

Typical Piedmontese first course dishes are *tajarin* (thin pasta noodles, often served with butter and sage), *agnolottini del Plin* and the square *agnolotti* (both stuffed pasta). Local *toma* and ricotta cheeses may be served with gnocchi and pasta, or with risotto. *Cruset* are fresh pasta shapes, often served with Sambucano lamb. *Zuppa di trippa* (tripe soup) comes with plenty of vegetables.

Cruset, *a pasta speciality from Valle Stura di Demonte, is similar to orecchiette pasta from Puglia in Italy's south.*

Pasta with local ricotta cheese *is a simple but tasty dish. Stuffed cannelloni and farfalle pasta are also good.*

Agnolotti alla Piemontese

Tartufo bianco *is white truffle. It is sliced very thinly and may accompany pasta or be served in salad and main dishes. It is a very highly prized ingredient.*

MAIN COURSES (SECONDI)

Meat, particularly beef and veal, appears in many main dishes, such as *fritto misto* (mixed fried meat and vegetables) and *bollito misto*. Fish comes from local lakes and rivers, and nearby Liguria, and frogs come from the rice fields of Vercelli. Corn is used to make polenta.

Chicken

Spiced sausage

Beef

Veal

Bollito misto *is a rich winter dish in the Piedmontese tradition which demonstrates the excellence of the local meat, such as beef, veal and chicken. The boiled meats may be served with potatoes.*

Yellow polenta, made with maize

Carne cruda *all'albese* is raw veal served with olive oil, Parmesan cheese and lemon, with white truffle in autumn.

Capretto *is tender kid fed only on its mother's milk. It is cooked with rosemary, garlic, sage and a glass of grappa.*

Tortino di bietole e patate *from Val di Susa is chard and potato pie, made with local ingredients, including ricotta.*

GRISSINI
Turinese breadsticks are a popular alternative to bread. The "stretched" type are made with ordinary wheat flour, water, milk, olive oil and acid yeast. The sticks are rolled by hand and are irregular in shape.

Rolled grissini

Funghi (mushrooms), *found in all the valleys, are often offered as side dishes.*

CHEESE
A great variety of cheeses is produced in Piedmont and the best examples come from alpine pastures at higher altitudes. Some of the most typical are *seirass* from Fen, *toma* and *murianengo* from Val Pellice, *blu* from Moncenisio and *tomino* from Talucco.

Murianengo, *a herb-flavoured cheese, is made from cows' milk in the area of Moncenisio. It is yellowish in colour with blue mould.*

Seirass del Fen, *a ricotta cheese aged in hay, is made with the whey left over from making toma cheese.*

Piedmontese ricotta *may be added to leftover salted cheese, herbs and spices, resulting in a mixture called Frachet. Ricotta cheese is produced in the valleys.*

Torta al cioccolato *is a delicious chocolate cake. Torta Gianduja is made with chocolate and hazelnuts.*

Nocciolini di Chivasso *are made with sugar, hazelnuts and egg whites.*

DESSERTS
Torta Zurigo from Pinerolo and Torta Novecento (Ivrea) are both very good. Locally made *giandujotti* (hazelnut chocolates) are very popular.

WINES
Piedmont produces a range of good red wines such as Barbera and Dolcetto, as well as some of Italy's finest reds, including Barolo. The zone also produces vermouth, made from wine and herbs.

Pinerolese *wine may be either red or rosé, such as Doux d'Henry, made from local vines, and Ramiè, made from Avanà, Avarengo and Neretto grapes.*

Vermouth *is a wine flavoured with herbs, such as wormwood. Carpano has made vermouth since 1786, but it was Martini who made it famous.*

The Iced Mint of Pancalieri *is a basic ingredient in syrups and liqueurs. It is also ideal for cocktails and other refreshing drinks.*

Choosing a Restaurant

L IKE ANY OTHER LARGE CITY, Turin offers a wide range of
restaurants and types of cuisine. The places here are listed
according to the geographical divisions used in this guide and
were chosen to offer readers a range of choices, from simple,
authentic trattorias to top quality restaurants. Rural restaurants
are listed under the name of the nearest main town.

	CREDIT CARDS	PARKING	OUTDOOR DINING	TRADITIONAL CUISINE	GOOD WINE LIST

TURIN

Agrifoglio   €€
Via Accademia Albertina 38. **Map** 7 B1. 🛈 *011 837 064.*
This small and elegant restaurant is in the historic centre of the city. Specialities
vary according to the season, but the cooking is always authentic and fairly
priced. Agrifoglio is known for its dishes of game, mushrooms and truffles.
Delicious desserts. ● *lunch, Sun, Mon; Easter, 15 Aug–15 Sep, 22 Dec–3 Jan.* ▤

| ● | | | ▨ | ● |

Al Garamond   €€€
Via Pomba 14. **Map** 7 B1. 🛈 *011 812 27 81.* Ⓦ www.algaramond.it
This small, elegant and romantic restaurant intelligently updates the staples of
Piedmontese cooking: for example, quail carpaccio with foie gras and black
truffle; lasagnetta with seafood; paniscia risotto with saffron; scampi with
lime and rice timbale; bison with smoked black tea and burrata cheese;
crème brûlée. Try the 8-course tasting menu. ● *Sat lunch, Sun, 1st wk Jan, Aug.* ▤

| ● | | | | ● |

Antiche Sere   €
Via Cenischia 9. **Map** 1 A5. 🛈 *011 385 43 47.*
One of the most authentic trattorias in Turin, with paintings on the walls and
cotton tablecloths. Classic Piedmontese specialities include *vitello tonnato*
(veal with tuna sauce), tajarin pasta with chicken livers; braised donkey; roast
pig shank. Good desserts include soufflé with Moscato wine and zabaione.
Tables are set out on the patio in summer. ● *lunch, Sun; Aug, Christmas.*

| | | | ▨ | ● |

Arcadia   €€
Galleria Subalpina 29. **Map** 3 B5. 🛈 *011 561 38 98.* Ⓦ www.ristorantearcadia.com
A simple restaurant, popular with shoppers at lunchtime, with single-dish meals
or a "subalpine" menu. In the evening, sushi and sashimi. ● *Sun; 1st wk Jan.* ▤

| ● | | | | |

Barrique   €€€
Corso Dante 53a. **Map** 6 D4. 🛈 *011 657 900.*
A Turinese institution, justifiably popular. Dishes might include sauté of crispy
vegetables in clam sauce; guinea fowl with foie gras mousse and cherries;
lasagnette with seafood and peas; *ombrina* (a local fish) with beans, capers and
parsley; rabbit with peppers and balsamic vinegar; apple tatin with ice cream.
● *Sat, Sun lunch, Mon; Aug.* ▤

| ● | | | | ● |

Birilli   €€
Strada Val S. Martino 6. **Map** 8 F1 off map. 🛈 *011 819 05 67.* Ⓦ www.birilli.com
A refreshing alternative to classic dining, Birilli offers an imaginative menu at
friendly prices, served by young staff. Begin with stuffed calamari, trout tartare;
ravioli with ricotta cheese; tagliolini pasta with sausage. Main courses include
tuna steaks, also a good range of meats. Cheese and traditional cakes. ● *Sun.*

| ● | | | | ● |

Bue Rosso   €€
Corso Casale 10. **Map** 8 D1. 🛈 *011 819 13 93.*
Across the river from the centre, but worth the walk. Reasonably priced,
unpretentious regional cuisine: delicious gratins; fish; mushrooms *all'albese*;
green gnocchetti with Castelmagno cheese; agnolotti with truffles; fondue with
truffles; braised beef; game; with panna cotta, bonet (chocolate, rum and
amaretti dessert) or zabaione to finish. ● *Mon, Sat lunch; Aug.*

| ● | | | ▨ | ● |

Caffè San Tommaso 10 – Lavazza   €€€€
Via San Tommaso 10. **Map** 3 A4. 🛈 *011 534 201.*
This historic café, the home of Lavazza coffee, is a well-known and popular
place to eat. The beautifully restored dining room offers a varied,
creative and traditional menu of fish and meat dishes. Strengths
include pasta, desserts and, of course, the coffee. ● *Sun; Aug.* ▤

| ● | | | | ● |

Price categories for a three-course meal for one, including a half-bottle of house wine, tax and service:
€ under 30 euros
€€ 30–40 euros
€€€ 40–50 euros
€€€€ 50–60 euros
€€€€€ over 60 euros

CREDIT CARDS
Major credit cards are accepted at these restaurants.

PARKING
Restaurant has its own parking area or garage.

OUTSIDE DINING
Garden, courtyard or terrace with outside tables.

TRADITIONAL CUISINE
Restaurant serves mainly traditional local cuisine.

GOOD WINE LIST
Wide range or a special selection of good wines.

Restaurant		CREDIT CARDS	PARKING	OUTDOOR DINING	TRADITIONAL CUISINE	GOOD WINE LIST
Capannina — €€		●			■	●
Carignano — €€€€		●	■	●	■	●
Casa Vicina — €€€€€		●				●
Combal.Zero — €€€€€		●	■	●	■	
Consorzio Montagna Viva — €		●			■	●
Da Bacco — €						●
Del Cambio — €€€€€		●		●	■	●
Gatto Nero — €€€		●				●

Capannina   €€
Via Donati 1. **Map** 2 E5. **(** 011 545 405.
An unassuming trattoria, Capannina has rustic furnishings and is located in a historic building. Mushrooms, game and white truffles are used to prepare authentic, typical dishes from the Alba area: risotto with Barolo wine; tajarin; *bollito misto*; cakes from the Langhe area. ● *Sun; Aug.*

Carignano   €€€€
Via Carlo Alberto 35. **Map** 3 B5. **(** 011 517 01 71. **W** www.thi.it
Tucked away at the back of the Gran Hotel Sitea, this is that rarity: a hotel restaurant worth seeking out. Piedmontese and international dishes are executed with flair: Fassone beef fillet with ricotta cheese; tajarin with courgette flowers and prawns; sea bass ravioli; lamb cutlets with sesame seeds; bonet (a chocolate, rum and amaretti dessert). Good service. ● *Sat lunch.* ▤

Casa Vicina   €€€€€
Via Massena 66. **Map** 6 F1. **(** 011 221 68 12.
Chef Claudio Vicina is a rising star. His menu, which changes according to availability, consists of well-presented modern cuisine: rabbit in oil; pork shanks; agnolotti; chicken with a leek fondant; Fassone beef in an onion crust; escalope of liver; creamed stockfish; kidneys. ● *lunch, Sun, Mon, 1st 10 days Aug.*

Combal.Zero   €€€€€
Piazza Mafalda di Savoia, Rivoli (To). **Road Map** D3. **(** 011 956 52 25.
Beyond the wood, slate and chrome of this minimalist location, chef Davide Scabin's utterly original hand fashions some of Italy's most striking dishes. Choose from three menus: Classic, Creative or Territory – expensive but worth the price. Don't miss the opportunity to try this genuinely innovative cuisine. Booking essential. ● *Mon, Tue, 10 days Christmas, 3 wks Aug.* ▤ ⮜ ▮

Consorzio Montagna Viva   €
Piazza Emanuele Filiberto 3/a. **Map** 3 A3. **(** 011 521 78 82. **W** www.montagnaviva.it
A greengrocer, delicatessen and restaurant all rolled into one, the CMV is run by farmers from the Val di Susa. Affordable, authentic produce includes meat, mushrooms and truffles, polenta *concia* (with fontina cheese), cheeses and salamis, to eat in the restaurant or take away. ● *Sun; 15 Aug.*

Da Bacco   €
Via Madama Cristina 82/C. **Map** 7 A2. **(** 011 650 51 46.
Simple, but endlessly popular wine bar. People drop in to munch a pastry or a filled roll or choose from the daily specials for something more substantial. Quality meats, *agnolotti* and stockfish with polenta. The wine list is excellent and the coffee superb. ● *Sun; Aug.*

Del Cambio   €€€€€
Piazza Carignano 2. **Map** 3 B5. **(** 011 546 690. **W** www.thi.it
As much a museum as a restaurant, Del Cambio, with its stuccowork, mirrors and red velvet, was once patronized by Camillo Cavour, and is quintessential, classic Turin. Traditional cuisine is imaginatively handled: stuffed courgette flowers; asparagus tart; pasta with quail and truffles; fillet of beef with wine; beef braised in Barolo; apples and *gianduja*. ● *Sun; 1st wk Jan, 1 wk Aug.* ▤ ▮

Gatto Nero   €€€
Corso Filippo Turati 14. **Map** 6 D3. **(** 011 590 477.
The Vanelli family are from Tuscany and the menu remains a mix of Tuscan and Piedmontese ingredients. A wood fire is used to grill fish and meat, the menu might also feature baked anchovies with cherry tomatoes, capers and origano; prawns with cannellini beans; tripe *alla fiorentina*; spelt soup with borlotti beans; angler fish or calamari; peach and amaretti tart. ● *Sun; Aug.*

Price categories for a three-course meal for one, including a half-bottle of house wine, tax and service: € under 30 euros €€ 30–40 euros €€€ 40–50 euros €€€€ 50–60 euros €€€€€ over 60 euros	**CREDIT CARDS** Major credit cards are accepted at these restaurants. **PARKING** Restaurant has its own parking area or garage. **OUTSIDE DINING** Garden, courtyard or terrace with outside tables. **TRADITIONAL CUISINE** Restaurant serves mainly traditional local cuisine. **GOOD WINE LIST** Wide range or a special selection of good wines.	CREDIT CARDS	PARKING	OUTDOOR DINING	TRADITIONAL CUISINE	GOOD WINE LIST

Grassi €€

Via Grassi 9. **Map** 2 D4. 011 434 54 30.

An unassuming local, a short taxi ride from Piazza Carignano, serving excellent fish dishes influenced by the cooking of Puglia in southern Italy. The traditional exterior belies an innovative kitchen. Very good *carne cruda all'italiana*, red mullet, scallops, tuna and *ricciola* (amberjack). ● *Sun; Aug.*

CREDIT CARDS	PARKING	OUTDOOR DINING	TRADITIONAL CUISINE	GOOD WINE LIST
●				●

Il Gatto e la Volpe €€

Via Fontanesi 33. **Map** 4 E4. 011 812 68 82.

Veneto and Pugliese traditions combine in this busy and popular trattoria, where the fish is straight from the day's market. Try the salmon and angler fish roll; the swordfish and provola cheese roulade served on a fish sauce; orecchiette pasta with broccoli and clams; angler fish *alla provenzale*. ● *Sun; 10–30 Aug.* ▤

CREDIT CARDS	PARKING	OUTDOOR DINING	TRADITIONAL CUISINE	GOOD WINE LIST
●				●

Lanterne €€€

Via Lagrange 47. **Map** 7 A1. 011 517 67 56.

This somewhat dated restaurant, part of the Hotel Concord, serves Piedmontese dishes with a Mediterranean touch: spinach with caprino cheese and elderberry jelly; puff pastry tart with toma cheese from Bra served on a black truffle sauce; *tajarin* of beetroot with rabbit ragù; swordfish with herbs; white chocolate mousse with raspberry sauce. ▤

CREDIT CARDS	PARKING	OUTDOOR DINING	TRADITIONAL CUISINE	GOOD WINE LIST
●				●

La Pista €€€€

Via Nizza 262 (pedestrian), Via Nizza 294 (with car). **Map** 6 E5 off map. 011 631 35 23.

Perched high above Lingotto in the old FIAT building, La Pista commands a stunning panorama over Turin and the old FIAT race track (*la pista*). The food is every bit as exciting as the view and well warrants the trek down Via Nizza. ● *Tue.* ▤ ▮

CREDIT CARDS	PARKING	OUTDOOR DINING	TRADITIONAL CUISINE	GOOD WINE LIST
●	■			●

La Prima Moreno €€€

Corso Unione Sovietica 244. **Map** 5 C5. 011 317 91 91. www.laprimamoreno.it

This modern, elegant restaurant serves innovative, uncomplicated Mediterranean dishes: lobster *alla catalana*; prawn kebabs with porcini mushrooms in a sweet-and-sour sauce; *straccetti* (meat patties) with lemon, sage and green beans; beef with juniper berries; *sanato* (Piedmontese veal) with Castelmagno cheese; iced raspberries. Decent wine list. ● *Aug.* ▤

CREDIT CARDS	PARKING	OUTDOOR DINING	TRADITIONAL CUISINE	GOOD WINE LIST
●		●		●

'L Birichin €€€

Via V Monti 16. **Map** 6 F5. 011 657 457.

The clean lines of the thoroughly modern interior reflect an accomplished and confident kitchen that draws its inspiration from the length and breadth of the country. Anyone tired of *vitello tonnato* should head for this urbane establishment in the heart of a fashionable suburb. ● *Sun, 10 days Aug.* ▤ &

CREDIT CARDS	PARKING	OUTDOOR DINING	TRADITIONAL CUISINE	GOOD WINE LIST
●	■			

Locanda Mongreno €€€–€€€€€

Strada Mongreno 50. **Map** 4 F4 off map. 011 898 04 17.

Locanda Mongreno is undoubtedly one of the city's most thought-provoking restaurants. There are three menus: Medium, Hard and Extreme. Each is a provocative reflection of Piemontese cuisine and there are few better qualified to push culinary boundaries than chef Pier Bussetti. Although some of the dishes wander off into the experimental wilderness, they remain challenging and unforgettable. The wine list is extensive. ● *Mon; 2 wks Jan, 2 wks Sep.* ▤ ▮

CREDIT CARDS	PARKING	OUTDOOR DINING	TRADITIONAL CUISINE	GOOD WINE LIST
●	■	●	■	●

Mina €€

Via Ellero 36. **Map** 6 F5 off map. 011 696 36 08.

An upmarket, elegant restaurant serving imaginative versions of Piedmontese classics including roulade *dello chef*; *agnolottini del Plin*; "orchid" risotto; gnocchi *di Italo*; pan-fried kid; braised kid with artichokes; Piedmontese *fritto misto* (which must be ordered ahead). ● *Mon; Aug.* ▤

CREDIT CARDS	PARKING	OUTDOOR DINING	TRADITIONAL CUISINE	GOOD WINE LIST
●		●	■	●

Monferrato €€

Via Monferrato 6. **Map** 8 D1. ☎ *011 819 06 61.*
Around the corner from Bue Rosso (*see p186*), this restaurant enjoys a deservedly favoured spot in the locals' affections for its rich selection of local specialities. If you're in this part of town there is little to choose between the two – Monferrato is perhaps the more polished of the two but it is also more expensive. ● *Sat lunch, Sun.* 🔲

Montecarlo €€€

Via San Francesco da Paola 37. **Map** 7 A1. ☎ *011 888 763.*
This restaurant is popular with an arty set, drawn by the atmospheric, vaulted cellars. Try the excellent liver paté with Tropea onion marmalade, puréed stockfish, soused eel, sardines in saôr (sweet and sour); spaghetti with mullet roe. Carnivores need not worry: stews and steaks are on offer as well as dishes such as fried lamb cutlets and courgettes or tripe. ● *Sat lunch, Sun; Aug.*

Neuv Caval 'd Brons €€€€

Piazza San Carlo 151. **Map** 3 A5. ☎ *011 562 74 83.*
Perched above the café of the same name, this damask-heavy restaurant commands a stunning location above Piazza San Carlo. Classic cuisine: half-moon ravioli with aubergine and caprino cheese, tagliolini pasta made with almond flour, grilled turbot with red onions and leeks, Fassone beef with juniper berries, scallops with thyme, prawns with ginger; foie gras with truffles. Excellent desserts and also a good vegetarian menu. ● *Sat lunch, Sun; Aug.* 🔲 🔲

Perbacco €€€

Via Mazzini 31. **Map** 7 A1. ☎ *011 882 110.*
The seasonal menu makes the most of local cheese, pasta and fish, served up in a friendly atmosphere. Recommended dishes include pie with ricotta cheese and basil, roulade of courgette *ai tre gusti* (three flavours), Sardinian gnocchetti with aubergine salad and loin of lamb with basil. ● *lunch, Sun Aug.*

Porta Rossa €€€€

Via Passalacqua 3B. **Map** 2 E3. ☎ *011 530 816.*
Although now in need of a facelift, Porta Rossa continues to offer seriously fresh fish, albeit at a price. Fish dishes are combined with regional produce such as truffles from Alba and mushrooms. Try the baby calamari, raw tuna and swordfish, *paccheri* pasta with *ombrina* (a local fish) sauce, sturgeon served on a bed of chicory and angler fish in red wine. ● *Sat lunch, Sun, Aug.* 🔲

Porticciolo €€€€

Via Barletta 58. **Map** 5 A5. ☎ *011 321 601.*
Expertly prepared langoustines, lobster, sea bass and salmon are served in this small, romantic restaurant. Try the fish mousse with Moscato and salmon fumé, salmon and sea bass with artichokes in pastry, ravioli with sea bass, pistachio nuts and pureed asparagus, gilthead bream in a potato crust. Follow up with rich chocolate cake with mint ice cream. ● *Sat lunch, Mon; Aug.* 🔲

Torricelli €€

Via Evangelista Torricelli 51. **Map** 5 C3. ☎ *011 599 814.*
Another Turinese favourite. Authentic Piedmontese food is generously served in a bright, if dated, dining room or on the attractive pavement terrace. Try the courgette flowers with pesto, octopus with black truffles, rabbit ravioli, tagliolini pasta with cuttlefish ink and moscardini octopus, suckling pig cooked in hay. Panna cotta with mint and fruit to end. ● *Sun, Mon lunch; 10–31 Aug, 1st wk Jan.* 🔲

Trait d'Union €€€€

Via degli Stampatori 4. **Map** 2 F4. ☎ *011 56 12 506.*
Housed in the converted stables of Palazzo Scaglia di Verrua, this restaurant has antique furniture and beamed ceilings. In summer you can eat in the small courtyard. Chef Antonino Crudo offers stylish cuisine and the wine list features hundreds of Italian and foreign wines. 🔲 ● *Sat lunch, Sun; 15 Aug.*

Tre Galline €€

Via Bellezia 37. **Map** 3 A3. ☎ *011 436 65 53.*
No visit to Turin would be complete without a visit to Tre Galline in the ancient Porta Palazzo quarter. In operation since 1575, it claims to be the city's oldest restaurant. The ultra-traditional menu features *bollito misto* every evening supplemented by a range of daily specials including *bagna cauda* on Saturdays. ● *Mon lunch, Sun, 1st wk Jan, 1st wk Aug.* 🔲

Price categories for a three-course meal for one, including a half-bottle of house wine, tax and service: € under 30 euros €€ 30–40 euros €€€ 40–50 euros €€€€ 50–60 euros €€€€€ over 60 euros	**CREDIT CARDS** Major credit cards are accepted at these restaurants. **PARKING** Restaurant has its own parking area or garage. **OUTSIDE DINING** Garden, courtyard or terrace with outside tables. **TRADITIONAL CUISINE** Restaurant serves mainly traditional local cuisine. **GOOD WINE LIST** Wide range or a special selection of good wines.

Columns: CREDIT CARDS · PARKING · OUTDOOR DINING · TRADITIONAL CUISINE · GOOD WINE LIST

Vigna Reale — €€€€
Via Sacchi 8. **Map** 6 F1. ☎ 011 562 55 11.
The Turin Palace hotel is home to Vigna Reale, furnished in the Belle Epoque tradition. Correct interpretations of all the Piedmontese classics are served: marinated salmon with dill; *carne cruda* with celery and Parmesan; pasta and porcini mushrooms; squash ravioli and sea bass with thyme; swordfish with spelt wheat. ● *Sat, Sun lunch; Aug.* 🍴 🛏
[Credit Cards · Good Wine List]

Villa Sassi — €€€€€
Strada al Traforo di Pino 47. **Map** 4 F4 off map. ☎ 011 898 05 56.
This restaurant is set in a beautiful 18th-century villa surrounded by an ancient park. Traditional Ligurian and Piedmontese dishes make up the menu. Dishes are reliable rather than exciting: salmon carpaccio; turbot with basil; ravioli with nettle sauce; carré of lamb with herbs; angler fish with pepper and saffron; soufflé *al gianduja*. Very good wine list with some bargains. ● *Sun; Aug.* 🍴 🛏
[Credit Cards · Parking · Outdoor Dining · Good Wine List]

Vintage 1997 — €€€€€
Piazza Solferino 16 H. **Map** 2 F5. ☎ 011 535 948. 🅆 www.vintage1997.com
The serious tone of Vintage 1997 is set by the clubby interior – all oak panelling and armchairs. Inspiration is drawn from around the globe but food retains a Piedmontese tone: crème caramel of foie gras; *vitello tonnato*; scampi and porcini mushrooms; Fassone beef with Carmagnola peppers; black strawberries from San Mauro in Brachetto jelly. ● *Sat lunch, Sun; Aug.* 🍴 🛏
[Credit Cards · Good Wine List]

VAL DI SUSA

BARDONECCHIA (To): *Biovey* — €€
Via Gen Cantore 2. **Road Map** A3. ☎ 0122 999 215. 🅆 www.biovey.it
Situated in a villa from the 1930s, this restaurant's menu offers venison carpaccio, cheese soufflé; ravioli *ai tre arrosti* (three roasts), lasagnette, pillow of bacon; prawns, chocolate desserts. ● *Tue; May, Oct.*
[Credit Cards · Traditional Cuisine · Good Wine List]

BARDONECCHIA (To): *Smith* — €€€€€
Località Molino 9. **Road Map** A3. ☎ 0122 999 861.
Smith is part of a hotel complex. The airy, elegant restaurant offers courgette soufflé with fondue, prawns, risotto with gorgonzola cheese, ravioli, venison and horse meat fillet, with *gianduja* soufflé to finish. ● *Wed; May, Oct.*
[Credit Cards · Outdoor Dining · Traditional Cuisine · Good Wine List]

OULX (To): *Vecchio Mulino* — €
Via del Mulino 12 - Beaulard. **Road Map** B3. ☎ 0122 851 669.
Friendly and atmospheric, this restaurant serves a menu of hearty dishes which might include venison, wild boar; rabbit terrine; tagliolini, gnocchi or braised venison. ● *Mon; May, Oct.*
[Credit Cards · Outdoor Dining · Traditional Cuisine · Good Wine List]

SAN GIORIO DI SUSA (To): *Adrit* — €
Località Adrit. **Road Map** C2. ☎ 339 253 04 03.
The menu at this trattoria includes pork with wine and tuna, courgette pie, risotto with chicory and sausage, tagliolini pasta with game, chestnut desserts. ● *Mon–Fri.*
[Traditional Cuisine]

SAUZE D'OULX (To): *Capricorno* — €€€
Località Les Clotés-Case Sparse 21. **Road Map** B3. ☎ 0122 850 273.
An elegant, wood-panelled hotel-restaurant, housed in a mountain chalet. Try the potato soufflé, Mariarosa's vegetable speciality, or chicken breasts with courgette flowers. Follow up with hazelnut ice-cream cake.
[Credit Cards · Outdoor Dining · Traditional Cuisine · Good Wine List]

SUSA (To): *Meana* — €
Piazza IV Novembre 2. **Road Map** B2. ☎ 0122 323 59. 🅆 www.ristorantemeana.it
The menu at this old-fashioned but friendly place includes warming soups, good risottos and pasta dishes. Quality cured meats and cheeses. ● *Wed.*
[Good Wine List]

VILLAR FOCCHIARDO (To): *Giaconera* €€
Strada Antica di Francia 1. **Road Map** C3. 011 964 50 00. W www.lagiaconera.it
In an old converted post house, Giaconera serves gnocchetti with tuna; porcini
mushrooms; river salmon; rabbit; hazelnut cake. *Mon, Tue, 3 wks Aug.*

THE CHISONE AND GERMANASCA VALLEYS

CESANA TORINESE (To): *Croce Bianca* €
Via Roma 33. **Road Map** A3. 0122 891 92. W www.crocebianca.com
Croce Bianca offers good, simple alpine cooking using seasonal ingredients.

CESANA TORINESE (To): *Locanda di Colomb* €
Fr. Champlas Seguin 27. **Road Map** A3. 0122 832 944.
A rustic-style restaurant with stone walls in converted 18th-century stables.
Typical mountain cuisine, excellent cured meat and cheese. *Mon; May, Oct.*

CESANA TORINESE (To): *Selvaggia* €€
Fr. Mollieres 43. **Road Map** A3. 0122 892 90.
The Piedmontese cooking is by an excellent chef from Ischia (in the bay of
Naples), who combines creativity with tradition. *Wed; 15–30 Jun, 10–30 Nov.*

CLAVIÈRE (To): *L'Gran Bouc* €
Via Nazionale 24/a. **Road Map** A3. 0122 878 830.
L'Gran Bouc serves Piedmontese dishes and some alpine specialities, such as
raclette and fondue, as well as excellent pizza. *Wed; May, Nov.*

SESTRIÈRE (To): *Du Grand Père* €€
Via Forte Seguin 14 Champlas-Janvier. **Road Map** B3. 0122 755 970.
A rustic-style restaurant in a 17th-century house, with tasty traditional pasta
dishes, braised meats, game and specialities of the valley.
Tue; spring, autumn.

SESTRIÈRE (To): *La Baita* €€
Via Louset 4a. **Road Map** B3. 0122 77 496.
A popular, unpretentious trattoria serving seasonal dishes such as venison, wild
boar, rabbit or risotto. Pizza is also served. Good range of grappas.

VAL PELLICE

BOBBIO PELLICE (To): *Alpina* €
Via Maestra 27. **Road Map** C4. 0121 957 747.
Excellent ravioli; *pierrade tartiflette* (potatoes and cheese); mountain cheese
dishes such as raclette or fondue; rabbit cooked in herbs; roast lamb;
home-made desserts. *Thu; Jun.*

CAVOUR (To): *Locanda la Posta* €€
Via dei Fossi 4. **Road Map** D4. 0121 699 89. W www.locandalaposta.it
This 18th-century post house serves satisfying fare such as Fassone beef,
vegetable flan, *agnolotti del Plin*; boiled and roast meat; pheasant and wild
boar. *Fri; last wk Jul, 1st wk Aug.*

LUSERNA SAN GIOVANNI (To): *Enoteca Sarti* €
Via Gianavello 29. **Road Map** C4. 0121 905 66.
Tasty appetizers and snacks are accompanied by good wines. *Mon; Aug.*

PINEROLO (To): *La Taverna degli Acaja* €€€
Corso Torino 106. **Road Map** C4. 0121 794 727. W www.tavernadegliacaja.it
Try fish or meat from the varied menu at this elegant restaurant: prawns' tails,
vegetables with caprino cheese and bacon, stockfish risotto or pork shanks;
hazelnut cream to round things off. *Sun, Mon lunch; Aug, 1–6 Jan.*

PINEROLO (To): *Locanda della Capreria Occitana* €€
Loc. Abbadia Alpina - Via Nazionale 370B. **Road Map** C4. 0121 201 139.
This atmospheric inn offers rabbit roulade, *agnolotti*, buckwheat pasta with
cabbage and cheese, kid in oil, caramel ice cream. *Mon–Thu.*

TORRE PELLICE (To): *Flipot* €€€€€
Corso Gramsci 17. **Road map** C4. 0121 912 36. W www.flipot.com
The creative menu here at this Art Nouveau hotel-restaurant includes pie of wild
flowers, roll of *salmerino* trout, lasagne with angler fish, ravioli, carp fillet, carré
of lamb. *Mon, Tue; Jun, Dec.*

For key to symbols see back flap

BARS AND CAFÉS

Cappuccino, the Italian breakfast

URIN'S CAFÉS are popular meeting places. The oldest cafés are to be found around the city's historic centre. Since the 1800s, many of these stuccoed rooms have been meeting places for activists and intellectuals, and important events of the Risorgimento must have been discussed among the mirrors and the elegant furnishings. Each place has its own history and particular story to tell, and an old-world atmosphere has been carefully maintained in many cases. While the older buildings have charm and some are historically important, Turin is also seeing a new breed of modern, trendy café-bar. Stop in for a variety of tasty snacks and a range of drinks while out sightseeing.

PIAZZA SAN CARLO

THIS SQUARE in the centre of Turin is bordered by some of the city's most famous cafés and *pasticcerie* (pastry shops). The Art Nouveau Caffè Torino was once patronized by international celebrities, and personalities such as Brigitte Bardot and James Stewart have sat beneath its Belle Époque stuccowork.

On the same side of the square is Caffè San Carlo, a Neo-Classical triumph of mirrors, capitals and columns, and the first café in Europe to install gas lighting, in the 19th century. Opposite is the *pasticceria* Stratta, famous for its cakes and sweets, including *gianduja* cream and *marrons glacés*. Neuv Caval'd Brôns takes its name from the equestrian statue of Emanuele Filiberto. It opened in the mid-1900s and today is also a restaurant (*see p189*).

San Tommaso 10 café, where the Lavazza company was founded in 1895

QUADRILATERO ROMANO

IN PIAZZA DELLA CONSOLATA, opposite the sanctuary of the same name, right in the historical centre, stands Al Bicerin. This small café opened in 1763 and still has its original period furnishings – the same eight marble tables, the wood panelling decorated with mirrors, and the original wooden counters. The café's success is due mainly to the invention of a drink called *bicerin* in the 1800s, which is made with hot chocolate, coffee and cream, and served hot.

Given the size of the premises and its position, it is not surprising that Al Bicerin became a haunt for people of both the nobility and lower classes. The politician Cavour often took a table here while he waited for the royal family to come from mass.

The same area is also home to San Tommaso 10, the shop where the Lavazza coffee company was founded in 1885. It offers a wide selection of good coffees.

Many fashionable and ethnic cafés and bars have also sprung up in this area. You can drink mint tea at 23c Via Sant'Agostino at the Hafa Café, which has a Moroccan atmosphere. For delicious cakes and different varieties of tea, try the Olsen café at 4b Via Sant'Agostino.

Sweets made by the old Stratta *pasticceria* in Piazza San Carlo

The Baratti & Milano *pasticceria* in the Galleria Subalpina

PIAZZA CASTELLO

A FTER Piazza San Carlo, you reach Piazza Carignano, where Pepino's café was founded by an enterprising Neapolitan in 1903. A favourite haunt of the Savoy family, it is renowned for its home-made ice cream (try the "penguin" ice cream, with cream and chocolate).

Between the Galleria Subalpina and the porticoes of Piazza Castello, the hub of city life, is the *pasticceria* Baratti & Milano. It still has its old marble tables, and little has changed in its luxurious surroundings since it opened in 1875. It is a good place for a coffee, an aperitif or a reasonably-priced lunch.

Mulassano, which originally specialized in selling vermouth, opened in 1907 and was once patronized by the House of Savoy. It was also here that the sandwich was made fashionable in the 1920s.

VIA PO AND PIAZZA VITTORIO VENETO

I N Via Po is Caffè Fiorio, known in the 1800s as the *caffè dei codini* (café of the ponytails) because it was the haunt, not only of scholars, but also of aristocrats and high-ranking officials. The ice-cream cone was invented and patented in Turin, and Fiorio is famous for *gianduja*-flavoured ices. At 52 Via Po is the Ghigo *pasticceria*, famous for its chocolate with cream, hot

zabaione and meringue. In Piazza Vittorio, the newly-renovated Caffè Elena is popular with young people. In the past it was a favourite haunt of the writer Cesare Pavese and the philosopher Nietzsche.

CORSO VITTORIO EMANUELE II

A T THE CORNER OF Corso Vittorio Emanuele II and Corso Re Umberto is Caffè Platti, which opened in 1875 as a wine shop. Today it is also renowned for its restaurant. The interior is reminiscent of the Louis XVI style and the rooms retain the atmosphere of that era.

Gerla, which opened in 1927 at No. 88, stocks 42 types of chocolates and six chocolate creams. Other famous sources of *giandujotto* and praline chocolates are Peyrano-Pfatisch at No. 76, and Avvignano in Piazza Carlo Felice.

The sumptuous interior of Caffè Platti in Corso Vittorio Emanuele II, Turin

CHOCOLATE

Since the early 1700s, Turin's chocolate makers have produced pralines, chocolates and Easter eggs. This world-famous symbol of Easter also originated in Turin with the widow Giambone who, in 1725, had the idea of filling eggs with liquid chocolate. Possibly the most famous speciality is *giandujotto*, which is made with a mixture of chocolate and pounded hazelnuts. It was created in 1806 to compensate for a lack of cocoa due to Napoleon's embargo on English imports. Moulding chocolate in a segmented shape was the invention of the Caffarel-Prochet company in 1865. Its name comes from the Turinese *commedia dell'arte* figure of "Gianduja" and has been a successful product ever since. Traditional chocolatiers keep the art of making chocolate alive, and the high quality is appreciated all over the world. Between February and March a big trade fair is held: CioccolaTO, with exhibitions, concerts and chocolate tastings.

Candied fruit, hazelnuts and chocolate

Bars and Cafés

TURIN HAS THE HIGHEST NUMBER of historic cafés and wine bars of any town in Italy. Taking an aperitif is a regular ritual and chocolate is a long tradition dating from the 1700s. This guide lists cafés, *pasticcerie* and wine bars where you can also have a light meal. The centre has been divided into five areas where most of the places to eat and drink are located.

	HISTORIC CAFÉ	PASTICCERIA	WINE BAR	OUTSIDE TABLES	HAPPY HOUR

PIAZZA SAN CARLO

Neuv Caval 'd Brôns
Piazza San Carlo 157. **Map** 3 A5. **(** *011 545 354.*
Historic café-*pasticceria* with typical cakes. Wide selection of savoury snacks, rolls and special pastries. ○ *7am–1am.* ● *Wed.*
| ■ | | | ● | ■ |

San Carlo
Piazza San Carlo 156. **(** *011 532 586.*
First opened in 1822, and long the haunt of artists and intellectuals. Exclusive coffees. Buffet lunch. In the evening, music is played. ○ *8am–2am.* ● *Aug.*
| ■ | | | ● | ■ |

Stratta
Piazza San Carlo 191. **Map** 3 A5. **(** *011 547 920.*
An institution since 1836: traditional sweets, *turineis* and the original jelly drops. Stratta was the supplier to royalty. ○ *9.30am–1pm, 3–7.30pm.* ● *Sun, Mon am; Aug.*
| | ● | | ● | ■ |

Torino
Piazza San Carlo 204. **Map** 3 A5. **(** *011 545 118.*
This elegant café from 1903 was the haunt of the Savoys, Cesare Pavese, Einaudi and others. Also a snack-bar and restaurant. Literary evenings. ○ *7.30am–1am.*
| ■ | | | ● | ■ |

QUADRILATERO ROMANO

Al Bicerin
Piazza della Consolata 5. **Map** 3 A3. **(** *011 436 93 25.*
Opened in 1763. Famous for Cavour's favourite drink. Good cakes and zabaione. ○ *8.30am–7.30pm Mon–Fri; 8.30am–1pm, 3.30–7.30pm Sat, Sun.* ● *Wed; Aug.*
| ■ | | | ● | ■ |

L'Albero di Vino
Piazza della Consolata 9/C. **Map** 3 A3. **(** *011 521 75 78.*
Wine bar with 350 different wines, hams and cheeses. ○ *9am–2am.* ● *Mon pm.*
| | | ■ | ● | ■ |

San Tommaso 10
Via San Tommaso 10. **Map** 3 A4. **(** *011 534 201.*
The Lavazza coffee company began here in 1885. Elegant café-restaurant with quality food. ○ *8am–8pm bar; 12 noon–2.30pm, 8–10.30pm restaurant.* ● *Sun; Aug.*
| ■ | | | ● | ■ |

Tre Galli
Via Sant'Agostino 25/B. **Map** 3 A3. **(** *011 521 60 27.*
A real Piedmontese wine bar, offering good food and wines. Relaxed atmosphere, music. ○ *12 noon–2.30pm, 6pm–midnight (12 noon–3pm Sat).* ● *Sun.*
| | | ■ | ● | ■ |

PIAZZA CASTELLO

Baratti & Milano
Piazza Castello 27. **Map** 3 B4. **(** *011 561 30 60.*
This place began as a *pasticceria* in 1875: chocolate, *giandujotti*, cream-filled chocolates and sweets. The restaurant is only open at lunchtime. ● *Mon.*
| ■ | | | | ■ |

Mulassano
Piazza Castello 15. **Map** 3 B4. **(** *011 547 990.*
Splendid marble and floral friezes adorn this café, opened in 1907. Famous for having invented special hot and cold sandwiches. ○ *7.30am–11pm.* ● *Sun; Aug.*
| ■ | | | ● | ■ |

Pepino
Piazza Carignano 8. **Map** 3 B5. **(** *011 542 009.*
Dating from 1873. Ice cream, cakes, Sunday brunch, lunchtime buffet. ● *Mon.*
| ■ | ● | | ● | ■ |

VIA PO AND PIAZZA VITTORIO VENETO

Caffè Elena
Piazza Vittorio Veneto 5. **Map** 7 C1. **(** *011 812 33 41.*
Antique furnishings, outside tables. Wine, rolls, hot meals. ○ *9am–2am.* ● *Wed.*
| ■ | | ■ | ● | ■ |

HISTORIC CAFÉS
Historic cafés which have retained the decor and atmosphere of the past.

PASTICCERIA
Shop selling pastries, sweets and chocolate, often with a bar.

WINE BAR
Piedmontese wine can be drunk in the many *vinerie* which also serve cheese and salami boards.

OUTSIDE TABLES
In spring, summer and autumn, many cafés have tables outside.

HAPPY HOUR
The ritual *aperitivo* is taken between 6pm and 9pm; pay for your drink and snack from the buffet.

	HISTORIC CAFÉ	PASTICCERIA	WINE BAR	OUTSIDE TABLES	HAPPY HOUR
Fiorio Via Po 8. **Map** 3 B5. 011 817 32 25. Historic café and meeting place of politicians since 1780. Famous for ice cream (particularly *gianduja*, torroncino and hazelnut flavours) and hot chocolate. Also rolls and light meals. 8am–1am. Mon; Aug.	■			●	■
Gran Bar Piazza Gran Madre di Dio 2. **Map** 8 D1. 011 81 30 871. This enormous café has sumptuous soft furnishings, cedar wood decor and minimal use of steel. In summer, outdoor tables offer splendid views. Gran Bar specializes in aperitifs and after-dinner drinks. 7am–2am, Mon–Sun.				●	■
Le Vitel Etonné Via San Francesco da Paola 4. **Map** 7 A1. 011 812 46 21. Good food and wines in a pleasant atmosphere. 10.30am–12 midnight Mon–Tue; 10.30am–3pm Wed; 10.30am–12 midnight Thu–Sat; 10.30am–12 midnight Sun.			■	●	■
La Drogheria Piazza Vittorio Veneto 18. **Map** 7 C1. 011 81 22 414. Comfortable atmosphere and original furnishings. Wines, liqueurs, tasty snacks, breakfast and late-morning brunch. A popular spot for an aperitif. 11am–2am Mon–Sun.				●	■
Taberna Libraria Via Bogino 5. **Map** 3 B5. 011 836 515. This well-stocked wine bar specializes in Piedmontese wine. Drink, eat, read and buy food, wine and much more. 10am–9pm.			■		

CORSO VITTORIO EMANUELE II

	HISTORIC CAFÉ	PASTICCERIA	WINE BAR	OUTSIDE TABLES	HAPPY HOUR
Avvignano Piazza Carlo Felice 50. **Map** 7 A1. 011 541 992. Original furnishings from 1883. A sweet-lover's paradise: *giandujotti* and *gianduja* cream chocolates. 8.30am–12.30pm, 3.30–7.30pm. Mon am; Aug.		●		●	■
Gerla Corso Vittorio Emanuele II 88. **Map** 1 A1. 011 545 422. Opened in the 1950s. Forty types of chocolates, cakes and other delicacies. 9am–7.30pm Tue–Fri; 9am–1pm, 3.30–7.30pm Sat; 8.30am–1pm Sun. Mon; Aug.		●			
Gertosio Via Mazzini 38. **Map** 7 A1. 011 812 25 12. Excellent chocolates (a different colour for each flavour) and cakes (Valentina with *gianduja* cream). 9am–1pm, 3.30–7.30pm. Mon; Aug.		●			
Giordano Piazza Carlo Felice 69. **Map** 7 A1. 011 547 121. Home-made products made from traditional recipes. *Giandujotti*, truffles, *boeri* (liqueur-filled chocolates). 9am–12 noon, 3–7.30pm. Sun pm; 20 Jul–31 Aug.		●			
Pfatisch Via Sacchi 42. **Map** 6 F1. 011 503 154. Opened in the 1920s, Pfatisch still has the original marble shelves. Savoury snacks and *gianduja* pralines. 8.30am–12 noon, 3.30–7.30pm. Mon; Aug.		●		●	■
Pfatisch-Peyrano Corso Vittorio Emanuele II 76. **Map** 1 A1. 011 538 765. Art Nouveau decor. Chocolate, special savarin cakes, exotic fruit and traditional *colombe* (Easter cakes). 9am–12.45pm, 4–7.30pm. Sun pm, Mon; end Jul.		●		●	■
Platti Corso Vittorio Emanuele II 72. **Map** 1 A1. 011 506 90 56. This sumptuous café began as a wine shop and is now a very popular place for breakfast, aperitifs or tea with biscuits. 7.30am–9pm.	■	●			■

For key to symbols see back flap

SHOPPING

VIA ROMA, Via Garibaldi, Via Po and the streets in the old city centre are the best places to buy clothes, antiques and a whole variety of objects. Some of the streets are pedestrian precincts and almost all are flanked by porticoes. The shop fronts are often the original wooden ones with decorated signs. Famous brand names can be found in the shops beneath the porticoes of Via Roma. Via Po has many antique bookshops

Wood carving of a bunch of fruit

and CD and record shops, while many of the shops in the Quadrilatero Romano district sell local products, gifts and accessories by young designers. The nearest shopping centres are those in Via Lagrange and at Lingotto. The outdoor market in Porta Palazzo is the largest in Europe. It is also possible to buy wines, *giandujotti* chocolates, clothes, trainers and fabrics at bargain prices in the outlet stores of Turin's famous brands.

The interior of Dobhran's in Via San Massimo

Around Via Maria Vittoria, Via Bogino, Via San Francesco da Paola and Via Principe Amedeo there are antique shops where you can buy furniture, crystal, lamps, candelabra and frames.

Football fans might like to visit the Turin football club shop in Via Costa and Via Allioni, or the Juventus club shop in Via Garibaldi.

Students can buy sweat shirts and other products of the University of Turin, founded in 1404, in the shop in Via Po. Products with the Torino 2006 logo can be bought at the Olympic stores.

OPENING HOURS

SHOPS IN TURIN are usually open from 9.30am to 12.30pm and from 3.30pm to 7.30pm. Some shops are open all day. Most shops are closed on Monday morning; food shops are closed Wednesday afternoon, and butchers close on Thursday afternoon. Many shops in the city centre and some **shopping centres** are also open on Sunday.

GIFTS AND SOUVENIRS

IT WOULD BE DIFFICULT to leave Turin without buying some of its delicious *giandujotti* or hand-made chocolates. Local food and wines are probably what visitors buy most and there are many well-stocked shops selling wine, cheese, salami, fresh pasta and *grissini* (breadsticks).

Some of the most famous Turinese aperitifs are made by

Carpano, Marchesi di Barolo, Cinzano and Martini & Rossi. In the valleys you can find Genepy liqueur, which is made from a medicinal herb which grows at the foot of the glaciers. In Turin you can also buy *bicerin*, the special local drink made with coffee, milk and chocolate.

HANDICRAFTS IN THE VALLEYS

THE WORKING and carving of wood is an ancient craft in the valleys which is still passed on from generation to generation. The Melezet

The old shop front of the Stratta *pasticceria* in Piazza San Carlo

Hand-carved wood made at the Melezet school in Bardonecchia

wood carving school, in the municipality of Bardonecchia, plays an important role in training craftsmen and making decorations. One of its most typical articles is a "cascade" of fruit and flowers, inspired by the 18th-century versions in the church of Melezet. Many carpenters in the valleys make wood carvings, do restoration work or make furniture and utensils.

Luserna San Giovanni, in Val Pellice, is renowned for the extraction and the working of a variety of gneiss called Luserna stone, which was also used to build the dome of the Mole Antonelliana, at Stupinigi and the Basilica di Superga.

The embroidery and lace from Sauze d'Oulx and the entire Val di Susa are famous. In many of the valley towns there is a strong tradition of wrought-iron work and in Val Chisone they work talc. Many craftsmen make stringed instruments and the *ghironda*, or hurdy-gurdy. In Pinerolo, a major craft meeting has been held annually since 1977.

MARKETS IN TURIN

Turin boasts the largest open-air market in Europe, at **Porta Palazzo**, which is held every morning from Monday to Friday and extends until the evening on Saturdays. Of the many local markets, the one held in Corso Palestro is well-stocked and is open daily except Sunday, 8am–2pm (on Saturday 7.30pm). The Crocetta market (8.30am–2pm Mon–Fri, 8.30am– 6.30pm Sat) has good prices for clothes.

There is a covered fish market in Piazza della Repubblica (8am–2pm Mon–Fri, 8am–7.30pm Sat). Other markets are those in Piazza Benefica and Piazza Madama Cristina.

Those who enjoy browsing among stalls of antiques and various junk will like the **Balôn** market, in Borgo Dora, a bustling, up-and-coming district. This traditional flea market, now more than 200 years old, is held on Saturdays. A Christmas market is held in

Lingotto shopping centre sign

the Cortile del Maglio. On the second Sunday in the month, the market at Porta Palazzo becomes the **Gran Balôn**. On the second Saturday in the month in Piazza Carlo Alberto about 30 stall-holders selling antique and modern articles assemble for a "Vintage" market.

DIRECTORY

SHOPPING CENTRES

[8] Gallery
Lingotto, Via Nizza 230, Turin.
☎ 011 663 07 68.
🕐 2–10pm Mon, 9am–10pm Tue–Sun. ⬤ public hols.

Lagrange-Rinascente
Via Lagrange 15, Turin.
☎ 011 517 00 75.
🕐 1–8.30pm Mon,
9.30am–8.30pm Tue–Fri,
9.30am–10pm Sat, 10am–8pm Sun (only some Suns).

Shopville Le Gru
Via Crea 10, Grugliasco (To).
☎ 011 770 97 03.
🕐 12 noon–10pm Mon,
9am–10pm Tue–Sat.
⬤ some Suns.

MARKETS

Balôn
Borgo Dora. 🕐 Sat.

Gran Balôn
Porta Palazzo.
🕐 2nd Sun in month (am).

Porta Palazzo
Piazza della Repubblica.
🕐 Mon–Fri am, Sat.

Hats on a stall in the Gran Balôn flea market

ENTERTAINMENT

Turin's proximity to the Alps makes it a convenient starting point for the 400 km (250 miles) of ski slopes in the valleys. In the summer, the mountain forests and paths are ideal places for excursions and all types of sporting activities, and the rivers and streams are great places for rafting. The river Po is good for canoeing, and the more than 40 km (25 miles) of cycle paths in Turin

Logo of the Turin Book Fair

offer ideal opportunities for long bicycle rides. In the hills around the city there are large golf courses. As well as sporting activities, many musical, artistic and cultural events take place throughout the year, both indoors and out. Turin hosts film festivals and various international trade fairs take place at Lingotto. The city also boasts a full and varied programme of theatre, dance and concerts.

THEATRE AND DANCE

The venues for theatrical performances are the Carignano, Alfieri, Colosseo, Nuovo, Gobetti and Gioiello theatres. The **Teatro Stabile** of Turin does not have its own premises, but its artistic productions can be enjoyed in the city's major theatres. Torino Danza is popular with fans of contemporary dance.

MUSIC

Turin's chief opera house is the **Teatro Regio**, which has its own calendar. Concerts by RAI Symphony Orchestra and the Philharmonic Orchestra are important events, and the Conservatorio is an outstanding venue for their concerts. The Giovanni Agnelli Auditorium at Lingotto hosts concerts and events organized by the **Associazione Lingotto Musica**, such as Sintonie and Torino Settembre Musica.

The city has long been famous for its contribution to the avant-garde music scene, from which successful groups such as Subsonica, Mau Mau and Africa Unite have

A concert at the Agnelli Auditorium at Lingotto in Turin

emerged. Live concerts take place in venues which have become institutions, such as Hiroshima Mon Amour, Barrumba and Mazda Palace.

In the summer, the Stadio delle Alpi and other outdoor venues, such as the Parco della Pellerina, host pop and rock music events, some of them part of the Traffic Torino Free Festival. Musica 90 and Torino Settembre Musica are occasions for many more excellent concerts.

Jazz music prevails in some of the events organized in and around Turin, such as Linguaggi Jazz, Eurojazz Festival and the Due Laghi Jazz Festival. The Torino Cultura website is a good source of information.

Ethnic and folk music have their roots in the valleys, where music is created with lutes, harps, *ghironda* and tambourines. Folk music has a good following thanks to groups such as Lou

Dalfin. In the Chisone-Germanasca valleys traditional, Italian and foreign music concerts are performed at the spring Cantavalli event.

CINEMA

Cabiria poster

Turin is also the capital of cinema. The first Italian film companies began here, producing important early films such as *Cabiria* (1914). This tradition continues with the city's numerous film festivals. The Torino Film Festival is the second in Italy after Venice. Festivals deal with various themes: homosexuality, women, the environment, youth and the mountains.

The number of cinemas in the city has risen in recent years, and there are a dozen cinemas for experimental and foreign films, including the Sala Massimo at the Museo del Cinema.

The Valsusa Filmfest is dedicated to historical recollections and environmental protection.

The interior of Teatro Carignano in Turin

FOOTBALL MATCHES

TURIN HAS a strong football tradition and has two important home teams: Torino, which has made football history since 1906, and Juventus. The football season runs from September to May, and matches are held at the Stadio delle Alpi. This stadium has over 70,000 seats and was built for the 1990 World Cup. Matches for the European Cup are all also held in Turin. Tickets for matches can be bought online through the relevant team's website, at Lottomatica offices, ticket offices and a number of authorized banks.

SKIING

THE PROVINCE OF TURIN offers numerous opportunities for skiing. Towards the Colle del Monginevro and Frejus, the resorts with the best facilities are: Sauze di Cesana, Clavière, Oulx, Cesana, Sestrière, Sauze d'Oulx, Prali, Bardonecchia and Pragelato. Between Val di Susa and Valle d'Aosta there are the slopes of Balme, Chiomonte, Usseglio, Viù, Ala di Stura and Ceresole Reale. Near Ivrea you can ski at Traversella.

Many resorts have both ski slopes and trails for cross-country skiing, and it is often possible to brush up skills at local ski schools.

HIKING AND CLIMBING

THE MAIN SOURCE OF information regarding hiking in the mountains is the **Club Alpino Italiano** (CAI), which has one of its most active branches in Turin. There are many other

Climbing a frozen waterfall in Valle Argentera

branches in the towns in the valleys. Many alpine refuges and paths are run by CAI, which also takes care of maintenance. There are various trails to follow or there is the Italian Alps Traverse, which branches off in various directions, enabling people to visit the abbeys and forts in the area.

The "Sentiero dei Franchi", probably the route used by Charlemagne's troops, is interesting culturally and environmentally and takes in the Sacra di San Michele, which can also be reached by train. The large nature reserves have facilities for various activities, while it is possible to explore the woods on horseback or follow the paths on a mountain bike.

Climbing is also a good way to explore the mountains, and beginners' courses and guided outings are available. In Val di Susa and Val Pellice there are practice rock faces and rock climbing schools.

OTHER SPORTS

IN THE PROVINCE OF TURIN there are golf courses around the city and at

Pecetto, Fiano, Carmagnola, Moncalieri, Sestrière, Clavière, Avigliana, Bardonecchia (nine holes) and Oulx.

Water sports such as canoeing and rafting are increasingly popular. In Novalesa and Venaus you can also go hang gliding and you can paraglide from the peaks in all the valleys.

In Turin, 40 km (25 miles) of cycle paths make for pleasant bicycle rides by the Po and Dora rivers, or you can make an excursion out of the city to Stupinigi. There are also riding stables. The city's summer heat can be escaped at one of the ten or so open-air swimming pools.

DIRECTORY

EVENTS IN TURIN

Torino Cultura
W www.torinocultura.it

THEATRE

Teatro Stabile di Torino
Via Roma 49. C 011 517 62 46. W www.teatrostabiletorino.it

MUSIC

Teatro Regio
Piazza Castello 215. C 011 8815 246. W www.teatroregio.torino.it

Ass. Lingotto Musica
Via Nizza 262. C 011 664 04 52.

SKIING

Via Lattea
Via del Colle 13, fraz. Borgata Sestrière (To). C 800 016 645.
W www.vialattea.it

HIKING

CAI, Turin Branch
Via Barbaroux 1. C 011 546 031.
W www.caitorino.it

One of the golf courses in the province of Turin

Skiing in Val di Susa, with Monte Niblè in the background

Nightlife

THE RANGE OF NIGHT SPOTS in Turin is vast, and mirrors the cultural variety of the city. The most popular places to meet before the night begins in earnest can be found in the city centre, the former industrial sites or the areas along the river, and they range from literary cafés to ethnic bars. Evenings start with an aperitif, when cocktails, beer and wine or sparkling prosecco are accompanied by savoury snacks. The next stop is likely to be a dance club or a live music venue.

Fruit cocktail

has become popular. The New York-style **Alcatraz** has all the latest trends in music and **Jammin'** has live concerts. **Dual**, also in the New York mould, is in Piazza Carlo Alberto. Another popular area is Docks Dora, which is in the old sheds of the Turin-Milan railway on an early-20th-century industrial site. This area is now used by artists and architects as studios and has trendy shops and cafés, such as **Café Blue** and **Shock Club**.

ETHNIC SPOTS

COMPLEMENTING the home-grown places are the numerous ethnic bars, restaurants and cafés which have sprung up in the Quadrilatero district. Highlights include the **Hafa Café**, inspired by the famous café in Tangier, **Las Rosas** (Mexican), **El Mir** (Lebanese) and **Mercante di Spezia**, an exotic tearoom with international, spiced cuisine. At **Achè** and **Sabor Latino** you can dance to Central and

Dancing under the arches at Jammin' in Via Murazzi

FASHIONABLE PLACES

THE STREETS around Via Garibaldi, which traces the layout of the Roman *castrum* to Porta Palazzo, have developed into the most fashionable area to be in recent years. From morning to night it is a place to stroll, have a coffee or a snack with a glass of good wine, or sit and enjoy an aperitif.

Besides the classic cafés such as Il Bicerin, many lively new spots have sprung up,

and these often have background music. Some of the most popular are the high-tech-style **Fusion Café**, Pastis, Km 5 and L'Obelix.

Night life is also to be found at the Murazzi: Giancarlo's, popular with young musicians and artists, has become an institution and is open until dawn. More recently **The Beach**, with its deckchairs facing the Po in the summer and good views of the Gran Madre church and Monte dei Cappuccini,

Moroccan atmosphere and furnishings at the Hafa Café

PAUSING FOR AN APERITIF

The aperitif has become fashionable almost everywhere, from Madrid to New York, but the tradition began in Turin, with vermouth. Surrounded by the best wine-producing areas in Italy – Langhe, Monferrato, Canavese – and the birthplace of world-famous products (such as Martini), it was in Turin that vermouth (wine flavoured with alpine herbs) was created. It is said that it was invented in a shop under the porticoes of Piazza Castello, owned by

Signor Marendazzo, assisted by Antonio Benedetto Carpano. Using Moscato wine as a base, Marendazzo and Carpano produced a drink flavoured with herbs from the Biella valleys. The shop soon became a meeting place for the people of Turin, and since that time Martini, Cinzano, Cora, Gancia and Riccadonna have joined the name of Carpano. Aperitifs have changed since that time – people now choose wine, cocktails or long drinks – but the ritual has remained. The Turinese still regularly meet after work to chat, nibble on snacks and enjoy a relaxing drink.

A barman preparing a cocktail

A crowded open-air spot at Murazzi, on the river Po

South American music. In Via Carlo Alberto, the **Kirkuk Café** serves Turkish, Kurdish and Greek food.

DANCE CLUBS, DISCO BARS AND LIVE MUSIC

TURIN IS a ferment of innovative sounds with music to listen or dance to in the most avant-garde night spots. Every evening, Alcatraz offers a different musical theme, while some of the best DJs and Italian and foreign groups perform at **Barrumba**. Do not miss Friday nights at the **Officine Belforte**, one of Turin's liveliest clubs, or the historic **Hiroshima Mon Amour**, a culture association begun in 1986 which now has three rooms for parties, concerts, and events and is also used for literary meetings and theatrical performances. The **Magazzino di Gilgamesh** offers a rich programme of blues, jazz and rock concerts.

Places to go for techno and house music are **La Gare**, **Rock City** and **Notorius**. Finally, for those who prefer to listen rather than dance there is the **Folk Club** which, since 1988, has seen many major Italian and foreign songwriters perform.

LITERARY AND ART CAFÉS

AN ALTERNATIVE WAY to spend an evening is at one of the art or literary cafés where you can visit exhibitions by emerging artists or attend literary or musical evenings. These include Diwan Café,

which organizes literary evenings, Paris Texas, a 1960s–70s lounge bar which holds musical evenings and exhibitions of works by new artists, and Machè, where you can look through the books and contemporary art magazines. Café Procope, where you can often dance the tango, began as a *café chantant* and Pastis has set aside part of its 1950s premises for exhibitions.

WINE BARS

TURIN'S NUMEROUS wine bars *(see pp192–5)* offer a friendly, welcoming atmosphere and a good selection of wines, from Italy and abroad. Drinks are often served with snacks, and you can stop to eat and drink at any time of day. The following are very popular with locals: Parola, Tre Galli, Le Vitel Etonné, Sapordivino, Al Sorji, the Casa del Barolo and the historic L'Ostu.

Some of the wine on offer at the Parola wine bar in Turin

(see pp192–5)

DIRECTORY

NIGHT SPOTS

Alcatraz Via Murazzi del Po 37. ☐ *10pm–4am.*

Café Blue Via Valprato 68. ☐ *11pm–4am.*

Dual Via Battisti 17/d. ☐ *8pm–2am.*

Fusion Café Via Sant'Agostino 17. ☐ *7pm–2am.*

Giancarlo Via Murazzi del Po 49. ☐ *10pm–5am.*

Jammin' Via Murazzi del Po 17. ☐ *9pm–4am.*

Shock Club Via Valprato 68. ☐ *10pm–3am.*

The Beach Via Murazzi del Po 18. ☐ *10am–4am.*

ETHNIC SPOTS

Achè Via Montebello 21. ☐ *10pm–3am.*

Ambhara Bar Via Borgo Dora 10. ☐ *8pm–2am.*

Café Procope Via Juvarra 15. ☐ *9pm–3am.*

El Mir Piazza Corpus Domini. ☐ *8am–11pm.*

Hafa Café Via Sant'Agostino 3/c. ☐ *11am–2am.*

Kirkuk Café Via Carlo Alberto 16. ☐ *12 noon–1am.*

Las Rosas Via Bellezia 15/F. ☐ *5.30pm–2am.*

Sabor Latino Via Stradella 10. ☐ *10pm–3am.*

LIVE MUSIC & DISCOS

Barrumba Via S Massimo 1. ☐ *10.30pm–4.30am.*

Folk Club Via Perrone 3/bis. ☐ *8pm–12 midnight.*

Hiroshima Mon Amour Via Bossoli 83. ☐ *9pm–3am.*

La Gare Via Sacchi 65. ☐ *10.30pm–4am.*

Magazzino di Gilgamesh Piazza Moncenisio 13. ☐ *8pm–3am.*

Notorius Via Stradella 10. ☐ *10pm–4am.*

Rock City Via Bertini 2. ☐ *10.30pm–4am.*

Officine Belforte Corso Venezia 30/a. ☐ *10pm–4am.*

SURVIVAL
GUIDE

PRACTICAL INFORMATION 204-207
TRAVEL INFORMATION 208-215

PRACTICAL INFORMATION

Turin has good facilities for tourists, and preparations for the Winter Olympics have created an opportunity for providing further services for visitors, such as guided theme tours and other initiatives run by the transport companies. The Atrium Torino in Piazza Solferino is often the first point of contact for visitors. This wood, glass and steel structure, by Giugiaro Design,

Logo of Turin's tourist board

is home to Turismo Torino, which provides visitors with all the information they need during their stay, from hotel booking services to a list of programmed events, shows and exhibitions. What will undoubtedly strike the visitor is the great number of cultural events that the city offers; it is a good idea to plan your visit according to the cultural events that most interest you.

The Atrium, the innovative tourist information centre, Piazza Solferino

TOURIST INFORMATION

The two key sources of tourist information are **Turismo Torino** and **Montagne Doc**. The first is the tourist board, which deals with and promotes tourism in the metropolitan area of Turin, while the second agency deals with the area between the Pinerolese district and Val di Susa. Visitors can contact these agencies before beginning their journey or on their

arrival. In either case, both Turismo Torino and the Montagne Doc are able to take care of all aspects of your stay in the area.

Turismo Torino information centres can be found at Turin airport (Caselle) and Porta Nuova railway station. However, the Atrium in Piazza Solferino is the most striking of the new tourist services and all the information

you could possibly need to know about the city can be found in these two innovative pavilions.

The information centres of the Montagne Doc agency are spread over a wider area. There are two branches in Pinerolo and Oulx, as well as information centres in the 11 main tourist resorts of the region. In other parts of the Turinese valleys, information can be found at the local tourist offices.

TOURIST SERVICES

Turismo Torino offers the visitor a variety of services, including free hotel and guesthouse booking services for accommodation in Turin and the surrounding area. There is also a free booking service for guided tours (available in various languages) for adults, groups and school parties.

Another special initiative is the ChocoPass. This is a book of tickets (costing 10 euros) which can be bought at the Turismo Torino information points and entitles the holder to ten "tastings" of chocolate cake, *giandujotti*, pralines, cakes or ice creams at participating historic cafés and *pasticcerie* within 24 hours.

Other campaigns have also been promoted to meet tourists' needs, including special weekend discounts in certain hotels and restaurants –

Logo of the Montagne Doc tourist agency

◁ **View of Turin with Piazza Vittorio Veneto and Mole Antonelliana**

The Turismo Bus Torino, a good way of seeing the historic centre

"Week-end a Torino" (*see p174–5*) – and "Le Tavole del Sapore".

For resorts in the Turinese valleys, Montagne Doc is a good source of information. It specializes in natural history, the mountains of the region, hiking, excursions and outdoor activities in general.

The Torino Card, a pass for the museums and city transport

VISITING THE CITY AND ITS MUSEUMS

A GOOD WAY to save money on a visit to Turin is to buy the Torino Card, a pass valid for 48 hours (15 euros) or 72 hours (17 euros) which gives you access to 120 museums and historic buildings in the Piedmontese region, as well as public transport and other tourist services. The card also entitles people to reductions for guided tours, various events, bicycle hire and car parking fees. The Torino Card can be purchased before departure by writing to Turismo Torino or it can be bought at the information points in the city, at hotels, or at the airport.

For those staying in Turin for longer periods, there is a very reasonably-priced Abbonamento Musei (museum season ticket),

which is valid for 13 months for museums in the city and Piedmont. It costs 40 euros.

A convenient way to visit the main sights of Turin is to take the Turismo Bus Torino: the circular route has 14 stops and costs 5 euros (free with the Torino Card) with multi-lingual commentary. Other tourist transport services are: the panoramic lift at Mole Antonelliana, the Sassi-Superga rack-rail tram car, the boats on the river Po and the vintage trams.

Guided tours are also available and there is a wide range of theme tours on offer by Turismo Torino (Tour of the City, Egyptian Museum, Aperitif beneath the Mole, Torino Golosa, Literary Turin and more). Tours take place on Saturday mornings (in Italian) or in the afternoons (bilingual). Prices are at 6 euros per person (reductions for Torino Card holders).

EXHIBITIONS AND EVENTS

THE CULTURAL EVENTS on offer in the city are very varied and it is worth planning a trip so as to take in an art exhibition or a wine or gastronomic event.

Information about what's on in the city and the surrounding areas can be found in the local paper, *La Stampa*. The Friday supplement, *Torino Sette*, is one of the best sources of information about shows, cultural and sports events in the province. Before departure it is a good idea to

consult some of the websites which have good up-to-date information, such as those of the city of Turin and the local areas (www.torinocultura.it, www.extratorino.it).

La Stampa's Friday supplement, with information about events

Health, Safety and Currency

Turin is a large european city and can offer visitors a full range of services and facilities. This section provides advice about everyday needs, such as the opening hours of the post offices, banks and pharmacies, information on the public phone system and which credit cards are most commonly accepted. To help with using the local currency, coins and banknotes are illustrated. The city itself is quite safe, and the towns in the valleys are very peaceful and quiet. It is important to be well-prepared for excursions into the mountains, particularly in winter.

The façade of the Mauriziano Umberto I Hospital (1885) in Corso Turati

HEALTH

Anyone unlucky enough to have health problems while staying in Turin can go to one of the city hospitals. In serious cases, call 118 for an ambulance. If you wish a doctor to make a house call, contact the **Guardia Medica** (duty physician).

All pharmacies display a list of chemists that are open at night or on public holidays. There are four night chemists in Turin: Boniscontro (Corso Vittorio Emanuele 66, near Porta Nuova station), Comunale 21 (Corso Belgio 151/b), Nizza (Via Nizza 65) and Piazza Massaua 1.

SAFETY IN THE MOUNTAINS

It is important to be well informed and properly equipped for trips into the mountains: hiking boots, warm clothes and rainwear, food and water, a detailed map and a first-aid kit are essentials. When choosing your route take into account your own physical abilities and the weather conditions, and always tell someone where you are going and when you plan to be back. Experienced guides can be contacted via Club Alpino Italiano (CAI).

EMERGENCIES

Unfortunately unpleasant incidents are always possible, but they can be

Entrance to the pharmacy of the Ospedale Mauriziano in Turin

dealt with by contacting the appropriate services. For any type of emergency, call 113. In the event of a road accident, contact the city or traffic police (for breakdowns and road emergencies call 112). If you are the victim of a robbery or have been defrauded in some way, report the incident to the *carabinieri* (call 118), who are responsible for public order and have jurisdiction at a municipal, provincial and regional level, or the state police (who deal with major crimes at a national level).

If you lose your documents or other personal items, it is advisable to report the loss at the nearest police or *carabinieri* station as soon as possible. After 48 hours you can contact the Lost Property Office. The fire brigade (call 115) intervenes in the event of fire, as well as other accidents of various kinds, in co-ordination with the police forces.

Stamps for the normal postal service and for priority mail

COMMUNICATIONS

The public telephone network is run by Telecom Italia and other smaller companies. As well as telephones that use phone cards (on sale at tobacconists and newsagents), some Telecom phones also accept credit cards or cash, while Albacom phones also accept foreign currency. To call directory enquiries call 412 (4176 for international information) and to make a reverse-charge call, dial 170. Post offices are open from Monday to Friday, 8am–2pm, and on Saturday, 8.30am–12 noon. The post offices Centrale, Porta Nuova (Via

Telecom Italia telephone booths in Piazza Carlo Emanuele II

Sacchi 2), 15 (Via Avogadro 8) and some other less central offices stay open until 7pm. All post offices offer the basic services and a number of other services are becoming more common, such as recharging mobile phone cards, online telegrams and banking services. Stamps are sold in post offices and at tobacconists.

BANKS AND ATMS

BANKS ARE USUALLY open from 8.30am to 1.30pm and from 3pm to 4pm, from Monday to Friday (they often close earlier the day before public holidays). Credit cards are generally accepted for purchasing goods or for making withdrawals. VISA, American Express, Diners Club and MasterCard are the most commonly-accepted cards. Automated teller machines (ATMs) are common in the city and larger towns in the valleys.

Offices of the Turinese bank group San Paolo IMI in Piazza San Carlo

CURRENCY EXCHANGE

THE CURRENCY in Italy is the euro. Banknotes come in denominations of 5, 10, 20, 50, 100, 200 and 500 euros and they all bear the star of the European Union. There are 1 and 2 euro coins, and 50, 20, 10, 5, 2 and 1 cent coins. There are banks and a bureau de change at the airport. However, it is a good idea to have a certain amount of local currency with you when you arrive. For more competitive rates it is best to change money at a bank.

If you use travellers' cheques, it is best to change them at a bank; a fee is charged for every transaction so it is not economic to change small sums. Exchange offices usually keep the same opening hours as shops. Card holders can also withdraw cash from ATMs.

BANKNOTES AND COINS

Seven banknotes are issued in denominations of 5 (grey), 10 (pink), 20 (blue), 50 (orange), 100 (green), 200 (yellow), and 500 (violet) euros. There are eight denominations of coin.

1 cent   2 cents   5 cents   10 cents   20 cents   50 cents

1 euro   2 euros   5 euros

10 euros
20 euros
50 euros
100 euros
200 euros
500 euros

TRAVEL INFORMATION

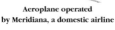

Aeroplane operated by Meridiana, a domestic airline

TURIN and the province are served by the international airport at Caselle, which offers connections to many European and Italian cities. The city is also directly connected to France and Spain by fast trains and to the rest of Europe via Milan. The motorway system around Turin is very good and you can travel around the region comfortably by car or by using the numerous services provided by Italian and other bus companies. The alpine tunnels of Frejus, Gran San Bernardo and Mont Blanc shorten the distances to the rest of Europe.

Dawn breaking at Turin's Caselle Airport

ARRIVING BY AIR

TURIN IS DIRECTLY connected by air to many European cities (including London Gatwick, Luton and Stansted, Frankfurt, Munich, Paris, Amsterdam, Brussels, Madrid, Lisbon and Barcelona), as well as major cities in Italy.

The budget airline **Ryanair** operates two daily direct flights from London Stansted to Turin, **Easyjet** runs a daily flight from London Luton and **British Airways** offers two flights a day from London Gatwick. Flying time is about two hours. Some charter airlines such as Monarch and Britannia offer seasonal flights from UK airports such as Birmingham and Manchester.

There are no direct international flights to Turin from the US, Canada, Australia or New Zealand; passengers will need to fly to a major European hub such as Frankfurt, Milan or Rome, and change to a domestic flight or train. There are frequent fast trains from Milan to Turin and the journey time is around 80–100 minutes.

TURIN AIRPORT

THE Sandro Pertini airport at Caselle, outside Turin, is 16 km (10 miles) from the centre and can be reached in about half an hour by car via a ring road that also links the main cities in Piedmont, northern Italy and the south of France (the border is only 112 km/70 miles from Turin).

There is a railway link to the airport from Dora station in Turin, with trains leaving every half-hour for the 20-minute trip. The train ticket is 3 euros and includes one trip on the inner city network.

An alternative is to use the buses run by Sadem, which connect the airport to the city's two main railway stations. The service runs from early in the morning until late in the evening. The trip takes about 40 minutes and buses leave every 30 or 45 minutes. Tickets cost 5 euros (less for Torino Card holders). Tickets can also be bought on board but there is a surcharge of 52 cents. There is also a coach service to and from Aosta twice a day.

The airport taxi rank is in front of the airport arrivals area. The usual price is from around 30 to 35 euros. There is also a personalized taxi and limousine service available 24 hours a day.

The airport has many useful services for travellers, such as airline ticket offices and the Turismo Torino centre. Many hire-car companies have desks in the arrivals hall. There are banks and

Passengers queuing at the check-in desks at Turin airport

exchange offices in both the arrivals and departures areas. The airport terminal is directly connected to a multi-storey car park which has around 3,000 parking places. The airport is being extended and will be able to offer more facilities in future, including a terminal for private planes and a four-star airport hotel.

By Car

TURIN'S POSITION, close to France and Switzerland, and its close links with the mountain passes and alpine tunnels, make the city an easy place to reach by car from many European cities: Lyon is only 307 km (190 miles), Munich 650 km (405 miles) and Paris 765 km (475 miles). Turin can be reached from Grenoble and Lyon via Susa and the Frejus tunnel.

Turin is part of a trans-European motorway network system and has the following connections with the Italian motorway network: the A6 from Savona, Nice, Côte d'Azur; A7 and A26 from Genoa; A4 from Milan, Venice, Trieste; A21 from Piacenza, Bologna, the Adriatic coast, Brescia; A5 from Aosta, Geneva,

Bird's-eye view of the railway station of Porta Susa in Turin

Lausanne; A32 from Grenoble and Lyon, via the Frejus alpine tunnel. The city ring road allows you to reach the city centre in just a short time: coming from the north you should take the exit for Corso Regina Margherita. Arriving from the south, the most suitable exit is the one signposted Corso Francia.

By Train

THE MAIN railway stations in Turin are Porta Nuova and Porta Susa. Porta Nuova is at the moment the main station for national and international connections with Eurostar, Intercity, Inter-regional, Direct and Express trains. The station is at the southern end of Via Roma, and therefore just a short distance from the centre.

Porta Susa station has more regional and inter-regional connections, which efficiently cover the Piedmont network. This station is near Piazza Statuto, and therefore close to the city centre. Over the next few years, work on Porta Susa station will probably make it the main station in Turin, and the structure will have a futuristic design. The most frequent rail service are the connections to Milan, which can be reached in about 80–100 minutes.

DIRECTORY			

By Air

Caselle Airport
Strada San Maurizio 12, Caselle Torinese (To).
📞 011 567 63 61.
ℹ️ 011 567 81 24.
🌐 www.aeroportodi torino.it

Air France
📞 8488 844 66.
🌐 www.airfrance.it

Alitalia
📞 8488 656 42 (international reservations).
🌐 www.alitalia.it

British Airways (Gatwick)
📞 199 712 266.
🌐 www.ba.com

Easyjet (Luton)
📞 848 887 766.
🌐 www.easyjet.com

Lufthansa
📞 199 400 044.
🌐 www.lufthansa.it

Meridiana
📞 199 111 333.
🌐 www.meridiana.it

Ryanair
📞 899 678 910.
🌐 www.ryanair.com

By Car

Motorway Torino–Milano
📞 800 80 60 26.
🌐 www.autostradatomi.it

Motorway Torino–Savona
📞 011 971 31 82.
🌐 www.tosv.it

Motorway Torino–Valle d'Aosta
📞 0125 739 585.
🌐 www.ativa.it

CCISS
📞 1518; 800 331 518.

Tunnels
📞 012 290 90 11 (Fréjus).
🌐 www.sitaf.it
📞 016 578 09 02 (Gran San Bernardo).
📞 016 589 04 11 (Mont Blanc).

AVIS
📞 011 470 15 28.
🌐 www.avis.com

Easy Car
📞 011 996 32 57.
🌐 www.easycarspa.com

Europcar
📞 011 567 80 48.

Hertz
📞 011 567 81 66.
🌐 www.hertz.it

Maggiore
📞 011 470 19 29.
🌐 www.maggiore.it

Targarent
📞 011 567 80 90.
🌐 www.targarent.it

By Train

Trenitalia
📞 89 20 21; 166 105 050 (national and international info).
🌐 www.trenitalia.it

GTT
📞 800 990 097.
🌐 www.gtt.to.it

By Bus

Sadem
Corso Siccardi. 📞 011 538 967 (Sadem Express).
🌐 www.sadem.it

Eurolines
📞 055 357 110
🌐 www.eurolines.it

The out-of-town bus service, covering the province of Turin

From the Dora railway station, further to the north, trains leave for Turin airport.

Travellers coming from Waterloo station in London must change at Gare de Lyon in Paris. Trains from Germany arrive at Porta Nuova station, after a change in Milan at Milano Centrale or at Verona Porta Nuova. There are direct rail connections to some French and Spanish cities.

ITALIAN TRAINS

IN ITALY, most of the trains are run by **Trenitalia**. In the province of Turin there is another company, Satti, which is part of the Consorzio Torinese Trasporti and is responsible for the management of Dora railway station, from where trains leave for the airport and for Ceres, Agliè, Avigliana, Racconigi and Ivrea. Another railway company which runs many of the trains coming from Switzerland and Germany, arriving in Milan, is Cisalpino.

Trenitalia offers various services. The fastest but most expensive trains are the Eurostar, for which bookings are obligatory. There are around a dozen daily trains for Milan and the journey only takes about 80 minutes. There are fewer Eurostar trains for Rome.

Intercity trains link the main cities and although slower than Eurostar, are comfortable express trains, only making a few intermediary stops along

Logo of Trenitalia

the way. There are also night trains. The journey from Rome to Turin takes around seven hours.

The inter-regional trains are cheaper but much slower as they make numerous stops along the route and are usually used by commuters. There is an inter-regional train service from Turin to Milan which runs every hour.

Regional trains are slower again, covering shorter distances, but they serve many destinations and smaller towns in the province and in the alpine region.

Tickets and any necessary supplements can be bought and reservations made at ticket offices, from the automatic ticket machines found in the stations, at authorized travel agents, or by telephone or by using a computer to access the internet. Most train tickets are valid for two months and must be date-stamped (validated), along with any

additional supplementary tickets, before boarding the train. This can be done at one of the many yellow machines which are placed at strategic points in the stations. However, Eurostar tickets are only valid for the particular day and for the specific train for which they were purchased. Journeys on Cisalpino trains require reservations, but it is also possible to pay a surcharge and board the train without booking a seat.

BY COACH

THE COACH TERMINAL in Turin is currently located in Corso Siccardi. It is possible to reach Turin directly by coach from many cities outside Italy: Amsterdam, Athens, Barcelona, Brno, Alicante, Budapest, Chamonix, Cracow, Geneva, London, Madrid, Marrakesh, Montpellier, Nice, Paris, Prague and Radom. By changing in Milan you can also reach other destinations, particularly those in eastern Europe. The ticket office is in the bus terminal.

Companies that offer connections outside Italy are **Eurolines** and **Sadem Express**. There are numerous connections to Italian towns and cities, especially in Piedmont. There are also direct connections outside the region to Aosta, Courmayeur, Cervinia, Briançon, Diano Marina, Gallipoli, Lidi Ferraresi, Porto Tolle, Rho, Pray, Rimini, Cattolica, Gabicce, Saint Vincent, Senise and Taranto.

Comfortable coaches, serving many tourist resorts

Getting to the Valleys

I T IS VERY EASY TO GET TO PIEDMONT'S SKI RESORTS from Turin. There are decent train and bus services, or travellers may choose to arrive by car via the motorway, which runs through the Val di Susa westwards to the Frejus alpine tunnel. Other important main roads *(strada statale, or SS)* are those to the hills of Monginevro and Moncenisio. For Val Pellice and Val Chisone-Germanasca, the main transport hub is Pinerolo, where buses and trains arrive from Turin and where you can also pick up coach links to other towns.

The entrance to the Frejus tunnel linking Italy and France

DIRECTORY

BY BUS

SAPAV
(800 801 901.
w www.sapav.it.

Cavourese
(0121 690 31.
w www.cavourese.it.

BY TAXI

Pinerolo
(0121 397 900 / 321 000.

Oulx
(0122 831 224.

also serves Susa, Oulx and Pinerolo. The service is fairly frequent, but it is best to check the timetables before setting out. The Torino-Sestrière line takes about three hours. From Pinerolo you can continue with the Sapav and **Cavourese** bus services which connect the smaller towns in the valley.

BY CAR

T O REACH Susa and Bardonecchia by car you can either choose to take the fast A32 Torino–Bardonecchia–Frejus motorway or the SS24 road to Monginevro, which is open all year round. The SS25 Moncenisio road is only open from May to October, however.

The town of Pinerolo is the key hub for routes to towns in Val Pellice. From here you can pick up the main roads to Cavour, Bricherasio and the other towns in Val Pellice as well as those in Val Germanasca, including Perosa Argentina and Villar Perosa.

Towns in Val Chisone-Germanasca can be reached by either taking the SS23 Sestrière state main road from Stupinigi or the newly-constructed Orbassano-Volvera motorway.

The Val Chisone area can easily be reached from France through the Sestrière hills by using either the Monginevro pass or the Sestrière tunnel (Traforo del Frejus in Italian), which links the two countries.

BY TRAIN

T HE TORINO-BUSSOLENO-Bardonecchia railway line enables you to get to the Alta Val di Susa in under an hour. The train stops at Salbertrand and Oulx, from which you can go on to Cesana, Clavière and Sestrière by bus. There are direct trains or you can change at Bussoleno.

Trains leave from Turin every hour and the direct train to Bardonecchia takes about 90 minutes. Trains for Pinerolo leave from Turin about every hour and the journey takes around 50 minutes. There is also an alternative bus service from Pinerolo to Torre Pellice. The trip takes around 35 minutes and the buses leave from the railway station.

BY BUS

T HE **SAPAV** BUS COMPANY runs the service from Turin to Pinerolo, Perosa Argentina, Pragelato and Sestrière. The Cavourese company connects Pinerolo with Torre Pellice, Cavour and Luserna San Giovanni. The same company

BY TAXI

Y OU CAN ALSO REACH resorts in the valleys directly from Turin airport by taxi. With very long trips it is advisable to establish a price before setting off. Visiting one of the forts or the abbeys out in the countryside is easy by taxi and there is a taxi or minibus service at all the railway stations in the valleys. Some drivers also speak English and French. In Pinerolo, taxis can be found in Corso Torino, and there is a taxi rank near the hospital in Via Inghilterra in Susa.

The Turin-Lyon railway line crossing the Val di Susa

GETTING AROUND TURIN

ALTHOUGH TURIN is a large metropolis, it is a city on a human scale. Miles of bicycle paths cross the various districts and parks and a number of projects are under way, aimed at reducing the traffic and making getting around the city easier for visitors and residents alike. A new underground system will radically

GRUPPO TORINESE TRASPORTI
Logo of Turin's public transport company

change the city's public transport map, and more areas will be designated as pedestrian precincts and limited traffic zones. However, getting around by car is also not a problem. There are many underground car parks and the city has characteristic wide avenues. Visitors can also make use of Turin's charming vintage trams.

TRAMS AND BUSES

BOTH URBAN AND SUBURBAN areas benefit from a good network of bus and tram services. The service, run by Gruppo Torinese Trasporti (GTT), begins at about 5am in the morning and finishes at around midnight.

You must have a ticket before boarding any of the buses or trams and it should be punched in one of the orange machines on board as soon as you get on. Tickets can be bought from tobacconists, newsagents and cafés displaying the logo of the company which runs the service, or you can buy them from the automatic ticket machines. A single ticket for the urban area is valid for 70 minutes and costs 90 cents. It is also possible to buy a booklet of ten tickets or a weekly or monthly ticket. If you do

**A single ticket
for the urban area**

not validate your ticket on boarding, you will be liable to a fine.

The GTT transport company also serves the 26 municipalities around Turin, including Rivoli and Moncalieri. The transport network will be reorganized when the new Turin underground system comes into service.

A bus stop in Piazza Statuto in Turin

In the meantime, tram no 4 crosses the city from north to south along an 18-km (11-mile) route, which the new underground (*metropolitana*) will follow.

The Linea Star 1 shuttle bus connects designated parking areas to the city centre. It passes through Piazza San Carlo and the area where many of the city's museums are located, as well as the area around the Mole Antonelliana.

Comprehensive timetables are displayed at all bus and tram stops and some have a complete map of the entire transport network for reference. Important notices concerning changes to routes or times are displayed at stops and on board.

VISITING TURIN ON FOOT

THE HISTORIC CENTRE of Turin can be visited on foot, but it is worth remembering that some of the important monuments and museums, such as the Pinacoteca

A new Cityway tram crossing the city

The lift in the Mole Antonelliana, rising up to the dome of the building

Giovanni e Marella Agnelli at Lingotto, or the Fondazione Sandretto Re Rebaudengo in Via Modane, are outside the city centre.

A good zone for strolling is the area between Piazza Carlo Felice and Piazza Vittorio Veneto, passing through Piazza Castello and the area called Quadrilatero Romano.

TOURIST SERVICES

THERE ARE MANY interesting tourist services on offer to visitors to the city and they are all free to Torino Card holders. No visitor should pass up a chance to visit the panoramic lift in the Mole Antonelliana, which goes up to the dome of the building that has become the symbol of Turin. It passes through the Museo Nazionale del Cinema and climbs 85 m (280 ft) up to the balcony from which you can enjoy a 360-degree panoramic view of the city and the Alps. The glass elevator also allows you to admire the building's impressive dome.

Another interesting service is the Sassi-Superga rack-rail tram car which goes to the basilica and park of Superga along a charming route. This track was laid down at the beginning of the last century and the tram car has old-fashioned carriages.

Sassi station, in Piazzale Modena, also has a restaurant and a museum where the first horse-drawn carriages to be used in Milan are on display.

The vintage tram connecting Sassi station and the Basilica di Superga

Embarkation point at Murazzi with boats Valentino and Valentina

A trip on the great river Po which crosses Turin is also a relaxing way to view the city from a different perspective. Two boats, one called Valentino and the other Valentina, leave from the jetty at Murazzi (a short distance from Piazza Vittorio Veneto). The boats also make a stop at the Borgo Medioevale and go as far as Moncalieri. Another stop is made at Italia '61 near Palazzo a Vela and the Museo dell'Automobile. Tickets can be bought on board the boat or at the main embarkation points. The boats may also be booked separately for groups. The frequency with which the boats run changes according to the season, so it is a good idea to check departure times before setting out.

A convenient way to visit the museums, monuments and the streets of Turin is to make use of a tourist bus service called "TurismoBus Torino". These buses run every hour and with just a single ticket passengers can get on or off at any of the 14 stops along the route. A guide on board tells visitors something of the many sights and attractions along the way. The terminus is in Piazza Solferino and the route is aimed at entertaining visitors to Turin, taking in the major attractions in the city. Tickets can be bought on board and cost 5 euros for the whole day. This service is free for

turismobus torino

Logo of Turismo Bus Torino

Torino Card holders. You may also see vintage trams and painted carriages on the streets in the centre of the city. These are historic trams which can be hired for parties or meetings. They date from the 1930s and the 1950s.

TAXIS

In every district of the city there is at least one taxi rank. However, it is also possible to call for or book a taxi by phoning companies such as Radio Centrale (call 011 5737) or Radio Taxi (call 011 5730, 011 3399). The main taxi ranks can be found at the main railway stations of Porta Nuova and Porta Susa.

The GTT transport company runs a special taxi service for the disabled.

PARKING

There are places to park all over the city centre. Parking fees in the so-called "blue zone" decrease the further away from the city centre you park. The price per hour varies from 50 cents to 2 euros. An hourly parking voucher can be bought at tobacconists, newsagents and cafés, or you can use the automatic ticket machines which are usually located at the end of the streets marked with blue parking lines.

There are about 20 car parks in the city, and these cost from between 40 cents and 1.30 euros per hour. The largest car park is located at Lingotto, where there are some 4,000 parking spaces. Other large parking areas closer to the city centre are near the Tribunale in Corso Vittorio Emanuele II, in Corso Bolzano (Porta Susa), in Corso Stati Uniti (near the Galleria d'Arte Moderna) and in Corso XI Febbraio (Piazza della Repubblica-Porta Palazzo).

PEDESTRIAN AREAS

Via Garibaldi and the streets adjacent form the main pedestrian areas in Turin. Via Garibaldi leads to Piazza Statuto, which can be reached by many forms of public transport, and is close to Porta Susa railway station and Piazza Castello. The 18 km (11 miles) of porticoes make strolling around the centre of

One of the vintage trams used to provide a tourist service

Turin a pleasant pastime. Via Roma and Via Po are also sometimes closed to car traffic. Traffic access is limited in parts of the historic centre known as *zona a traffico limitata* (ZTL). These areas, which have closed-circuit cameras, are closed to regular traffic from Monday to Friday from 7.30 to 10.30am.

CYCLING

A GOOD WAY TO SEE the city and the surrounding areas is by bicycle. Bikes can be hired in the city parks (Parco del Valentino, Viale Ceppi, ATM parking area; Parco della Pellerina, Corso Appio Claudio 106; Parco Ruffini, Viale Bistolfi 20/a; Parco Colletta and Via Carcano 26). Torino Card

Cycling along the Po, with Superga in the background

holders are entitled to a 50 per cent discount. A cycle path from the centre leads to the lodge at Stupinigi, while the paths along the Po pass through lovely green areas of the city. Turin is one Italian

city where 65 km (40 miles) of cycle paths and 1,800 cycle racks mean that bicycles are most commonly used. It is estimated that six per cent of the city's inhabitants use a bicycle to get around.

THE NEW METROPOLITANA

Logo of Turin's new *metropolitana*

Line 1 of Turin's underground railway (*metropolitana*) is under construction. It will connect the Lingotto area with the town of Collegno and pass through the Molinette hospital area, Via Nizza, Corso Marconi, Corso Vittorio Emanuele II and the railway stations of Porta Nuova and Porta Susa. In the meantime, anyone interested in new technology can go on a guided tour of the construction sites and view the latest techniques being used for the excavations. The *metropolitana* will use a system called VAL (*veicolo automatico leggero*) which guarantees all-round safety. Each train can carry 440 passengers and will have a maximum speed of 80 kph (50 mph). The journey from Lingotto to Porta Nuova will take eight minutes, taking a further 16 minutes to reach Collegno.

□ **Deposito**

Fermi

Paradiso **Marche** **Massaua** **Pozzo Strada** **Monte Grappa** **Rivoli** **Racconigi** **Bernini** **Principi d'Acaja**

XVIII Dicembre
Porta Susa
Vinzaglio
Re Umberto
Porta Nuova
Marconi
Nizza
Dante
Carducci-Molinette
Spezia
Lingotto

KEY

▮▮ Line 1 Collegno-Porta Nuova (from 2006)

▮▮ Line 1 Porta Nuova–Lingotto (under construction)

▮▮ Extension, towards Rivoli (project)

▮▮ Extension, towards Piazza Bengasi (project)

One of the new Turin *metropolitana* trains

TURIN STREET FINDER

THE MAP REFERENCES shown in this guide, both in the sightseeing sections and in *Travellers' Needs*, refer to the eight maps in this *Street Finder (pp220–27)*. The grid below shows which parts of Turin are covered by maps in this section. The names of the streets can be found in the index which follows *(pp217–19)*. The maps also show other public buildings, including post offices, police stations, hospitals, railway stations, sports fields, public parks and all the main places of worship in the city. Major sights are shown in pink.

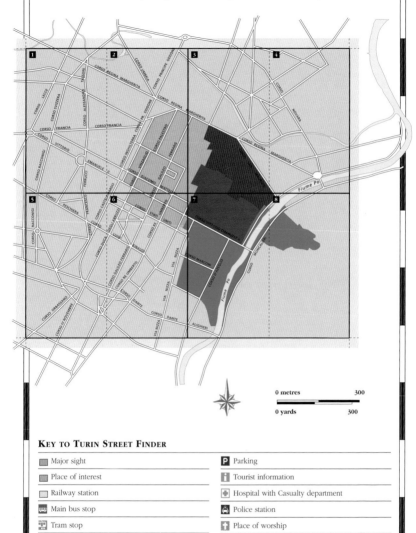

| 0 metres | 300 |
| 0 yards | 300 |

KEY TO TURIN STREET FINDER

▣ Major sight		🅿 Parking	
▣ Place of interest		ℹ Tourist information	
▢ Railway station		✚ Hospital with Casualty department	
🚌 Main bus stop		▣ Police station	
🚋 Tram stop		✝ Place of worship	

Street Finder Index

A

Accademia Albertina (Galleria dell')	3 B5
Accademia Albertina (Via)	7 B1
Accademia delle Scienze	3 A5
Accademia delle Scienze (Via)	3 A5
A.C.I. (Automobile Club)	7 B1
Adriatico (Corso)	5 B4
Adua (Piazzale)	8 E3
A.E.M. (Electricity Company)	2 F4
Aglié (Via)	3 C1
Agostino da Montefeltro (Via)	6 E4
Agrigento (Lungo Dora)	3 A1
Airasca (Via)	5 B3
Ala (Via dell')	2 F5
Albarello (Piazza)	1 B4
Alberto del Belgio (Ponte)	2 F1
Alessandria (Via)	3 B1
Alfiano (Via)	5 B4
Alfieri (Teatro)	2 F5
Alfieri Vittorio (Via)	3 A5
Alimonda (Via)	3 B1
Allioni (Via)	2 E3
Almese (Via)	1 B3
Alpi (Via delle)	2 D3
Alpignano (Via)	1 B3
Amalfi (Via)	4 D2
Amedeo di Savoia (Ospedale)	1 C1
Amendola (Via)	7 A1
Amministrazione Provinciale	3 B5
Ancona (Via)	3 B3
Andorno (Via)	4 F4
Andreis (Via)	3 A2
Antinori (Via)	6 D3
Antonelli (Lungo Po)	4 F5
Aosta (Via)	3 B1
Aporti Ferrante (Via)	8 E1
Appio Claudio (Corso)	1 A1
Aquila (Via)	2 D1
Arcivescovado (Via)	2 F5
Arcivescovado (Via)	6 D5
Ardigò (Via)	2 D1
Arezzo (Via)	6 E4
Argentero (Via)	6 E4
Argonne (Via)	7 C3
Arimondi (Corso)	6 D2
Ariosto (Via)	3 A3
Arona (Via)	1 A2
Arquata (Via)	6 D4
Arsenale (Via)	3 A5
Arte Moderna (Galleria d')	6 E1
Artiglieri di Montagna (Giardino)	1 C5
Artisti (Via degli)	3 C5
Ascoli (Via)	2 D1
Asmara (Piazza)	8 F1
Assaretti (Via)	2 F4
Assietta (Via)	6 F1
Asti (Via)	8 E1
Auditorium	3 C4
Aurora	3 B1
Avellino (Via)	2 D1
Avezzana (Via)	1 C5
Avigliana (Via)	1 C4
Avogadro (Istituto)	3 C4
Avogadro Amedeo (Via)	2 E4
Azzi (Via)	1 A5

B

Bagetti (Via)	2 D3
Bagnasco (Via)	5 B3
Balbo Cesare (Via)	4 D4
Balme (Via)	1 A2
Banca d'Italia	3 A5
Bandiera Fratelli (Via)	5 C1
Barbaro (Via)	1 C3
Barbaroux (Via)	3 A4
Barcellona (Piazzale)	2 D2
Bardassano (Via)	8 F1
Bardonecchia (Via)	1 A4
Baretti (Via)	7 A2
Barge (Via)	1 B5
Bari (Via)	2 E2
Barletta (Via)	5 B4
Barriera Ponte Isabella	7 B5
Barriera Val Salice	8 E2
Barriera Villa della Regina	8 E2
Barriti (Via)	6 D5
Bartolini (Via)	3 B3
Basilica (Via della)	3 A4
Battisti Cesare (Via)	3 A5
Bava (Via)	4 D5
Bazzi (Via)	3 B3
Beaumont (Via)	2 D3

Beccaria (Corso)	2 E3
Beinasco (Via)	3 A1
Belfiore (Via)	6 F4
Belgio (Corso)	4 E4
Belgio (Largo)	4 D4
Belle Arti (Promotrice di)	7 B4
Bellezia (Via)	3 A3
Bellini (Via)	6 E1
Belli Pietrino (Via)	1 A1
Bellotti Bon (Via)	1 C1
Belluno (Via)	1 C1
Benaco (Via)	4 D1
Bene Vagienna (Via)	5 A5
Benevento (Via)	4 F4
Bergamo (Via)	3 C2
Bernini Lorenzo (Piazza)	1 C3
Bersezio (Via)	3 C1
Berta (Via)	5 B2
Berthollet (Via)	7 A2
Bertini (Via)	2 E4
Bertola (Via)	2 E4
Bertolotti (Via)	2 F5
Bertrandi (Via)	2 F4
Bezzecca (Via)	8 D2
Biamonti (Via)	8 D2
Biancamano (Via)	2 F5
Bianzè (Via)	1 B3
Bicocca (Via)	7 C3
Bidone (Via)	6 F3
Biella (Via)	2 F1
Bioglio (Via)	3 C1
Birago di Vische (Ospedale)	2 D1
Bixio Nino (Via)	1 C5
Bligny (Via)	2 F3
Bobbio (Via)	5 B2
Bodoni (Piazza)	7 A1
Bogetto (Via)	2 D2
Boggio Pier Carlo (Via)	1 C5
Bogino (Via)	3 B5
Bognanco (Via)	3 A1
Boiardo Matteo Maria (Viale)	7 A5
Bologna (Largo)	4 E1
Bologna (Ponte)	3 B2
Bologna (Via)	3 B1
Bolzano (Corso)	2 D4
Bona Bartolomeo (Via)	6 E5
Bonafous (Via)	7 C1
Bonelli (Via)	3 A3
Bonzanigo (Via)	2 E2
Borgo Dora (Piazza)	3 A2
Borgo Po	8 E1
Borg Pisani (Via)	5 B2
Borriana (Via)	4 E1
Borromini (Piazza)	4 F5
Borsa Valori	7 B1
Bossi (Via)	1 C2
Bossolasco (Via)	5 B1
Botero (Via)	2 F4
Botta (Via)	2 F3
Bottego (Via)	5 C3
Bottesini (Piazza)	4 D1
Boucheron (Via)	2 E3
Bove (Via)	6 D2
Boves (Via)	5 A1
Bra (Via)	3 B1
Braccini Paolo (Via)	5 A2
Bramante (Corso)	6 D5
Brescia (Corso)	3 B2
Brescia (Largo)	3 C2
Bricca (Via)	8 E1
Bricherasio (Via)	6 D1
Brindisi (Via)	2 F2
Brione (Via)	1 A3
Brocca (Via della)	7 C3
Brofferio (Via)	2 F5
Brugnone (Via)	6 E4
Bruino (Via)	1 C3
Brunetta (Via)	1 A4
Buniva (Via)	4 D4
Buonarroti Michelangelo (Via)	6 F4
Buon Pastore (Istituto del)	2 D4
Buozzi (Via)	7 A1
Buronzo (Via)	1 B2
Burzio (Via)	2 E3
Buscalioni (Via)	4 D3
Bussoleno (Via)	1 A4
Buttigliera (Via)	8 F1

C

Caboto Sebastiano (Via)	5 C3
Cadorna (Lungo Po)	8 D1
Cadorna (Via)	5 A5
Cagliari (Via)	3 C3
Cagni (Via)	7 B3
C.A.I. (Club Alpino Italiano)	3 A4
Cairoli (Corso)	7 C2

Calandra Fratelli (Via)	7 B1
Calvo (Via)	6 F4
Camandona (Via)	1 A3
Camerana (Via)	6 F1
Camino (Via)	3 B1
Camogli (Via)	6 D5
Campana (Via)	7 A5
Campidoglio	1 B2
Campurzano (Via)	1 A3
Candelo (Via)	4 D2
Canova Antonio (Via)	6 E5
Cantello (Strada Comunale del)	8 F2
Cantore (Via)	6 D1
Capellina (Via)	2 D2
Cappel Verde (Via)	3 A4
Cappuccini (Monte dei)	8 D2
Caprera (Via)	5 A4
Caprie (Via)	1 B4
Capua (Via)	2 D1
Carceri Giudiziarie	1 C5
Cardinal Cagliero (Via)	3 A3
Cardinal Maurizio (Via)	8 E1
Carena (Via)	2 E2
Caresana (Via)	4 E1
Carabinieri HQ	2 E4
Carignano (Palazzo)	3 B5
Carignano (Piazza)	3 B5
Carignano (Teatro)	3 A5
Carisio (Via)	1 A2
Carle Fratelli (Via)	5 C3
Carlo Alberto (Piazza)	3 B5
Carlo Alberto (Via)	3 B5
Carlo Emanuele I (Ponte)	4 E3
Carlo Emanuele II (Piazza)	7 B1
Carmagnola (Via)	3 B1
Carmine (Via del)	2 E3
Carrara Mario (Parco)	1 A1
Carrù (Via)	5 A1
Casalborgone (Via)	4 F5
Casale (Corso)	8 D1
Casalis (Via)	2 C2
Caselle (Via)	2 F2
Caserta (Via)	2 E2
Cassini (Largo)	6 D2
Cassini (Via)	5 C2
Castagnevizza (Via)	5 A5
Casteggio (Via)	7 C2
Castelfidardo (Corso)	5 C1
Castellamonte (Via)	2 E3
Castello (Piazza)	3 B4
Catania (Via)	3 C3
Catone (Viale)	8 D4
Cavalieri di Vittorio Veneto (Parco)	5 B5
Cavallermaggiore (Via)	1 B4
Cavalli Giovanni (Via)	1 C4
Cavallo (Heliport)	5 B5
Cavezzale (Via)	4 E5
Cavour (Via)	7 A1
C.C.I.A.A. (Chamber of Commerce)	7 B1
Cecchi Antonio (Via)	3 A1
Cenischia (Via)	1 A5
Cenisia	1 A4
Centre	3 B4
Ceppi (Viale)	7 A4
Cernaia (Via)	2 E4
Cervignasco (Via)	5 B1
Cesana (Via)	1 B4
Cesare Augusto (Piazza)	3 A3
Ceva (Via)	2 D1
Chiabrera (Via)	7 A5
Chianocco (Via)	1 A4
Chimica (Istituto di)	7 A4
Chiomonte (Via)	5 A1
Chisone (Via)	6 E3
Chiuse (Via le)	1 C2
Chivasso (Via)	3 B2
Cialdini Enrico (Via)	1 B3
Cibrario (Largo)	2 D3
Cibrario (Via)	1 C2
Cigliano (Via)	4 F4
Cigna (Largo)	3 A1
Cigna (Via)	3 A1
Cignaroli (Via)	3 B3
Cimarosa (Via)	4 E1
Cimitero Generale	4 E2
Cinema (Museo del)	3 A4
Cinzano (Via)	4 F5
Ciriè (Corso)	2 F1
Ciriè (Via)	2 B1
Ciriè-Lanzo (Stazione)	3 A2
Cirio (Via)	3 A2
Cittadella	2 F4
Cittadella (Giardino)	2 F4
Cittadella (Via)	2 F4
Clemente (Via)	1 C3
Clementi (Via)	3 C1
C.L.N. (Piazza)	3 A5

Coazze (Via)	1 B4
Cocchi (Via)	8 F1
Colleasca (Via)	1 B2
Collegno Giacinto (Via)	1 C3
Colletta Pietro (Lungo Dora)	4 E3
Colli (Via)	6 D1
Colombo Cristoforo (Giardino)	6 D3
Colombo Cristoforo (Via)	5 C4
Como (Via)	3 C1
Condove (Via)	5 C4
Confienza (Via)	2 F5
C.O.N.I. (Olympic Committee)	6 F2
Consolata (Piazza)	3 A3
Consolata (Via della)	2 F4
Conte Rosso (Via)	2 F5
Conte Verde (Via)	3 A4
Contini Innocenzo (Viale)	8 F2
Cordero di Pamparato (Via)	1 B3
Corpus Domini (Chiesa)	3 A4
Correggio (Via)	7 A5
Cortanze (Via)	3 C5
Corte d'Appello (Via)	3 A4
Cosmo (Via)	8 D1
Cosseria (Via)	7 C2
Cossila (Via)	4 E4
Costa (Via)	7 B1
Costantino il Grande (Piazza)	5 C4
Costigliole (Via)	5 A1
Cottolengo	3 A2
Cottolengo (Via)	3 A2
Cremona (Via)	3 B1
Crimea	7 B3
Crimea (Piazza)	7 C3
Crimea (Via)	7 C3
Crissolo (Via)	5 A1
Crivelli Balsamo (Viale)	7 B4
Crocetta (la)	5 C3
Crocetta (Via)	6 D2
Cumiana (Via)	5 A1
Cuneo (Via)	3 A1
Curreno Giacomo (Via)	7 C3
Curtatone (Via)	3 A1

D

Damiano (Via)	2 F5
Dante Alighieri (Corso)	6 D4
D'Azeglio Massimo (Corso)	7 A2
De Cristoforis (Via)	5 C5
De Gasperi Alcide (Corso)	5 C2
Del Carretto Luisa (Via)	8 E1
Del Sarto (Via)	1 C2
De Nicola Enrico (Corso)	5 C4
Denina (Via)	5 C4
Denza (Via)	3 C1
Des Ambrois (Via)	3 B5
De Sonnaz (Via)	2 E5
Diaz (Lungo Po)	7 C1
Diciotto Dicembre (Piazza)	2 E4
Digione (Via)	1 B3
Di Nanni (Via)	1 B5
Di Robilant Carlo (Piazza)	5 A2
Doberdo (Via)	3 C1
Dogliani (Via)	3 A1
Domodossola (Via)	1 A3
Don Albera Paolo (Piazza)	3 B3
Don Minzoni (Via)	2 F5
Don Prinotti (Via)	5 B2
Donatello (Piazza)	6 F3
Donati (Via)	2 E5
Donizetti (Via)	6 F4
Dorè (Via)	2 D4
Doria Andrea (Via)	7 A1
Dronero (Via)	2 E1
Drovetti (Via)	2 D4
Duca d'Aosta (Corso)	6 D2
Duca d'Aosta (Piazzale)	6 D1
Duca degli Abruzzi (Corso)	5 C1
Duca degli Abruzzi (Ponte)	5 A2
Duchessa Jolanda (Via)	1 C3
Durandi (Via)	1 C2

E

Educatorio della Provvidenza	6 D2
Egeo (Via)	6 E4
Egidi (Via)	3 A3
Einaudi Luigi (Corso)	5 C2
Elba (Via)	5 B4
Emanuel (Via)	1 A5
Emanuele Filiberto (Piazza)	3 A3
Emanuele Filiberto (Ponte)	4 F4
Emilia (Corso)	3 B2
E.N.E.L. (Electricity Co.)	1 B1
E.N.E.L. (Electricity Co.)	2 F4
E.N.E.L. (Electricity Co.)	3 B2
Envie (Via)	5 A1

F

Fabrizi Nicola (Largo) 1 A2
Fabrizi Nicola (Via) 1 A2
Fabro (Via) 2 F4
Facoltà di Medicina e
  Chirurgia 7 A4
Facoltà di Veterinaria 6 F4
Fagnano (Via) 2 D1
Fanti (Via) 6 E1
Farini (Corso) 4 D4
Febo (Via) 7 B4
Felice Carlo (Piazza) 7 A1
Ferrari (Via) 4 D1
Ferrari Gaudenzio (Via) 3 C5
Ferraris Galileo (Corso) 5 C1
Ferrere (Via) 1 A4
Ferrero (Via) 1 C5
Ferrucci Francesco (Corso) 1C4
Fiano (Via) 1 B2
Fieramosca (Via) 5 A5
Figlie dei Militari (Via) 8 E1
Filangieri (Via) 6 E3
Finance Office 2 E4
Fiochetto (Via) 3 B3
Fiorano (Via) 4 F5
Fire Brigade HQ 3 B3
Firenze (Lungo Dora) 3 B3
Fiume (Corso) 7 C3
Foà (Via) 6 F5
Foggia (Via) 3 C3
Fontanesi (Piazza) 4 F4
Fontanesi (Via) 4 E4
Foresto (Via) 1 A4
Forlanini (Via) 6 D5
Fortino (Strada del) 2 F1
Fortunato (Via) 2 D4
Foscolo Ugo (Via) 6 F5
Fossano (Via) 2 D1
Francia (Corso) 1 A3
Francia (Largo) 1 A3
Frassineto (Via) 1 A5
Frejus (Via) 1 A4
Frescobaldi (Via) 3 C1
Frinco (Via) 5 B4
Frossasco (Via) 1 A5
Frugarolo (Via) 6 D5

G

Gabetti Giuseppe (Corso) 8 F1
Gaeta (Via) 7 C3
Galleria d'Arte Moderna 6 E1
Galleria dell'Accademia
  Albertina 3 B5
Galleria Nazionale 7 A1
Galleria Subalpina 3 B5
Galliano Giuseppe (Via) 6 D2
Galliari Bernardino (Via) 7 A2
Galluppi (Via) 5 C5
Galvagno Filippo (Piazza) 5 A2
Galvani (Via) 1 C2
Gamalero (Via) 5 A4
Gambasca (Via) 5 B1
Garibaldi Giuseppe (Via) 2 F3
Garizio (Via) 1 A4
Gastaldi (Via) 6 E1
Gatti (Via) 8 D3
Gattinara (Via) 4 E4
Genè (Via) 3 B3
Genovesi (Via) 6 E3
Gerdil (Via) 2 F2
Germanasca (Via) 1 B5
Gessi (Via) 5 B4
Gesù Adolescente (Chiesa) 1 A5
Gesù Bambino (Chiesa di) 5 A4
Gesù Nazareno (Chiesa) 2 D4
Giacosa Giuseppe (Via) 7 A3
Giannone (Via) 2 F5
Giardino Gaetano (Via) 7 C2
Giardino Reale 3 B4
Giardino Zoologico 8 E1
Giaveno (Via) 2 F1
Gioannetti (Via) 8 D2
Gioberti Vincenzo (Via) 6 E1
Gioia Melchiorre (Via) 6 F1
Giolitti (Via) 7 B1
Giotto (Via) 6 F5
Giulia di Barolo (Via) 3 C5
Giulio Carlo (Via) 2 F3
Giulio Cesare (Corso) 3 A1
Giuria Pietro (Via) 6 D4
Giusti (Via) 2 D5
Giustizia (Palazzo di) 3 A4
Gobetti (Via) 7 A1
Goito (Via) 7 A2
Goldoni (Via) 3 C4
Governolo (Via) 6 D2
Govone Generale (Corso) 6 D1
Gozzano Guido (Piazza) 8 F1
Gozzi (Via) 2 D5
Gradenico (Ospedale) 4 E5

Gradisca (Via) 5 A4
Graf Arturo (Piazza) 6 F5
Graglia (Via) 5 A4
Gramsci (Via) 7 A1
Grandis (Via) 2 E4
Gran Madre di Dio (Chiesa) 8 D1
Gran Madre di Dio
  (Piazza della) 8 D1
Grassi (Via) 2 D4
Grattoni (Via) 2 D4
Gropello (Via) 2 D3
Groscavallo (Via) 1 B4
Grossi Tommaso (Via) 6 E5
Guarini (Via) 7 A1
Guastalla (Via) 4 D4
Guicciardini (Via) 2 E4

H

Hermada (Piazza) 8 F1

I

Immacolata Concezione
  (Istituto) 6 F3
Industria (Via dell') 2 E2
Ingegneria
  (Istituto Superiore d') 7 B3
Inghilterra (Corso) 2 D4
I.N.P.S. (Social Insurance) 3 A5
Israelita (Tempio) 7 A2
Istituto Avogadro 3 C4
Istituto del Buon Pastore 2 E2
Istituto di Chimica 7 A4
Istituto Immacolata
  Concezione 6 F3
Istituto Missioni della
  Consolata 1 B4
Istituto Protette San
  Giuseppe 8 E1
Istituto Salesiano 2 F2
Istituto Superiore
  d'Ingegneria 7 B3
Istituto Tecnico Sommeiler 6 D1

J

Juvarra (Via) 2 E4

L

Lagrange (Piazza) 7 A1
Lagrange (Via) 7 A1
Lamarmora Alfonso (Via) 6 D1
Lambruschini (Via) 1 C2
Lancia (Gruppo Sportivo) 5 A2
Lancia Vincenzo (Via) 5 A2
Lanfranchi (Via) 8 D2
Lanino (Via) 3 A3
Lanza Giovanni (Corso) 7 C2
La Salle (Via) 3 B2
Lascaris (Via) 2 F5
Lecce (Corso) 1 A1
Legnano (Via) 6 D1
Leoncavallo (Via) 4 D1
Leopardi Giacomo (Parco) 7 B5
Lepanto (Corso) 5 C4
Lesegno (Via) 5 A4
Lessona Michele (Via) 1 A2
Levanna (Via) 1 B2
Limone (Via) 5 A2
Lione (Corso) 5 B3
Livorno (Via) 2 E1
Locana (Via) 1 B2
Lodi (Via) 3 B1
Lodovica (Via) 8 D1
Lombriasco (Via) 1 B5
Lombroso Cesare (Via) 7 A3
Loria (Via) 6 E4
Lugaro (Via) 6 E4
Luserna di Rorà (Via) 1 A5
Lussimpiccolo (Via) 5 A3

M

Macerata (Via) 2 E1
Machiavelli (Lungo Po) 4 D5
Madama (Palazzo) 3 B4
Madama Cristina (Piazza) 7 A2
Madama Cristina (Via) 7 A2
Maddalene (Via) 4 E1
Magellano (Via) 6 D4
Magenta (Via) 6 D1
Magistrates' Court 3 A4
Malta (Via) 5 A2
Mamiani (Corso) 4 F1
Manara (Via) 7 C3
Mancini (Via) 8 D2
Manin (Via) 4 E4
Mantova (Via) 4 D3
Manzoni (Via) 2 E3
Marconi Guglielmo (Corso) 7 A3

Marenco Carlo (Via) 7 A5
Maria Adelaide (Ospedale) 3 C3
Maria Ausiliatrice (Piazza) 2 F2
Maria Ausiliatrice (Via) 2 F2
Maria Teresa (Piazza) 7 C1
Maria Vittoria (Ospedale) 1 C2
Maria Vittoria (Via) 7 B1
Marmolada (Piazza) 5 A3
Marsala (Via) 7 B4
Martinetto (Via) 1 C1
Martiniana (Via) 5 A1
Martini Luigi (Giardino) 2 D4
Martiri della Libertà (Via) 8 D1
Massena (Via) 6 F1
Matteotti Giacomo (Corso) 2 D5
Mattioli (Viale) 7 B3
Mauriziano (Ospedale) 6 D4
Mazzini Giuseppe (Via) 7 A1
Medaglie d'Oro (Viale) 7 A4
Medail (Via) 1 C1
Medici Giacomo (Via) 1 A2
Medicina e Chirurgia
  (Facoltà di) 7 A4
Medievale (Borgo) 7 A4
Mediterraneo (Corso) 5 B2
Menotti (Corso) 5 C1
Mentana (Largo) 7 C3
Mentana (Via) 7 C3
Mercanti (Via) 3 A4
Mercantini (Via) 2 F5
Messina (Via) 3 C3
Meucci (Via) 2 F5
Mezzenile (Via) 1 B4
Micca Pietro (Via) 3 A5
Michelotti (Parco) 4 A5
Migliara (Via) 1 C3
Miglietti (Via) 2 E2
Milano (Via) 3 A4
Milazzo (Via) 7 C3
Militare (Ospedale) 5 B5
Mille (Via dei) 7 B1
Millio Francesco (Via) 5 A2
Millo (Viale) 7 A5
Missioni della Consolata
  (Istituto) 1 B4
Modane (Via) 5 B3
Modena (Via) 3 C2
Mole Antonelliana 3 C5
Mombarcaro (Via) 5 A5
Mombasiglio (Via) 5 A4
Moncalieri (Corso) 7 B1
Moncalvo (Via) 8 D1
Moncenisio (Piazza) 1 B2
Mondovì (Via) 3 A1
Monfalcone (Via) 5 A4
Monferrato (Via) 8 D1
Monforte (Via) 1 B4
Monginevro (Via) 5 A1
Mongrando (Via) 4 E4
Montagna (Museo della) 8 D2
Montalto (Via) 4 E4
Montano (Via) 1 B3
Monte Albergian (Via) 1 A4
Montebello (Largo) 3 C4
Montebello (Via) 3 C4
Montecuccoli (Via) 2 E5
Monte di Pietà (Via) 3 A4
Montefeltro Agostino da
  (Via) 6 E4
Montemagno (Via) 8 F1
Monte Rosa (Via) 3 C1
Montevecchio (Via) 6 D1
Montezemolo (Via) 5 A5
Montiglio (Via) 8 F1
Monti Vincenzo (Via) 7 A5
Monumento a Vittorio
  Emanuele II 6 E1
Monza (Via) 3 C2
Moretta (Via) 1 A5
Morgari Oddino (Via) 7 A3
Morghen (Via) 1 C2
Moris Giuseppe (Via) 2 F2
Morosini (Via) 6 D1
Mosca (Ponte) 3 B2
Mottalciata (Via) 4 D2
Municipio 3 A4
Muratori (Via) 6 E5
Murazzano (Via) 5 A3
Muriaglio (Via) 5 A1
Museo del Cinema 3 A4
Museo della Montagna 8 D2
Musinè (Via) 1 B2

N

Napione (Via) 4 D5
Napoli (Lungo Dora) 3 A1
Nazionale (Galleria) 7 A1
Nazzaro (Via) 1 B3
Netro (Via) 1 B2
Nievo (Via) 4 F3
Nizza (Piazza) 6 F4

Nizza (Via) 6 F2
Nobile (Strada del) 8 F4
Noè Carlo (Via) 3 B3
Nostra Signora del Santissimo
  Sacramento (Chiesa) 4 F5
Nostra Signora del Suffragio
  (Chiesa) 8 E1
Nota (Via) 2 E3
Novalesa (Via) 1 A4
Novara (Corso) 3 B1
Novi (Via) 3 C1

O

Oftalmico (Ospedale) 2 E4
Omegna (Via) 1 A2
Orbassano (Corso) 5 A4
Orbassano (Largo) 5 C4
Orfane (Via delle) 3 A3
Ormea (Via) 7 A2
Ornato (Via) 8 E1
Ornavasso (Via) 1 A2
Oropa (Via) 4 F4
Orta (Via) 1 A2
Orto Botanico 7 B3
Osasco (Via) 5 B1
Ospedale Amedeo di
  Savoia 1 C1
Ospedale Birago di Vische 1 D1
Ospedale Gradenico 4 E5
Ospedale Maria Adelaide 3 C3
Ospedale Maria Vittoria 1 C2
Ospedale Mauriziano 6 D4
Ospedale Militare 5 B5
Ospedale Oftalmico 2 E4
Ospedale San Giovanni 7 B1
Ospedale San Vito 7 B4
Ospedale San Vito (Strada) 7 B4
Ospedale Valdese 7 A2
Ovidio (Via d') 6 D2

P

Pacini Giovanni (Via) 4 D1
Pacinotti (Via) 2 D2
Paciotto (Via) 2 E4
Padova (Via) 3 C2
Paesana (Via) 5 B1
Paganini (Via) 4 E1
Pagano (Via) 5 A1
Pagano Mario (Via) 6 E4
Palatina (Porta) 3 A3
Palazzo Carignano 3 B5
Palazzo di Città (piazza) 3 A4
Palazzo di Città (Via) 3 A4
Palazzo di Giustizia 3 A4
Palazzo Madama 3 B4
Palazzo Reale 3 B4
Palazzo Torino Esposizioni 7 A4
Paleocapa (Piazza) 6 F1
Palermo (Corso) 3 C1
Palermo (Largo) 3 C1
Palestro (Corso) 2 E4
Palladio (Via) 8 E2
Pallavicino (Via) 4 D4
Palmieri (Via) 2 D3
Palmieri (Via) 1 C4
Paolini (Via) 1 B4
Papacino (Via) 2 E5
Paravia (Via) 1 C1
Parella 1 A2
Parini (Via) 6 F1
Parma (Via) 3 B2
Partigiani (Viale) 3 B4
Paruzzaro (Via) 3 C1
Pascoli (Corso) 5 C4
Passalacqua (Via) 2 E3
Pastrengo (Via) 6 E2
Pavia (Via) 3 C2
Peano (Via) 5 C2
Pedrotti (Via) 4 C2
Pellice (Via) 1 A5
Pellico Silvio (Via) 7 A2
Perosa (Via) 1 A5
Perotti Giuseppe (Piazza) 1 B2
Perrero (Via) 1 A5
Perrone (Via) 2 F4
Perugia (Via) 3 C2
Pesaro (Via) 2 F1
Pescatore Matteo (Via) 7 C1
Peschiera (Corso) 5 A1
Petitti Ilarione (Via) 6 E5
Petrarca Francesco (Via) 6 F4
Petrocchi (Via) 2 D5
Peyron Amedeo (Piazza) 2 D3
Peyron Amedeo (Via) 1 C2
Pezzana (Via) 4 D1
Pianfei (Via) 2 D1
Piave (Via) 2 F3
Piazzi Giuseppe (Via) 5 C3
Picco Alberto (Corso) 8 E1
Piemonte (Lungo Po) 7 C2

Piffetti (Via) 1 C3
Pigafetta Francesco (Via) 5 C2
Pilo Rosalino (Via) 1 A3
Pinasca (Via) 1 C4
Pindemonte (Via) 4 F1
Pinelli (Via) 1 C2
Pinerolo (Via) 3 B1
Pingone (Via) 2 E3
Piossasco (Via) 3 A1
Pisa (Via) 3 B2
Pisano Andrea (Via) 3 B3
Pistoia (Via) 2 E1
Plana (Via) 7 C1
Po (Via) 3 B5
Police Headquarters 2 E5
Politecnico 6 D1
Poliziano (Via) 4 F3
Pollenzo (Via) 5 A1
Pollone (Via) 4 D2
Polo Marco (Via) 5 C2
Polonghera (Via) 1 B5
Pomaro (Via) 5 B4
Pomba (Via) 7 B1
Pomponazzi (Via) 6 D5
Ponchielli (Via) 4 D1
Ponza (Via) 2 F5
Porporati (Via) 3 B3
Porro (Via) 4 E5
Porta Nuova (Stazione) 6 F2
Porta Palatina (Via) 3 A3
Porta Susa (Stazione) 2 E4
Poste e Telegrafi 3 A5
Pragelato (Via) 1 A5
Prarostino (Via) 1 B3
Prati (Via) 1 A5
Prefecture 3 B4
Prestinari (Via) 2 F5
Pria (Via) 1 C1
Primo Maggio (Viale) 3 B4
Principe Amedeo (Via) 3 A5
Principe Eugenio (Corso) 2 E1
Principe Oddone (Corso) 2 E1
Principessa Clotilde (Ponte) 3 A2
Principessa Clotilde (Via) 2 D2
Principessa Felicita di
  Savoia (Via) 8 D2
Principessa Isabella
  (Ponte) 7 A5
Principe Tommaso (Via) 7 A2
Principi (Via) 2 D3
Priocca (Via) 3 B3
Promis (Via) 2 F5
Promotrice di Belle Arti 7 B3
Protette San Giuseppe
  (Istituto) 8 E1
Provvidenza
  (Educatorio della) 6 D2

Q

Quartieri (Via dei) 2 F3
Quattro Marzo (Via) 3 A4
Quattro Novembre (Corso) 5 B5
Quittengo (Via) 4 D1

R

Racagni (Via) 4 E3
Racconigi (Corso) 5 A1
Racconigi (Largo) 5 A2
Raffaello (Corso) 6 F4
R.A.I. (Television Company) 4 D4
R.A.I. (Television Company) 3 C5
Ramello Candido (Ponte) 1 C1
Rapallo (Via) 6 D5
Rattazzi (Via) 7 A1
Ravenna (Via) 2 F2
Ravina (Via) 4 F3
Reale (Giardino) 3 B4
Reale (Palazzo) 3 B4
Reale (Piazzetta) 3 B4
Reale Accademia Militare 3 A5
Reano (Via) 5 A1
Regaldi (Via) 4 D1
Reggio (Via) 3 C3
Regina (Villa della) 8 B3
Regina Margherita (Corso) 3 B2
Regina Margherita (Piazzale) 4 E5
Regina Margherita (Ponte) 4 E5
Regio (Teatro) 3 B4
Regione Piemonte 3 A4
Regio Parco (Corso) 3 C1
Regio Parco (Largo) 3 C3
Regio Parco (Ponte) 3 C3
Renier Rodolfo (Via) 5 A2
Repubblica (Piazza della) 3 A3
Re Umberto (Corso) 6 D1
Re Umberto (Largo) 6 D3
Revello (Via) 1 A4
Riberi (Via) 3 C5
Ribet (Via) 6 F3
Ricaldone (Via) 5 A4

Ricasoli (Via) 4 E4
Righino
  (Strada Consortile di) 8 D3
Rio de Janeiro (Via) 5 B2
Risorgimento (Piazza) 1 B2
Ristori (Via) 4 E1
Rivalta (Via) 5 B3
Rivara (Via) 1 B2
Rivarolo (Via) 3 B2
Rivoli (Piazza) 1 A3
Roasio (Via) 1 A2
Robassomero (Via) 3 A2
Rocca (Via della) 7 B1
Roccabruna (Via) 6 D5
Rocciamelone (Via) 1 B2
Rodi (Via) 2 F4
Rolando (Via) 7 B1
Roma (Via) 3 A5
Romagnosi (Via) 6 E3
Romani (Via) 8 D1
Rosine (Via delle) 7 C1
Rosmini Antonio (Via) 6 E4
Rossana (Via) 5 A1
Rosselli (Corso) 5 A3
Rossini (Ponte) 3 C4
Rossini (Via) 3 B4
Rosta (Via) 1 B3
Rovigo (Via) 2 F1
Ruffini (Via) 2 E4

S

Sabotino (Piazza) 5 A1
Saccarelli (Via) 2 D2
Sacchi (Via) 6 F1
Sacro Cuore (Chiesa del) 7 C3
Sacro Cuore di Maria
  (Chiesa) 6 F3
Saffi (Via) 1 B3
Sagliano Micca (Via) 2 E5
Salerno (Via) 2 F1
Salesiano (Istituto) 2 F2
Saluggia (Via) 1 B2
Saluzzo (Largo) 7 A2
Saluzzo (Via) 6 F3
San Bernardino (Chiesa) 5 A2
San Bernardino (Via) 5 A1
San Carlo (Piazza) 3 A5
San Dalmazzo (Via) 2 F4
San Domenico (Via) 2 E3
San Donato (Via) 2 D3
San Donato (Via) 1 C2
San Fermo (Via) 7 C3
San Francesco da Paola
  (Via) 7 A1
San Francesco d'Assisi
  (Via) 3 A4
San Giorgio (Via) 6 D5
San Giovanni (Chiesa) 3 B4
San Giovanni (Ospedale) 7 B1
San Giovanni (Piazza) 3 A4
San Giovanni Bosco (Via) 1 C1
San Giuseppe (Chiesa) 3 A5
San Lorenzo (Chiesa) 3 B4
San Martino (Corso) 2 E3
San Massimo (Chiesa) 7 B1
San Massimo (Via) 7 B1
San Maurizio (Corso) 3 C4
San Paolo (Via) 5 A2
San Paolo (Via) 5 A1
San Pellegrino (Chiesa) 1 A4
San Pietro in Vincoli (Via) 3 A2
San Pio Quinto (Via) 7 A2
San Quintino (Via) 6 E1
San Rocchetto (Via) 1 B2
San Rocco (Chiesa) 3 A4
San Salvario (Via) 7 A4
San Salvario (Chiesa) 6 F3
San Secondo (Piazza) 6 F2
San Secondo (Via) 6 E1
San Tommaso (Via) 3 A4
San Vincenzo (Strada) 8 F5
San Vito (Ospedale) 7 B4
San Vito (Strada Antica di) 7 C5
San Vito a Revigliasco
  (Strada Comunale da) 7 C5
San Vito a Revigliasco
  (Strada Consortile da) 8 F3
Sanctus (Chiesa Il) 1 A3
Sanfront (Via) 1 B5
Sangano (Via) 1 B3
Sant'Agostino (Via) 3 A3
Sant'Anselmo (Via) 7 A2
Sant'Antonio da Padova
  (Via) 2 D5
Sant'Ottavio (Via) 3 C5
Santa Chiara (Chiesa) 3 A3
Santa Chiara (Via) 2 E3
Santa Croce (Chiesa) 7 B1
Santa Croce (Via) 7 B1
Santa Giulia (Piazza) 4 D5
Santa Giulia (Via) 3 C4

Santa Margherita
  (Strada Comunale di) 8 E2
Santa Maria (Via) 2 F4
Santa Maria del Monte
  (Chiesa) 8 D2
Santa Marta (Chiesa) 3 A4
Santa Pelagia (Chiesa) 7 B1
Santa Rita (Chiesa) 5 A5
Santa Rita da Cascia (Piazza) 5 A5
Santa Teresa (Chiesa) 5 C3
Santa Teresa (Via) 3 A5
Santa Zita (Chiesa) 2 D2
Santarosa Santorre (Via) 8 D1
Santi Angeli (Chiesa) 7 A1
Santi Angeli Custodi (Chiesa) 2 E5
Santi Pietro e Paolo (Chiesa) 7 A2
Santissima Annunziata
  (Chiesa) 3 C5
Santissima Trinità (Chiesa) 3 A4
Santissimo Redentore
  (Chiesa) 8 F1
Santo Sudario (Chiesa) 2 F3
Sardegna (Lungo Po) 7 B3
Sassari (Giardino) 2 F2
Sassari (Via) 2 F2
Savigliano (Via) 2 E2
Savio (Via) 2 E5
Savoia (Piazza) 2 F3
Savona (Lungo Dora) 3 B2
Savonarola (Via) 6 E4
Scalenghe (Via) 5 B1
Schina (Via) 2 D3
Schio (Via) 3 A1
Scienze (Accademia delle) 3 A5
Sclopis (Corso) 7 A5
Scuola di Guerra 2 E4
Sebastopoli (Corso) 5 A5
Segre Corrado (Via) 6 D2
Seguranda (Via) 2 E1
Sei Ville (Strada delle) 8 F2
Sella Quintino (Corso) 8 E1
Sempione (Via) 4 F1
Seneca (Via) 8 D4
Settimio Severo (Viale) 7 C4
Sforzesca (Via) 7 C3
Siccardi (Corso) 2 F4
Siena (Lungo Dora) 3 C3
Sineo Riccardo (Via) 4 E5
Sismonda Angelo (Via) 1 A1
Sobrero (Via) 2 D2
Solero (Piazza) 6 D5
Solferino (Piazza) 2 F5
Somis Giovanni (Via) 2 D3
Sommacampagna (Via) 7 C2
Sommeiller (Corso) 6 E3
Sommeiller (Ist. Tecnico) 6 E3
Sondrio (Via) 1 C1
Sordevolo (Via) 4 D2
Spalato (Via) 5 B2
Spallanzani (Via) 6 D4
Spanzotti (Via) 1 A4
Spoleto (Via) 1 B1
Staffarda (Via) 5 A1
Stampatori (Via degli) 2 F4
Stati Uniti (Corso) 6 D1
Statuto (Piazza) 2 E3
Susa (Via) 1 C4
Svizzera (Corso) 1 B1

T

Tadini (Strada Consortile dei) 8 F4
Talucchi (Via) 1 C3
Tarino (Via) 3 C4
Tassoni Alessandro (Corso) 1 C2
Teatro Alfieri 2 F5
Teatro Carignano 3 A5
Teatro Regio 3 B4
Telecom (Phone Company) 2 D4
Telecom (Phone Company) 2 E5
Tempio Israelita 7 A2
Tenivelli (Via) 2 D2
Teramo (Via) 3 C3
Ternengo (Via) 3 C1
Thaon di Revel (Via) 2 E5
Thesauro (Via) 6 F3
Thovez Enrico (Via) 8 D3
Ticineto (Via) 5 A4
Tiepolo (Via) 7 A5
Tirreno (Largo) 5 B4
Tirreno (Via) 5 A3
Tiziano (Via) 6 E5
Tollegno (Via) 4 D1
Tolmino (Via) 5 A2
Tommaseo (Via) 4 D4
Torino Esposizioni
  (Palazzo) 7 A4
Torricelli Evangelista (Via) 5 C3
Tortona Pietro da (Corso) 4 E2
Toselli (Via) 6 D2
Toselli Giovanni (Via) 8 F1
Traffic Police 2 E4

Trana (Via) 1 B4
Tre Galline (Via) 3 A3
Trento (Corso) 6 D2
Treviso (Via) 2 E1
Trieste (Corso) 6 D1
Trinità (Via) 5 B2
Tripoli (Via) 5 A4
Tronco (Via) 8 E2
Turati Filippo (Corso) 6 D3
Turati Filippo (Largo) 6 D4
Turr (Viale) 7 A5

U

Udine (Via) 2 F1
Umberto I (Ponte) 7 C2
Umbria (Corso) 2 E1
Umbria (Piazzale) 2 E1
Undici Febbraio (Corso) 3 B3
Unione Sovietica (Corso) 5 C5
Università 3 B5
Università degli Studi 3 C5
Urbino (Via) 2 F1

V

Vagnone (Via) 2 D2
Valdese (Ospedale) 7 A2
Valdieri (Via) 1 B5
Valdocco (Corso) 2 F3
Valeggio (Via) 6 D2
Valentino (Castello del) 7 B3
Valentino (Parco del) 7 A3
Valerio (Via) 2 F3
Valfrè Sebastiano (Via) 2 E4
Valperga Caluso (Via) 6 F3
Valperga di Masino
  (Giardino) 6 D4
Val Salice 8 D4
Val Salice
  (Strada Comunale di) 8 E4
Vanchiglia 4 D4
Vanchiglia
  (stazione merci) 4 D2
Vanvitelli (Via) 4 D5
Varallo (Via) 4 F4
Varano Alfonso (Via) 4 E2
Varese (Via) 3 C1
Vassalli Eandi (Via) 2 D3
Vedove e Nubili (Convitto) 8 D3
Vela Vincenzo (Via) 6 D1
Venasca (Via) 1 B5
Venti Settembre (Via) 3 B4
Verazzano Giovanni da (Via) 5 C2
Vercelli (Corso) 3 B1
Verdi Giuseppe (Via) 3 B5
Vernazza (Via) 5 A5
Verona (Corso) 3 C2
Verrocchio (Via) 3 B3
Verrua (Via) 8 D1
Verzuolo (Via) 1 A5
Vespucci Amerigo (Via) 5 C2
Veterinaria (Facoltà di) 6 F4
Vicenza (Via) 2 D1
Vico Gian Battista (Via) 6 D3
Vidua (Via) 1 C2
Vigili del Fuoco 3 B3
Vigliardi Paravia (Piazza) 2 D2
Vignale (VVia) 8 F1
Vigne di San Vito
  (Strada Vicinale) 8 D5
Vigone (Via) 1 A5
Villa della Regina (Piazzale) 8 E2
Villa della Regina (Via) 8 D2
Villarbasse (Via) 5 B1
Villarfocchiardo (Via) 1 A3
Vinadio (Via) 1 B5
Vinzaglio (Corso) 2 E4
Viotti (Via) 3 A5
Virgilio (Viale) 7 B2
Virle (Via) 1 B5
Vittone (Via) 8 F1
Vittorio Amedeo II (Via) 2 F4
Vittorio Emanuele I (Ponte) 8 D1
Vittorio Emanuele II (Corso) 1 A4
Vittorio Emanuele II (Largo) 6 E1
Vittorio Emanuele II
  (monumento a) 6 E1
Vittorio Veneto (Piazza) 7 C1
Vittozzi (Via) 3 A5
Vochieri (Via) 5 C1
Voghera (Lungo Dora) 4 E4
Volta (Via) 6 F1
Volturno (Via) 7 C3
Volvera (Via) 5 A1

Z

Zanella 4 F1
Zoologico (Giardino) 8 E1
Zumaglia (Via) 1 A2

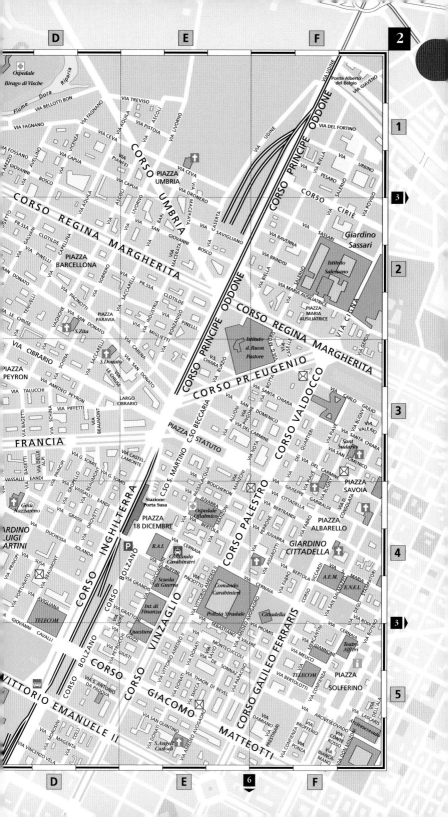

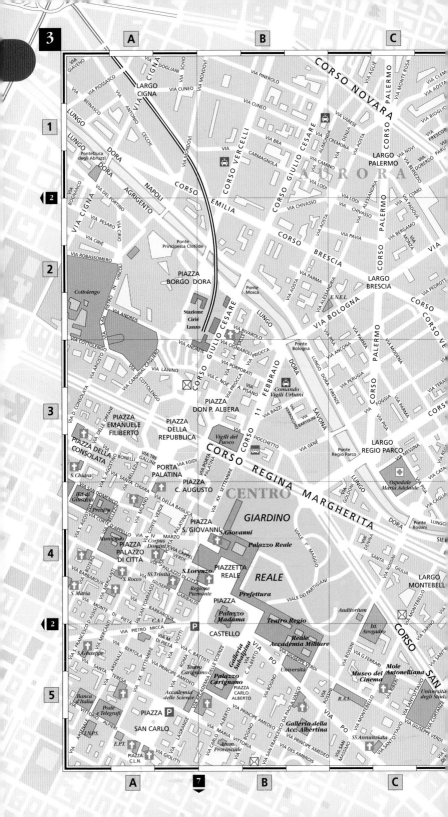

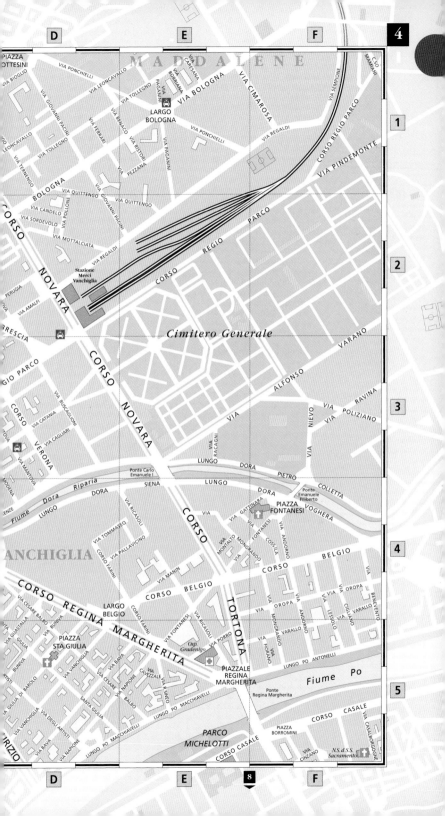

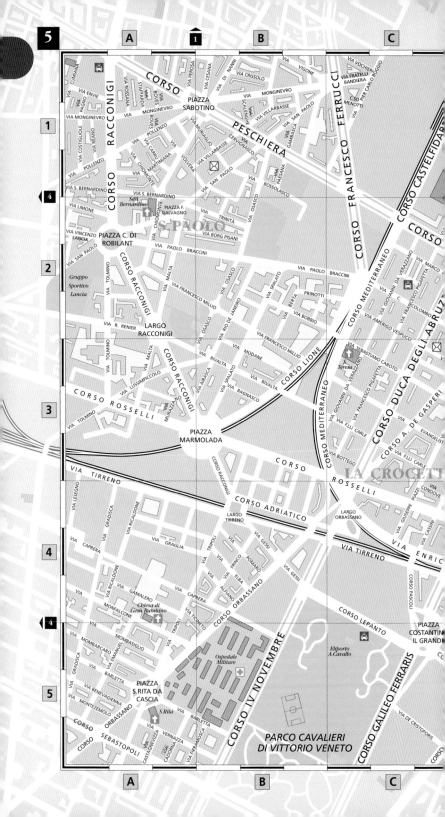

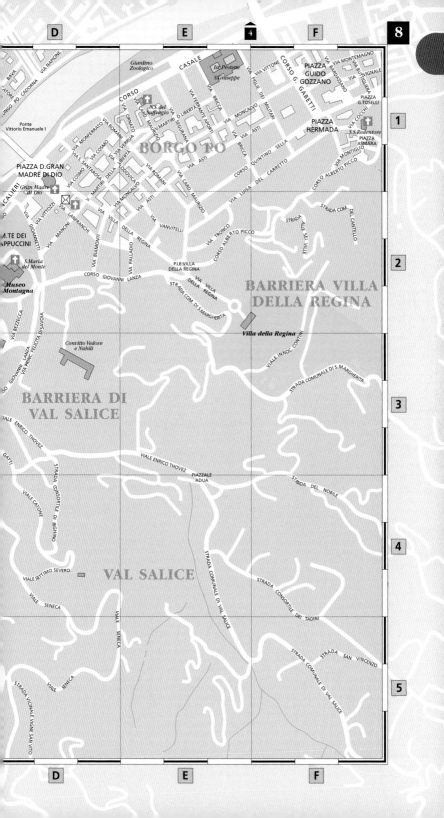

General Index

Page numbers in **bold** type refer to main entries.

A

Accorsi, Pietro 59
Achè 200, 201
Africa Unite 198
Agilulfo 38
Agliè 17, 210
Agritourism 174, 175, 183
Airline companies 209
  Air France 209
  Alitalia 209
  British Airways 209
  Easyjet 209
  Lufthansa 209
  Meridiana 209
  Ryanair 209
Airò, Mario 31
Aitken, Doug 30
Al Bicerin 12, 82, 192, 200
Al Sorj 201
Ala di Stura 199
Alba 47
Albugnano 105
Alcatraz 200, 201
Alfieri Benedetto 54, 55, 80, 81, 100
Alps 22–3
  Cozie 10, 22, 149, 155, 170
  Graie 10
Angrogna 155, 156, 159, **162**
Antonelli, Alessandro 60, 91
Apartments for rent 175
Architecture **26–9**
Ariperto 38
Arnaud, Enrico 109, 163
Arpino, Giovanni 16
Art **30–31**
Asti 42
Augusta Taurinorum 37, 81, 104
Augustus 37
Aulenti, Gae 27
Avigliana 32, 34, 86, 89, 112, 113, **114**, 115, 182, 199, 210
  Casa di Porta Ferrata 114
  Casa Senore 114
  Hotels 178
  Piazza Conte Rosso 114

B

Balla, Giacomo 30, 94
  Compenetrazioni Iridescenti 30
Balmat, Jacques 22
Balme 199
Balôn 79, **80**, 197
Banks and ATMs 207
Bars and cafés 192–5
Bardonecchia 20, 24, 108, 111, 112, 113, **130**, 132–3, 196, 199, 210
  Chapels in the valley of Bardonecchia 131
  Hotels 178

Bardonecchia (cont.)
  Restaurants 190
  Skiing facilities **132–3**
Bardot, Brigitte 192
Barillet-Deschampes, Pierre 86
Baroncelli, Gian Francesco 81
Barrumba 198, 201
Battle of Assietta 43, 129
Battle of Bezzecca 44
Battle of Custoza 40
Battle of San Quintino 40
Bauduc, Cerruti Felice 73
  Battle of Sommacampagna 73
Beato, Angelico 70
  Madonna and Child 70
Beaumont, Claudio Francesco 96
Beckwith, Charles 161
Bed & breakfast 175
Bellotto, Bernardo 71
  Palazzo Reale in Turin 71
Benso Camillo, Conte di Cavour 12, 16, 44, 45, 58, 72, 73, 75, 183, 192
Bernero, Giovan Battista 96
Bertola, Antonio 57, 125
Bertola, Ignazio 83
Bibiana
  Hotels 181
Bicerin **82**, 183, 192
Birilli (restaurant) 183
Bobbio Pellice 109, 155, 156, **164**, 183
  Restaurants 191
Bollati, Giuseppe 72
Bonaparte, Napoleon 43, 54, 193
Bonsignore, Ferdinando 88
Borgognone 122
Borgone 113
Bossoli, Carlo 45
Botticelli (studio of) 71
  Venus 71
Bottino, Vittorio Bonadè 29
Bousson 131, 151, 153
  Casa delle Lapidi 151
Brayda, Riccardo 80
Bricherasio 156, 157, **159**
Bronzino 70
  Portrait of a Lady 70
Brueghel de Velours, Jan 70
Buildings
  Palazzo Barolo 78
  Palazzo Bricherasio 63, **75**
  Palazzo Carignano 26, 41, 42, 63, 64, 65, **72–3**
  Palazzo Carpano 74
  Palazzo Cavour 63, **75**
  Palazzo Dal Pozzo Della Cisterna 63, 65, **74–5**
  Palazzo degli Stemmi 53, 58
  Palazzo dei Conti (Luserna San Giovanni) 160
  Palazzo dell'Accademia delle Scienze 66
  Palazzo dell'Università 53, 58
  Palazzo della Regione 27
  Palazzo della Vittoria 27

Buildings (cont.)
  Palazzo Faletti di Barolo 77, **81**
  Palazzo Fenoglio-La Fleur 27
  Palazzo Madama 12, 26, 41, 51, 52, **55**, 78, 80
  Palazzo Martini di Cigala 82
  Palazzo Reale 12, 27, 41, 51, 52, **54**, 70, 71, 74
  Palazzo Roero di Guarene 59
  Palazzo Saluzzo Paesana 77, 78, **82**
  Palazzo Solaro del Borgo 12
Buren, Daniel 31
Bus services 209
Bussoleno 121
Buttigliera Alta 114

C

Cabiria 198
Café Blue 200, 201
Café Procope 201
Caffarel-Prochet 193
Caffè Elena 193
Caffè Fiorio 58, 193
Caffè Mulassano 27, 193
Caffè Platti 193
Caffè San Carlo 16, 64, 192
Caffè Torino 192
Cairo, Francesco 71
Cametti, Bernardino 96
Camping sites 175
Canalupa
  Hotels 181
Carema 183
Carena, Antonio 161
Carignano 199
Canaletto 71, 94
  The Bucentaur at the Wharf on Ascension Day 94
Canavesio, Giovanni 70
Cane, Ottaviano 70
Canova, Antonio 94
Cantalupa
  Hotels 181
Carema 183
Carena, Antonio 161
Carmagnola 199
Carpano, Antonio Benedetto 200
Casorati, Daphne 161
  Paese Alpino 161
Casorati, Francesco 31, 83
Castellaro 115
Castles and mansions
  Castello de la Mandria 41
  Castello del Valentino 13, 15, 17, 32, 41, 85, 87, **89**
  Castello di Govone 41
  Castello di Moncalieri 41, 93, 100, 101, **104**
  Castello di Pollenzo 41
  Castello di Racconigi 17, 41, 101
  Castello di Rivoli 17, 27, 30, 31, 41, 93, 96, 100, **105**, 114
  Castello di Susa 123
  Castello Ducale di Agliè 17, 41,100, 101
  Castello Reale di Casotto 41
  Mandria di Chivasso 41

Castles and mansions (cont.)
Palazzina di Caccia Stupinigi 5, 17, 26, 41, 93, 100, **102–3**
Reggia di Venaria Reale 41, 100, 126
Cateau-Cambrésis (Treaty of) 40, 42
Cattelan, Maurizio 104
Caval' d brôns 64
Cavour 156, 158, **160**, 182, 183
Hotels 181
Restaurants 191
Celts 122
Ceppi, Carlo 82
Ceres 210
Ceresole Reale 199
Cesana Torinese 24, 108, 111, 136, **151**, 152, 182, 199
Hotels 179
Restaurants 191
Chanforàn (Council of) 39, 162, 165
Charlemagne 124, 199
Charles of Anjou 39
Cherchi, Sergio 161
Chiambretti, Piero 183
Chianocco 19, 20, 113, 121
Chieri 93, **105**, 183
Chiomonte 25
Chocolate 193
Christmas 35
Churches
Abbazia di Novalesa 108, 111, 112, **124–5**, 129
Abbazia (Sacra) di San Michele 108, 109, 111, 112, 113, 114, 115, **116–7**
Abbazia di Santa Maria (Cavour) 160
Abbazia di Santa Maria (Pinerolo) 144
Abbazia di Vezzolano 93, **105**
Basilica di Superga 17, 26, 32, 41, 93, **96–7**, 126
Cattedrale di San Donato (Pinerolo) 158
Cattedrale di San Giusto (Susa) 122, 123
Certosa di Banda 115
Certosa di Monte Benedetto 18, 112, 115, 121
Duomo (Chieri) 105
Duomo (Turin) 13, 26, 51, 52, 54, **56–7**
Gran Madre di Dio 10, 27, 59, 85, **88**, 90, 200
La Consolata 12, 26, 42, 78, 79, **82**
Madonna del Pilone 90
Monastero Benedettino di Sant'Egidio (Moncalieri) 105
Nôtre Dame de Coignet (Les Arnauds) 131
Parrocchiale di San Giovanni Battista (Cesana Torinese) 151
Parrocchiale di Sant'Andrea

Churches (cont.)
(Millaures) 131
Parrocchiale di Sant'Antonio Abate (Sestrière) 150
Parrocchiale di Santa Maria Assunta (Bricherasio) 159
Parrocchiale di Santa Maria Assunta (Oulx) 129
Parrocchiale di Salbertrand 112, 126
San Carlo 64, 74
San Domenico 26, 77, 79, **80**
San Filippo Neri 63, 65, 74
San Francesco (Susa) 122, 123
San Giacomo (Luserna San Giovanni) 160
San Giovanni (Avigliana) 114
San Giovanni Battista (Sauze d'Oulx) 129
San Lorenzo 4, 26, 42, 51, 52, **55**
San Maurizio (Pinerolo) 158
San Pietro (Rochemolles) 131
San Pietro in Vincoli (Villar Perosa) 138
San Restituto (Sestrière) 150
Sant'Agostino 26
Sant'Andrea 26
Sant'Antonio Abate (Melezet) 131
Sant'Antonio di Ranverso 93, **104**
Santa Chiara 81
Santa Cristina 64, 74
Santa Croce (Rivoli) 59, 104
Santa Maria del Monte 88, 90
Santa Teresa 64, 74
Santissimi Martiri e Cappella della Pia Congregazione 77, 78, **81**
SS. Sudario 78
Cignaroli, Vittorio Amedeo 59, 103
Pleasures of the Country life 59
Ciriè 183
Claudio (bishop) 38
Clavière 22, 24, 25, 136, **151**, 152, 199
Hotels 179
Restaurants 191
Club Alpino Italiano 17
Coassolo Torinese 183
Coazze 132, 159
Communications 206
Conca Cialancia 20
Condove 183
Constantine 122
Cordero, Riccardo 161
Corio 183
Cottolengo 16
Cozio 23, 37, 122, 123
Crissolo 168
Croce, Benedetto 64
Cuneo 160, 168
Cuisine 182–5

D
D'Alba, Macrino 70
D'Andrade, Alfredo 80, 89, 116
D'Azeglio, Massimo 46, 73
Da Camaino, Tino 55
Da Messina, Antonello 52, 55, 59
Portrait of an Unknown Man 52, 55, 59
Da Roreto, Gandolfino 70
Da Varallo, Tanzio 55
Da Vinci, Leonardo 52, 54
Self Portrait 54
Codex on Bird Flight 54
Da Volterra, Daniele 124
Deposition 124
De Amicis, Edmondo 64, 155
De Bello Gallico 37
De Bernardi, Arnaldo 27
De Maistre, Xavier 142
De Pisis, Filippo 83
Del Cambio (restaurant) 183
Del Caprino Meo 39, 56
Di Buoninsegna, Duccio 71
Madonna and Child Enthroned with Angels 71
Di Castellamonte, Amedeo 54, 55, 58, 75, 88, 89, 100
Di Castellamonte, Carlo 64, 74, 88
Dauphin, Charles 71
Discos 201
Diwan Café 201
Docks Dora 200
Don Bosco 16
Donati, Vitaliano 16
Donno 37, 122
Dou, Gherard 70
Drovetti, Bernardino 16, 66, 68
Dual 200, 201
Dumas, Alexandre 64
Dupré, Giovanni 58

E
El Mir 200, 201
Einaudi (publishers) 16
Emergencies 206
Entertainment 198–201
Entertainment venues 200
Events *see* Exhibitions
Exchange offices 207
Exhibitions and events 32–5
Artissima 34
Automotoretrò 35
Bal do Sabre 33
Cantavalli 32, 198
Christmas market 35
Cineambiente 34
CioccolaTò 32
Concorso Ippico Internazionale (International Horse Race) 34
Da Sodoma a Hollywood 32
Danza degli Spadonari 35
Danza delle Spade 32
Due Laghi Jazz Festival 34, 198
Eurojazz Festival 198
Experimenta 33

Exhibitions and events (cont.)
Festival Cinema delle Donne 32
Festa dei Valdesi 35
Festival delle Colline Torinesi 33
Festa di San Giovanni 33
Festivalmontagna 33
Fiera Internazionale del Libro 32
Identità e Differenza 34
Il Mistero della Maschera di Ferro 34
Immagini dell'Interno 33
L'Orso della Candelora 35
Le Fenestrelle 33
Linguaggi Jazz 198
Luci d'Artista e Arte Contemporanea 34
ManifesTO 31
Mostra Mercato dell'Artigianato (handicrafts) 33
Musica 90 32, 198
Parchi Storici Fioriti 32
Racchettinvalle 35
Salone del Vino 34
Salone Europeo della Montagna 34
Salone internazionale del Gusto 34, 183
Sentinelle delle Alpi 33
Sintonie 35
Sottodiciotto Film Festival 34
Tastar de Corda 32
Teatro Festival Sauze d'Oulx 33
Torino Danza 35
Torino Film Festival 34
Torino Settembre Musica 34, 198
Traffic Torino Free Festival 33, 198
Turin Marathon 32
Valsusa Filmfest 32
Vincoli Sonori 33
Exilles 125, 130

F

Fantini, Guglielmetto 105
Fattori, Giovanni 83
Fenestrelle
Hotels 179
Ferrari, Defendente 56, 58, 70, 114, 116, 117
Renaissance Polyptych 56
Adorationof the Magi 58
Triptych 116–7
Ferrari, Eusebio 70
Ferrari, Gaudenzio 58, 70
Lamentation of the Dead Christ 58
Crucifixion 70
Ferrero 16
Ferri, Gaetano 72
Festivals 183
Fiano 199
FIAT 15, 27, 46, 47, 75, 91, 138
Flora and fauna 18–9

Folklore 128
Folk Club 201
Fontana dei Mesi 86
Fontana del Tritone e delle Nereidi 53
Fontana, Lucio 83
Fontanesi, Antonio 83
Formento, Luigi 91
Forts and fortresses
Forte di Exilles 5, 33, 43, 108, 111, 112, **125**, 127, 135
Forte di Fenestrelle 33, 43, 108, 111, 120, 135, 136, 137, **142–3**
Forte Variselle 111, 125
Francesco I 39
Frejus 22, 44, 46, 130, 132, 133, 199
French border 60, 61
Frezzi, Giuseppe 59
Fusion Café 200, 201

G

Galvano, Albino 161
Galleries see Museums
Garelli, Franco 161
Garibaldi, Giuseppe 44, 45, 46, 73
Garove, Michelangelo 100
Giaglione 35
Gianavello, Giosuè 164
Giancarlo 200, 201
Giaveno 32
Hotels 179
Gioberti, Vincenzo 45, 46, 72
Giolitti, Giovanni 160
Giovenone (family) 70
Glorious Repatriation 109, 163, 165
Gobetti, Piero 16
Gole del Rouspart 19
Gozzano, Guido 16
Grammorseo, Pietro 80
Gramsci, Antonio 59
Gran Balôn 197
Granges 29
Green Count see Amedeo VI
Griffa, Giorgio 161
Griffier, Jan 70
Guarini, Guarino 26, 42, 51, 52, 55, 56, 57, 65, 66, 72, 82
Guercino 71, 80
Madonna of the Rosary and Saints Dominic and Catherine of Siena 80
Guttuso, Renato 83
Execution of Partisans 83

H

Hafa Café 192, 200, 201
Handicrafts 196
Hannibal 37
Hardwick, James 94
Health 206
Hills see Mountains

Hiroshima Mon Amour 198, 201
Horn, Rebecca 31
Hotels 174–5, 176–181
Hotels, characteristic and historic 174

I

Il Castelvecchio 102
Il Risorgimento (newspaper) 75
Industria (city) 57
Istituto Elettrotecnico Nazionale 16
Ivrea 35, 210

J

Jam Club 200, 201
Jaquerio, Giacomo 104
Fresco cycle (St Anthony of Ranverso) 104
Jewish Ghetto 59
Julius Caesar 23, 37, 55, 122, 130
Juvarra, Filippo 26, 52, 54, 55, 56, 64, 65, 74, 81, 82, 96, 97, 100, 102
Juventus 16, 64, 196, 199

K

Kirkuk Café 200, 201

L

L'Ostu 201
La Casa del Barolo 201
La Gare 201
La Ruà 29, 145
La Stampa 16, 46, 205
La Tuccia 148
Ladatte, Francesco 103
Lakes
Avigliana 18, 19, 20, 114
Borello 20
Del Beth 149
Grande di Viso 168
Nero 29, 152
Paradiso delle Rane 121
Lanino, Bernardino 70
Lanzo Torinese 183
Las Rosas 200, 201
Lateran Council (IV) 39
Laval 148
Lavazza 16, 192
Le Gru (Grugliasco) 196
Le Nôtre André 53, 54, 101
Le Vitel Etonné 201
Legnanino 81
Les Arnauds 131, 132
Les Horres 131
Cavalcade of Vices and Virtues 131
Levi, Carlo 161
Levi, Corrado 81
LeWitt, Sol 31
Ligurians 122
Lyon (Treaty of) 42

Lippi, Filippo 58, 70
  *The Fathers of the Church
  Augustine and Ambrose* 58
  *The Fathers of the Church
  Gregory and Jerome* 58
  Three Archangels and Tobias 70
Lombards 38, 109, 116, 124, 128, 130
Lou Dalfin 198
Luserna San Giovanni 156, 160, 164, 197
  Ala Pubblica 160
  Convento dei Serviti 160
  Convento di San Francesco 160
  Restaurants 191

M

Machè 201
Madonna del Ponte (Susa) 123
Magazzino di Gilgamesh 201
Maglione 183
Manet Edouard 94
  La Négresse 94
Maniglia 139
Mantegna, Andrea 71
  Madonna and Child and Saints 71
Manzù, Giacomo 83
Maps
  Along the Po 85
  Alps 22–3
  Further Afield 93
  Centre of Susa 123
  Centre of Turin 12–3
  Chisone and Germanasca Valleys 136
  Giro del Monviso 168
  Parco del Valentino 86–7
  Parco Naturale del Gran Bosco di Salbertrand 126
  Parco Naturale della Val Troncea 148
  Parco Naturale Orsiera-Rocciavré 120
  Parks and Reserves 20–21
  Piazza Castello 51–3
  Piazza San Carlo 63–5
  Quadrilatero Romano 77–9
  Savoy residences 100–1
  Skiing facilities in Bardonecchia 132
  Skiing facilities in Val Chisone 152
  Val di Susa 112
  Val Pellice 156
Maratta Carlo 74
  Virgin and Child 74
Marchesi di Asti 39
Marchesi di Monferrato 39
Marendazzo 200
Markets 197
  Opening times 197
Marocchetti, Carlo 64, 74
Martinez, Simone 53
Martini, Arturo 83

Massello 139
Mastroianni, Umberto 161
Matisse, Henri 94
Mattie 179
  Hotels 179
Mau Mau 198
Mazda Palace 198
Mazzini, Giuseppe 45, 46, 73
Melezet 112, **131**, 132
  Cappella di Nostra Signora del Carmine 131
  School of wood carving **131**, 196
Melotti, Fausto 83
Memling, Hans 70
  Passion of Christ 70
Menzio, Francesco 161
Merz, Mario 30, 31, 161
  Fountain-Igloo 30
Micca, Pietro 43, 83
Miel, Jan 71
Millaures 121
Miniere di Fontane (Prali) 140
Modigliani, Amedeo 30, 94
  Head of a Woman with Red Hair 30
  Nu couché 94
Mollino, Carlo 29
Moncalieri 93, **105**, 199
Moncenisio 113
Monferrato 42
Monfol 126
Montagne Doc 204, 205
Montgenèvre 24, 152
Mountains and hills
  Adamello 23
  Adula 23
  Argentera 22
  Bernina 23
  Cervedale 23
  Cervino 22
  Chaberton 18, 22, 152
  Cima del Vallonetto 133
  Col d'Armoine 168, 169
  Colle Barant 165
  Colle Boucie 165
  Colle del Lys 159
  Colle della Croce 165
  Colle della Maddalena 22, 90
  Colle di San Chiaffredo 168
  Colle Gallarino 168
  Colle Selliere 168
  Colle Vaccera 162
  Colomion 132, 133
  Corno Bianco 23
  Frioland 156, 164
  Genevris 129, 136
  Gran Costa 127
  Gran Paradiso 22
  Gran Pilastro 23
  Granero 165
  Jafferau 133
  Marmolada 23
  Moncenisio 15, 22, 125
  Monginevro 15, 37, 43, 128, 199

Mountains and hills (cont.)
  Monte Bianco 22
  Monte Rosa 15, 23
  Monti della Luna 108, 151, 152, 153
  Monviso 15, 17, 22, 109, 155, 156, 165, **168–171**
  Niblé 129, 133
  Orsiera 22, 120, 136, 142
  Ortles 23
  Palavas 165
  Palla Bianca 23
  Pezzulano 114
  Picco dei Tre Signori 23
  Pirchiriano 113, 114, 117
  Pizzo Bernina 23
  Platasse 18
  Pra Catinat 120
  Punta della Mulattiera 132
  Punta Ramière 22
  Punta Sommeiller 133
  Robinet 121
  Rocca d'Abin 22
  Rocca Sbarua 159
  Rocciamelone 4, 15, 18, 22, 122
  Rocciavré 120, 136
  Rognosa 18, 148
Morandi, Giorgio 83
Motorways 209
Murals 44
Museums and galleries
  Castello di Rivoli - Museo di Arte Contemporanea **31**
  Centro di Documentazione delle Meridiane (La Ruà) 145
  Ecomuseo Colombano Romean (Salbertrand) 126, 128
  Ecomuseo del Dinamitificio Nobel (Avigliana) 115
  Ecomuseo "Di Filo in Filo" (Perosa Argentina) 139
  Ecomuseo della Pietra (Rorà) 164
  Ecomuseo della Resistenza (Bricherasio) 159, 162
  Ecomuseo Scopriminiera (Prali) 140
  Fondazione Sandretto Re Rebaudengo 30, 93, **94**
  Galleria Civica di Arte Contemporanea 30
  Galleria Civica di Arte Moderna Filippo Scroppo (Torre Pellice) 161
  Galleria Sabauda 63, 64, 65, **70–71**
  GAM Galleria Civica di Arte Moderna e Contemporanea 10, 30, 77, **83**
  Museo Civico di Arte Antica 52, 55
  Museo Civico di Susa 123
  Museo Civico Pietro Micca 77, **83**

Museums and galleries (cont.)
Museo del Costume e delle
Tradizioni delle Genti Alpine
(Pragelato) 145
Museo del Grande Torino 97
Museo del Risorgimento 63, 64,
65, **72–73**
Museo del Tessile (Chieri) 105
Museo dell'Automobile 93, **95**
Museo dell'Osservatorio di
Apicoltura (Pragelato) 145
Museo della Donna (Angrogna)
162
Museo della Marionetta 63, 64,
74
Museo della Meccanica e del
Cuscinetto (Villar Perosa) 138
Museo della Radio e della
Televisione 51, **58**
Museo della Sindone 77, 78, **82**
Museo di Antichità 4, 37, 52,
57
Museo di Arte
e Ammobiliamento 100, 102
Museo di Arte Contemporanea
100, 104
Museo di Arte Preistorica
(Pinerolo) 158
Museo di Arte Religiosa Alpina
(Melezet) 131
Museo di Arte Sacra di
Giaglione 123, **124**
Museo di Arte Sacra di Novalesa
123, **124**, 125
Museo di Arti Decorative
Fondazione Accorsi 51, **59**
Museo di Prali e della Val
Germanasca (Prali) 141
Museo di Rodoretto (Prali)
141
Museo Diocesano d'Arte Sacra
(Susa) 122
Museo Egizio 13, 16, 43, 63, 64,
65, **66–9**, 70
Museo Etnografico
(Bardonecchia) 130
Museo Nazionale del Cinema 15,
47, 51, 59, **60–61**
Museo Nazionale della
Montagna 85, **88**, 90
Museo Odin-Bertot (Angrogna)
162
Museo Regionale di Scienze
Naturali 63, 75
Museo Storico dell'Arma della
Cavalleria (Pinerolo) 158
Museo Storico Nazionale di
Artiglieria 77, **83**
Museo Storico Valdese della
Balsiglia 139
Museo Valdese (Rorà) 164
Museo Valdese (Torre Pellice)
161
Nuovo Centro per l'Arte
Contemporanea 30
Osservatorio Meteorologico Real

Museums and galleries (cont.)
Collegio Carlo Alberto
(Moncalieri) 105
Pinacoteca dell'Accademia delle
Belle Arti 51, **58**
Pinacoteca Giovanni e Marella
Agnelli 93, **94**
Società Promotrice delle Belle
Arti 87
Mussolini, Benito 41, 47

N

Napoleon Bonaparte 43, 54, 193
Nature parks and protected areas
20–21
Palude del Lago Borello 20
Parco del Gran Paradiso 23
Parco Fluviale del Po 21, 33,
89, 90
Parco Naturale del Gran Bosco
di Salbertrand 4, 18, 20, 108,
112, 126–127, 133, 135, 144
Parco Naturale della Val Troncea
20, 135, 136, **148–9**
Parco Naturale di Superga
and Basilica 91
Parco Naturale Laghi di
Avigliana 21, 114, 115
Parco Naturale Orsiera-
Rocciavré 19, 21, 23, 108, 112,
115, **120–21**, 135, 137, 144
Parco Naturale Rocca di Cavour
21, 160
Parco Ornitologico Martinat 159
Parco Regionale la Mandria 21,
93, 100, **104**
Riserva Chianocco e Foresto 19,
20, 121
Rocca di Cavour 20, 21, 160
Nero 122
Nervi, Pierluigi 86
Neuv Caval'd Brôns 192
Nietzsche 193
Nizza 43
None 183
Novalesa 19, 37, 124, 125
Notorius 201

O

Obelix 200
Officine Belforte 201
Olderico, Manfredi 38, 122
Olivetan *see* Pietro Robert 161
Olsen 192
Olympic Store 197
Orchestra Sinfonica Nazionale
16, 198
Orpheus (mosaic) 57
Orrido di Foresto 19
Ostana 168
Ottaviano, Augusto 55
Ottone 130
Oulx 111, 112, 113, **128–9**,
199, 204

Oulx (cont.)
Casa des Ambrois 129
Casa Gally 129
Fontana della Vière 129
Hotels 179
Restaurant 190
Torre Saracena 128

P

Pacca, Bartolomeo 142
Paccard, Michel 22
Paris Texas 201
Passo del Moncenisio 111, 122,
124
Passo del Monginevro 22, 23, 37,
111, 122
Passo di Vallanta 168
Pasticcerie (pastry shops)
Avvignano 193
Baratti & Milano 193
Gerla 193
Ghigo 193
Gobino 174
Stratta 64, 192, 196
Pastis 200, 201
Pavese, Cesare 16, 193
Pecetto 199
Pelagi, Pelagio 80, 100
Pellico, Silvio 78, 81, 158
Pellizza da Volpedo 83
Pepe, Guglielmo (statue) 75
Pepino 193
Perosa Argentina 136, 137, **138**,
182, 183
Perrero 135, 136, 137, **139**
Petiti, Enrico 91
Peyrano-Pfatisch 193
Pian del Colle 131
Cappella di San Sisto 131
Pian del Frais 132
Pian del Prà 156
Pian del Re 169, 171
Pian del Sole 132
Pian Neiretto 132
Piano Renzo 94, 95
Picasso, Pablo 94
Pinerolo 24, 25, 32, 33, 34, 42, 86,
89, 109, 136, 144, 156, 157,
158–9, 182, 183, 197, 204
Hotels 181
Restaurants 191
Pino Torinese 91
Pistoletto, Michelangelo 161
Plantery, Gian Giacomo 44, 75, 80,
82
Pliny 37
Poirino 183
Pollaiolo 70
Archangel Raphael and Tobias
70
Pomodoro, Giò 31
Pozzo, Andrea 55, 81
Pradeltorno 165
Pragelato 24, 25, 29, 35, 108, 135,
136, 137, **144–5**, 152, 182, 183,

Pragelato (cont.)
199
Hotels 180
Prali 25, 135, 136, 137, **140–41**, 199
Hotels 180
Pralormo 32

R
Racconigi 17, 32, 210
Radio RAI 16
Ramondetti, Amato 174
Reano 114
Red Count *see* Amedeo VII
Reddocks 200
Refuges 156, 165, 168, 199
Rifugio Barbara Lowrie 156, 165,
168
Rifugio Battaglione Monte
Granero 165, 168
Rifugio Capanna Mautino 152
Rifugio Sella 168
Rifugio Vallanta 168
Rifugio Willy Jervis 156, 165,
168, 175
Rembrandt (attributed) 70
Portrait of a Man Sleeping 70
Renoir, Auguste 94
Republic of the Escartons 170
Republic of
Val San Martino 139, 141
Restaurants 183, 186–191
Hours and prices 183
Reycend, Enrico 10
Ricci, Sebastiano 96
Risorgimento 44–5
Rivalba 183
Rivalta di Torino 183
Rivers and streams
Angrogna 160, 165
Chiamogna 159
Chisone 19, 20, 135, 149
Dora 10, 37, 122, 151, 199
Dora Baltea 21, 37
Dora Riparia 104, 111, 151
Marderello 19
Pellice 19, 160, 164
Po 5, 10, 13, 15, 17, 18, 19, 22,
32, 33, 37, 43, 55, 57, **85**, 88, 89,
101, 111, 170, 171, 199
Prebèc 121
Rio Claretto 19
Ripa 151
Sangone 10, 21
Stura di Lanzo 10, 21
Rivoli 17, 32, 35, **104**, 111, 113,
114
Campanile of Santa Maria della
Stella 104
Casa del Conte Verde 104
Robert, Pietro *known as* Olivetan
161
Rochemolles 131
Rock City 201
Romans 37, 111, 122
Rorà 156, 164
Hotels 181

Rosso, Medardo 83
Rosta 114
Roure 135, 141, 144
Rouspart, Gole del 19
Rubens, Peter Paul 71, 124
Crucifixion of Peter 124
Deposition of Christ 124
Ruggeri, Piero 161

S
Sabor Latino 200, 201
Safety in the mountains 206
Salbertrand 18, 20, 112, 126, **128**
Piazza San Rocco 128
Salza di Pinerolo 144
San Giorio di Susa 20, 32, 124
Cappella del Conte 123, **124**
Restaurants 190
San Pietro Val Lemina 159, 183
San Sicario 24, 136, **151**, 152
San Tommaso 10, 192
Sant'Ambrogio 114
Santhià 42
Sapordivino 201
Sauze di Cesana 150, 199
Sauze d'Oulx 24, 29, 33, 108, 112,
126, **129**, 132, 152, 153, 197
Hotels 179
Restaurants 190
Savoy family 12, 13, 15, 17, 38,
40–47, 87, 89, 93, 97, 104
Adelaide di Susa 38, 122, 128,
130, 144
Amedeo I 40
Amedeo VI *known as* Green
Count 39, 54, 77, 79, 104
Amedeo VII *known as* Red
Count 39
Anne D'Orleans 88, 90
Bianca 55
Carlo Alberto 43, 44, 45, 46, 54,
58, 60, 70, 72, 91, 97, 101, 116,
129, 163
Carlo Emanuele I 42, 71, 88
Carlo Emanuele II 100
Carlo Emanuele III 71, 83, 142
Carlo Emanuele IV 43
Carlo Felice 44, 46, 66, 71, 101,
116
Emanuele Filiberto 40, 41, 42,
54, 55, 71, 83
Emanuele Filiberto II 54
Eugenio 42, 54
Eugenio di Savoia-Soissons
70
Luigi Duca degli Abruzzi 88
Margherita 88
Maria Adelaide of Habsburg
101
Marie Christine of France 13, 52,
71, 74, 87, 89, 101
Maria Vittoria 65, 74
Maurizio (cardinal) 88
Oddone 38, 122, 144
Tommaso III 39

Savoy family (cont.)
Umberto I Biancamano 38, 41,
54
Umberto III *known as* the
Blessed 104
Vittorio Amedeo II 27, 40, 42,
43, 71, 74, 88, 96, 100, 102, 163,
182
Vittorio Amedeo III 43
Vittorio Emanuele I 44, 46, 71,
88, 90, 158
Vittorio Emanuele II 45, 46, 54,
72, 101
Vittorio Emanuele III 41
Scroppo, Filippo 161
Sella, Quintino 17
Serra, Sebastiano & Bartolomeo
di Pinerolo 129
Last Judgment 129
Sestrière 17, 18, 24, 29, 46, 108,
111, 135, 136, 137, 138, **150**,
151, 152, 153
Hotels 180
Restaurants 191
Severini, Gino 94
Seytes 148
Shock Club 201
Shopping 196–7
Opening hours 196
Silvestrin, Claudio 30, 94
Sip (phone company) 16
Spanzotti, Giovanni Martino 56,
58, 70
Renaissance Polyptych 56
*St Francis, St Agatha
and a Donor* 58
Sport 132, 199
Biathlon 152
Canoeing 199
Climbing 132, 159
Cross-country skiing 141, 148,
151, 152, 153
Curling 25, 158
Freestyle 24, 129, 152
Golf 199
Hang gliding 199
Hiking 199
Hockey 24, 160
Horse riding 199
Ice skating 25
Nordic skiing 24
Off-piste skiing 133, 150,
151, 152, 153, 171
Paragliding 199
Rafting 199
Short track 25
Skiing 132, 199
Snowboarding 24, 130, 131, 132
Trekking 129
Spranger, Bartholomaeus 70
Last Judgment 70
Statue of Amedeo VI 80
Statue of Camillo Benso di Cavour
58
Statue of Emanuele Filiberto of
Savoy 12, 16, 64, 74, 192

Statute, Albertine 44
Stewart, James 192
Stingel, Rudolf 94
Stupinigi 17, **102–3**, 137, 157, 199
Subsonica 198
Superga 26
  Basilica di Superga 17, 26, 32, 41, 93, **96–7**, 126
  Palazzo Superga 26
Susa 22, 57, 111, 112, 113, **122–3**
  Anfiteatro 122, 123
  Arco di Augusto 23, 122, 123
  Cappella del Conte 123, 124
  Castello 123
  Hotels 179
  Porta Savoia 122–3
  Restaurant 190
  Tesoro di San Giusto 123

T

Taricco, Sebastiano 81
Taurini 37, 57
Teniers, David il Giovane 70
Teodolinda 38
Testa di Ferro *see* Emanuele Filiberto 40
The Beach 200, 201
Thures 153
Tiepolo, Gian Battista 94
  Halberdier in a Landscape 94
Tintoretto 71
  Trinity 71
Turin 10, **12–17**, 18, 21, 22, 24, 26, 27, 42, 44, 93, 96, 104
  Accademia delle Scienze 70
  Armeria Reale 51, 52, **54**
  Atrium 204
  Auditorium Agnelli 34, 35, 198
  Biblioteca Civica 27
  Biblioteca Nazionale 72
  Biblioteca Reale 51, 52, **54**
  Bicycles 215
  Borgo Dora 35
  Borgo e Rocca Medioevale 34, 85, 86, **89**
  Cappella dei Banchieri e dei Mercanti 78, **81**
  Cappella della Sacra Sindone 13, 17, 26, 42, 52, 56, 82
  Casa Macciotta 27
  Cittadella 42, 83
  Complesso della Cavallerizza Reale 51, 53, **55**
  Conservatorio 198
  Corso Castelfidardo 210
  Corso Francia 27
  Corso Galileo Ferrari 83
  Corso Turati 206
  Corso Vittorio Emanuele II 63, 83, 87
  Cortile del Maglio 35
  Cremagliera Sassi-Superga 205

Turin (cont.)
  Galleria Subalpina 65, 193
  Giardini Reali 52, 53, 57
  Gruppo Torinese Trasporti (GTT) 212
  Hotels 176–8
  Il Mastio 41, 83
  International airport, Caselle 204, 208
  Largo IV Marzo 26
  Lingotto 27, 32, 34, 35, 93, **95**
  Metropolitana 215
  Mausoleo di Giovanna d'Orlier de la Balme 56
  Mole Antonelliana 10, 13, 15, 27, 32, 46, 51, 58, 59, **60–61**, 91, 205
  Monte dei Cappuccini 32, 85, 88, 90, 200
  Murazzi 32, 85, 200
  Orto Botanico 85, 87, **89**
  Ospedale Le Molinette 207
  Ospedale Mauriziano Umberto I 206
  Oval-Lingotto 25
  Palasport 24, 25
  Palavela 25, 27
  Parco del Valentino 17, 32, 85, **86–7**, 91
  Parco della Pellerina 198
  Parco della Rimembranza 90
  Parco Michelotti 90
  Parking 214
  Pedestrian precinct 214
  Piazza Albarello 77
  Piazza Carignano 72, 193
  Piazza Carlina *see* Piazza Carlo Emanuele II 58
  Piazza Carlo Alberto 63, 65, 72, 200
  Piazza Carlo Emanuele II *known as* Piazza Carlina 51, **58–9**
  Piazza Carlo Felice 74, 193
  Piazza Castello 12, 16, 27, 42, 51, **52–3**, 55, 58, 63, 65, 74, 78, 80
  Piazza Cavour 63, **75**
  Piazza Consolata 77, **82**, 192
  Piazza della Repubblica 77, 80
  Piazza Maria Teresa 27, 63, 74, 75
  Piazza Palazzo di Città 77, 78, 79, **80**
  Piazza San Carlo 5, 12, 16, 26, 63, **64–5**, **74**, 183
  Piazza Savoia 77, 78, **81**
  Piazza Solferino 204
  Piazza Statuto 27, 46, 77, 80
  Piazza Vittorio Veneto 27, 51, 58, **59**, 85, 193
  Piazzetta Corpus Domini 80
  Piercing 80
  Ponte Principessa Isabella 86
  Ponte Umberto I 86, 87
  Ponte Vittorio Emanuele I 27
  Ponte Vittorio Emanuele II 85

Turin (cont.)
  Porta Nuova 42
  Porta Palatina 26, 38, 51, 52, **55**, 77
  Porta Palazzo 77, 79, 80, 197, 200
  Porta Pretoria 55
  Porta Susa 77
  Porticoes 16
  Quadrilatero Romano 5, 12, 77, 82, 192, 200
  Quartiere San Salvario 85, **91**
  Rack-rail tram car 90, 205
  Restaurants 186–190
  Sacra Sindone 17, 56, **82**
  Synagogue 85, **91**
  Stadio delle Alpi 33, 198, 199
  Station, Porta Nuova 12, 74, 85, 91, 204, 209
  Station, Porta Susa 12, 209
  Street Finder 216
  Taxi 214
  Teatro Alfieri 198
  Teatro Carignano 34, 198
  Teatro Colosseo 198
  Teatro Gianduja 74
  Teatro Gioiello 198
  Teatro Gobetti 34, 198
  Teatro Regio 47, 53, 198
  Teatro Stabile 34, 198
  Torino Card 174, 205, 214
  Torino Cultura 199
  Torino Esposizioni 25
  Torinosette 205
  Town Hall 77
  Turismo Bus Torino 205, 214
  Turismo Torino 174, 175
  Via Dora Grossa 80
  Via Garibaldi 12, 26, 37, 44, 77, **78–9**, **80**, 200
  Via Po 12, 51, 53, **58**, 59, 193
  Via Roma 12, 63, 64, **74**
  Via San Tommaso 77
  Via XX Settembre 71
  Villa della Regina 41, 85, **88**, 90
  Villino Raby 27
Torre Pellice 17, 25, 109, 155, 156, 157, **160–61**, 163, 183
  Hotels 181
  Restaurants 191
Tourist information 204
Tourist services 204
Tunnels 209
Trana 114
Transport 208–15
Trattorias 183
Traversella 199
Traverses 29, 145
Tre Galli 201
Triptych of the Madonna del Rocciamelone (Susa) 123
Trofarello 183
Troncea 149
Trucco, Mattè Giacomo 27, 95

U

Urbiano
  di Mompantero 35
Usseaux 28, 29, 135, 136, 137, **144**
  Hotels 180
Usseglio 199
Utet (publishers) 16
Utrecht (Treaty of) 40, 42

V

Val della Torre 183
Valdo 39, 155
Valleys
  Alta Val Pellice 156, 165
  Angrogna 39
  Argentera 136, 199
  Chisone 5, 10, 18, 21, 22, 24, 28, 32, 43, 108, 111, 120, 135, **136–7**, 138, 140, 142, 144, 148, 152–3, 197
  Dei Carbonieri 109, 165
  Del Thuras 108, 153
  Germanasca 5, 10, 17, 19, 22, 24, 32, 135, **136–7**, 138, 140, 141
  Monviso 10, 15, 17
  Noce 159
  Ossola 47
  Pellice 5, 10, 17, 18, 19, 22, 33, 42, 108, 109, 135, 136, 155, **156–7**, 159, 162, 171, 175, 197
  Po 23, 155, 160, 170
  Rochemolles 133
  Sangone 21, 121, 132, 159
  Stretta 132
  Susa 5, 10, 18, 20, 21, 22, 23, 32,

Valleys (cont.)
  37, 43, 104, 108, 109, **111**, **112–13**, 120, 127, 130, 135, 197
  Troncea 18, 20, 135, 136, 141, 148–9
  Varaita 170
Van der Werff 70
Van der Weyden, Rogier 71
  Worshipper in Prayer 71
  Visitation 71
Van Dyck, Anthony 71
Van Dyck, Jan 65, 70, 71
  The Children of Charles I of England 65, 71
Van Eyck, Jan 59, 70
  Illuminated Codex 59
  St Francis receiving the Stigmata 70
Van Loo, Carlo Andrea 103
  Repose of Diana 103
Vannier, Luigi 81
Van Wittel, Gaspard 71
Vercruysse, Jan 31
Verona (Council of) 39
Veronese, Paolo 71
  Feast in the House of Simon 71
Via Francigena 113, 122
Via Lattea 24, 152, 199
Vienna (Congress of) 43
Villafranca (armistice of) 45
Villafranca Piemonte 19
Villanova 165, 168
Villar Focchiardo 115
  Restaurants 191
Villar Pellice 19, 155, 156, **164**
Villar Perosa 136, 137, **138**, 140, 183

Villar Perosa (cont.)
  Hotels 180
Vineria Parola 201
Visconti (Family) 39
Visconti, Galeazzo 55
Vitozzi, Ascanio 42, 90
Vittone, Bernardo 81
Viù 199

W

Waldensians 10, 17, **39**, 44, 45, 108, 109, 135, 138, 139, 141, 144, 145, 155, 156, 159, 160, **163**
  Centro Culturale Valdese (Torre Pellice) 163
  Coulege del Barba (Angrogna) 162
  Festa dei Valdesi 35
  Gheisa d'la Tana (Angrogna) 162
  Great Repatriation 109
  Tempio Valdese 85, **91**
  Tempio Valdese (Massello) 139
  Tempio valdese (Torre Pellice) 157
  Tempio Valdese Vecchio (Prali) 141
Widow Giambone 193
Winter Olympics 2006
  17, **24–5**, 47, 108, 129, 130, 150, 151, 158, 161, 174, 204

Z

Zuccari, Federico 81
  St Paul, San Saverio and other Saints 81

Acknowledgments

THE PUBLISHER would like to thank all the institutions, associations and individuals whose contribution and assistance have made the preparation of this guide possible.

SPECIAL THANKS
Paola Musolino (Turismo Torino), Francesca Soncini (public relations, City of Turin), Elena Cottini (Studio Mailander), Monica Re and Roberta Rossetti (Montagnedoc).

Thanks also go to:
Antonella Angiono, Andrea Bruno, Anna Rosso, Claudia Negro, Marta della Rocca, (editorial office www.nordovest.it); Claudio Artico; Olivia Assereto (Lavazza); Associazione Progetto San Carlo Forte di Fenestrelle – onlus; Library of Torre Pellice; Angela Brunengo (Associazione Lingotto Musica); Linda Brizzolara (TOROC); Angelo Cappetti (*La Stampa*); Ufficio Cultura Comunità Montana Valli Chisone e Germanasca; Claudia Debernardi (Sestrières s.p.a.); Claudio De Consoli (Gruppo Torinese Trasporti); Delfina dell'Acqua (Fondazione Accorsi); Ecomuseo dell'Industria Tessile "Di Filo in Filo" at Perosa Argentina; Laura Gonella (Museo Nazionale del Cinema); Marco Fratini (Fondazione Centro Culturale Valdese); Marta Fusi (Servizio Patrimonio Storico Artistico - Mauritian order); FIAT press office; Juventus Football Club s.p.a., Isabella Grandis (Associazione La Maschera di Ferro di Pinerolo); Gabriele Mariotti (Museo di Scienze Naturali di Torino); Paola Masetta (Museo dell'Automobile); Daniela Matteu (Fondazione Torino Musei); Enrica Melossi; Massimo Melotti e Manuela Vasco (Castello di Rivoli press office); Roberta Balma Mion (Fondazione Sandretto Re Rebaudengo); the monks of the Abbazia di Novalesa; Valter Musso (Salone del Gusto-Slow Food); the Rosminian fathers of Sacra di San Michele; Parco Ornitologico Martinat at Pinerolo; Pinacoteca Giovanni e Marella Agnelli; Barbara Pons (Scopriminiera); Dario Seglie (Centro Studi e Museo d'Arte Preistorica); Laura Tori (Torino Settembre Musica); Torino Calcio 1906 s.p.a.; Turin Hotels International; Andrea Vettoretti (Photographic archive, Province of Turin); Giancarlo Zattoni (Turin airport); Andrea Zonato (Centro Culturale Diocesano Susa).

Credits

PHOTOGRAPHY PERMISSIONS
The publisher would like to thank all the churches, museums, hotels, restaurants, shops, art galleries and parks too numerous to thank individually for their co-operation and contribution to this publication. Although every effort has been made to trace copyright holders, the publisher would like to take this opportuntity of apologizing for any omissions, and would be happy to include them in future editions of this guide.

KEY TO PHOTOGRAPH POSITIONS
t = top; tl = top left; tlc = top left centre; tc = top centre; tr = top right; tla = top left above; ca = centre above; cra = centre right above; cla = centre left above; cl = centre left; c = centre; cr = centre right; clb = centre left below; cb= centre below; crb = centre right below; bl = bottom left; b = bottom; bc = bottom centre; bcl = bottom centre left; br = bottom right; d = detail.

LIST OF PHOTOGRAPHS
ALINARI: 8–9, 44–45c, 62.

ARCHIVIO FOTOGRAFICO PROVINCIA DI TORINO (Bruno Allaix): 109tr, 171tl.

ARCHIVIO FOTOGRAFICO CITTÀ DI TORINO (Claudio Penna): 13br, 15bc, 21bc, 26cra, 45tr, 55cl, 59t, 87cr, 87tl, 183bl.

ARCHIVIO FOTOGRAFICO CITTÀ DI TORINO (Michele D'Ottavio): 27cda, 48–49, 74as, 88ad, 89bs, 95bd, 193cd, 200acs, 200abs, 201as.

ARCHIVIO FOTOGRAFICO CITTÀ DI TORINO: 31br, 35bl, 100cl, 102bl (photo by Pino dell'Aquila), 197br.

DORLING KINDERSLEY PHOTOGRAPHIC ARCHIVE: 117cr.

ARCHIVIO MONTAGNEDOC IMAGE: 109br, 133bcr, 154, 155, 156tr, 156bl, 157bl, 159br, 160tl, 160br, 161t, 162b, 162cl, 163crb, 163bl, 164br, 165 (all), 168cl, 204br.

ARCHIVIO FOTOGRAFICO TURISMO TORINO (Claudio Penna): 174br, 182tc, 215tr.

ARCHIVIO FOTOGRAFICO TURISMO TORINO (Giuseppe Bressi): 26tla, 53tl, 54tl, 54br, 60bl, 64cr, 73tl, 79cr, 83tl, 86cl, 90tr, 101tc, 103tl, 105cr, 192tc, 196cl, 198bl.

ARCHIVIO FOTOGRAFICO TURISMO TORINO (Ramella&Giannese): 53tl.

ARCHIVIO FOTOGRAFICO TURISMO TORINO (Roberto Borgo): 32cra.

ARCHIVIO FOTOGRAFICO TURISMO TORINO: 27tl, 27crb, 52bl, 56tr, 56cl, 56cr, 57tl, 64bl, 65tl, 78cl, 78tr, 91tr, 174tc, 199cr, 204tc, 205tl, 205cl.

ARCHIVIO GEOMONDADORI: 11 tr, 32tc, 32cr, 37 (all), 38tc, 38br, 38br, 40tr, 40bl, 41tr, 41cl, 41bc, 41br, 43bl, 43br, 44tr, 44tl, 44cl, 44bl, 44br, 45tl, 45cr, 46tl, 47tr, 55br, 57br, 58br, 65bl, 70–71 (all), 73tr, 73cr, 73bl, 77tc, 80tr, 83cr, 90cl, 95cr, 97cr, 102tl, 103br, 170cl, 184clb, 184bl, 184cr, 185tl, 185tlc, 206cr, 207crb, 208tc, 210c.

ARCHIVIO SAGAT (Turin Airport): 208cl, 208br.

ARCHIVIO VIA LATTEA: 150tl, 153cr, 153tl, 198bl, 200tl.

FABRIZIO ARDITO, Rome: 38bl, 114t, 123tl, 124tr, 124tr, 137cr, 141ltr, 143cr, 160cr, 164tl, 168tl, 168bl, 169tr, 169cr, 170bc, 175bc.

ARMERIA REALE: Turin: 52tr, 54c.

ASSOCIAZIONE MASCHERA DI FERRO, Pinerolo: 34bc.

ASSOCIAZIONE PROGETTO SAN CARLO, Forte di Fenestrelle – onlus: 43tl, 142 (all), 143tl, 143br.

ATRIUM TORINO: 17tr, 30tr, 204cl.

MARCO BIANCHI, Milan: 170tr, 171cr.

BIBLIOTECA REALE, Turin: 52br.

GIAN LUCA BOETTI, Chivasso: 1, 2–3, 13tc, 15ca, 16cb, 17cr, 17bl, 18–19 (all except for 18 bcl), 20–21 (all except for 21bc), 22–23 (all except 23tr), 33tl, 33tr, 28–29 (all except for 29br), 35tr, 36, 42tc, 42cr, 42cl, 43tr, 43cr, 84, 102tr, 102cl, 103cr, 103bl, 105tl, 105bl, 106–7, 108cl, 108br, 109bc, 110, 111, 112tr, 112bl, 113tr, 113bl, 114br, 115tr, 115cr, 116tr, 116cl, 117bc, 118–9, 120–121, 124bc, 125bl, 126–127, 128, 129bl, 130tr, 131tr, 131br, 132tr, 132bcl, 133cra, 133bc, 134, 135, 136cl, 136br, 137tl, 139tr, 139br, 141bl, 144, 146–7, 148–9, 152cl, 152clb, 152br, 159tl, 170bl, 171tr, 171bl, 171br, 172–3, 182bl, 183tc, 184br, 185tr, 185bcl, 193bl, 196tc, 197tl, 199tc, 199bl, 201bc, 202–3, 209tc.

CENTRO COMMERCIALE [8]GALLERY: 197cl.

CENTRO CULTURALE DIOCESANO, Susa: 122cr, 124cl.

CeSMAP (Centro Studi e Museo di Arte Preistorica), Pinerolo: 158cr.

CIVICA GALLERIA D'ARTE
CONTEMPORANEA "FILIPPO SCROPPO",
Torre Pellice: 161br.

COLLEZIONE MUSEO NAZIONALE DEL
CINEMA, Turin: 60tr, 60cr (photo Bruna
Biamino), 60cb (photo A. Fanni), 61tl
(photo Bruna Biamino), 61c (photo Laura
Cantarella).

COURTESY CASTELLO DI RIVOLI MUSEO
D'ARTE CONTEMPORANEA, Turin: 31tl,
311tr (photo Paolo Pellion), 104tc.

ECOMUSEO DELL'INDUSTRIA TESSILE,
Perosa Argentina: 139tl.

EPAT (Esercizi Pubblici Associati di Torino
e Provincia): 200bl.

FARABOLAFOTO, Milan: 133tl, 169br,
170–1c.

FIERA INTERNAZIONALE DEL LIBRO DI
TORINO: 32br, 198tc.

FONDAZIONE ACCORSI, Turin: 59 br.

FONDAZIONE CENTRO CULTURALE
VALDESE, Torre Pellice: 35cl, 39cr, 139cl,
141cl, 162tr, 162tr, 163tc, 163cl, 163br.

FONDAZIONE PALAZZO BRICHERASIO,
Turin: 75br.

FONDAZIONE SANDRETTO RE
REBAUDENGO, Turin: 30bl (photo by Tom
Buzzi); 30 br, 94t, 94bl (Patrizia Mussa).

FONDAZIONE TORINO MUSEI: 30cr, 30cla,
30clb, 55tr, 83br, 86br.

FOTO ARCHIVIO COMUNITÀ MONTANA
VALLI CHISONE E GERMANASCA: 138tl.

PIO GEMINIANI, Milan: 18bcl.

ROBERTO GIUDICI (Archivio Fotografico
Provincia di Torino): 29br, 45br, 131bcl,
145bc, 151tr, 150bl.

GIEMME, Milan: 23tr, 79tl, 104bl, 117cr.

GRUPPO FIAT, Turin: 16tl, 46cr, 47bl, 47br.

GRUPPO TORINESE TRASPORTI: 85tc,
210tl, 210br, 212–213, 214-215 (all except for
215tr).

JUVENTUS FOOTBALL CLUB SpA., Turin:
16cl, 33br.

PASQUALE JUZZOLINO (Associazione
Lingotto Musica): 34tl, 198cra.

*LaPresse, TOROC: 14, 24–25 all, 27cl, 129tr,
130bl, 132cl, 145t, 151b, 152tl, 158br, 175tl.

LA STAMPA EDITRICE, Turin: 46br, 205br.

LAVAZZA, Turin: 192cr.

LINGOTTO FIERE, Turin: 95cl.

LUIGI LIZZI, Asti: 98–9, 101c, 150cr, 166–7.

MARKA, Milan: 51, 76, 92, 132br.

MUSEO DELL'AUTOMOBILE, Turin: 95tr.

MUSEO EGIZIO, Turin: 13cr, 65cr, 66–67
(all), 68–69 (all).

MUSEO REGIONALE DI SCIENZE
NATURALI, Turin: 75tl (photo by Gabriele
Mariotti).

PARCO DEI LAGHI DI AVIGLIANA: 114c.

PARCO ORNITOLOGICO MARTINAT,
Pinerolo: 157cr, 159c.

PINACOTECA GIOVANNI E MARELLA
AGNELLI, Torino: 47cr, 93c, 94c.

PHOTOSERVICE ELECTA: 3c.

DANIELE ROBOTTI, Alessandria: 10 tl,
12bc, 16 bl, 26tr, 26clb, 27br, 27 bl, 38cl,
39tc, 42bc, 50, 52cl, 53bl, 58tl, 63, 64tr, 72
br, 72tr, 74br, 78bl, 79br, 81bc, 86tr, 86bl,
87bl, 88bc, 89t, 89c, 90tl, 90bl, 96tl, 96cl,
96bl, 97tl, 100tl, 100bl, 192bl, 193tl, 196br,
216ca.

MATTEO RONCA, Chiaverano: 80tl, 206tl,
206bc, 207tl, 207bl.

ALBERTO SANTANGELO, Sciacca Terme:
12cr, 31cr, 39b, 46c, 80br, 81tl, 81cr, 82cl.

SCALA, Florence: 97cr.

SCOPRIMINIERA, Prali: 137br, 140bl, 140tr.

SITAF S.P.A., Susa: 211cl.

SLOW FOOD: 34cr.

GUIDO STECCHI, Montemarzino: 184tl, tr,
tlc, tc, cb; 185tc, cla, c, cl, cb, crb, bl, bc,
br.

TEATRO REGIO DI TORINO
(Ramella&Giannese): 53tr.

TORINO CALCIO 1906 S.P.A.: 97bc.

TRENITALIA: 211br.

TURIN HOTEL INTERNATIONAL, Turin:
174cl, 182cr.

ANDREA VETTORETTI (Archivio
Fotografico Provincia di Torino): 158tl,
122tlc, 122br.

Phrase Book

IN EMERGENCY

Help!	**Aiuto!**	eye-**yoo**-toh
Stop!	**Fermate!**	fair-**mah**-teh
Call a doctor.	**Chiama un medico**	kee-**ah**-mah oon meh-dee-koh
Call an ambulance.	**Chiama un' ambulanza**	kee-**ah**-mah oon am-boo-**lan**-tsa
Call the police.	**Chiama la polizia**	kee-**ah**-mah lah pol-ee-**tsee**-ah
Call the fire brigade.	**Chiama i pompieri**	kee-**ah**-mah ee pom-pee-**air**-ee
Where is the telephone?	**Dov'è il telefono?**	dov-**eh** eel teh-**leh**-foh-noh?
The nearest hospital?	**L'ospedale più vicino?**	loss-peh-**dah**-leh pee-oo vee-**chee**-noh?

COMMUNICATION ESSENTIALS

Yes/No	**Sì/No**	see/ noh
Please	**Per favore**	pair fah-**vor**-eh
Thank you	**Grazie**	**grah**-tsee-eh
Excuse me	**Mi scusi**	mee **skoo**-zee
Hello	**Buon giorno**	bwon **jor**-noh
Goodbye	**Arrivederci**	ah-ree-veh-**dair**-chee
Good evening	**Buona sera**	**bwon**-ah **sair**-ah
morning	**la mattina**	lah mah-**tee**-nah
afternoon	**il pomeriggio**	eel poh-meh-**ree**-joh
evening	**la sera**	lah **sair**-ah
yesterday	**ieri**	ee-**air**-ee
today	**oggi**	**oh**-jee
tomorrow	**domani**	doh-**mah**-nee
here	**qui**	kwee
there	**la**	lah
What?	**Quale?**	**kwah**-leh?
When?	**Quando?**	**kwan**-doh?
Why?	**Perchè?**	pair-**keh**?
Where?	**Dove?**	**doh**-veh?

USEFUL PHRASES

How are you?	**Come sta?**	**koh**-meh stah?
Very well, thank you.	**Molto bene, grazie.**	**moll**-toh **beh**-neh **grah**-tsee-eh
Pleased to meet you.	**Piacere di conoscerla.**	pee-ah-**chair**-eh dee coh-**noh**-shair-lah
See you later.	**A più tardi.**	ah pee-**oo** **tar**-dee
That's fine.	**Va bene.**	va **beh**-neh
Where is/are ...?	**Dov'è/Dove sono ...?**	dov-**eh**/doveh **soh**-noh?
How long does it take to get to ...?	**Quanto tempo ci vuole per andare a ...?**	**kwan**-toh **tem**-poh chee voo-**oh**-leh pair an-**dar**-eh ah ...?
How do I get to ...?	**Come faccio per arrivare a ...?**	koh-meh **fah**-choh pair arri-**var**-eh ah..?
Do you speak English?	**Parla inglese?**	**par**-lah een-**gleh**-zeh?
I don't understand.	**Non capisco.**	non ka-**pee**-skoh
Could you speak more slowly, please?	**Può parlare più lentamente, per favore?**	pwoh par-**lah**-reh pee-**oo** len-ta-**men**-teh pair fah-**vor**-eh?
I'm sorry.	**Mi dispiace.**	mee dee-spee-**ah**-cheh

USEFUL WORDS

big	**grande**	**gran**-deh
small	**piccolo**	**pee**-koh-loh
hot	**caldo**	**kal**-doh
cold	**freddo**	**fred**-doh
good	**buono**	**bwoh**-noh
bad	**cattivo**	kat-**tee**-voh
enough	**basta**	**bas**-tah
well	**bene**	**beh**-neh
open	**aperto**	ah-**pair**-toh
closed	**chiuso**	kee-**oo**-zoh
left	**a sinistra**	ah see-**nee**-strah
right	**a destra**	ah **dess**-trah
straight on	**sempre dritto**	**sem**-preh **dree**-toh
near	**vicino**	vee-**chee**-noh
far	**lontano**	lon-**tah**-noh
up	**su**	soo
down	**giù**	joo
early	**presto**	**press**-toh
late	**tardi**	**tar**-dee
entrance	**entrata**	en-**trah**-tah
exit	**uscita**	oo-**shee**-ta
toilet	**il gabinetto**	eel gah-bee-**net**-toh
free, unoccupied	**libero**	**lee**-bair-oh
free, no charge	**gratuito**	grah-**too**-ee-toh

MAKING A TELEPHONE CALL

I'd like to place a long-distance call.	**Vorrei fare una interurbana.**	vor-**ray far**-eh oona in-tair-oor-**bah**-nah
I'd like to make a reverse-charge call.	**Vorrei fare una telefonata a carico del destinatario.**	vor-**ray far**-eh oona teh-leh-fon-**ah**-tah ah **kar**-ee-koh dell dess-tee-nah-**tar**-ree-oh
I'll try again later.	**Ritelefono più tardi.**	ree-teh-**leh**-foh-noh pee-oo **tar**-dee
Can I leave a message?	**Posso lasciare un messaggio?**	**poss**-oh lash-**ah**-reh oon mess-**sah**-joh?
Hold on.	**Un attimo, per favore**	oon **ah**-tee-moh, pair fah-**vor**-eh
Could you speak up a little please?	**Può parlare più forte, per favore?**	pwoh par-**lah**-reh pee-oo **for**-teh, pair fah-**vor**-eh?
local call	**telefonata locale**	te-leh-fon-**ah**-tah loh-cah-leh

SHOPPING

How much does this cost?	**Quant'è, per favore?**	kwan-**teh** pair fah-**vor**-eh?
I would like ...	**Vorrei ...**	vor-**ray**
Do you have ...?	**Avete ...?**	ah-**veh**-teh.. ?
I'm just looking.	**Sto soltanto guardando.**	stoh sol-**tan**-toh gwar-**dan**-doh
Do you take credit cards?	**Accettate carte di credito?**	ah-chet-**tah**-teh **kar**-teh dee **creh**-dee-toh?
What time do you open/close?	**A che ora apre/ chiude?**	ah keh **or**-ah **ah**-preh/kee-**oo**-deh?
this one	**questo**	**kweh**-stoh
that one	**quello**	**kwell**-oh
expensive	**caro**	**kar**-oh
cheap	**a buon prezzo**	ah bwon **pret**-soh
size, clothes	**la taglia**	lah **tah**-lee-ah
size, shoes	**il numero**	eel **noo**-mair-oh
white	**bianco**	bee-**ang**-koh
black	**nero**	**neh**-roh
red	**rosso**	**ross**-oh
yellow	**giallo**	**jal**-loh
green	**verde**	**vair**-deh
blue	**blu**	bloo

TYPES OF SHOP

antique dealer	**l'antiquario**	lan-tee-**kwah**-ree-oh
bakery	**il forno /il panificio**	eel **forn**-oh /eel pan-ee-**fee**-choh
bank	**la banca**	lah **bang**-kah
bookshop	**la libreria**	lah lee-breh-**ree**-ah
butcher	**la macelleria**	lah mah-chell-eh-**ree**-ah
cake shop	**la pasticceria**	lah pas-tee-chair-**ee**-ah
chemist	**la farmacia**	lah far-mah-**chee**-ah
delicatessen	**la salumeria**	lah sah-loo-meh-**ree**-ah
department store	**il grande magazzino**	eel **gran**-deh mag-gad-**zee**-noh
fishmonger	**il pescivendolo**	eel pesh-ee-**ven**-doh-loh
florist	**il fioraio**	eel fee-or-**eye**-oh
greengrocer	**il fruttivendolo**	eel froo-tee-**ven**-doh-loh
grocery	**alimentari**	ah-lee-men-**tah**-ree
hairdresser	**il parrucchiere**	eel par-oo-kee-**air**-eh
ice cream parlour	**la gelateria**	lah jel-ah-tair-**ee**-ah
market	**il mercato**	eel mair-**kah**-toh
newsstand	**l'edicola**	leh-**dee**-koh-lah
post office	**l'ufficio postale**	loo-**fee**-choh pos-**tah**-leh
shoe shop	**il negozio di scarpe**	eel neh-**goh**-tsioh dee **skar**-peh
supermarket	**il supermercato**	eel su-pair-mair-**kah**-toh
tobacconist	**il tabaccaio**	eel tah-bak-**eye**-oh
travel agency	**l'agenzia di viaggi**	lah-jen-**tsee**-ah dee vee-**ad**-jee

SIGHTSEEING

art gallery	**la pinacoteca**	lah peena-koh-**teh**-kah
bus stop	**la fermata dell'autobus**	lah fair-**mah**-tah dell **ow**-toh-booss
church	**la chiesa**	lah kee-**eh**-zah
	la basilica	lah bah-**seel**-i-kah
closed for holidays	**chiuso per le ferie**	kee-**oo**-zoh pair leh **fair**-ee-eh
garden	**il giardino**	eel jar-**dee**-no
library	**la biblioteca**	lah beeb-lee-oh-**teh**-kah
museum	**il museo**	eel moo-**zeh**-oh
railway station	**la stazione**	lah stah-tsee-**oh**-neh
tourist information	**l'ufficio di turismo**	loo-**fee**-choh dee too-**ree**-smoh

STAYING IN A HOTEL

Do you have any vacant rooms?	**Avete camere libere?**	ah-**veh**-teh **kah**-mair-eh **lee**-bair-eh?
double room	**una camera doppia**	oona **kah**-mair-ah **doh**-pee-ah
with double bed	**con letto matrimoniale**	kon **let**-toh mah-tree-moh-nee-**ah**-leh
twin room	**una camera con due letti**	oona **kah**-mair-ah kon **doo**-eh **let**-tee
single room	**una camera singola**	oona **kah**-mair-ah **sing**-goh-lah
room with a bath, shower	**una camera con bagno, con doccia**	oona **kah**-mair-ah kon **ban**-yoh, kon **dot**-chah
porter	**il facchino**	eel fah-**kee**-noh
key	**la chiave**	lah kee-**ah**-veh
I have a reservation.	**Ho fatto una prenotazione.**	oh **fat**-toh oona preh-noh-tah-tsee-**oh**-neh

EATING OUT

Have you got a table for ...?	**Avete una tavola per ... ?**	ah-**veh**-teh oona **tah**-voh-lah pair ...?
I'd like to reserve a table.	**Vorrei riservare una tavola.**	vor-**ray** ree-sair-**vah**-reh oona **tah**-voh-lah
breakfast	**colazione**	koh-lah-tsee-**oh**-neh
lunch	**pranzo**	**pran**-tsoh
dinner	**cena**	**cheh**-nah
The bill, please.	**Il conto, per favore.**	eel **kon**-toh pair fah-**vor**-eh
I am a vegetarian.	**Sono vegetariano/a.**	soh-noh **veh**-jeh-tar-ee-**ah**-noh/nah
waitress	**cameriera**	kah-mair-ee-**air**-ah
waiter	**cameriere**	kah-mair-ee-**air**-eh
fixed price menu	**il menù a prezzo fisso**	eel meh-**noo** ah **pret**-soh **fee**-soh
dish of the day	**piatto del giorno**	pee-**ah**-toh dell **jor**-no
starter	**antipasto**	an-tee-**pass**-toh
first course	**il primo**	eel **pree**-moh
main course	**il secondo**	eel seh-**kon**-doh
vegetables	**il contorno**	eel kon-**tor**-noh
dessert	**il dolce**	eel **doll**-cheh
cover charge	**il coperto**	eel koh-**pair**-toh
wine list	**la lista dei vini**	lah **lee**-stah day **vee**-nee
rare	**al sangue**	al **sang**-gweh
medium	**al puntino**	al poon-**tee**-noh
well done	**ben cotto**	ben **kot**-toh
glass	**il bicchiere**	eel bee-kee-**air**-eh
bottle	**la bottiglia**	lah bot-**teel**-yah
knife	**il coltello**	eel kol-**tell**-oh
fork	**la forchetta**	lah for-**ket**-tah
spoon	**il cucchiaio**	eel koo-kee-**eye**-oh

MENU DECODER

l'acqua minerale gassata/naturale	lah-kwah mee-nair-ah-leh gah-**zah**-tah/nah-too-rah-leh	mineral water fizzy/still
agnello	ah-**niell**-oh	lamb
aceto	ah-**cheh**-toh	vinegar
aglio	**al**-ee-oh	garlic
al forno	al **for**-noh	baked
alla griglia	ah-lah **greel**-yah	grilled
l'aragosta	lah-rah-**goss**-tah	lobster
arrosto	ar-**ross**-toh	roast
la birra	lah **beer**-rah	beer
la bistecca	lah bee-**stek**-kah	steak
il brodo	eel **broh**-doh	broth
il burro	eel **boor**-oh	butter
il caffè	eel kah-**feh**	coffee
i calamari	ee kah-lah-**mah**-ree	squid
i carciofi	ee kar-**choff**-ee	artichokes
la carne	la **kar**-neh	meat
carne di maiale	**kar**-neh dee mah-**yah**-leh	pork
la cipolla	la chip-**oh**-lah	onion
i contorni	ee kon-**tor**-nee	vegetables
i fagioli	ee fah-**joh**-lee	beans
il fegato	eel **fay**-gah-toh	liver
il finocchio	eel fee-**nok**-ee-oh	fennel
il formaggio	eel for-**mad**-joh	cheese
le fragole	leh **frah**-goh-leh	strawberries
il fritto misto	eel free-toh **mees**-toh	mixed fried dish
la frutta	la **froot**-tah	fruit
frutti di mare	**froo**-tee dee **mah**-reh	seafood
i funghi	ee **foon**-ghee	mushrooms
i gamberi	ee **gam**-bair-ee	prawns
il gelato	eel jel-**lah**-toh	ice cream
l'insalata	leen-sah-lah-tah	salad

il latte	eel **laht**-teh	milk
lesso	**less**-oh	boiled
il manzo	eel **man**-tsoh	beef
la melanzana	lah meh-lan-**tsah**-nah	aubergine
la minestra	lah mee-**ness**-trah	soup
l'olio	loh-lee-oh	oil
il pane	eel **pah**-neh	bread
le patate	leh pah-**tah**-teh	potatoes
le patatine fritte	leh pah-tah-**teen**-eh **free**-teh	chips
il pepe	eel **peh**-peh	pepper
la pesca	lah **pess**-kah	peach
il pesce	eel **pesh**-eh	fish
il pollo	eel **poll**-oh	chicken
il pomodoro	eel poh-moh-**dor**-oh	tomato
il prosciutto cotto/crudo	eel pro-**shoo**-toh **kot**-toh/**kroo**-doh	ham cooked/cured
il riso	eel **ree**-zoh	rice
il sale	eel **sah**-leh	salt
la salsiccia	lah sal-**see**-chah	sausage
le seppie	leh **sep**-pee-eh	cuttlefish
secco	**sek**-koh	dry
la sogliola	lah **soll**-yoh-lah	sole
i spinaci	ee spee-**nah**-chee	spinach
succo d'arancia/ di limone	**soo**-koh dah-**ran**-chah/ dee lee-**moh**-neh	orange/lemon juice
il tè	eel **teh**	tea
la tisana	lah tee-**zah**-nah	herbal tea
il tonno	eel **ton**-noh	tuna
la torta	lah **tor**-tah	cake/tart
l'uovo	loo-**oh**-voh	egg
vino bianco	**vee**-noh bee-**ang**-koh	white wine
vino rosso	**vee**-noh **ross**-oh	red wine
il vitello	eel vee-**tell**-oh	veal
le vongole	leh **von**-goh-leh	clams
lo zucchero	loh **zoo**-kair-oh	sugar
gli zucchini	lyee dzu-**kee**-nee	courgettes
la zuppa	lah **tsoo**-pah	soup

NUMBERS

1	**uno**	**oo**-noh
2	**due**	**doo**-eh
3	**tre**	treh
4	**quattro**	**kwat**-roh
5	**cinque**	**ching**-kweh
6	**sei**	**say**-ee
7	**sette**	**set**-teh
8	**otto**	**ot**-toh
9	**nove**	**noh**-veh
10	**dieci**	dee-**eh**-chee
11	**undici**	**oon**-dee-chee
12	**dodici**	**doh**-dee-chee
13	**tredici**	**tray**-dee-chee
14	**quattordici**	kwat-**tor**-dee-chee
15	**quindici**	**kwin**-dee-chee
16	**sedici**	**say**-dee-chee
17	**diciassette**	dee-chah-**set**-teh
18	**diciotto**	dee-**chot**-toh
19	**diciannove**	dee-chah-**noh**-veh
20	**venti**	**ven**-tee
30	**trenta**	**tren**-tah
40	**quaranta**	kwah-**ran**-tah
50	**cinquanta**	ching-**kwan**-tah
60	**sessanta**	sess-**an**-tah
70	**settanta**	set-**tan**-tah
80	**ottanta**	ot-**tan**-tah
90	**novanta**	noh-**van**-tah
100	**cento**	**chen**-toh
1,000	**mille**	**mee**-leh
2,000	**duemila**	**doo**-eh **mee**-lah
5,000	**cinquemila**	**ching**-kweh **mee**-lah
1,000,000	**un milione**	oon meel-**yoh**-neh

TIME

one minute	**un minuto**	oon mee-**noo**-toh
one hour	**un'ora**	oon **or**-ah
half an hour	**mezz'ora**	medz-**or**-ah
a day	**un giorno**	oon **jor**-noh
a week	**una settimana**	oona set-tee-**mah**-nah
Monday	**lunedì**	loo-neh-**dee**
Tuesday	**martedì**	mar-teh-**dee**
Wednesday	**mercoledì**	mair-koh-leh-**dee**
Thursday	**giovedì**	joh-veh-**dee**
Friday	**venerdì**	ven-air-**dee**
Saturday	**sabato**	**sah**-bah-toh
Sunday	**domenica**	doh-**meh**-nee-kah

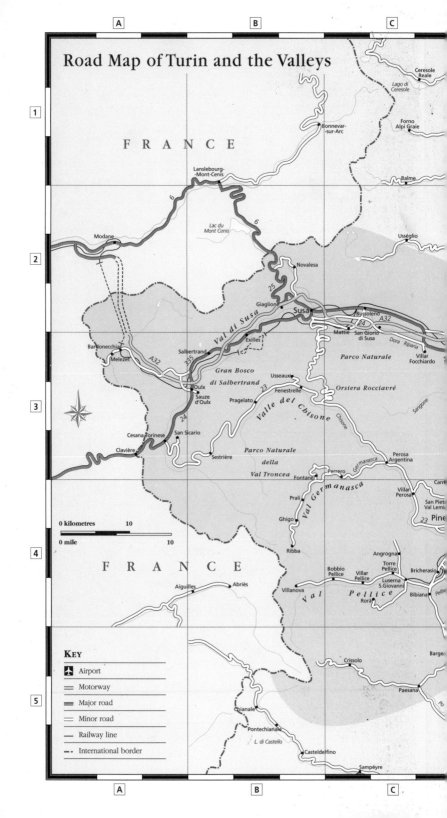

Road Map of Turin and the Valleys

FRANCE

Ceresole Reale
Lago di Ceresole
Forno Alpi Graie
Bonnevar-sur-Arc
Balme
Lanslebourg-Mont-Cenis
Usséglio
Modane
Lac du Mont Cenis
Novalesa
Giaglione
Susa
Bussoleno
A32
San Giorio di Susa
Mattie
Dora Riparia
Villar Focchiardo
Parco Naturale
Bardonecchia
Salbertrand
Exilles
Melezet
A32
Val di Susa
Gran Bosco di Salbertrand
Usseaux
Orsiera Rocciavré
Oulx
Sauze d'Oulx
Fenestrelle
Pragelato
Sangone
Cesana Torinese
San Sicario
Valle del Chisone
Chisone
Clavière
Sestrière
Parco Naturale della Val Troncea
Fontane
Perrero
Perosa Argentina
Germanasca
Prali
Val Germanasca
Villar Perosa
San Pietro Val Lemi
Cant
23 Pine
Ghigo
Angrogna
Ribba
Bobbio Pellice
Villar Pellice
Torre Pellice
Bricherasio
FRANCE
Villanova
Val
Pellice
Luserna S.Giovanni
Rorà
Bibiana
Pellic
Aiguilles
Abriès
Barge
Crissolo
Paesana
Chianale
Pontechianale
L. di Castello
Casteldelfino
Sampéyre

0 kilometres 10
0 mile 10

KEY

✈	Airport
═	Motorway
═	Major road
═	Minor road
─	Railway line
─·─	International border